Animals and Other People

Animals and Other People

Literary Forms and Living Beings
in the Long Eighteenth Century

Heather Keenleyside

PENN

UNIVERSITY OF PENNSYLVANIA PRESS

PHILADELPHIA

Published by
University of Pennsylvania Press
Philadelphia, Pennsylvania 19104-4112
www.upenn.edu/pennpress

Printed in the United States of America on acid-free paper
1 3 5 7 9 10 8 6 4 2

Cataloging-in-Publication Data is available from the Library of Congress
ISBN 978-0-8122-4857-9

Contents

Introduction

Animals and Other Figures

The task of this book is to recover what is most unique and still useful about eighteenth-century approaches to animal life. I do this by focusing on writers who people their poetry, novels, and children's literature with goats, mules, oxen, and hares; experiment with beastly genres like the fable; write the "lives" of mice as well as men. These writers turn to animals in works that call attention to their own formal devices: extensive poetic personifications, sentimental cross-species conversations, and fables that use speaking animals to teach children that speech is the sole property of human beings. Such devices can seem utterly conventional, having little to do with animals, and lacking significant conceptual or ethical stakes. My aim is to make the contrary case. I argue that the patently figurative animals in eighteenth-century literature have much to contribute to cultural and intellectual debates that are still with us—about the specificity of animals and the nature of species, about persons and their relationship to other sorts of creatures, and about what life is, which lives count, and how we might live together. They do this by making a point that eighteenth-century writers understood better than we: rhetorical conventions make real-world claims.

The philosophy and literature of the period is full of animal figures, from Hobbes's Leviathan and Locke's conversible parrot to Rousseau's natural man that is or is like an animal; from the "soft fearful People" and "houshold, feathery People" (sheep and chickens) of James Thomson's nature poetry to the Yahoos and Houyhnhnms of *Gulliver's Travels*; from the dogs, cats, goats, and parrots that inhabit Robinson Crusoe's otherwise solitary island to the talking animals of children's fiction.[1] These figures are distributed across the long eighteenth century and appear in a range of its favored genres—those that are on the rise, like the novel or the life narrative, and those that are ancient or even antiquated, like the animal fable. As diverse as they are, these works all suggest that we best apprehend the specificity of animal life—including, potentially, our own—by way of conspicuously figurative uses of language, generic literary forms, or recognizable rhetorical conventions. Moreover, all conceive literary form as an engine for incorporating individuals into a species or community, and thus for composing the quasi-figurative, quasi-natural beings that both animals and people are.

Over the course of this book, I pay considerable attention to the period's predilection for the rhetorical figure of personification, in poetry and beyond. It is in the eighteenth-century literature and criticism of personification that animals and persons are most pointedly and most curiously brought together, and conceived in distinctly literary terms. Broadly speaking, this book follows the fate of personification as it moves out from the pages of rhetorical treatises and poetry to genres like the novel, the life narrative, and the fable. As one would expect, the figure of personification takes different forms in these diverse genres, appearing at times as a local rhetorical ornament, at others, more capaciously, as the literary and imaginative operation of distributing personhood—and sometimes, as both at once. Take, for example, the following passage from Georges-Louis Leclerc, Comte de Buffon, one of the era's leading thinkers of animal life, also a preeminent theorist of literary style:

> Among the numberless objects with which the surface of this globe is covered and peopled, animals deservedly hold the first rank. . . . The senses, the figure, and the motions of animals, bestow on them a more extensive connection with surrounding objects than is possessed by vegetables. . . . It is this number of relations alone which render the animal superior to the vegetable, and the vegetable to the mineral. Man, if we estimate him by his material part alone, is superior to the brute creation only from the number of peculiar relations he enjoys by means of his hand and of his tongue.[2]

Like other writers in this book, Buffon identifies animal life above all with a particular sort of agency—that associated with "the senses, figure, and the motions of animals," and with the human hand and tongue—as well as with the relations it generates. In doing so, he pictures human relations as different in degree rather than in kind from those of other animate beings and so configures the order of nature in conspicuously social terms, as a realm composed of the relations between "the numberless objects with which the surface of this globe is covered and peopled."[3]

My title picks up on the usage of "people" that Buffon's English translator employs here—a common eighteenth-century usage, very often applied to animals, as both a noun that means inhabitants, group, or tribe, and a verb in the sense of "to populate." In *An Essay on Man*, for example, Alexander Pope directs his readers with the wholly familiar call to "'Learn each small People's genius, policies, / The Ant's republic, and the realm of Bees.'" He pictures "the green myriads in the peopled grass," much as Thomson, in *The Seasons*, will describe insects that "People the Blaze," or figure chickens as "houshold, feathery People" (*Su*, 250; *W*, 87).[4] The *OED* cites Thomson's "soft fearful People" (sheep) as an "extended" or "poetic" use of "people": "animals, living creatures (applied [chiefly *poet.* or *humourous*] to animals personified)."[5] I am interested in this sort of personification precisely because, as John Sitter remarks, "just how figurative or realistic some of these usages are is hard to know."[6] I argue that these usages are at least as realistic as they are figurative—or, that they defy any confident sorting of the realistic from the figurative, and that they are therefore important not only in the poetry of Pope or Thomson, but also in the pages of Buffon's natural history, and in the prosaic realism of the novel form. When Robinson Crusoe calls his parrot a "Person," for example, he makes playful and pointed use of the figure of personification to register something significant about what Poll *is*—above all, an animate creature, whose capacity to move of his own accord unsettles Crusoe's sense of living alone in unpeopled territory, in a state of nature that might be clearly sorted from any social realm.[7]

One of the central claims of the book follows from these examples. In many eighteenth-century texts, personification functions less as a figure that enacts "the change of things to persons," as Samuel Johnson would have it, than it does as Erasmus Darwin characterizes it at century's end: as a "poetic art" that serves "to restore . . . [an] original animality."[8] Unsurprisingly, the sense that animality needs restoring is a roughly post-Cartesian one, a response to what was widely characterized as the Cartesian assault on animal life. For many of the writers in this book, as for so many of their contemporaries, Descartes stood above all for a philosophical schema that established human uniqueness by identifying animals with things. This schema is encapsulated in a well-known section of the *Discourse on the Method* that identifies animals and machines and then describes "two very certain means" of distinguishing a machine from an apparently identical human twin:

> The first is that they could never use words, or put together other
> signs, as we do in order to declare our thoughts to others. For we

can certainly conceive of a machine so constructed that it utters words, and even utters words which correspond to bodily actions causing a change in its organs. . . . But it is not conceivable that such a machine should produce different arrangements of words so as to give an appropriately meaningful answer to whatever is said in its presence, as the dullest of men can do. Secondly, even though such machines might do some things as well as we do them, or perhaps even better, they would inevitably fail in others, which would reveal that they were acting not through understanding but only from the disposition of their organs. . . . Now in just these two ways we can also know the difference between man and beast.[9]

Citing this passage in isolation—as many others have done, and I do here—does little justice to the complexity even of Descartes's thesis of the animal-machine.[10] But it does register the astonishing move he makes when he collapses the distinction between speaking and acting into a uniquely human capacity for response or "meaningful answer" and so denies animals the very attribute for which they are named.[11] Identifying animals with machines—which is to say, with organized but essentially inanimate objects, set in motion by an agency not their own—Descartes ejects animals from the realm of acting altogether, not only from deliberative and intentional action but also from what was variously referred to as animation, self-motion, or motivity—the sort of acting that commonly distinguishes animate beings from inanimate things, and that was widely taken to imply some sort of mind or conscious purpose. (Acting "from the disposition of their organs," animals are pictured less as self-moving than as moved from without, by a structure of parts common to every member of a species, and the external stimuli that occasions their motion.) Some time ago, Julian Jaynes referred to this as Descartes's "rapier-like attack on the animism of animals"—his breathtaking intervention into seventeenth-century debates about the nature of animate motion itself.[12] As Jaynes details, the question of animate motion was so unsettled in the period before Newton that it could be attributed to the cosmos as a whole (as in Tommaso Campanella's response to Copernicus, "*Mundum esse animal, totum sentiens!*") or restricted, as in Descartes, to human begins alone.[13] In a familiar but not trivial sense, Descartes's rendering inanimate of the animal marks a decisive moment in the constitution of the "modern" division of all beings into (human) persons and (nonhuman) things.[14]

    This move may have been decisive, but it was met by considerable and often complicated dissent. John Locke frames his massively influential *Essay*

Concerning Human Understanding, for example, as an extended reply to Descartes, contesting the Cartesian commitment to innate ideas in particular, and more broadly, calling into question key aspects of Descartes's account of both human and animal cognition. "They must needs have a penetrating sight," Locke quips, "who can certainly see, that I think, when I cannot perceive it my self, and when I declare, that I do not; and yet can see, that Dogs or Elephants do not think, when they give all the demonstration of it imaginable, except only telling us, that they do so."[15] In part, Locke is resisting Descartes's collapse of demonstration into declaration (of action into speech), by insisting that animals demonstrate mind as certainly as we do—though how certainly we do this is, for Locke, a real question. Locke is also and perhaps more basically resisting Descartes's claim that "I" am essentially and substantively something that exists in and as thought—resisting, specifically, the implication that I always think, despite my own sense that sometimes I do not (as in sleep, or lapses in consciousness, or simply when my mind is empty). But the terms of Locke's objection—that I am in the best position to know whether and when I think—are themselves drawn from Descartes's own logic, from the roughly Cartesian insistence on the epistemological priority of the first person. Locke thus registers his disagreement with and debt to Descartes in one and the same moment, a moment that seeks to reconfigure the interrelationship of Descartes's twin figures of the animal-machine and the cogito.

Locke's quasi-Cartesian objection to Descartes begins to indicate what it meant to "restore animality" in this moment, and ultimately, why personification plays a role in this restoration. Most basically, Locke shows that while Descartes's "rapier-like attack on animism in animals" met with considerable resistance in eighteenth-century Britain, his sense of the epistemological and ontological primacy of the individual person—and of the first person in particular—was far more widely shared. This is not news. At least since Ian Watt, the literary and intellectual culture of eighteenth-century Britain has been characterized according to a narrative of modernization and rising individualism that begins with Descartes, a narrative that has been much disputed and revised, but that remains influential.[16] What I want to emphasize here is the close relation between the originary figure of this familiar narrative, Descartes's "I," and the animal-machine. Indeed, in the context of the *Discourse*, the animal-machine emerges at least in part to contain a possibility the cogito generates: the possibility that I might be alone in the universe, that there exist no other beings like me. Descartes's claims about animals—in particular, the claim that even animals that produce articulate sounds or skillful actions "cannot show that they are thinking what they are saying" (or doing)—largely serve to define human beings differently: securing other people from doubt by way of their capacity to transform thought into something we can, as Locke puts it, "certainly see" (115).

Unconvinced by the Cartesian account of animals but compelled by Descartes's sense of the primacy of first personhood, writers like Locke are left to grapple differently with the epistemological and ontological questions of other people that Descartes's animal-machine in part serves to address— questions about the relationship between the individual and the species, the first person and some larger kind or collective. This, finally, is what "restoring animality" means in this period, and in this book. It means restoring our own animality, in the sense either of a species identity that could shore up the newly unsettled relationship between myself and humankind, or of the more capacious and creaturely identity that inheres in the relation between the first person and the living body (a form of identity I share with other human beings, and perhaps with other animals). Restoring our animality in this way also means restoring animality as such: restoring animality as a unique form of being and relation, a mode of agency and generality in which it is diffi-cult to distinguish between moving and being moved, individual and species. Understood as part of this restorative effort, the works on which I focus in this book are not especially troubled by the skeptical prospect of my being alone in the universe, uncertain that the sounds I hear or the movements I see either declare or demonstrate mind. Instead, they repeatedly raise the inverse possibility: that among the numberless objects with which the globe is covered, animals may not simply be one sort of object among others—they might, instead, be people like me.

The possibility that animals are people like me is one that eighteenth-century writers repeatedly register by way of the figure of personification. In this tradition, personification is not anthropomorphism, at least as anthro-pomorphism is understood by Barbara Johnson (glossing Paul de Man)—as "a comparison, one of whose terms is treated as a given (as epistemologically resolved)."[17] Unlike anthropomorphism, eighteenth-century personification does not naturalize the human being by "treat[ing] as *known* the properties of the human."[18] At the same time, to adapt Johnson's formulation slightly, eighteenth-century personification does treat as known the properties of the *person*. The constitutive attributes of personhood are routinely identified in eighteenth-century texts: speech, action, and the social relations that both enable and result from speaking and acting. But there is much that remains epistemologically unresolved. What counts as evidence of speech, action, or sociality? Who or what might bear such attributes, or participate in such relations? The sort of knowing that would resolve such questions is itself an uncertain and contingent activity that takes place in the context of other people, in response to the movements of others. Personification, in this tradition, is a figure that registers the sort of quasi-natural, quasi-figurative creatures that all animate beings are.

By focusing on the "poetic art" of "restor[ing] . . . animality," I hope to recover a post-Cartesian moment that is not simply, or even chiefly, one of modern consolidation and triumphal human exceptionalism, but one that is marked by its own animal turn. Consider the opening of Denis Diderot and Louis Jean-Marie Daubenton's 1751 *Encyclopédie* entry on "Animal": "What is the *animal? Here is one of those questions by which one is all the more embarrassed, the more philosophy and knowledge of natural history one has.*"[19] Diderot and Daubenton are remarkably frank about the insufficiency of philosophical and natural-historical knowledge in apprehending animal life. Their self-consciousness about this insufficiency points toward an extraordinary aspect of the eighteenth-century animal turn: the conviction that if we are not to be embarrassed by the question of the animal, we need literary as well as scientific forms of knowledge. This is a point to which eighteenth-century writers repeatedly call attention. The protocols of empirical observation cannot tell us what the animal is (or who or what is an animal), because the constitutive attribute of animal life—animate motion—is not something we can "certainly see." To apprehend motion as self-motion—as meaningful answer or a demonstration of mind—the evidence of the senses alone will not serve. This is why patently figurative animals like Crusoe's Poll or Thomson's "houshold feathery People" are so central to any effort to restore animality. In an important sense, animals really are rhetorical figures, as well as living beings. Indeed, they are rhetorical figures because they are living beings.

Animals and Other People elaborates this crucial insight about animal life, so important to eighteenth-century writers and worth recovering more widely in our own. When we apprehend animals (including humans), we are never in the territory of strictly literal description, relying solely on the evidence of our senses. Any description of animals involves what we might call personification—if we understand personification not as a rhetorical ornament that could be stripped away, but as a fundamental part of our descriptive and conceptual repertoire.[20] It is a figure of words and of thought that is essential to apprehending certain kinds of beings, to distinguishing them from things.

Motions Discourse

I shall not ask Jean Jacques Rousseau
If Birds confabulate or no,
'Tis clear that they were always able
To hold discourse at least in fable
    —William Cowper, "Pairing Time Anticipated: A Fable"[21]

At this point, I want to begin to specify some of the claims I have been making about animal life, animate motion, and literary figuration by looking at the case of William Cowper, and his experiments with animal fable in particular. In its original publication, the opening lines of Cowper's poem "Pairing Time Anticipated: A Fable" directed readers to a note, perhaps Cowper's, perhaps his editor's, that sends up "the whimsical speculations of this Philosopher."[22] The poem and note refer to Rousseau's well-known caution against the use of fables in early education—a section of *Emile* that begins by imagining the puzzlement of a child reading La Fontaine: "Foxes speak, then? . . . the same language as crows?"[23] Over the past two and a half centuries, Rousseau's remarks on fable have generated their own considerable puzzlement, and readers continue to debate precisely how he understands the fable form, and the problems it poses for young readers. By contrast, the opening lines of Cowper's fable have not seemed to call for much comment. The original annotation offers a straightforward gloss of the poem's apparently straightforward point: to the philosopher who argues "that all fables which ascribe reason and speech to animals should be withheld from children," Cowper retorts, "what child was ever deceived by them, or can be, against the evidence of his senses?"[24] Perhaps a whimsical and speculative philosopher understands so little about literary conventions as "to interpret by the letter / A story of a Cock and Bull" (6–7). A poet, like a child, knows better. Cowper's birds can speak, as animals in fable have always been able to do, because they are not animals but vehicles for human beings or human meanings.

Poems like Cowper's "Pairing Time" can appear to offer little to readers interested in the lives of animals, for the simple reason that Cowper seems to articulate: the figures of fable have nothing to do with actual animals. For many scholars of the recent animal turn, the literary and philosophical culture of Cowper's era is especially guilty of generating fabulous animals—including the most fabulous creature of all, the generic figure of "the Animal" that functions, as Jacques Derrida puts it, to "corral . . . a large number of living beings within a single concept."[25] On this view, the eighteenth century—under the auspices of Cartesianism, the Enlightenment, or modernity—invents generic and fabulous animal figures at the same time and by the same logic that it occludes or oppresses living nonhuman beings. The proliferation of generic and figurative animals in this moment is a symptom of the violent disappearance of actual animals from the real world, or at least from the realm of meaningful ethical consideration. This is a view I argue against throughout the book, but one that is widely held by scholars of the current animal turn, who regard animal figures with suspicion, worrying that "the yoke of human symbolic service" renders animals in themselves invisible.[26]

For scholars who share this view, one of the central tasks of literary animal studies is to liberate animals from the confines of Enlightenment figuration and abstraction—to bring animals into view in our literary and cultural histories by recognizing that they are already there, not as figures for human beings or ideas, but as subjects in their own right. In Laurie Shannon's elegant shorthand, borrowed in part from Claude Lévi-Strauss, the turn from figurative animals to the real thing requires that we move from thinking *with* animals to thinking *about* them.[27] Animals may be "good to think [with]," as Lévi-Strauss put it, good figures for human arrangements, and good tools for human thought. But being good to think with has never been very good for animals. For such scholars, the literary liberation of the animal involves recognizing that "literal reading [is] a proper part of the critical repertoire"—a means of freeing animals from the confines of fable or the corralling of the general singular, to exist in all their particular and material reality.[28] In *The Accommodated Animal*, Shannon shows the considerable rewards of such an approach, demonstrating persuasively that for many early modern writers "the terms and conditions of human sovereignty over real animals operate as an example of tyranny—not just an emblem for it."[29] In this book, though, I am interested in writers like Cowper, for whom being an emblem is not necessarily opposed to being an example, nor always qualified by "just."[30]

It is difficult to see how we could recuperate a poem like Cowper's "Pairing Time" by reading literally; certainly the literal reading that Shannon calls for is not the sort of reading "by the letter" for which Cowper ridicules Rousseau, a mistaking of fabulous figures for descriptions of actual animals. Indeed, recuperating a poem like "Pairing Time" has not seemed especially worthwhile to scholars interested in animals, who take the figurative logic of fable to fix attention necessarily and exclusively on human beings. Over the course of this book, I argue that this assumption misunderstands the logic of literary forms like fable, as well as that of living beings. For writers like Cowper, manifestly fabulous animal figures do not abstract from actual animal lives, or "dematerialize their stakeholdership or participation" in our common world.[31] Instead, such figures are crucial to distinguishing animals from things, as uniquely animate and species creatures.

It would be somewhat surprising if Cowper's animal fable were wholly indifferent to the lives of actual animals, because elsewhere in his life and work, Cowper paid considerable attention to all kinds of living creatures. In his own day, he was well known for keeping a remarkable range of domestic animals: by one count, his household included three hares, five rabbits, two guinea pigs, two dogs, and no less than twenty-two birds (a magpie, a jay, a starling, a linnet, two goldfinches, and sixteen pigeons).[32] Cowper wrote movingly, humorously, and in considerable detail about his pets and those of his friends in his letters and journals, periodical essays, epitaphs, and major long poem, *The Task*. Many of his animal fables were themselves prompted by real-life incidents involving familiar animals, first recorded in his correspondence and then worked up into verse. And in much of his work, he takes evident care to chronicle the particular preferences and material exigencies of animal lives and activities—as in his "Epitaph on a Hare," which details the favorite pastimes and foods of Cowper's pet Tiny: "On twigs of hawthorn he regaled, / On pippins' russet peel / And, when his juicy salads fail'd, / Sliced carrots pleased him well" (17–20).

Readers interested in the lives of animals might be inclined to turn away from a fable like "Pairing Time," then, and toward this sort of creaturely tribute to Tiny. Or, they might look to a poem like "The Dog and the Water-Lily: No Fable," which explicitly repudiates the conventions of fable to recount an incident that occurs during a walk by a river. Cowper's spaniel, Beau, looks on as Cowper stops to admire a water lily, which he tries and fails to reach. Returning to the same spot a while later, Beau jumps into the water and retrieves the flower, setting it down at the poet's feet. Poems like "The Dog and the Water-Lily" often earn Cowper a place in a literary-historical story about the modernization of the animal fable, which charts a shift from conventional, generic, and abstract figures (of Cowper's "Pairing Time," say) to increasingly naturalistic, particularized, and sympathetic depictions of living or life-like animals (like Beau).[33] This narrative of the modernization-qua-naturalization of fable contributes to a larger historical narrative about the eighteenth century and animal life—one that emphasizes sensibility and the rise of ideals of kindness with and toward living things, as well as the emergence of a utilitarian ethics that potentially extends moral standing to any individual (human or nonhuman) capable of pleasure and pain.

This account of changing attitudes toward the lives of animals is an important story, which has been well and variously told by historians Keith Thomas and Ingrid Tague, philosopher Peter Singer, and literary critics and historians like David Perkins, Christine Kenyon-Jones, Kathryn Shevelow, and others.[34] It is also a specifically British story, which rightly reminds us that the eighteenth century was a more heterogeneous and in some respects more salutary era for animals than accounts of a human-exceptionalist Enlightenment would suggest. It is not, however, the story of this book. For this historical narrative of cultural, intellectual, and affective transformation very often shares a basic and common logic with the kind of Enlightenment critique it counters. It too understands thinking about (and caring for) the material participation of actual and individual animals to be fundamentally opposed to thinking with abstract rhetorical figures, always and only about human concerns.[35] *Animals and Other People* argues that this opposition occludes much of what is most promising about eighteenth-century approaches to animal life.

In doing so, this book builds on recent work in eighteenth-century studies, which has emerged in recent years as a particularly rich field for work at the intersection of literary and animal studies. For some time, eighteenth-century scholars have been generating exciting work on the way that particular literary forms think both with and about animals—by Frank Palmeri on fable, Anne Milne on laboring-class women's poetry, Tess Cosslett on children's fiction, and Markman Ellis and Laura Brown on the it-narrative—without quite arguing for the necessary role of literary form and figure in apprehending the lives of animals, and our obligations to them.[36] Tobias Menely's recent *The Animal Claim* makes this case more explicitly, as it charts the prehistory of animal rights legislation in the poetry of sensibility. Menely's argument rests on a nuanced and beautifully rendered account of the capacity of figurative language to translate creaturely voice into human language, and so to bring animal claims before a human public. Menely contrasts this sort of "figurative and passionate" poetic language with a more deleterious sort of figuration: the "figurative power to give life to abstractions" (especially, abstractions like "human" and "animal"). Following Giorgio Agamben, Menely associates this figurative power with sovereign violence: "figure follows force," as he puts it.[37] Menely's approach brilliantly illuminates the poems of "creaturely advocacy" on which he focuses, like Christopher Smart's *Jubilate Agno*, James Thomson's *The Seasons*, and Cowper's *The Task*.[38] It is an approach perfectly suited to a literary tradition of sensibility that, as Richard Nash writes elsewhere (quoting Menely), turns away from the long-standing conventions of animal fable to "read . . . animals as 'somatically legible subjects' rather than as undifferentiated representatives of an animal class."[39]

What to do, though, with a writer like Cowper, who writes the sort of creaturely verse that translates "the expressive joy of animals" and also animal fables, poems conspicuously organized around abstractions and animal species, and less clearly meant to reform community by "address[ing] us on the level of affect and association"?[40] My sense is that Cowper is quite interested in the role that conceptual abstractions and generic figures might play in "the reformation of community"—in writing poetry that makes us think with animals, as well as feel with them.[41] Certainly, the opposition between actual individual animals and generic rhetorical figures does little to account for much of Cowper's animal poetry, even for a putatively naturalistic poem like "The Dog and the Water-Lily." Cowper's subtitle may insist that this is "No Fable," and the poem might begin from an actual incident between a man and his dog—truly a little dog, *this* dog, as Derrida might say.[42] But this dog is always also "The Dog" of the title; it is at once a particular animal and a figure for the species in general. So too, its proper name, "Beau," designates a particular living dog and an abstract or typical figure (the incarnation of beauty, or a stock epithet for a canine companion). Throughout the poem, Cowper pictures this/the dog as an actual animal, doing what dogs do—running in the reeds, chasing swallows, "puzzling . . . his puppy brains." Despite its real life origins and its lifelike central character, however, "The Dog and the Water-Lily" is very much a fable, its narrative set in service of a final moral lesson meant to "mortify the pride / Of Man's superior breed": "myself I will enjoin / Awake at Duty's call, / To show a Love as prompt as thine, / To Him who gives me all" (39–44). Finally, Cowper's Beau is at once a subject in his own right and an emblem or figure—for Cowper himself, for the Christian subject before God, for the allegorical virtues of duty and love. This is a poem about animals (and about a particular animal, Cowper's pet Beau); it is also a poem about all kinds of abstract and fabulous beings (the Dog, the animal, the human, the Christian, Love).[43]

Poems like "The Dog and the Water-Lily" are more interested in the traffic than the distinction between literal and figurative, individual and general, material and abstract—in literature and also in everyday life. So too, and perhaps especially, is a poem like "Pairing Time Anticipated," with its narrative of an assembly of birds debating whether to mate out of season, on a warm winter's day. It may seem—and Cowper's rejoinder to Rousseau would seem to confirm—that the animal narrative of this apparently conventional fable is merely a means to a wholly human moral: "Chuse not alone a proper mate, / But proper time to marry" (64–65). From the start, however, Cowper's "Pairing Time" urges us to reconsider the genre of fable and its use of animal figures. He begins by announcing the poem's generic affiliation in its title ("Pairing Time Anticipated: A Fable") and then echoes this twice in its first four lines ("Birds confabulate . . . at least in fable"). In these disarmingly simple opening lines, Cowper reminds readers of the common etymology of fable and speech (fable, confabulate, from *fabulari*, to talk or discourse) and points toward a rather startling proposition: that confabulation, or speech, somehow depends on fabulation.[44] In part, this is simply to note that Cowper calls attention to the fundamental move of fable: fables enact, at the level of form, the coming to speech (humanity, politics, reason) of the animal.[45] Cowper goes on to thematize this move—the move from the state of nature into society, so familiar from seventeenth- and eighteenth-century theorists of social contract—in the narrative of his poem, staging the birds' marriage debate between two opposing figures. The first is an elder and rational Bulfinch counseling caution and prudence—an emblem of human reason and public discourse who, having "Entreated . . . / A moment's liberty to speak; / And silence publicly enjoin'd, / Deliver'd briefly . . . his mind" (19–22). He is pitted against (and at the assembly, bested by) a creature of animal appetite and motion—a young and impulsive female finch determined to "marry, without more ado," and who says so with a "tongue [that] knew no control" (36, 26). In the dispute between these figures, Cowper seems to stage at the level of content the same contest that the fable enacts at the level of form—between humanity (reason, publicity, masculinity, social contract, articulate speech) and animality (appetite, privacy, femininity, the state of nature, animal motion).

Described in this way, Cowper's fable begins to seem a literary approximation of what Agamben calls the "anthropological machine of humanism," in which the animal comes into being as an excluded and privative term, the internal exception that defines the human by what it is not.[46] But this characterization does not exhaust the point Cowper makes when he lingers over the connection between the genre of fable and its signal convention of animal speech. Crucially, it leaves out one speaker altogether—the addressee of the marriage proposal delivered by the female finch's uncontrolled tongue: "'I marry, without more ado, / My dear Dick Red-cap, what say you?'" (36–37). This is what Dick Red-cap says in response:

> Dick heard, and tweedling, ogling, bridling,
> Turning short round, strutting and sideling,
> Attested, glad, his approbation,
> Of an immediate conjugation. (38–41)

Dick Red-cap's "tweedling, ogling, bridling, / Turning . . . , strutting and sideling" cuts across the oppositions between humanity and animality, society and nature, speech and animal motion. On the one hand, Dick's speech is described in the conspicuously humanist vocabulary of social contract—his motions are a sign of consent, functioning to "attest …his approbation" to marriage, and to society more generally. On the other hand, and unlike the quoted speech of the elder Bulfinch and his female interlocutor, Dick's "speech" is composed wholly of animal motions. This is perhaps Cowper's spin on Michel de Montaigne's remark about the significance of animal movement: "their motions discourse."[47] But this sort of naturalistic animal discourse sits oddly inside fable, a genre in which animals speak directly in words, by way of the explicitly figurative conventions of the form.

By including Dick's discursive motions inside the genre of fable, as one variety of the articulate speech of fabulous animals, Cowper blurs the line between animal vehicle and human tenor, as well as between literal description and rhetorical figuration. In doing so, he raises a number of questions that are central to this book. Do Dick Red-cap's meaningful animal motions indicate that the fable—and the human society for which it clearly stands—might somehow accommodate actual animals? If animal motions can serve to attest approbation—if animal motions constitute a mode of discourse—could animals be parties to social contract, rather than simply figures for human participation? (Hobbes, among others, raises this question explicitly and answers clearly in the negative.)[48] Finally, before and alongside such questions—about whether animal motions might count as speech, and what it means if they do—are others, perhaps more basic still. Do birds really ogle? Are Dick's strutting, ogling, and sideling actually animal motions at all? Are Dick's discursive motions not further evidence of the straightforwardly figurative nature of fabulous animals—evidence that there really are no animals in this poem, but only people?

In literary terms, these last questions are crucial. When Cowper pictures animals performing conspicuously human activities—Dick Red-cap ogling, Beau puzzling his puppy brains, or Tiny regaling hawthorn—he enters the curiously complex rhetorical and philosophical territory of personification, in the eighteenth-century sense I have begun to outline. In doing so, Cowper complicates his own admonition to Rousseau, that "the evidence of his senses" is sufficient to distinguish rhetorical figures from actual animals, or to divide creatures with reason and speech (persons) from those without (animals). Cowper would seem to counter Rousseau's objections to fable ("Foxes speak, then? . . . the same language as crows?") with common sense. Animals cannot really speak, Cowper seems to say to Rousseau, just look or listen to an actual animal. But what *do* we see when we look at an animal? Montaigne thought we saw (or ought to see) "discourse." Descartes insisted that we see a complex machine, a coordinated set of movements indistinguishable, to the senses, from the movements of an automaton, an inanimate object set in motion from without. Cowper never does describe what ogling that "attests appro- bation" looks like—nor even what it looks like, more simply, to ogle. What is the visible or perceptible difference, we might wonder, between ogling and looking, or between strutting and, say, hopping or walking? For that matter, what is the visible difference between Cowper's Tiny eating oats and straw and Jacques de Vaucason's famous automaton, "The Digesting Duck," "eat- ing" grains (and then "eliminating" feces)? Intuitively, the animal motions of Vaucason's digesting and defecating duck would seem figurative in a way that Tiny's are not—an intuition registered by my use of scare quotes in describ- ing them. But in the wake of the Cartesian animal-machine, automata like the defecating duck captured the cultural imagination precisely because such intuitions were called into doubt.[49]

In poems like "Pairing Time Anticipated," Cowper registers the insight that hovers between Montaigne and Descartes: that animal life, as such, is not evident to the senses, because one cannot strictly see animate motion any more than one can strictly see reason or speech in humans. (This is what Cowper is getting at with the opening quip that confabulation—or simply, speech—depends on fable.) Some types of activities, and so some types of beings, are apprehended as and by way of figuration. Without the sort of generic and species figures we associate with literary forms like fable (the Dog, the Bird, the Hare), there are no dogs puzzling or birds strutting or hares regaling or even, simply, eating. There is no Beau pursuing swallows, or Tiny enjoying his straw. There are no animals but only objects among others. Phi- losopher Michael Thompson makes the same point in a different context and idiom, using "life form" where I have used "generic and species figure": "take away the life form and we have a pile of electrochemical connections; put it back in and we have hunger and pain and breathing and walking."[50] Cowper might put the point this way: take away the life form, the generic and species figure, and we have a succession of sounds and movement; put it back in and we have speaking and suffering and strutting and eating. In other words, Cowper does not picture the animal as a natural category before figuration—the raw stuff out of which human persons are made and into which they might ultimately resolve. Instead, he helps us to see that animals are made, much as persons are—or better, that animals, like persons, are at once given and made, both living beings and rhetorical figures.[51]

To put things this way is, finally, to link Cowper's fables back to Lévi-Strauss's remark that animals are good to think with. For with this phrase, Lévi-Strauss makes a point familiar to eighteenth-century writers like Cowper. Animals are good to think with, Lévi-Strauss argues, because they embody a peculiar sort of logic, in which neither literal and figurative, nor individual and species, are straightforward oppositions: "An animal, for all it is something concrete and individual, nevertheless stands forth as essentially a quality, essentially also a species."[52] On this view, the individual animal is always also a rhetorical, generic, and species figure—this cat is always also "the Cat" (and "the Cat" is always also "the Animal").[53] For Lévi-Strauss it is this "'specific' character" of animals that makes them uniquely good for thinking, and for thinking about social arrangements in particular.[54] Providing a "direct perception of the *class*, through the individual," animals are powerful figures for conceiving collectivity—for configuring what William Godwin calls the "due medium between individuality and concert" that so eludes human beings.[55] Like the other writers in this book, Cowper shares this sense of the "specific" character of animals—the sense that in literature and in life, animals come into view simultaneously as rhetorical and generic figures and as living and individual beings. It is for this reason that thinking with animals—thinking with animals about human beings and their social relations—so often shifts into, or simply overlaps with, thinking about them.

In the chapters that follow, restoring animality means thinking with writers like Cowper both with and about animals. It does not necessarily mean advocating for the interests of animals, in any direct or deliberate way—though repeatedly, it does result in some sense of the stakeholdership and participation of all kinds of animate beings in our common world. This is because literary animal figures provide a direct perception of a class that is not coterminous with any given or natural-historical sense of species, but that comes into being by way of representation and reading. In their use of overtly rhetorical figures and conventional literary forms, eighteenth-century texts help to restore the animal as a distinctive mode of being and relation, and one that is common to all kinds of people. Such an animal is indeed a powerful figure for conceiving social and political community. It is also a potential member of it.

Over the course of this book, I elaborate what it means to focus our attention on this lesson of eighteenth-century texts: that our capacity to think about animals, to recognize their participation and their claims, depends on the figures we use. I do this by centering each chapter on a form of life and a literary form or genre: the person and personification; the creature and the emerging realist novel; the human and satire; the animal and the life narrative; the child and the fable in early juvenile literature. Throughout, I read literary writers alongside philosophers like Shaftesbury, Hobbes, Locke, Buffon, and Rousseau, in order to elaborate the conceptual stakes of what can appear conventional or ornamental aspects of literary form or genre. I am more interested in the possibilities raised by particular works, and in local connections between writers who read and respond to one another, than I am in charting an overarching narrative of progress or change over the course of the century. My hope is that by dislodging key works from some of the intellectual and literary-historical narratives through which we tend to receive them (the rise of the novel, the literature of sensibility, the philosophy of social contract, the history of children's literature, etc.), common threads and sometimes unexpected emphases will come more clearly into view.

The book begins by taking up the cosmopolitical project of James Thomson's *The Seasons* as the focus of Chapter 1, "The Person: Poetry, Personification, and the Composition of Domestic Society." In this chapter, I chart the complex ways in which Thomson uses personification to depict all kinds of beings united in explicitly social, economic, and political relations, joining "soft fearful People" and "houshold, feathery People" (sheep and chickens) with "lively people" and "mighty people" (Greeks and Romans) into one great natural-historical and social system (*Su*, 378; *W*, 87, 448, 498). What interests me about Thomson's extravagant and varied use of personification is that he associates "people" not with human beings but with a mode of agency modeled on animal motion—a mode of animation that is not structured around a subject and the object it acts upon (a structure linked, for Thomson, to violence), but in which the distinction between moving and being moved is difficult to parse. Thomson is the most conspicuously poetic writer I consider in this book—not only because he writes poetry but because of the kind of poetry he writes, the famously "florid and luxuriant" diction by which he animated or personified all of nature.[56] This combination goes to the heart of *Animals and Other People*, and the kind of rhetorical strategies and conceptual resources of which it seeks to make sense. Above all, Thomson's massive and difficult poem introduces the central concerns I elaborate in the succeeding chapters: a sweeping and capacious vision of a domestic and multispecies society along with worries about both its external and internal limits; the centrality of the animal and of animation to imagining how this society takes shape; and the work of literature, and especially personification, in composing its people.

In Chapter 2, "The Creature: Domestic Politics and the Novelistic Character," I follow personification—construed as critics like Lord Kames and Hugh Blair construe it, as a figure of animation as well as of speech—to the novel, and to Defoe's *Robinson Crusoe* in particular. The chapter argues that the many animals that surround Defoe's solitary human figure—dogs, cats, goats, and Poll, the parrot Crusoe refers to as both a "person" and a "sociable Creature"—play a central and unsettling role in the novel's social and political imaginary (116, 112). It begins by looking at Locke's lesser-read *First Treatise of Government*, in which Locke sets out to separate human beings from other creatures, and thus to construct the very being on which his politics depends: the sovereign human person, a type of creature who speaks and cannot be eaten. It demonstrates that the person that grounds the Lockean political order is not a natural being, as Locke often seems to insist, but a product of representation—in effect, a personification. Defoe discloses this fact in the course of Crusoe's conversations with Poll and with Friday, associating the human faculty of speech with the animal faculty of self-motion. He discloses it too by constituting its central character around the capacious, radically nonspecific category of "the creature." While Locke takes speaking and eating to stand synecdochally for two forms of putatively natural being (the person and the thing) and two paradigmatic modes of political relation (contract and property), Defoe conceives civil society quite differently—as a process of domestication that is surprisingly uncertain about how to separate persons from animals, speaking from eating. Like Thomson, Defoe uses the figure of personification to bring animals inside the bounds of a society peopled by fellow creatures. But while Thomson does this in the service of an explicit ethical and ecological ideal of a harmonious multispecies society, Defoe does it obliquely, as he worries the limits of political relations constituted around speech. In a nightmare version of Thomson's promiscuous personification, Crusoe comes to imagine that all animate creatures might be or become persons, and to see society as grounded not in contract but in the domestic—and cannibalistic—logic of eating and being eaten.

Both Thomson and Defoe critique visions of human exceptionalism with which they nonetheless have some sympathy, poignantly depicting the desire of individual human beings to set themselves, and their species, apart from others. In Chapter 3, "The Human: Satire and the Naturalization of the Person," I turn to Jonathan Swift, who made a career of satirizing that desire—the delusive and dangerous longing to see ourselves as other and as better than we are. And yet, more than any other writer in this book, Swift is committed to setting human beings definitively apart from animals, by identifying that which is essentially and exclusively human. For Swift, I argue, this is personhood understood as a matter of grammar and point of view, in the minimal and also inalienable sense of the first-person perspective. This chapter reads Swift's "The Beasts' Confession to a Priest" and *Gulliver's Travels* as meditations on the problematic relation between the first person and the animal species. In *Gulliver's Travels*, Gulliver undergoes repeated species transformations—at different moments, he is an insect, a kitten, a clock, a pet, a man-mountain, a *lusus naturae*. Whatever else Gulliver is or becomes, he is the "I" that narrates the story. Gulliver's first personhood is crucial, I suggest, because Swift follows Hobbes in identifying the first person as the basis of a uniquely human form of generality, a mode of individuation that is simultaneously a mode of speciation. In the persona of Gulliver, Swift seeks to unite the (first) person and the species in a form of life and representation that is specifically and solely human. But he also acknowledges that the union of these orders—self and species—is always experienced as violence: the inescapable indictment of satire, which yokes the individual to the species from which she would be set apart.

In Chapter 4, "The Animal: The Life Narrative as a Form of Life," I continue to focus on first personhood and the sort of generality proper to animal life, and I link this focus back to the capacity for animate motion I consider at length in my first two chapters. I do this by reading Laurence Sterne's *The Life and Opinions of Tristram Shandy* in light of Locke's discussion of personal identity and Buffon's natural history. Attending both to the first-person form of Tristram's *Life* and to the many animal figures it features (mules, bulls, asses, horses, oxen), I argue that Sterne picks up on a tentative strain of Locke's thought—one in which first personhood is not conceived against animality (as it is in Swift, Hobbes, and much of Locke himself), but is itself a form of animal life. I argue Sterne develops this strain of Lockean thought both within and alongside new midcentury notions of life and of species, best described as Buffonian and vitalist notions. Buffon did as much as anyone in this period to generate new thinking and writing about life, and he shares with Sterne an interest in the intersection between literary and living form. For all of Buffon's reflections on writing and life, however, it is in *Tristram Shandy* that we find the form of *Life* that Buffon's vitalism would seem to require. It is the form that Sterne glimpses, at times, in Locke: a vital, first-person form of agency and generality associated with the living animal.

In my final chapter, "The Child: The Fabulous Animal and the Family Pet," I follow eighteenth-century thinking about animals and other people into children's literature, the realm in which we most often encounter it today. Imaginative literature written specifically for children rises to prominence in the second half of the eighteenth century, and from the start, it is filled with animals. This chapter seeks to forestall the apparent self-evidence of this development and asks why and how so many eighteenth-century writers turned to animals when they began to produce literature for young readers. In answering this question, I argue that early children's writers take up the insights of both Locke and Rousseau about the political centrality of children and animals, adapting the preferred literary genres of the period's two leading philosophers of childhood to the real world project of making people out of animals. From the Aesopic fable that Locke recommends comes a strain of children's literature that combines elements of fable, natural history, and the life narrative to create a new genre around a new type of being: the fabulous life history of the family pet. Works in this tradition—by writers like Sarah Trimmer, Dorothy Kilner, and Mary Wollstonecraft—compose a multispecies domestic sphere around a mode of speech widened to include the intelligible, suffering bodies of children and of animals, attributing to them the sort of honorary subjectivity and quasi-figurative status frequently associated with pets. I close by reading Anna Barbauld's experimental and ambitious *Lessons for Children*, alongside Rousseau's critique of fable and his recommendation of a redacted version of *Robinson Crusoe*, as a formally inventive meditation on what it might mean to model persons on pets in this way. For writers like Trimmer, Kilner, and Wollstonecraft, the reader alone is exempt from the domestic economy their fictions depict, his or her humanity secured by the capacity to read and to personify others, to regard (some) other creatures as intelligible, interpretable beings. By contrast, Barbauld's writing for children makes conspicuous and shifting use of the second person to constitute reading as an activity that identifies every one of us with the dependence and vulnerability of the animal.

In each of these chapters, I focus on eighteenth-century writers who seek to make sense of the sort of creaturely domestic sphere that Crusoe begins to apprehend, or that Barbauld imagines—a realm that at times would expand to incorporate all of nature (as in Buffon, or Thomson), and at others more anxiously contracts to the narrow bounds of the household.[57] The domestic has long been a central political-philosophical trope in eighteenth-century studies, but only recently have critics and historians begun to take seriously what writers from Defoe to Barbauld make plain: the eighteenth-century domestic sphere housed more than human beings.[58] Attending to forms of life and association that do not fit neatly into dominant political models of the period, writers as different as Thomson, Sterne, and Barbauld construe society in domestic terms, understanding domestication as an operation in which agency is widely if unevenly distributed, in ways that do not assert the force of an absolute sovereign, or the freedom and self-sovereignty frequently associated with social contract. Indeed, attending to animal forms of life and association—to creaturely relations of call and response, reproduction, and eating, feeding, and being eaten—can make the period's dominant political models themselves look quite different. I return to Locke and Defoe in particular throughout the book not for their role in establishing the cultural myth of social contract, at least as it is typically understood, as a "liberal contractual model of political obligation" centered on the self-possessed human subject and his capacity to represent his thoughts and will in words.[59] Locke and Defoe are important, instead, for their sense that animal life and motion both underwrite and disrupt what counts as speech, and as community. It is this aspect of their writing and influence that I hope to bring out in the following pages: not their consolidation of a human-exceptionalist model of social contract, but their attunement to its animal limits.

I have been arguing that eighteenth-century writers very often explore the problems and the possibilities of multispecies sociality where we'd least expect: in their adherence to formal conventions, their fondness for self-conscious and often stylized rhetoric, and their play with established genres and generic figures. If we discount these aspects of eighteenth-century literature as preoccupations with merely poetic, rhetorical, or generic conventions, we miss the force of the poetic, the rhetorical, and the generic in this period. We miss that "figures of words" are often also, in the words of Lord Kames, "figures of thought"—the figures by which and as which we live.[60] The works I discuss in this book are populated by a host of diverse and often conflicting animal figures, with which writers think about the ground and the limits of social and political relations: favorite pets, wild predators, and invasive vermin; household feathery people and sociable persons like Poll; exceptional individuals and the species figures that would seem indifferent to them. Some eighteenth-century writers openly embrace the task of composing society beyond human beings. Others, quite decisively, do not—or, they acknowledge this task only implicitly or anxiously, as the logical and uneasy conclusion of some other thought or commitment. The literature and philosophy of this period offer no clear prescriptions for resolving the conflicts that come with interspecies association. Nor do they cohere into a portrait of a better time for animals. But they do show us that figuring animals is crucial to acknowledging the difficult task of cohabitation across as well as within species, of regarding animals among the people who inhabit our common world.

Chapter 1

The Person

Poetry, Personification, and the Composition of Domestic Society

When William Wordsworth launched a revolution in poetry by identifying personification with the old regime, he inaugurated a move that is echoed in the founding texts of a host of modern disciplines.[1] From sociology and anthropology (Auguste Comte and E. B. Tylor), to political economy, law, and psychoanalysis (Karl Marx, Oliver Wendell Holmes, and Sigmund Freud), writers turn to personification to establish their own modernity, repeatedly defining this modernity against a primitive confusion of persons and things.[2] After Wordsworth, literary historians have centered their own tale of primitivism and progress on the figure of personification. In a typical articulation of this story, *The New Princeton Encyclopedia of Poetry and Poetics* locates the line between old and new in the eighteenth century: a moment when "rational attitudes superseded the primitive imagination" and personifications lost much of the "emotional and quasi-mythical power" that they had enjoyed "in medieval morality plays or in Milton."[3] In this compressed version of a familiar Enlightenment narrative, something happens in the eighteenth century that reveals persons (humans) and things (nonhumans) to be the essentially different kinds we (moderns) know them to be. On this view, personification is both a product and a casualty of this revelation: cut off from myth and authentic animism, it survives only as a conventional device that is employed without conviction or consequence. Personification becomes merely poetic.

The persistent appearance of personification at the threshold of the modern suggests that we might be wary of dismissing the figure so quickly. Personification is not simply an empty archaism or vestigial remnant, as many modernizers would claim. Instead, the figure of personification appears peculiarly apposite to modernity itself, an order that Bruno Latour identifies with two logically interconnected but notionally segregated practices: purification, which fixes human persons and nonhuman things as distinct ontological kinds, and translation or mediation, which mixes these two kinds together.[4] Indeed, the term "personification" is newly invented in the eighteenth century: the *OED* identifies Samuel Johnson's dictionary entry as the first English use of the term. There, Johnson brings Latour's modern practices together in a single phrase. Personification, Johnson writes, is "the change of things to persons."[5] After Johnson, critics and rhetoricians devote considerable time and space to charting the broad terrain of "things" and "persons" that this new figure is meant to bring together. Poets, in turn, take up the figure in a variety of different ways: from the vices and virtues of Johnson's *Vanity of Human Wishes*, Pope's *Dunciad*, and Gray's *Elegy Written in a Country Churchyard*, to the situations and emotions of Collins's odes, to the animate vegetation and natural processes of Erasmus Darwin's *Botanical Garden*.[6] Personification emerges as a term and a central poetic practice in a period that proclaims itself newly modern. And the eighteenth-century fondness for personification reveals modernity to be marked less by the clear distinction between persons and things than by the persistent instability of these terms—an instability that often turns on the figure of the animal.[7]

In this chapter, I turn to one of the most widely read poems of the era, James Thomson's *The Seasons*. In a period known for personification, Thomson is a peculiarly copious and various personifier, using this unmistakably literary device to pose ontological and ethical questions about the composition of persons, and about the relationship between different forms of life. Then, as now, Thomson's poem was known for its precise natural descriptions and its technical literacy in a striking range of natural-philosophical discourses (including microscopy, hydrology, geology, optics, and natural history). It was also known for its use of all manner of personifications, from the allegorical personifications of abstract ideas, to the ascription to animals, objects, and elements characteristics that are more often associated with human beings, to the periphrases that designate birds, sheep, insects, bees, and chickens as, in turn, plumy, peaceful, unseen, happy, household, and feathery "people." Critics have tended to laud Thomson's achievements in natural description—to celebrate him as Wordsworth does, for returning British poetry to "external nature."[8] They have tended to dismiss his personifications much as William Hazlitt does, as "trite and mechanical common-places of imagery and diction."[9]

My contention in this chapter is that Thomson's personifications are neither mechanical nor trite. They are not an example of the "vicious style" or "false ornaments" that Wordsworth derides in Thomson's poetry, nor of the unnecessarily "florid and luxuriant" diction of which Samuel Johnson complains.[10] Instead, Thomson uses personification to do serious natural- and social-philosophical work. More specifically, he draws on the wider context of eighteenth-century discussions of the figure, as well as its much older prehistory, to connect uncertainties about both persons and things with animation—a mode of action that Thomson associates with animal life, and extends to all kinds of beings. In doing so, he registers the sorts of questions that emerge when the newly coined figure of "personification" creates its two grand realms of persons and things by uniting what classical rhetoric had considered separately: roughly, figures that represent speech and figures that represent action. In Quintilian, for example, "*Prosopopoeia*" or "personating Characters," designates a figure that occurs whenever we "speak, as it were, by the Mouth of others," and "speak, as we suppose they would have spoken."[11] Quintilian imagines a striking variety of mouths by which one might speak: one's own, or that of an adversary, a god, a ghost, a town, or Fame, as well as of "Boys, Women, People, [and] inanimate Objects."[12] And he distinguishes this figure that represents speech from a species of trope that represents action: those "bold, and what we may call dangerous, Metaphors, [that occur] when we give Life and Spirit to inanimated Objects."[13] Quintilian's examples of this type of metaphor include poetic phrases like Virgil's "*The wond'ring Shepherd's Ears drink in the Sound*" and colloquial expressions like "the Fields are *thirsty.*"[14] In classical rhetoric, then, there is one figure that has to do with speech; there is another that confers "life and spirit," the animation implied in the act of drinking, or sense of thirst.

Over the course of the eighteenth century, Quintilian's two rhetorical kinds are increasingly brought together, first under the heading of "prosopopoeia," sometimes as "personation," and finally, as "personification."[15] Critical discussions of the figure are marked by difficulties that stem from this move, as writers try to work out what it means to set action or animation (notions that are themselves not clearly distinguished) alongside speech and on the side of persons, as attributes that are figuratively conferred on other kinds of beings. Lord Kames defines personification, then, as "the bestowing of sensibility and voluntary motion upon things inanimate."[16] James Beattie identifies it as "those figures of speech that ascribe sympathy, perception, and other attributes of animal life, to things inanimate, or even to notions merely intellectual."[17] Hugh Blair calls personification "that figure by which we attribute life and action to inanimate objects," which occurs whenever we "speak of stones and trees, and fields and rivers, as if they were living creatures, and . . . attribute to them thought and sensation, affections and actions."[18] And Joseph Priestley characterizes the figure similarly: personification, he writes, "converts every thing we treat of into thinking and acting beings. We see *life*, *sense*, and *intelligence*, every where."[19]

These definitions are remarkable for two reasons. First, all register a shift in emphasis. Unlike Quintilian, eighteenth-century rhetoricians do not detail a multitude of possible personifieds, extensive lists of all the things that might be treated by this figure (ideas, objects, dead human beings, women, children, cities, gods). Instead, they seem content with vaguely comprehensive epithets like Kames's "things inanimate," Blair's "inanimate objects," or Priestley's "every thing we treat of." But now there is a proliferation on the other side of the figure, in the range of attributes that it is imagined to bestow: sensibility, voluntary motion, life, action, affection, sympathy, perception, intelligence. The second remarkable feature of these accounts is the kinds of attributes they catalog. Even though eighteenth-century rhetoricians define personification with the attribution of both speech and action, their definitions focus primarily on action, in its broadest sense of animation. While Johnson defines "person" as "human being," the attributes that personification bestows properly belong, for Kames, to "sensible beings" and for Beattie, to "animal life." Personification may change things to persons, as Johnson proclaimed. But very often, in these discussions, the attributes of personhood have more to do with sensible or animal life than with any specifically human being. The question that emerges from these discussions, then, is this: Is *person*ification distinct from *anim*ation?[20]

Descartes famously claimed that it was not, collapsing the distinction between speech and action into a solely human capacity for response or meaningful answer. Eighteenth-century discussions of personification follow Descartes in taking both speech and action to be the constitutive attributes of human personhood, and thus in aligning animals with things, as inanimate objects moved from without. But with their extensive lists of the kinds of actions that personification might bestow, these accounts also register uneasiness with Descartes's conclusions, embedding epistemological and ontological questions about animal life and motion in their rhetorical definitions. Later literary critics and historians, by contrast, repeatedly imagine personification to operate as though the Cartesian divide between human and nonhuman, person and thing, were straightforward and set. Personification, in the *Princeton Encyclopedia*'s quite standard definition, is "a manner of speech endowing nonhuman objects, abstractions, or creatures with life and human characteristics."[21]

Understood according to this sort of definition, the figure of personification can appear duplicitous, cloaking ontological uncertainty in a rhetorical move. Writing about Wordsworth's attitude toward (at least some types of) personification, Frances Ferguson suggests that for Wordsworth, "personification in its simplest forms fails to recognize the difficulty of comprehending humanness" by suggesting "that there is a stable form to be projected."[22] Or, as Adela Pinch puts it, "personifications can suggest that we know what a person is."[23] On this formulation, the ontological uncertainty that personification conceals concerns the human being, who is falsely reduced to a set of conventional characteristics. If this formulation underlies Wordsworth's objection to personification, it elides the more extensive uncertainty on which poets like Thomson (as well as rhetoricians like Kames, Beattie, Priestley, and Blair) insist. Thomson acknowledges that we may not know what a person is. But he also suggests that we may not know what a person is not; or, who (or what) is a person. In what follows, I argue that Thomson develops a model of both personhood and society that privileges species over individuals, and animal motion over Cartesian response. Thomson's ideas about persons and the society that they constitute will, I think, appear rather strange: his person looks nothing like Descartes's human subject, and his society bears little resemblance to Latour's modern constitution. As we look for ways to move beyond such familiar humanist forms, however, the oddity of Thomson's vision is valuable. Aligning personhood and animal life, he sets literature to the task of domestication, understood most basically as a project of peopling a common world with more than human beings.[24]

Personification for the People

Jonathan Swift did not care for Thomson's *Seasons* because, as he put it, "they are all Descriptions and nothing is doing."[25] Contrary to Swift's complaint, however, *The Seasons* is a poem in which everything is doing. Animation is the primary mode of being in and of Thomson's poem, which presents an elaborate vision of the whole "Earth animated" (*Su*, 296). Critics have repeatedly noted that Thomson's descriptions teem with verbs or verbs-made-adjectives (the first fifteen lines of the poem, for example, describe a "dropping Cloud,"

"shadowing Roses," a "howling Hill," a "shatter'd Forest," and a "ravag'd Vale")
(*Sp*, 2, 4, 13, 14). But most understand Thomson to animate his descriptions
of natural objects in order to emphasize his own perception, focusing on the
operations of his mind rather than on the world outside.[26] This kind of reading can be traced back to Romantic critics like Hazlitt, who applauds Thomson because he "humanises whatever he touches. He makes all his descriptions
teem with life and vivifying soul."[27] On such readings, the life and soul of *The
Seasons* are always the poet's own, human attributes projected onto the natural
world. Thus when John Barrell notes "the activity, the motion, of Thomson"
(in particular, of Thomson's syntax), he locates the source of this activity in
the poet's will to order the landscape and its objects, to act upon the landscape
by composing it.[28] The Thomsonian poet projects or forces his own animation
onto the inert landscape as he works it into shape, "recognizing the stretch of
land under [his] eye not, simply, as that—as an area of ground filled with various objects, trees, hills, fields—but as a complex of associations and meanings
. . . in which each object bore a specific and analyzable relationship to others."[29] For Barrell, then, Thomson is not quite the poet that returned British
poetry to nature. Instead, he is the poet that would overwrite human activity
(poetic, political, economic) as natural process, disguising aesthetic and also
social organization as natural order: to effect what Kevis Goodman has called
"the pastoralization of the georgic."[30]

Barrell's is an especially compelling and acute recent reading of Thomson,
and its account of the political implications of Thomson's poetics has been rightly
influential. Most basically, Barrell argues that Thomson's "idea of landscape" sub-
ordinates sense and particularity to abstract or conventional form: "For the idea
to have any concrete existence it has to be applied to, or discovered in, a tract of
land, but this tract of land is to be understood as hostile to the notion of being
thus organized. The synthesis Thomson arrives at is one in which the objects
retain to some extent their individuality—each landscape is different from any
other—and yet appear to be organized within a formal pattern."[31] In passages
like this one, Barrell objects to Thomson's idea of landscape because it fails to
free a particular place from formal organization, to fully depict "individuality."
He thus dismisses as wrongheaded ideology the common eighteenth-century
idea that "'natural objects readily form themselves into groups'" (the phrase is
Kames's).[32] Barrell's sense that composition is always imposition marks a major
difference with Thomson and (as Barrell himself makes clear) with much of
eighteenth-century nature poetry. This difference is aesthetic, ideological, and
perhaps most basically, ontological. Barrell's Marxism—his alertness to systems

that benefit the rich at the expense of the poor—entails viewing Thomson's poetry in fundamentally humanist terms, insisting that there is no activity or association outside the social domain of human beings. To grant nonhuman beings a capacity for activity—a capacity for form or forming relations—is an act of personification as obfuscation, attributing to nonhuman nature something that properly belongs to human beings.

Curiously, Barrell critiques Thomson's personifying poetics—and behind him, the mainstream of eighteenth-century poetic and landscape aesthetics—by invoking a vocabulary that often enacts its own kind of personification. Throughout Barrell's reading of Thomson, the landscape and its objects "suffer," "demand," and "retaliate"; they are "hostile," "subjected," "governed," "subordinated," and "imposed" on; they are "prevent[ed] . . . from asserting themselves at all."[33] The logic and the stakes of Barrell's personifications begin to come into focus when, quoting Kenneth Clark, Barrell remarks that Claude's notebook drawings of trees "were not 'ends in themselves . . . his mind was always looking forward to their use as part of a whole composition.'"[34] This Kantian language begins to indicate something important about the way that Barrell's personifications differ from Thomson's. Taking the individual human person to be the primary unit of both reality and moral life, Barrell uses personification first to transform things into individuals or ends, and then to shift attention from vehicle to tenor, from particular places to particular human beings. Barrell makes this move explicit when he contends that poets like Thomson could abstract from particular places so effectively because they "had very little sense of what can perhaps be called the 'content' of a landscape—I mean, they gave little evidence of caring that the topography of a landscape was a representation of the needs of the people who had created it."[35] In a reading like Barrell's, particular places represent and give way to particular human beings, those who actually "suffer," "demand," and "retaliate," who are in fact "subjected," "governed," "imposed" on, and "subordinated." By suppressing the individuality of a place, poets like Thomson support the oppression of its people; they "manipulated the objects in [the landscape] . . . without any reference to what the function of those objects might be, what their use might be to the people who lived among them."[36] Defining the individuality or identity of a place with its function, its use, or the "intellectual, emotional, historical associations evoked" by its features, Barrell ultimately returns to human beings as the proper subjects of ethics.[37] It is these individuals that Barrell is ultimately concerned to portray and protect—not particular tracts of land, but the human beings who call them home.

I am reading Barrell's account of Thomson somewhat against its own spirit and interests in order to suggest that Barrell's quite modern and humanist ontology departs from Thomson's in important and instructive ways. The basic unit of Thomson's ontology is not the unique individual, and it is not necessarily human. As a result, Thomson's personifications, unlike Barrell's, do not begin (or end) with individual human persons. Instead, they start with the technique of periphrasis, which configures all kinds of beings as *people*—as well as, in Thomson's other terms, as tribes, nations, troops, races, or kinds—rather than as *persons* in the sense of individuals, ends, or human beings. Critics who think about Thomson's "people" have sometimes noted that the form of Thomson's periphrases resembles the emerging form of natural-historical taxonomy. Ralph Cohen, for example, suggests that Thomson uses periphrasis to create a coherent binomial nomenclature, in which the "personification is implicit in the substantive, and the natural description in the adjective."[38] On this interpretation, Thomson's use of periphrasis would preserve the boundaries between humans and other kinds of beings, even as it brings them together in one classification system.[39] To my mind, though, Thomson apes taxonomic conventions in ways that confound rather than shore up distinctions between human and nonhuman beings. He calls sheep "soft fearful People" and chickens "houshold feathery People" just as he calls Greeks "lively People" and Romans "mighty People" (*Su*, 378; *W*, 87, 448, 498). He writes of "the Tulip-Race" in the same terms as he does of the "human Race" (*Sp*, 539; *A*, 1021); he refers to "the finny Race" of fish and the "soaring Race" of birds as well as to the "boisterous Race" and "Thrice happy Race" of Laplanders, and to "the toiling Race" or "the never-resting Race" of men (*Sp*, 395, 753; *W*, 836, 881; *Su*, 36, 726). He describes "the busy Nations" of bees and "the tuneful Nations" of birds just as he does "the guilty Nations" of humans (*Sp*, 510, 594; *Su*, 1711). "Human" is not the stable term in Thomson's system of periphrastic personifications. If sheep and bees and flowers are personified in these phrases, so too are human beings.[40]

Thomson does not use periphrasis to construct a Linnaean table of fixed and essential differences. Instead, he develops a system that seeks to replace natural-historical classification with his own taxonomical operation, using personification to define all kinds of beings as people—a term of relation rather than being, of sociality rather than individual essence. In this, the system created by Thomson's periphrastic personifications comes closer to the classification systems Claude Lévi-Strauss describes in *The Savage Mind*. The "people" constituted by Thomson's periphrases function as "species" do for Lévi-Strauss, to motor a perpetual movement between universalization and particularization, a movement in which species and individuals are not opposed, but terms that follow on one another.[41] Lévi-Strauss describes this dynamic, which he calls the totemic operator: "It can be seen that the species admits first empirical realizations: Seal species, Bear species, Eagle species. Each includes a series of individuals . . . : seals, bears, eagles. Each animal can be analysed into parts: head, neck, feet, etc. These can be regrouped first within each species (seals' heads, seals' necks, seals' feet) and then together by types of parts: all heads, all necks. . . . A final regrouping restores the model of the individual in his regained entirety."[42] In the totemic operation that Lévi-Strauss outlines, species are logically prior to individuals (as "people" are to "persons," in Thomson's terms): "the detotalization of the concept of a species into particular species, of each species into its individual members, and of each of these individuals into organs and parts of the body . . . issue into a retotalization of the concrete parts into abstract parts and of the abstract parts into a conceptualized individual."[43] In such a system, moreover, the individual is not the unit of maximum difference or particularity, but a relational term that resolves difference into equivalence.[44] Heads, necks, and feet create individuals that are like every other, because they are composed of like parts.

I have invoked Lévi-Strauss because his account of the totemic operation provides a helpful model for what goes on in *The Seasons*—a poem that begins with all kinds of "people," and then composes individual persons out of the parts and the actions of their composite bodies. In *The Seasons*, the body part that appears most often is the eye. Readers have tended to identify the myriad "eyes" in Thomson's poem (eighty-one, on Cohen's count) as Barrell does, with the eye of a poet-speaker.[45] For readers like Barrell, this eye is the primary instrument by which the poet tries to subdue a recalcitrant landscape, surveying objects and features from a distance and composing them into an alien and abstract form. Yet while some of Thomson's "eyes" are identified as the speaker's ("my searching Eye" [*A*, 785]), many are clearly attached to other human figures: "the conscious Eye" of Britannia's daughters; the "downcast Eye" of Musidora; the "sad Eye" of the Russian exile (*Su*, 1594, 1280; *W*, 802). Others are explicitly not human: the "glancing Eye" of a dove, the "stedfast Eye" of a horse, the "deploring Eye" of cattle (*Sp*, 788; *Su* 510, 1125); or the "Eye" of Scotland, the "sacred Eye" of Day, the "kindling Eye" of Time, or the "*ever-waking Eye*" that is Providence (*A*, 932; *Su*, 916, 1520; *W*, 1020). Finally, most of Thomson's eyes are oddly detached from either human or nonhuman beings. Thus when Thomson describes the pleasures of the shade to an eye and ear and heart, his repeated use of the definite article rather than a possessive adjective reminds readers of all the bodies that could be made up of such parts: "The Heart beats glad; the fresh-expanded Eye / And Ear resume their Watch; the Sinews knit; / And Life shoots swift thro' all the lighten'd Limbs" (*Su*, 477–79). Like these different parts, the eye that sees a coming storm or struggles in the dark could belong to any body: "'Tis listening fear, and dumb Amazement all: / When to the startled Eye the sudden Glance / Appears far South, eruptive thro' the Cloud"; "A faint erroneous Ray, / Glanc'd from th' imperfect Surfaces of Things, / Flings half an Image on the straining Eye" (*Su*, 1128–30, 1687–89).[46] Thomson's eyes do not impose human form on a hostile and alien nature, abandoning concrete particularity by assigning natural creatures and objects to preconceived classes. Instead, they link concrete and abstract by claiming equivalence between these many different eyes, and between the individual doves, horses, and humans that see through them. In this, Thomson's poem again resembles Lévi-Strauss's totemic system: first, using periphrasis to compose all kinds of people; then, decomposing people into parts, into eyes and ears and hearts; and finally, recomposing those parts on a different plane, into persons.

Person is not a term that appears in *The Seasons*, and this absence sets Thomson apart from the terms of Barrell's critique, as well as from Kantian ideas of dignity, autonomy, or freedom. Like Barrell, Thomson uses personification to claim value for nonhuman nature, but he proceeds by way of "people," a term above all for the kind of relation that Thomson calls "social." The individual person, for Thomson, is not the foundation but the effect of relation; in *The Seasons*, to borrow and invert Barrell's formulation, beings "retain to some extent their individuality" not although but because they are "organized within a formal pattern." Working outside of familiar models of being and relation, Thomson's poem generates remarkable conceptual as well as ethical possibilities. For his peculiar effort to compose all sorts of people into one great social whole takes the animal rather than the human being as its foundational term. And it understands the animal less as a type of being than as a mode of relation and of motion—the animation that is everywhere the method and aim of Thomson's poetics.

Animation and the Composition of Domestic Society

In Thomson, I have been arguing, form is not something imposed on hostile individuals, whether human or animal. It is what enables individuals to come into being, as effects of the animation Thomson associates with animals and other people. This means that the persons precipitated from Thomson's system of peoples are composed not only of corresponding body parts, but also of the motions and emotions of those parts: deploring, gazing, loving, demanding, musing. Such actions and affections link Thomson's periphrasis to the more common form of personification described by Kames, Beattie, Blair, and Priestley: the figure of animation that ascribes sensibility, voluntary motion, life, action, affection, sympathy, or perception to "things inanimate," an ever shrinking category in Thomson's nature. Animation is the most pervasive type of personification that appears throughout *The Seasons*, and it is also the most fugitive—very often difficult to pin down, or to confidently distinguish from straightforward natural description.[47] At times, Thomson clearly signals the ascription of action or affection as ascription: in the summer heat, "Streams look languid from afar" and "seem / To hurl into the Covert of the Grove" (*Su*, 448–50). Thomson similarly distinguishes the responses of different creatures to an approaching rain shower:

> Th' uncurling Floods, diffus'd
> In glassy Breadth, seem thro' delusive Lapse
> Forgetful of their Course. 'Tis Silence all,
> And pleasing Expectation. Herds and Flocks
> Drop the dry Sprig, and mute-imploring eye
> The falling Verdure. Hush'd in short Suspense,
> The plumy People streak their Wings with Oil,
> To throw the lucid Moisture trickling off;
> And wait th' approaching Sign to strike, at once,
> Into the general Choir. Even Mountains, Vales,
> And Forests seem, impatient, to demand
> The promis'd Sweetness. Man superior walks
> Amid the glad Creation, musing Praise,
> And looking lively Gratitude. (*Sp*, 159–72)

In this section, floods, mountains, vales, and forests seem "Forgetful" or "impatient" or "to demand." By contrast, neither herds nor flocks nor humans *seem* to do, to think, or to feel: herds and flocks simply "mute-imploring eye" the verdure; man walks "musing Praise." In such passages, Thomson accords different faculties to different kinds of beings. Describing the motions and emotions of both humans and animals, moreover, he locates the crucial line of difference not between human and nonhuman but between animate and inanimate beings. Forests only seem to demand; herds and humans actually do.

At other moments, however, Thomson suggests that even this difference is not certain. He makes this point as he pictures insects brought to life by the sun:

Swarming they pour; of all the vary'd Hues
Their Beauty-beaming Parent can disclose.
Ten thousand Forms! Ten thousand different Tribes!
People the Blaze. To sunny Waters some
By fatal Instinct fly; where on the Pool
They, sportive, wheel; or, sailing down the Stream,
Are snatch'd immediate by the quick-eyed Trout,
Or darting Salmon. Thro' the green-wood Glade
Some love to stray; there lodg'd, amus'd and fed,
In the fresh Leaf. Luxurious, others make
The Meads their Choice, and visit every Flower,
And every latent Herb: for the sweet Task,
To propagate their Kinds, and where to wrap,
In what soft Beds, their Young yet undisclos'd,
Employs their tender Care. (*Su*, 247–61)

Many of the insectan actions that Thomson charts here might be easily explained by "fatal instinct," while others—actions that involve faculties commonly reserved for human beings—might simply mix rhetorical modes. On this sort of reading, phrases like "They, sportive, wheel" or "Some love to stray," embed personification ("sportive" or "love") in natural description ("They wheel," "Some stray"). Yet with the several terms for motion that he uses in this passage, Thomson hedges against this reading. Physical actions are not consistently kept separate from those that imply some higher or mental faculty, but often come together in single terms: terms like "stray" and "visit," which describe physical motion—the path of insects from glade to flower—and, at the same time, faintly suggest the kind of intentionality that a word like "choice" asserts more directly. And just as terms like "stray" and "visit" unsettle clear distinctions between different modes of animation, other terms complicate even the basic divide between animate and inanimate: terms like "wheel," "sail," and "dart," in which—with the contraction that transforms a phrase such as "move like a wheel" into "wheel"—nouns become verbs, things become actions. By confounding efforts to separate mind from motion or moving from being moved, Thomson reminds us that one cannot see love or amusement, know whether flocks "mute-imploring eye" or merely "eye," whether man "walks / . . . musing Praise" or merely "walks." In careful juxtapositions of human and nonhuman creatures and of perceptible and imperceptible actions, Thomson suggests that personification and natural description are not clear and distinct modes. Every action is in some sense an animation: something that is described by means of personification.

In part, this is an epistemological point about the perceptual difficulty of apprehending action. Thomson suggests that "seem" may not always need to be qualified by "only" (as in, forests only seem to demand, while humans actually do). Some things *seem* a certain way because that is simply what they are. In the case of animate beings in particular, appearance is the best indication of—or, simply *is*—essence. For Thomson, this is also a point about what action is: something less clearly agentive than we tend to think, and less clearly set apart from other modes of motion or movement. Thomson makes this point in part by using personification to do something besides attribute "human" or mental actions to other creatures—very often, to do something like the inverse. While birds sympathize and insects sport and make choices, Thomson's humans often perform actions typically associated with other kinds. Like the "fluttering Wing" of a fly, men "flutter on / From Toy to Toy, from Vanity to Vice"; so too a fop is "a gay Insect . . . light-fluttering," and a human mother holds her child "to her fluttering Breast" (*Su*, 278, 348–49; *W*, 644–45; *Su*, 933). Like the insects "Swarming" forth in *Summer*, a Village "swarms . . . o'er the jovial Mead"; again in *Winter*, "The City swarms intense" (*Su*, 247, 352; *W*, 630). Thomson's terms do not only traverse the territory between humans and nonhuman animals; they also cut across other distinctions of kind. As insects and humans do elsewhere, birds "Thick-swarm" over floods, this time "Like vivid Blossoms" (*Su*, 734–35). Human agency is in turn often cast as vegetable growth: humankind begins, "With various Seeds of Art deep in the Mind / Implanted"; the Sun "rears and ripens Man, as well as Plants" (*A*, 50–51; *W*, 939). Parents are gardeners who cultivate a "human Blossom," working "to rear the tender Thought, / To teach the young Idea how to shoot, / To pour the fresh Instruction o'er the Mind" (*Sp*, 1147, 1152–54). Like much of Thomson's poem, these lines derive something of their logic from the second book of the *Georgics*, where Virgil uses terms of child rearing to instruct the husbandman on how to cultivate vines: advising, in Dryden's translation, that he teach young plants how to "lift their Infant Head[s]"; use stakes as crutches to help them "learn to walk"; show tenderness to his "Nurseling[s]" in their "Nonage," and "Indulge their childhood."[48] But Thomson does not counsel farmers to rear plants like children; rather, he advises parents to rear children (and ideas) like plants.

The crossings that Thomson enacts between human, animal, and vegetable begin to indicate the strangeness of what we might think of as Thomson's philosophy of action, as well as the kind of ethical and social relations that he envisions. If blossoms swarm like humans and humans grow like blossoms, then humans, like flowers, frequently require external force to be moved. Man remained idle, Thomson declares, "till INDUSTRY approach'd / And rous'd him from his miserable Sloth," "breathing high Ambition thro' his Soul" (A, 72–73, 93). Even in *Liberty* and *The Castle of Indolence*, poems explicitly concerned with political action, Thomson depicts action not as the product of agentive individuals but as an effect of personified motives: of Liberty, "whose vital Radiance calls / From the brute Mass of Man an order'd World"; and of Industry, who stirs a crowd into action as the sun melts snow:

> Strait, from the Croud,
> The better Sort on Wings of Transport fly.
> As when amid the lifeless Summits proud
> Of *alpine* Cliffs, where to the gelid Sky
> Snows pil'd on Snows in wintry Torpor lie,
> The Rays divine of vernal *Phoebus* play;
> Th' awaken'd Heaps, in Streamlets from on high,
> Rous'd into Action, lively leap away,
> Glad-warbling through the Vales, in their new Being gay.[49]

Moving human beings from without, allegorical personifications like Liberty and Industry might seem to dispersonify or to reify human beings, much as Stephen Knapp suggests in his study of eighteenth-century personification. Knapp argues that Milton's personifications of Sin and Death troubled eighteenth-century readers because of the reversibility they risked. By permitting personifications to act like persons—by allowing Sin and Death to act like Adam and Eve—Milton threatened what Coleridge would later refer to as "the sacred distinction between things and persons."[50] As Knapp puts it, "Once the boundaries between literal and figurative agency were erased, it seemed that nothing would prevent the imagination from metaphorizing literal agents as easily as it literalized metaphors."[51] For my purposes, a central insight of Knapp's account is that of all the "human characteristics" that personification might confer, agency is peculiarly unsettling. By according agency indiscriminately to all kinds of beings, personification threatens accounts of personhood that depend on distinguishing human action from the movements of other kinds.

For Thomson, this is precisely personification's promise: the capacity to reconfigure agency as animation, and thus to distribute it more widely. Like Knapp, Thomson understands personification to confer agency, and like Kames, Beattie, Priestley, and Blair, he connects this agency to sentiment: to mental actions or affections like imploring or musing or being amused. For Thomson, however, these attributes are proper not to human beings but to persons and to peoples—proper, in other words, not to some given natural kind, but to beings constituted by means of personification. Further, Thomson does not define the agency of persons with a Cartesian capacity for response, the capacity to move with meaning. Instead, he runs agency and sentiment together, defining persons by a capacity to be moved. In this, he identifies persons with something that looks very much like animal motion: a mode of action in which moving and being moved is difficult to parse, because its source straddles the line commonly drawn between individual and species, between inside and out.

The eighteenth-century term for this mode of both motion and feeling is passion; it is a type of agency that is not exactly agentive.[52] Thomson thus depicts the central passion of *The Seasons*—Love—less as an internal feeling than as an external force, an animating principle that extends from God to bind "this complex stupendous Scheme of Things" (*Sp*, 858). In *Spring*, "the Soul of Love is sent abroad"; it moves "Warm thro' the vital Air, and on the Heart / Harmonious seizes" (*Sp*, 582–84). Love first seizes on the hearts of birds, who are bound by this "soft Infusion" into pairs and then to the offspring they produce: "O what Passions then, / What melting Sentiments of kindly Care, / On the new Parents seize!" (*Sp*, 588, 674–76). Love proceeds to "seize" on the hearts of bulls, sea creatures, and finally, human beings, who are similarly moved by "th'infusive Force of Spring" (*Sp*, 868). In his turn with the theme of the passions of the groves, Thomson once again both draws on and departs from a Virgilian model. In the *Georgics*, Virgil also pictures the influence of love over "every Creature, and of every Kind"; as in Thomson, "Love is Lord of all; and is in all the same."[53] Yet if the reach of love is similar in both poets, the nature and effects of the passion differ widely. In Virgil, love is a "rage" that affects one creature after another, turning each away from family and its fellows: he relates that "with this rage, the Mother Lion stung / Scours o'er the Plain; regardless of her Young"; and that "to battle Tygers move; / . . .

enrag'd with love."[54] In Thomson, by contrast, the primary effect of love is homemaking. Thomson describes a bird under the more gentle and sociable sway of this animal passion, moved not to battle or the plain but "to build his hanging House," to construct his "Habitation" and "airy City" (*Sp*, 655, 660, 769). The proper work of love, in Thomson, is to construct social relations conceived in explicitly domestic terms: the poet thus takes up his "rural Seat" that he "might the various Polity survey / Of the mixt Houshold-Kind" (766, 771–72). This "polity" of "mixt Houshold-Kind" is the crux of Thomson's social vision: a domestic society that extends well beyond humanity to include all the beings under the influence of "Love."

Thomson's domestic society is composed of the affective ties of couple, kin, and kind. This is the work of love, as Thomson conceives it. This society is also composed of commercial and economic relations, in both a narrow and an expansive sense. This is the work of industry, a passion that Thomson aligns closely with love. (Indeed, *Autumn*—the book devoted to Industry, as *Spring* is to Love—opens with a tale that unites these passions in the persons of Palemon and Lavinia, a farmer and the maid who gleans in his fields. Their industry gives rise to love, which in turn gives rise to industry.) For Thomson, industry and love are both forces of domestication. Without industry, Thomson writes, man is "Naked, and helpless, out amid the Woods, / And Wilds," nothing more than a "sad Barbarian, roving / . . . / For Home he had not" (*A*, 48–49, 57, 65). If love gives rise to the couple and so to the household, then industry gives rise to commerce, which Thomson pictures as an expanded domestic sphere, a household that might incorporate all of nature. In *Liberty*, for example, Thomson celebrates the Roman and British empires for enlarging domestic relations, for moving "Round social Earth to circle fair Exchange, / And bind the Nations in a golden Chain" (4.436–38); in *The Castle of Indolence*, he lauds the Knight of Industry because he "Bade social Commerce raise renowned Marts, / Join Land to Land, and marry Soil to Soil, Unite the Poles" (2.174–76). *The Seasons* similarly extols the civilizing force of empire, as that which in "generous Commerce binds / The Round of Nations in a golden Chain," which "in unbounded Commerce mix'd the World" (*Su*, 138–39, 1012).

In such passages, Thomson invokes the image of the great chain of being to describe and to justify empire.[55] He is often and understandably charged with thereby attempting to naturalize social relations. At the same time, the relationship between the natural and the social is complicated in Thomson, and his effort moves equally in the opposite direction: Thomson seeks to socialize nature, to constitute the whole of the earth as one great domestic society. The same attitude that underwrites his praise of "generous" or "social" empire thus informs his critique of those who act against the ethos of his domestic vision. These include agents of human empire that Thomson sees as neither generous nor social—those who "Rush into Blood, the Sack of Cities seek; / . . . / By legal Outrage, and establish'd Guile, / The social Sense extinct" (*A*, 1281, 1288–89). They also include "the guilty Nations" of human beings that plunder "the busy Nations" of bees, gathering honey by robbery and murder rather than the more peaceable relations of commercial exchange (*Sp*, 510; *Su*, 1711). The same principle directs Thomson's polemic against mistreating and even eating domestic animals:

> The Beast of Prey,
> Blood-stain'd, deserves to bleed: but you, ye Flocks,
> What have you done; ye peaceful People, What,
> To merit Death? You, who have given us Milk
> In luscious Streams, and lent us your own Coat
> Against the Winter's Cold? And the plain Ox,
> That harmless, honest, guileless Animal,
> In What has he offended? He whose Toil,
> Patient and ever-ready, clothes the Land
> With all the Pomp of Harvest; shall he bleed,
> And struggling groan beneath the cruel Hands
> Even of the Clowns he feeds? And That, perhaps,
> To swell the Riot of th'autumnal Feast,
> Won by his Labour? (*Sp*, 357–70)

Thomson contends that because "peaceful People" like sheep and oxen contribute to human well-being (with milk and coats and labor), human beings are bound to contribute to the well-being of sheep and oxen. In Thomson's configuration, sheep shearing becomes a model act, replacing "the Knife / Of horrid Slaughter" with an instrument of industry and commerce, "the tender Swain's well-guided Shears" (*Su*, 417–18). As Thomson explains to the "dumb complaining" sheep, this is a fair trade: the swain, "to pay his annual Care, / Borrow'd your Fleece, to you a cumbrous Load" (*Su*, 416, 419–20).

In such moments, Thomson's domestic system brings humans and animals together on a model that resembles contract, as he explains the terms of agreement to sheep. But more often, Thomson's mixed household polity is composed not by the consent of discrete individuals (whether human or no), but by allegorical personifications like Love and Industry—passions that bind all sorts of beings in affective and economic relations that very often exceed one's assent or even knowledge. For all that such personifications are clearly and conspicuously figurative, they create real obligations in Thomson. At least, they register the fact that, like sheep who do not consent to trade fleece for care nor even understand that they do, humans may be obliged to all kinds of things from which they unknowingly benefit. Thomson's description of "The various Labour of the silent Night" and "the Frost-Work fair," for example, refers to "The pendant Icicle" that this labor produces, along with a whole series of beneficial and far-reaching effects: frost fertilizes soil, purifies air, strengthens our bodies and our spirits (W, 747, 750). Describing the products of frost work in the same terms (of labor and work) that he uses to demand ethical consideration for domestics like sheep and oxen, Thomson implies that such consideration might extend beyond humans and animals to all the elements that toil for some greater good. Thomson's domestic social vision—his image of a great chain that binds both nations and natural elements—seeks to incorporate all kinds of beings in a system of both economic and ethical obligation.

In many respects, this vision resembles the model of natural sociability associated with the moral sense tradition, and with Anthony Ashley Cooper, third Earl of Shaftesbury, in particular—"generous ASHLEY," whom Thomson sets alongside Bacon, Boyle, Locke, and Newton in his roll of great British philosophers (Su, 1551). In its simplest and perhaps most familiar form, Shaftesburian philosophy grounds ethics in the natural affections of every creature, aligning private and public good, self-love and social affection. "In the passions and affections of particular creatures, there is a constant relation to the interest of a species or common nature," Shaftesbury writes in *An Inquiry Concerning Virtue or Merit*; "nature has made it to be according to the private interest and good of everyone to work towards the general good."[56] Private and general interest line up in this way because for Shaftesbury, as for Thomson, every particular creature essentially *is* an element in some composition. Whether one is a human or an animal or even an organ, one's virtue and one's identity depend on "that whole of which he is himself a part."[57] At times, Shaftesbury calls this whole the "public" or "society"; sometimes one's "kind," "species," or "common nature"; sometimes he calls it an "economy" or "system"; sometimes it is simply the "general" or the "whole."[58] Shaftesbury's various terms would seem to designate wholes of significantly different scope and kind (some social, some natural). But Shaftesbury does not discuss these differences, or even appear to view them as such. Instead, he insists that the same logic underwrites what might look like different types of relation: between two bodily organs, between the male and female of a species, between spider and fly, and potentially, between all living and nonliving beings. Everything in nature, Shaftesbury suggests, is a part of an ever-expanding whole, which he calls "an animal order or economy": "If a whole species of animals contributes to the existence or well-being of some other, then is that whole species, in general, a part of some other system. . . . Now, if the whole system of animals, together with that of vegetables and all other things in this inferior world, be properly comprehended in one system of a globe or earth and if, again, this globe or earth itself appears to have a real dependence on something still beyond, as, for example, either on its sun, the galaxy or its fellow-planets, then is it in reality a part only of some other system."[59] Ultimately, Shaftesbury suggests, one might be comprehended by a system of uncertain and potentially unlimited proportions.

Thomson takes up Shaftesbury's expansive vision as both an epistemological challenge and an ethical imperative. Like Shaftesbury, Thomson wants to ground a universal ethics on an ontology in which one's identity essentially depends on the whole of which one is a part—a whole that again is alternately presented in economic, social, and ecological terms. But Thomson's Shaftesburian vision takes some peculiar turns, not least because of the central role Thomson accords personification in composing the great system of nature, the vast animal order or economy of which every one is a part. Some of the most heavily personified sections of *The Seasons* are those in which Thomson is most closely engaged with matters of natural-philosophical knowledge— with describing nature as it actually is. When Thomson sets out to replace the older hydrologic theory of percolation with the new theory of condensation, for example, he begins by depicting the former as the product of improper personification:

> But hence this vain
> Amusive Dream! Why should the Waters love
> To take so far a Journey to the Hills,
> When the sweet Valleys offer to their Toil
> Inviting Quiet, and a nearer Bed?
> Or if, by blind Ambition led astray,
> They must aspire; why should they sudden stop
> Among the broken Mountain's rushy Dells[?] (*A*, 756–63)

This passage does not suggest that percolation theory is a "vain / Amusive Dream" because it personifies a natural object, attributing agency and affections to water. Instead, Thomson insists that percolation theory is an amusive dream because it attributes a particular kind of agency and affection: water is led by "blind Ambition" to toil alone, ignoring the invitations of the "sweet Valleys." Thomson supplants this picture of a solitary self with a vision of harmonious system:

> I see the Rivers in their infant Beds!
> Deep deep I hear them, lab'ring to get free!
> I see the leaning *Strata*, artful rang'd;
> The gaping Fissures to receive the Rains,
> The melting Snows, and ever-dripping Fogs.
> Strow'd bibulous above I see the Sands,
> The pebbly Gravel next, the Layers then,
> Of mingled Moulds, or more retentive Earths,
> The gutter'd Rocks and mazy-running Clefts;
> That, while the stealing Moisture they transmit,
> Retard its Motion, and forbid its Waste. (*A*, 808–18)

In this passage, Thomson does not replace personification with a more naturalist mode of description. Instead, he reconfigures personification so that it does not picture a central agent toiling without regard to others, but instead composes a system of relations that unites its elements and directs their movement:

> United, thus,
> Th' exhaling sun, the Vapour-burden'd Air,
> The gelid Mountains, that to Rain condens'd
> These Vapours in continual Current draw,
> And send them o'er the fair-divided Earth,
> In bounteous Rivers to the Deep again,
> A social Commerce hold, and firm support
> The full-adjusted Harmony of Things. (*A*, 828–35)

Throughout this section, Thomson uses personification to compose a Shaftesburian animal economy, a "social Commerce" in which all sorts of "Things" are animated by affections that are directed to the good of the whole. Sun, air, mountains—and even more intricately, rivers, strata, fissures, rain, snows, fogs, sands, gravels, rocks, and clefts—all work together toward one end.

At the same time that this kind of passage envisions sociability on an explicitly Shaftesburian model, it also brings the uniqueness of Thomson's social vision into focus. Throughout his work, Shaftesbury often turns to the figure of the animal in a way that is fairly familiar: in order to naturalize social organization, granting the authority of nature to everything from heterosexual coupling, to class distinctions, to a carnivorous diet. Thomson does something more unusual. Like Shaftesbury, Thomson takes the animal as a model for the kind of society he is after, and for the movement that brings such society into being. But in Thomson, the animal and its economy is not natural in the way that it is for Shaftesbury—something given, logically prior to the material labor of social organization or the figurative work of poetic composition. The Thomsonian animal—and so, Thomsonian nature—is a self-consciously rhetorical product, the effect of personification understood as a literary, social, and material operation. This vision of nature distinguishes Thomson from Shaftesbury, and the difference is marked by their respective key terms: Thomson's "people" and Shaftesbury's "species," a term that Thomson, despite his interest in natural history, does not use.[60] In other words, if Thomson seems to follow Shaftesbury in suggesting that the social order is natural, this is in part because he everywhere imagines the natural order in social terms. On Thomson's view, nature is indeed one great domestic society, a "full-adjusted Harmony of Things" supported by "social Commerce." But although this social commerce extends (at least ideally) to all of nature, it is not exactly natural. It is both made and made visible by means of personification.

Wilderness, Selfhood, and the Limits of Domestic Society

If Thomson does not separate nature from society in *The Seasons*, he does single out figures that appear incompatible with his vision of social nature: figures like the "Beast of Prey, / Blood-stain'd," or "The villain Spider" who waits "in eager Watch" for a fly and who, "fixing in the Wretch his cruel Fangs, / Strikes backward grimly pleas'd" (*Sp*, 357–58; *Su*, 268–78). Such figures dominate the landscape in "the *torrid Zone*," where, Thomson remarks, "the Wilderness resounds, / From *Atlas* Eastward to the frighted *Nile*" (*Su*, 632, 937–38). In this wilderness, Thomson sees no system of reciprocity or toil for the general good but only solitary predators like the serpent, tiger, leopard, hyena, lion—animals who are moved by "rage" rather than love as they, "scorning all the taming Arts of Man, / . . . / Demand their fated Food" (*Su* 920, 928).[61] Thomson punctuates his description of the harmonious hydrologic system with a repeated exclamation of perceptual achievement: "I see the rivers," "I see the strata," "I see the sands." In his description of the wilderness, by contrast, Thomson's triumphant "I see!" becomes an anxious "what?":

> But what avails this wondrous Waste of Wealth?
> This gay Profusion of luxurious Bliss?
> This Pomp of Nature? what their balmy Meads
> Their powerful Herbs, and *Ceres* void of Pain?
> By vagrant Birds dispers'd, and wafting Winds,
> What their unplanted Fruits? What the cool Draughts,
> Th' ambrosial Food, rich Gums, and spicy Health,
> Their Forests yield? Their toiling Insects what,
> Their silky Pride, and vegetable Robes?
> Ah! what avail their fatal Treasures, hid
> Deep in the Bowels of the pitying Earth,
> *Golconda*'s Gems, and sad *Potosi*'s Mines;
> Where dwelt the gentlest Children of the Sun?
> What all that *Afric*'s golden Rivers rowl,
> Her odorous Woods, and shining Ivory Stores? (*Su*, 860–74)

Here—in Africa—Thomson sees no chain of being bound by love or commerce, but only disconnected parts, rage, cruelty, and waste.

In the foreign wilderness of the torrid zone, Thomson's domestic vision seems to reach its limits. At the same time, Thomson's anxious "what?" intimates that this vision of disconnected parts may be the poet's version of the percolation theorists' error, his own "Amusive Dream." For this passage echoes an earlier section of *Summer*, in which Thomson chides a "Critic-Fly" for "dar[ing] to tax the Structure of the Whole," "as if Aught was form'd / In vain, or not for admirable ends":

> Shall little haughty Ignorance pronounce
> His Works unwise, of which the smallest Part
> Exceeds the narrow Vision of her Mind?
> . . . .

And lives the Man, whose universal Eye
Has swept at once th'unbounded Scheme of Things;
Mark'd their Dependance so, and firm Accord,
As with unfaultering Accent to conclude
That *This* availeth nought? (*Su*, 321–33)

By looking at elements of the wild African landscape and asking of each, "what avails this?" Thomson does not simply proclaim the superiority of European civilization (though he does also do this). He also casts himself as a critic-fly, presuming to suggest that anything could "availeth nought." There is something here of Pope's well-known question from the *Essay on Man*: "Why has not Man a microscopic eye? / For this plain reason, Man is not a Fly" (1.193–94). But while Pope counsels acceptance of the bounds of human perception, Thomson brings man and fly together to worry the problem of perceptual limits. Thomson's critic-fly falters because he sees only partially, and he sees only parts. He fails to apprehend the whole, as Thomson (unlike Pope) insists he ought. Thomson thus suggests that the problem of the torrid zone may not lie first with hyenas, serpents, and spiders, but with Thomson, and with "Man." Unable to picture the value or role of seemingly solitary predators, Thomson fears that he might fail to perceive and to personify correctly. Like percolation theorists, he might commit an error that is at once ontological, epistemological, and rhetorical: using personification to depict solitary (and sanguinary) selves rather than to compose the social system that enables both peoples and persons to come into being, and to live harmoniously together.

This is what "wilderness" ultimately signals for Thomson: not only the outside but also the underside of his attempt to compose all of nature into one great society. The torrid zone is a site of particular trouble for Thomson, replete as it is with predators like hyenas and spiders, or with the apparent waste of a natural profusion that "availeth nought." But for Thomson, the problem of wilderness exceeds the bounds of any geographical region, or of narrowly predatory relations. It is a notion he invokes again and again in moments when his capacity for composition strains against elements that seem to defy any vision of a harmonious domestic sphere. Such elements sometimes appear quite close to home. At the start of *Summer*, for example, just before the poem's journey to the tropics, the domestic breakfast table becomes the site of Thomson's most elaborate and also most crowded vision of nature as "one wondrous Mass / Of Animals, or Atoms organiz'd" (*Su*,

289–90). Here, Thomson imagines that even "the Stone / Holds Multitudes," that fruit is inhabited by "nameless Nations," that the air itself is filled with "unseen People" (298–99, 302, 311). According to the logic of Thomson's expansive social harmony, this might be a positive vision—of extending domestic society to even the microscopic, atomic level. But Thomson's system seems overwhelmed by all these people, and he notes with relief that our senses shield us from their presence:

> for, if the Worlds
> In Worlds inclos'd should on his Senses burst,
> From Cates ambrosial, and the nectar'd Bowl,
> He would abhorrent turn; and in the dead Night
> When Silence sleeps o'er all, be stun'd with Noise. (*Su*, 313–17)

In her reading of *The Seasons*, Kevis Goodman suggests that the abhorrence registered in passages like this one disrupts Thomson's ideal of one great social whole with the noise of history, the cacophony of dissonant and dissident colonial subjects on whom an imperial Britain feeds. Goodman's reading is beautifully attuned to Thomson's unease with eating. But it is less interested in the literal scene of leaves, fruit, and nectar than it is in the way that Thomson's diction "renders a weird human presence." As Goodman puts it, phrases like "'nameless nations,' 'unseen people,' the 'inhabitants' of the 'winding citadel' . . . [run] the reification of commodities in reverse. There are people in that food."[62]

Powerful as Goodman's reading is, its emphasis on human presence occludes Thomson's commitment to constituting all kinds of beings as nations or as peoples, parts of a social and ethical system that takes neither the human being, nor the individual person, as its foundational term. This is no easy commitment, as Thomson acknowledges in moments like this one. From the perspective of any particular animal, atom, or person—of any of the manifold eyes that compose his poem—his great domestic society looks less like a "full-adjusted Harmony of Things" and more like wilderness, a realm characterized by predation and consumption, by overwhelming and abhorrent "Noise." Thomson does insist, in the closing "Hymn" to *The Seasons*, that even in "distant barbarous Climes," "GOD is ever present"—"In the void Waste as in the City full; / And where HE vital spreads there must be Joy"—but this remains an article of faith, of what must be ("Hymn," 101, 105–7). Nowhere in the poem does he ascend to the sort of God's-eye view that might affirm the rightness of the social order on which he nevertheless insists. Instead, Thomson uses so many forms of personification to expose the difficult poetic labor, as well as the perceptual and ethical perplexity, that is entailed in composing a vision of the whole from necessarily individuated (if not specifically human) points of view.[63]

One of the most intricate elaborations of what this perplexity means for Thomson comes in his depiction of a summer storm, an episode that follows immediately on the poem's return from the African wilderness to a domestic and pastoral setting. In this episode, Thomson makes particularly complex use of personification to signal the way that "wilderness" not only impinges on seemingly innocent forms of eating, but also threatens Thomson's ideal form of relation and movement—love. This time it is not the poet or the percolation theorist but the lover, Celadon, who errs in setting persons outside of and prior to the order of things. The scene begins not with Celadon's error, but with a description of the storm:

> Th' unconquerable Lightning struggles thro',
> Ragged and fierce, or in red whirling Balls,
> And fires the Mountains with redoubled Rage.
> Black from the Stroke, above, the smouldring Pine
> Stands a sad shatter'd Trunk; and, stretch'd below,
> A lifeless Groupe the blasted Cattle lie:
> Here the soft Flocks, with that same harmless Look
> They wore alive, and ruminating still
> In Fancy's Eye; and there the frowning Bull,
> And Ox half-rais'd. Struck on the castled Cliff,
> The venerable Tower and spiry Fane
> Resign their aged Pride. The gloomy Woods
> Start at the Flash, and from their deep Recess,
> Wide-flaming out, their trembling Inmates shake. (*Su*, 1147–60)

Thomson's depiction of the storm begins with what seem straightforward personifications: lightning is "fierce," it "struggles" with "Rage"; a pine tree is "sad"; flocks wear a "harmless Look"; the Bull is "frowning"; a tower and fane "Resign" their "Pride"; woods "Start." Using personification to identify tree and cattle and tower according to the ways in which they are acted upon by lightning, Thomson might appear to call attention to the difference between such personifications and the actual human persons who appear on the scene, or, between (onto)logical objects and (onto)logical subjects. But to read the section in this way is to make the same error as Celadon commits, when he assures his beloved Amelia that she need not fear the storm because she is a "'Stranger to Offence'" (*Su*, 1205). Celadon reasons that because Amelia has committed no wrong, "'HE, who yon Skies involves / In Frowns of Darkness, ever smiles on thee, / With kind Regard'" (*Su*, 1206–8). At that moment, Amelia is struck dead by lightning:

> From his void Embrace,
> (Mysterious Heaven!) that moment, to the Ground,
> A blacken'd Corse, was struck the beauteous Maid.
> But who can paint the Lover, as he stood,
> Pierc'd by severe Amazement, hating Life,
> Speechless, and fix'd in all the Death of Woe!
> So, faint Resemblance, on the Marble-Tomb,
> The well-dissembled Mourner stooping stands,
> For ever silent, and for ever sad. (*Su*, 1214–22)

In this episode, Celadon is rebuked for the same error that Thomson makes in the torrid zone: for singling out individuals, and for doing so, in Celadon's case, out of a sense of both species and individual exceptionalism. Celadon is rebuked, that is, for thinking that human beings in general and Amelia in particular are unique—for imagining that Heaven will spare Amelia as it does not spare other creatures, even though they are also, presumably, "Stranger to Offence." To separate Thomson's account of the storm's effects on human beings from his account of its effects on other kinds of things is to echo Celadon's ironic assurance that Amelia is different from a tree or a sheep or a tower. Thomson insists that she is not.

Celadon's error should urge us to proceed carefully when we think about the work of personification in this scene. For throughout his description of lightning and its effects, Thomson's syntax both complicates and intensifies the work of the figure, ultimately blurring rather than shoring up the distinction between human persons and personified things. To begin, Thomson's lines often break between subject and verb, unsettling the relation between these terms and granting a degree of independence to action: "the smouldring Pine / Stands"; "The venerable Tower and spiry Fane / Resign"; "The gloomy woods / Start." Moreover, before something is the subject of an action, it is the object of an act of lightning (the only autonomous—because heavenly—agent in the scene): the pine is "Black from the Stroke" and "smouldring" before it "Stands"; the cattle are "blasted" before they "lie"; the tower and fane are "Struck" before they "Resign." Similarly, Thomson presents positions before the entities that occupy them: "above" before pine, "below" before cattle, "here" before flocks, "there" before bull or ox. Throughout his description of the storm, Thomson turns syntax and line to the task of his peculiar mode of personification, using both to attribute a form of agency that is again understood not as a Cartesian capacity for response, but rather as the capacity to be moved. In doing so, he proposes a radical leveling: suggesting that what something *is* proceeds from what something *does*, that what it does proceeds from what *is done* to it, and finally, that what is done to it proceeds from *where* it is. To put this another way: Thomson uses personification in this section to elevate the identity of qualities over and against the difference of subjects, to grant sentiment and agency to pine trees, towers, and sheep, and crucially, to Amelia and to Celadon as well. Thus, as Thomson charts the effect of lightning on Amelia, he proceeds both passively and in reverse, moving from position, to action, to "the beauteous maid." Amelia is "struck" as the tower is "Struck," "blacken'd" as the pine is "Black"; Celadon is "sad" as the tree trunk is "sad," "Pierc'd" as the cattle are "blasted."[64]

In this episode, Celadon is derided because he gets personification wrong, imagining that "Mysterious Heaven" acts like a person, and that persons act unlike things. In doing so, he not only mispersonifies heaven, imagining that it operates in the same manner and on the same plane as a person. He also mispersonifies Amelia, imagining that she operates in a different manner and on a different plane from a pine tree or a bull. Imagining human persons to be unique, prior to, and separable from the system that enables their individuation, Celadon enacts what Lévi-Strauss identifies as the characteristic transformation of human society:

> All the members of the species *Homo sapiens* are logically comparable
> to the members of any other animal or plant species. However, social
> life effects a strange transformation in this system, for it encour-
> ages each biological individual to develop a personality; and this is
> a notion no longer recalling specimens within a variety but rather
> types of varieties or of species, probably not found in nature . . . and
> which could be termed "mono-individual." What disappears with the

death of a personality is a synthesis of ideas and modes of behaviour as exclusive and irreplaceable as the one a floral species develops out of the simple chemical substances common to all species. When the loss of someone dear to us or of some public personage such as a politician or writer or artist moves us, we suffer much the same sense of irreparable privation that we should experience were *Rosa centifolia* to become extinct and its scent to disappear for ever.[65]

For Frances Ferguson, what Lévi-Strauss describes in this passage is one version of personification: an operation that transforms persons into exclusive and irreplaceable "personalities."[66] While Lévi-Strauss imagines that, at least in modern society, this transformation of person into personality is inevitable, Thomson wants to avoid the process of "mono-individuation" that affixes affection to any one "exclusive" personality. Apprehensive about the ethical implications of this affective exclusivity, he looks to Shaftesburian systematicity precisely for its capacity to resolve difference into equivalence, to make it possible, as Lévi-Strauss puts it, "both to define the status of persons within a group and to expand the group beyond its traditional confines."[67] But Thomson worries, in a way that Shaftesbury does not, about love.

Love is at once the prime mover of Thomson's great social harmony and troubling threat to his domestic vision. Thomson repeatedly calls into doubt the smooth passage from self to society imagined by moral-sense philosophers like Shaftesbury or a poet like Pope, by way of the ever-widening concentric circles of the *Essay on Man*, moving "from individual to the whole" to finally "Take every creature in, of every kind" (4.362, 370). Picturing a self more squarely at odds with the whole of which it is nevertheless a part, Thomson conceives social love as a "Godlike Passion," which, "the bounds of *Self* / Divinely bursting, the whole Public takes / Into the Heart, enlarg'd, and burning high / With the mix'd Ardor of unnumber'd *Selves*" (*Liberty*, 3.107–10). Rather than proceed outward from the individual, proper Thomsonian love comes from without to explode the self. This is true of the Roman people, whose "generous Hearts, / Unpetrify'd by *Self*, so naked lay / And sensible to *Truth*" (*Liberty*, 3.207–9). It is also true of his ideal lovers, Lyttelton and Lucinda, in whom "The tender heart is animated Peace" (*Sp*, 941). Linked directly to the species by an impersonal, abstract organ—they are animated by "the heart" rather than by their own particular hearts—these lovers are "happiest of their Kind," directed by "Harmony itself / Attuning all their Passions into Love" (*Sp*, 1113, 1118–19).

The passion that Thomson celebrates under the name of "love"—the social passion of the Roman people, or of the ideal couple—is sharply distinguished from self-love, a passion that Thomson often denominates with the Virgilian "rage," or simply qualifies as "wild." The most extreme instance of this sort of self-directed love in Thomson is rape or enforced marriage: the kind of love he depicts as common in those "barbarous Nations, whose inhuman Love / Is wild Desire," where a tyrannical and predatory lover is "meanly posses'd / Of a meer, lifeless violated Form" (Sp, 1130–31, 1133–34). Thomson wants to distinguish "The cruel Raptures of the Savage Kind" from the animating passion that composes domestic and civilized society (Sp, 826). But love repeatedly threatens to slide toward what Thomson calls wilderness—love as inhuman possession, a mode of lifelessness, inanimacy, or death. Spring thus closes its celebration of domestic love with a caution to youth to "beware of Love" (983), warning that "Love deludes into . . . thorny Wilds" (1108). It is for such wild delusion that Thomson faults "the guileless" Celadon and Amelia: "Devoting all / To Love, each was to each a dearer Self" (Su, 1183). Celadon and Amelia may be in some sense "guileless," but Thomson insists they are also guilty—of imagining that their guilelessness matters, that nature is a personal order, that who and what persons are is, most fundamentally, singular selves.

For Thomson, the problem is that when love personifies in this way—when it singles out what Thomson calls a "self" and Lévi-Strauss calls a "personality"—it fractures rather than binds the social whole, constricts rather than enlarges its bounds. It becomes a principle of obstruction and rupture rather than motion and composition. This is the fate not only of the barbarian tyrant-lover but of the lovesick boy, whose beloved "alone / Heard, felt, and seen, possesses every Thought, / Fills every Sense, and pants in every Vein," and who thus sits "amid the social Band . . . / Lonely, and unattentive" (Sp, 1013–18). When love is fixed on one person rather than directed in and by an ever expanding whole, Thomson warns that it leaves a "Semblance of a Lover, fix'd / In melancholy Site," a "Wretch, / Exanimate by Love" (Sp, 1022–23, 1051–52). Thomson insists that it does not matter if love is fixed on oneself or on one's "dearer Self." Identifying the capacity to move with the capacity to be moved, Thomson understands the self not as the seat or source of agency but as its arrest: the lovesick boy is "fix'd / In melancholy Site" just as Celadon "stood / Pierc'd . . . and fix'd." As these phrases indicate, Thomson decries self-love not because it misdirects emotion, but because it cuts emotion off from direction or motion altogether. If (e)motive forces become fixed in one personality or self, then movement stops and the form of personhood that grounds Thomson's domestic society is suspended: one is made "Exanimate by Love."

In his remarks on love, selfhood, and wilderness, Thomson acknowledges the troubling potential of personification to transform human beings into exclusive personalities, a petrified figure, on Thomson's view, that undoes personhood and the forms of sociability with which it is associated. This is a potential that Thomson does not entirely contain in *The Seasons*, but to which he does provide an alternative. This comes in the form of yet another type of personification, which seeks to avoid the production of personality by transforming human beings into allegorical personifications. Personified thus, human persons appear not as unique individuals but as types, designated by common nouns instead of proper names: "A Drake," "a Bacon," "a steady More," "The generous Ashley," "The gentle Spenser" (*Su*, 1495, 1535, 1488, 1551, 1573). The move from Thomson's catalog of British patriots to his roll of allegorical virtues and passions like Love and Charity is a seamless one, because for Thomson, patriots *are* virtues: More is "steady," Walsingham is "frugal, and wise," Raleigh is "active," Russel is "temper'd," and Algernon Sidney is "fearless" (*Su*, 1488, 1494, 1505, 1523, 1528). Making persons grammatically identical to personified virtues, Thomson makes the final move in a poetic system that looks to personification to both constitute and expand the bounds of society: he composes persons into peoples or kinds, as he indicates when he praises classical luminaries as "First of your Kind! Society divine!" (*W*, 541). To make a person a people or kind is for Thomson to render him reproducible, a motive for the movement of others: like Socrates "the Sun, / From whose white Blaze emerg'd each various Sect / Took various Teints, but with diminish'd Beam," or like Homer, "the Fountain-Bard, / When each Poetic Stream derives its Course" (*Liberty*, 2.223–25, 272–73). Rather than the sexual reproduction of erotic love, it is this sort of reproduction with which Thomson is most comfortable, as more reliably working against the exanimating logic of selfhood. In *The Seasons* as in *Liberty*, then, Thomson everywhere personifies human persons in order to produce other people, casting British heroes from and as classical types: More is "Like Cato firm, like Aristides just, / Like rigid Cincinnatus nobly poor"; Algernon Sidney is "the British Cassius"; Bacon is "in one rich Soul, / Plato, the Stagyrite, and Tully join'd" (*Su*, 1491–92, 1528, 1541–42). *The Seasons* thus composes society as a dynamic system that proceeds from periphrastic to allegorical personification: a system in which persons and personifications are collapsed and constantly producing each other.[68]

Coda: Patient Persons

Throughout this chapter, I have argued that Thomson does not take the individual to be a primary ontological or even ethical term. He does, however, take individuality seriously as both an epistemological and an affective reality—one that he calls wild, and yet acknowledges at the center of his domestic vision. Thus while Thomson affirms, with Shaftesbury, that every being is fundamentally an element in some composition, he does not think that we experience ourselves (or others, at least beloved others) that way. In the end, wilderness is best understood to designate this limited or simply partial point of view: the point of view of the individual—whether human or no—that senses itself not as a part of a whole but as a particular life, even a unique personality. Thomson may be uncomfortable with the claims made from this point of view, but he does not entirely set them aside. Along with discomfort, there is sympathy for the guilelessness of Celadon and Amelia—for what it feels like to be part, or to care for one individual person. This sympathy is most powerfully expressed in *The Seasons* when individual persons are subject to violence at the hands of human beings.

In its own time, Thomson's poem was probably most famous for its polemic against hunting, which centers on the personified figure of a solitary hunted stag.[69] With this figure of an acutely singular individual, we encounter a form of individuation that Thomson presents not as an ethical problem, but as a good. Thomson's hunt scene in some ways reprises the episode of the summer storm, which ended by indicting Celadon's personification of Amelia as an ontological and ethical error. But Thomson's depiction of the hunt replaces divine or natural forces like heaven and lightning—which Celadon wrongly imagined to act like persons, or to care about particular personalities—by human agents, who are themselves wholly dehumanized and pictured as natural forces. In this, the hunt scene picks up on Thomson's wider effort, in *The Seasons*, to fundamentally recast the nature of action, ejecting useless, self-directed, or rapacious acts from the category altogether. It is to this end that Thomson figures as an "idle Blank" the "cruel Wretch" who "squander'd vile, / Upon his scoundrel Train, what might have chear'd / A drooping Family of modest Worth"; so too the "luxurious Men" who "pass / An idle Summer-Life in Fortune's Shine," who "flutter on / From Toy to Toy, from Vanity to Vice" (*Su*, 1635–40, 346–49). Thomson depicts hunting as the exemplary case of such idleness or inaction, using the conventions of the mock-heroic to send up the lowly status not of the hunted fox but of the predatory hunter: "O glorious he, beyond / His daring Peers!" who, with a pack of "an hundred Mouths," triumphs over one "Villain" (*A*, 490–93). Thomson continues his burlesque of heroic agency in his description of the post-hunt meal. He personifies all kinds of things: "the strong Table groans"; ale is "not afraid . . . to vie" with wine; whist "Walks his grave Round"; dice are "leaping from the Box" (*A*, 503, 522–27). At the same time, Thomson depicts humans sinking into stupor, and then falling asleep:

> Their feeble Tongues,
> Unable to take up the cumbrous Word,
> Lie quite dissolv'd. Before their maudlin Eyes,
> Seen dim and blue, the double Tapers dance,
> Like the Sun wading thro' the misty Sky.
> Then, sliding soft, they drop.
> . . . .
> The *lubber* Power in filthy Triumph sits,
> Slumbrous, inclining still from Side to Side,
> And steeps them drench'd in potent Sleep till Morn. (*A*, 552–64)

This scene of what Thomson calls "social Slaughter" is clearly marked by the reversal of agency that Knapp identifies as the primary consequence of personification (*A*, 561). In Thomson, however, the combination of animate things and inanimate humans does not result from an invasion of ontological territory, as Knapp would have it: human beings are not reified because things are personified. Instead, Thomson's human beings have themselves abdicated their claim to personhood, by operating in a mode to which Thomson denies the status of action.

This abdication occurs during the hunt, when men are cast together with dogs as a "Storm," a "Tempest," and an "inhuman Rout" (*A*, 417, 428, 439). It happens elsewhere when humans plunder a beehive, and are described as "some dread Earthquake" (*A*, 1205). In *The Seasons*, these epithets are not only figures: to an apiarian eye, human beings *are* "some dread Earthquake" that seizes "a proud City, populous and rich"; to the "folded Ears; unsleeping Eyes" of a hunted hare, human beings (and dogs) are not persons, but a turn in the weather: "With every Breeze she hears the coming Storm" (*A*, 1201, 411, 417). With these shifts in point of view, Thomson makes body parts not only the objects or the means but also the subjects of personification, granting the eyes and ears of a bee or a hare the power to dispersonify humans. It is against the backdrop of these dispersonified human beings—human beings depicted and denounced as inanimate and destructive natural forces—that Thomson personifies the hunted stag. Driven by "the Tempest," the stag is pictured "sobbing," recalling good times with his "Friends" and "his Loves," relations who now abandon him as they "With selfish Care avoid a Brother's Woe." When the stag finally surrenders, "The big round Tears run down his dappled Face; / He groans in Anguish" (*A*, 428, 441–44, 448, 454–55). In various scenes of conquest, human beings who exercise what we typically think of as agency become an impersonal and inanimate force: a movement of air or of earth. By contrast, as the stag is "singled from the Herd" by a "Tempest" that pushes him forward, he becomes an individual, a singular, even psychological subject (*A*, 426). He becomes a person, in other words, by being a patient.

Critics have often censured Thomson for prescribing patience: for urging readers to "yet bear up a While," assuring them that this "bounded View" will pass and disclose "*The great eternal Scheme*" (*W*, 1065, 1066, 1046). On this reading, Thomson's vision of social harmony and his personification of human beings denies both the necessity and the possibility of action.[70] Yet Thomson aims to do something more complicated than evacuate action from his poetry and the society that it envisions. At its most challenging—from *The Castle of Indolence*'s allegory of the dangers of idleness, to *Liberty*'s effort to track the movement of a political idea through various persons and peoples, to the personifying system building that *The Seasons* performs—Thomson's poetry works to conceive a social order that might include everything under the sun, and to imagine an ethics that could serve such an expanded system. In doing so, Thomson's poetry insists that the kind of agency that we often ascribe to human persons is proper not to persons but to impersonal and divine forces like an earthquake, a tempest, or the indiscriminate and "unconquerable Lightning" (*Su*, 1147). Thomson advocates patience as an alternative not to action, but to this mode of agency that is structured around a subject and the objects that it necessarily acts upon: a structure that, Thomson suggests, leads inevitably to harm. Thomson advocates patience—which he alternately conceives of as passion and as animal motion or animation—as a mode of agency in which moving and being moved are impossible to parse, and a model of personhood that might harmonize the movements of all kinds of people. But he is not always hopeful, or sure. For this person is the product of often perplexing poetic labor, and it is a figure of vulnerability that is conceived against but also out of violence. In part, this is what Robinson Crusoe comes to sense during his sojourn in the wilderness: how easily the "Social Commerce" of all sorts of people can appear, to any particular person, like cannibalism. As *The Seasons* everywhere reminds us, wilderness surrounds.

Chapter 2

The Creature

Domestic Politics and the Novelistic Character

In Robert Zemeckis's film *Cast Away* (2000), Tom Hanks plays Chuck Noland, a modern-day Robinson Crusoe who does what Thomson does with wilderness, though on a smaller and more intimate scale: he composes society, and he does so by way of personification. When his plane goes down somewhere in the Pacific, Noland is marooned for four years on an uninhabited desert island, where he survives with the aid of material remnants of the society he has lost: the contents of FedEx packages that wash ashore. Frustrated by his efforts to make fire, Noland picks up the contents of one of these packages—a Wilson volleyball—and flings it against a tree. Later, he notices that his bloodied handprint has given the ball a kind of face, whose features Noland then accentuates, highlighting the outlines of eyes, nose, and mouth. Finally, Noland animates this figure with a question posed in the second person: "you wouldn't have a match, by any chance, would you?"[1] In Hanks's account of the film, from the moment that Noland addresses "Wilson" with this question, "there is a new person created in Chuck's head."[2] Noland spends the rest of his time on the island in Wilson's company. When Wilson is lost at sea, Noland grieves his loss.

In many respects, *Cast Away* is remarkably faithful to Defoe's original castaway narrative. But there are significant differences between Zemeckis's film and *Robinson Crusoe*. As Hanks tells it, he first conceived of *Cast Away* as a film of "pure behavior and action": the tale of "a character who would spend the bulk of his time onscreen doing rather than talking."[3] He remembers being assaulted by "suggestions on how to embellish his spare drama by helping the protagonist find somebody to trade quips with. 'It would be like, "Well, what if he had a monkey?""⁴ As one critic remarks, the "closest thing Chuck gets to a Man Friday"—or, to a monkey—"is a Wilson volleyball."⁵ Noland's island is notable for its lack of any living creatures. Crusoe's, by contrast, is populated by all kinds of animals: "two or three household Kids," "several tame Sea-Fowls," which were "very agreeable," three parrots including Poll, whom Crusoe describes as "a sociable Creature," a dog that he calls "a very pleasant and loving Companion," and "two or three Favourites" out of the cats on the island which, Crusoe says, "were part of my Family" (112, 141).

Despite the presence of so many animate creatures whom he describes in explicitly social terms, Crusoe, like Noland, often complains of his "solitary Condition" (110). Crusoe makes clear what is missing when a passing ship is wrecked on the rocks: "O that there had been but one or two; nay, or but one Soul sav'd out of this Ship, to have escap'd to me, that I might but have had one Companion, one Fellow-Creature to have spoken to me, and to have convers'd with! In all the time of my solitary Life, I never felt so earnest, so strong a Desire after the Society of my Fellow-Creatures, or so deep a Regret at the want of it" (147). Crusoe boards the wreck to see if "there might be yet some living Creature on board," but is "disturb'd" and "desperate" with "Disappointment" when he discovers only a dog, "where I had been so near the obtaining what I so earnestly long'd for, viz. Some-Body to speak to" (154). By "the Society of . . . Fellow-Creatures," then, Crusoe does not mean the company of "some living Creature" like a dog, but the conversation of someone to whom he might speak. By limiting society to those who can speak, Crusoe would seem to designate a solely human domain, quite different from the expansive animal system of Thomson's animated earth.

As the narrative proceeds, however, Defoe brings the company of animate creatures and the society of "Some-Body to speak to" much closer together. According to his own narration, at least, Crusoe does seem to have "Some-Body to speak to" on the island, and this somebody is both like and unlike Noland's Wilson. Early during his island sojourn, Crusoe reports that "I diverted my self with talking to my Parrot, and teaching him to Speak, and I quickly learn'd him to know his own Name, and at last to speak it out pretty loud P O L L, which was the first Word I ever heard spoken in the Island by any Mouth but my own" (94). Crusoe continues to pass his time on the island both speaking and being spoken to: "I had taught my Poll, as I noted before, to speak; and he did it so familiarly, and talk'd so articulately and plain, that it was very pleasant to me; and he liv'd with me no less than six and twenty years" (141). In spite of such descriptions of his creaturely company and conversation, critics frequently take Crusoe's complaints of his solitary "silent Life" at face value (123). As Irene Basey Beesemeyer puts it, "not withstanding 'conversations' with Poll, the dog and cats, maybe even the goats, Crusoe is his own sole correspondent for much of the text."[6] David Marshall and Eric Jager similarly set Crusoe's conversations with animals in scare quotes, identifying Poll as Crusoe's "talking signature," or his own "'othered' voice."[7] Such readings understand Crusoe's animal companions not as "Some-Body to speak to," but as products of Crusoe's own projective imagination—"poignant yet humorous reminders of the absent conversation that he desires during his many years of solitude."[8] For Jager, most explicitly, Crusoe's conversations are "conversations" because they proceed by means of personification. By "personifying the other," Jager writes, "Crusoe acquires a 'diverting' semblance of society, though it is no more than a semblance."[9]

Jager's comments get at an important aspect of *Robinson Crusoe*: its interest in the operation that constitutes persons and society around conversation or the capacity to speak, an operation that is usefully thought of in terms of personification. Yet *Cast Away* helps us to be more precise about Defoe's use of this device. For if Noland and Crusoe both personify the beings to whom they speak, the status of their personifications differs. Made from Noland's handprint, of Noland's blood, Wilson is literally an effect of his creator's physical and psychological state, a projection that results from but does not end Noland's isolation. Despite the vividness of Wilson's persona or the animation of Noland's address, there is never any question that Wilson is, in a strong sense, only in Chuck's head. Neither monkey nor man, Wilson never does become "somebody to trade quips with" (in Hanks's terms) or "Some-Body to speak to" (in Crusoe's). The same is not true of an animate creature like Poll. Poll may be imprinted (and so given speech) by Crusoe's voice, much as Wilson is imprinted (and so given face) by Noland's hand. But Defoe locates this imprinting in the interaction of two living creatures, rather than with the action of a human being upon an inanimate object. The difference between talking to a volleyball and talking to a parrot signals that Defoe uses personification neither to index Crusoe's psychological state nor, as critics often imagine, to divide true society from its mere semblance. Instead, Crusoe's personification of Poll arises from uncertainty about the distinction between speaking and moving, and it ultimately opens the possibility that "the Society of . . . Fellow-Creatures" might be composed of animals as well as human beings. With its focus on a lone individual and a putatively presocial state of nature, Defoe's novel seems a long way from Thomson's vision of the great "social Commerce" of the whole "Earth animated" (*A*, 834; *Su*, 292). But like Thomson, Defoe suggests that personhood itself is a quasi-figurative status, and one that might extend to all animate creatures.

The stakes of this suggestion, for Defoe, are explicitly political. In particular, the connections Defoe draws between personification, speech, and animal motion make significant trouble for the Lockean political philosophy he is frequently seen to endorse. Locke's account of civil society turns on the distinction between political authority (a relation between human persons that is constituted by consent) and property right (a relation between persons and things that is constituted by appropriation). In condensed form, Locke construes these two modes of relation as speaking and eating; these relations in turn rest on the putatively natural distinction between human persons and all other things. Locke's own work often undercuts this simplified Lockean schema, as I argue in this chapter and at greater length in Chapter 4. But it is this basic Lockean paradigm that Defoe both invokes and undermines in *Robinson Crusoe*. Rather than picture a world divided into persons and things—on the model of Locke's *Second Treatise*, and also Zemeckis's *Cast Away*—*Robinson Crusoe* composes a domestic and creaturely society that does not clearly sort humans from animals, speaking from eating, consent from coercion, family from food. In this respect, Defoe's social vision resembles Thomson's, imagining as it does a society that extends beyond human beings, and granting personification a central role in its constitution. But the domestic society that emerges on Crusoe's island is not the expansive and affirmative social vision of *The Seasons*. Instead, it is a sign of the breakdown, or the impossibility, of Lockean politics.

The claim that Defoe sketches a distinctly un-Lockean world may sound strange to readers of *Robinson Crusoe*, more accustomed to viewing Defoe's text as a sympathetic novelization of Lockean political philosophy. There are good reasons to hold this customary view. It is certainly the case that Crusoe wants society to work as Locke outlines. An obsessive maker of contracts even in the most unlikely of circumstances, he seeks both to secure and to legitimate his dominion over other people by construing his dominion as Locke would construe it, in terms of consent. But Defoe undercuts the Lockean longings of his own protagonist. He does this in the narrative by replacing Locke's category of the human person with the more capacious category of the creature, and by associating speech with the figure of personification, and with the creaturely activities of moving and eating. He does this too at the level of form—particularly, in the creaturely form of his "Allegorical, though also Historical" central character, a direct representation of the species "Man," or even the more abstract and nonspecific "Life." I will have more to say about what this means in the next section. For now, I mean to note simply that it is by novelizing Locke's political philosophy that Defoe undercuts its logic. Character is the formal site of a conclusion that sets *Robinson Crusoe* apart from the political individualism of Locke's *Second Treatise* (and, from the psychological individualism of *Cast Away*): the conclusion that it is impossible to be solitary or sovereign, secure in oneself and in one's species, one who speaks and is not eaten. It does not matter where we are—on a desert island, at the center of an English metropolis, on a plantation in Brazil—we are incorporated in the kind of domestic society that *Robinson Crusoe* pictures, for this is simply what we are: lives made of and by others.

Fellow Creatures and the Novelistic Character

In his remarks on *Robinson Crusoe*, Samuel Taylor Coleridge commented that the greatness of Defoe's character is that he is a "representative of humanity in general": he "makes me forget my *specific* class, character, and circumstances, [and] raises me into the universal man."[10] Though in some respects Defoe clearly does attend to specificities of class, character, and circumstance, Coleridge's kind of claim has followed the novel since its inception. Readers from Rousseau to James Joyce have continued to assert Crusoe's representative status.[11] In doing so, they celebrate an achievement that can seem at odds with Ian Watt's still influential account of the genre, in which Defoe is the first novelist in part because he—like Locke, on Watt's account—privileges "the discrete particular, the directly apprehended sensum, and the autonomous individual" over "the ideal, the universal, and the corporate."[12] Certainly, one might read Coleridge's remark in a way that is wholly compatible with Watt's individualist logic—if, for example, Defoe arrives at universal representativeness by way of an inductive process of aggregation, adding together so many discrete particulars to compose first smaller groups (Coleridge's "*specific* class") and then the species as a whole. The greatness of *Crusoe*, on this view, would consist in its greatness of scope: Crusoe moves past "the various forms of traditional group relationship, the family, the guild, the village, the sense of nationality" to stand for the whole of the species, conceived of as an even bigger group.[13] By this account, the difference between family, guild, nation, and species is a quantitative one.

All are collectives differentiated by degree, and the basic unit, in each case, is the discrete and particular individual. This would be to take Coleridge (and Defoe) to articulate a modern logic of generalization associated with the empiricism of Locke or Bacon before him, in which individuals come first, and are then composed or collected into groups.

In *Robinson Crusoe*, however, Defoe develops something quite different: a representative novelistic character that is not derived from empirical particulars but is a direct representation of the species—a character that is at once abstract and realistic or, in Defoe's terms, both allegorical and historical. It is Crusoe who describes his character this way, in the third volume of his narrative, *Serious Reflections During the Life and Adventures of Robinson Crusoe*:

> I have heard, that the envious and ill-disposed Part of the World have rais'd some Objections against the two first Volumes, on Pretence . . . that (*as they say*) the Story is feign'd, that the Names are borrow'd, and that it is all a Romance; that there never were any such Man or Place, or Circumstances in any Mans Life; that it is all form'd and embellish'd by Invention to impose upon the World.
>
> I *Robinson Crusoe* being at this Time in perfect and sound Mind and Memory, Thanks be to God therefore; do hereby declare, their Objection is an Invention scandalous in Design, and false in Fact; and do affirm, that the Story, though Allegorical, is also Historical; and that it is the beautiful Representation of a Life of unexampled Misfortunes, and of a Variety not to be met with in the World, sincerely adapted to, and intended for the common Good of Mankind, and designed at first, *as it is now farther apply'd*, to the most serious Uses possible.
>
> Farther, that there is a Man alive, and well known too, the Actions of whose Life are the just Subject of these Volumes, and to whom all or most Part of the Story most directly alludes, this may be depended upon for Truth, and to this I set my Name.[14]

Few readers make much of Crusoe's peculiar assertion that his story "though Allegorical, is also Historical."[15] From Charles Gildon to Catherine Gallagher, they tend to argue that Defoe is caught in a lie and belatedly tries to switch genres, recasting Crusoe's castaway narrative as the secret history of Defoe's own life.[16] This reading resolves the apparent incompatibility between Crusoe's two claims—that his adventures are "literally true" and also that they are "allegorical"—by taking Crusoe to mean that his adventures refer indirectly but truthfully to a particular living person.

Such a reading has the benefit of resolving Crusoe's curious formulation into good common sense. But it does not exhaust the possibilities of this passage. Against those who charge that "there never were any such Man . . . or Circumstances in any Mans Life," Crusoe insists that *Robinson Crusoe* is the true "Representation of a Life," the real and historical story of "a Man." In light of the novel's interest in the logic that organizes both inter- and intra-species relations, I think we are invited to read the indefinite article as such, and take "a Man" to mean not *this* man (Defoe) but simply *a* man. In other words, we might read *Robinson Crusoe* as Coleridge suggests, as the story of "a representative of man in general." Though Gallagher herself does not read *Crusoe* in this way, her work on the novelistic character is helpful in considering what it would look like if we did. In "The Rise of Fictionality," Gallagher begins where Watt's account of the novel's rise most clearly falters: with Fielding, and in particular, with Fielding's claim (from *Joseph Andrews*) "that he describes 'not men, but manners; not an individual, but a species" (341). Gallagher identifies Fielding's claim as a major turning point in the emergence of fiction, which clearly distinguishes the realist novel from the factual historical narrative by articulating a set of ambitions for the new genre—above all, its capacity to "refer to a whole class of people in general" (342). Against Watt's sense of the novel's commitment to particular individuals, Gallagher gives us the realist novel as a genre shaped by the logic of the general, the type, or the species.[17] Intriguingly, novelistic generality takes two slightly different forms in Gallagher's account. On the one hand, Gallagher presents Fielding's "species" as "a whole class of people," understood as a collection of logically prior individuals—much like Coleridge's "*specific* class" or Watt's "aggregate of particular individuals having particular experiences at particular times and at particular places."[18] On the other hand and more unusually, she presents Fielding's "species" not as an effect of aggregation but as an entirely different kind of figure: "the form of the fictional Nobody, a proper name explicitly without a physical referent in the real world."[19] Citing Barthes and Searle for different versions of the idea that in fiction, proper names "refer to what they . . . are simultaneously creating," Gallagher suggests that this new novelistic character is not a collection of particular and prior persons, composed by aggregation or induction (353). Created in and by the fictional text, the novelistic character is a general but crucially not a collective form. It is the nonempirical and indefinite species creature that Gallagher calls a "Nobody."

On Gallagher's view, Defoe comes too early to participate in the Fielding-led rise of fictionality. Still, he articulates something close to the general form of Gallagher's Nobody when he has Crusoe identify his story as both allegorical and historical, the real story of "a Man" or "a Life," "to which I sign my Name." Crusoe's allegorical logic is not simply the one-to-one correspondence of secret history (Crusoe stands for Defoe), nor is it the one-to-many correspondence of class (Crusoe as the sum of many individuals, their lowest common denominator, their average or mean). It is a species logic that understands "species" not as a collection of particular individuals, but as an abstract and indefinite term: a Man, a Life.[20] At stake here is a logic of literary characterization that is neither individualist nor humanist but is nonetheless realist, claiming some reference to historical and material reality. As a representative of man in general, Crusoe is closer to an allegorical personification than a particular person, the embodiment of an abstraction (Man) rather than an aggregate or average term (a representative of men).[21] What's more, in the indefinite generality that forgoes the specifics of class, character, and circumstance, even the specificities of species begin to give way. A general form that does not start from individuals need not stop, it would seem, with the human species. Crusoe is thus the representation of not only "a Man" but also "a Life"—a more inclusive and indeterminate category, which Defoe designates by the term "creature."

Turning to the narrative itself, we can start to apprehend more precisely what it means to conceive the character Crusoe on the model of the creature, as the (abstract and material, allegorical and historical) "Representation of a Life." Creatureliness is a major thematic preoccupation of the novel, and the central telos of its plot.[22] At the start of his adventures, Crusoe is a "young Man" in the company of men (6): his father, "a wise and grave Man" (5), a host of "Seafaring Men" who are also called "Seamen" or simply "Men" (8, 10–13), the ship captain, "an honest and plain-dealing Man" (16), and the Moor and Xury, whom Crusoe calls "the Man and Boy" (19). Yet the moment that Crusoe departs from known territory, making his escape with Xury—the "Boy" whom Crusoe promises to make "a great Man" but ends up selling to slavery—he encounters other beings, which he calls "creatures" (21). These appear for the first time when Crusoe and Xury drop anchor for the night, at the mouth of a river near shore:

> We heard such dreadful Noises of the Barking, Roaring, and Howl-
> ing of Wild Creatures, of we knew not what Kinds. . . . In two or

three Hours we saw vast great Creatures (we knew not what to call them) of many sorts, come down to the Sea-shoar and run into the Water. . . . We were both more frighted when we heard one of these mighty Creatures come swimming towards our Boat, we could not see him, but we might hear him by his blowing to be a monstrous, huge and furious Beast; Xury said it was a Lyon, and it might be so for ought I know. . . . I perceiv'd the Creature (whatever it was) within Two Oars Length, which something surpized me, and taking up my gun fir'd at him. (22)

In this passage, Crusoe seems to use "creature" to mark the epistemological pre-dicament that results from conditions of both perceptual obscurity ("we could not see") and conceptual uncertainty. Even when they "saw" the creatures, Crusoe reports, "we knew not what to call them"; again, when he "perceiv'd" the creature at only two oars' length, he still could not identify it ("whatever it was"). Crusoe's arrival on the island is marked by a series of similarly indis-tinct creaturely encounters—with "two or three Creatures like Hares" and "a Creature like a wild Cat," as well as with "two Fowls like Ducks," "a Sea Fowl or two, something like a brand Goose," and "Hares, as I thought them to be, and Foxes, but they differ'd greatly from all the other Kinds I had met with" (44, 45, 58, 76, 87). In all these moments, Crusoe would seem to use "creature" to mark his uncertainty in the face of the new.[23]

From the start, however, Defoe indicates that "creature" signals some-thing more than a terminological solution to the problem of classifying unfa-miliar particulars. A few pages after Crusoe and Xury encounter the "vast great Creatures" that Crusoe shoots at but does not name, they meet natives, whom Crusoe calls "People" and "Negroes" (25, 26). This second encounter suggests that whatever the earlier "vast great Creatures" were, they were not human, a species that Crusoe seems able to recognize and to designate as such. But this designation falters momentarily when Crusoe describes what happens when "two mighty Creatures" once again run into the water, and Crusoe once again fires his gun: "It is impossible to express the Astonishment of these poor Creatures at the Noise and Fire of my Gun; some of them were ready to dye for Fear, and fell down as Dead with the very Terror. But when they saw the Creature dead and sunk in the Water, and I made Signs to them to come to the Shore; they took Heart and came to the Shore and began to search for the Creature" (26). Only after a moment of indistinction between "these poor Creatures" and the "two mighty Creatures" does Crusoe distinguish human from animal, going on to relate how the "Negroes" dragged the creature's body to shore to discover "a most curious Leopard" (27). In his descriptions of both nonhuman and human responses to his gun, Crusoe extends this sort of creaturely indeterminacy further still. Of the first encounter (with the "vast great [nonhuman] Creatures" at the mouth of the river), Crusoe writes: "it is impossible to describe the horrible Noises, and hideous Cryes and Howlings, that were raised . . . upon the Noise or Report of the Gun, a Thing I have some Reason to believe those Creatures had never heard before" (22). Of the second encounter (with the "poor [human] Creatures" on the shore), he writes: "it is impossible to express the Astonishment of these poor Creatures at the Noise and Fire of my Gun" (22, 26). Human and nonhuman creatures alike are astonished by Crusoe's gunfire in a way he finds "impossible to express" and "impossible to describe."

Set together, these scenes signal that the term "creature" does more than index Crusoe's epistemological uncertainty. It is also the novel's word for an ontological determination effected by exposure to external force. The creatures in these episodes are identified as such because that is what they are, not simply because Crusoe does not know what else to call them. The humans who are astonished by Crusoe's gunfire, the "vast great Creatures" at which Crusoe shoots—as well as the "Creatures like Hares" and "Creature like a Wild Cat" that will later come under Crusoe's fire—are all creatures in the sense that Julia Reinhard Lupton outlines in her discussion of "the politico-theological category of the creaturely," which associates the creature with embodiment, vulnerability, and especially, with subjection to a radically superior power (the Creator).[24] It might appear that Crusoe is patently unlike the creatures he encounters, given that he wields the gun that constitutes them as such. But in both of these scenes, Crusoe's gunfire is followed by a striking symmetry of response. Unable to describe or express the response of different creatures at the noise and fire of his gun, Crusoe is as incapacitated and astonished as they.[25] Ultimately, Crusoe's gun serves to indicate his insecurity rather than his sovereignty—to indicate, most simply, that that he is a creature too, one vulnerable living body among others. In Defoe, "creature" works much as Thomson's personifications do in *The Seasons*, to identify all beings under (and in contrast with) "Mysterious Heaven."

To make this claim is again to work against one dominant strain of both secular and religious readings of Defoe's novel. Critics often dispute the sincerity of Crusoe's religiosity, but they usually agree that he proceeds by means of a set of analogical relations—between literal and metaphorical, material and spiritual, human and divine—toward God, whom he becomes or becomes like, as he ultimately achieves a quasi-divine mastery over others.[26] Critics also agree that the turning point in Crusoe's movement toward mastery occurs during his illness, in the moment of conversion when he first conceives of himself in relation to God. Crusoe marks the start of this moment with a question: "Lord, what a miserable Creature am I?" (72). He marks its conclusion, in turn, with God's answer, which Crusoe discovers when he opens the Bible and reads at random: "*Call on me in the Day of Trouble, and I will deliver, and thou shalt glorify me*" (75). On this reading, Defoe configures a relation of resemblance that will come to facilitate Crusoe's movement between positions: a creature with respect to his Creator, Crusoe becomes Creator with respect to the rest of creation.[27]

I am arguing, by contrast, that over the course of the narrative Crusoe's development proceeds toward not divine omnipotence but creaturely identification with the humans, lions, leopards, hares, and cats that are subject to his gun. This is indicated by the vocabulary of creature indeterminacy that sets in as soon as Crusoe leaves European society. It is also signaled at the moment of his conversion, for the psalm to which Crusoe turns is as likely to prevent as to promote his identification with God:

> Hear, O my people, and I will speak; O Israel, and I will testify against thee: I am God, even thy God.
> I will not reprove thee for thy sacrifices or thy burnt offerings, to have been continually before me.
> I will take no bullock out of thy house, nor he goats out of thy folds,
> For every beast of the forest is mine, and the cattle upon a thousand hills.
> I know all the fowls of the mountains: and the wild beasts of the field are mine,
> If I were hungry, I would not tell thee: for the world is mine, and the fullness thereof.
> Will I eat the flesh of bulls, or drink the blood of goats?
> Offer unto God thanksgiving; and pay your vows unto the most High:
> And call upon me in the day of trouble: I will deliver thee, and thou shalt glorify me. (Ps. 50:7–15)

It is this last line that Crusoe cites in the text, and on its own, the line seems to accord with a fairly conventional schema in which one submits to God and becomes master of others. Defoe certainly invokes this schema here, but his particular textual choice complicates that gesture. By stressing the impropriety of merely physical sacrifice for a God who, unlike humans, does not feed on flesh, this psalm emphasizes a significant difference between Crusoe and God—a difference that turns on relations of owning and of eating. The way that the beast and cattle and fowls are God's is fundamentally unlike the way that Crusoe makes them his, with decidedly undivine acts of material eating and drinking. Similarly, Defoe does not simply mark a moment of regression into doubt when Crusoe goes on to compare himself to the children of Israel who asked, "when they were promis'd Flesh to eat, *Can God spread a Table in the Wilderness?*" (75). He also articulates a relation between creature and Creator that is not one of distance but of categorical difference, of kind and not degree: between God, who will not eat, and human beings, who must.

Eating may not seem a likely or sufficient ground for the sort of "radical separation of Creation and Creator" that Lupton outlines in her work on the creature, and around which Defoe organizes his novel.[28] But *Robinson Crusoe* is a novel obsessed with eating, in both its metaphorical and literal senses. This is most obvious in Crusoe's seemingly inordinate preoccupation with cannibalism. Many critics point out that Crusoe's fear of finding himself as food for another is less extravagant if one understands it as the displacement of his quite plausible fear of finding another as food for himself. In order to consider eating and being eaten together and in political terms, however, such readings move quickly into a metaphorics of consumption, in which "eating" figures various kinds of relations between human beings.[29] Crusoe's anxieties about cannibalism certainly intimate that his activities as capitalist, colonizer, or slave trader involve the metaphorical devouring of other people. But Defoe repeatedly insists that eating is not only a figure for human relations.[30] From the moment that Crusoe arrives on the island, his narrative is filled with frequent and extended accounts of what and how he literally eats: the effort he expends protecting his crops of barley and rice; gathering and drying grapes; mastering the tasks required to make a loaf of bread; and hunting or taming turtles, pigeons, and goats. And such activities occupy Crusoe's time as much as they do his narrative: he reports that his "Morning Walk with my Gun" to bring home "something fit to eat," "generally took me up three Hours each Morning"; the "great Part of the Day" was then spent "ordering, curing, preserving, and cooking what I had kill'd or catch'd for my Supply" (60, 91).

Just as eating occupies much of Crusoe's time on the island, it also plays a central role in the political-philosophical imaginary of the novel, in ways that bring Defoe's engagement with Locke into sharper focus. For Locke invokes eating as his first example of the natural dominion of persons over things, which he calls property: "The Fruit, or Venison, which nourishes the wild Indian, who knows no Inclosure, and is still a Tenant in common, must be his, and so his, i.e. a part of him, that another can no longer have any right to it, before it can do him any good for the support of his Life."[31] In his reading of this key passage from the *Second Treatise of Government*, Wolfram Schmidgen remarks that Locke uses "the ingestive act as a vivid figure for a property that is inalienable because it is physically tied to the body."[32] Indeed for Locke, eating is at once a "vivid figure" for property and also a primary mode of appropriation. This means that eating occupies a strangely central place in Locke's account of political society, and particularly, in his crucial distinction between political authority and property right. This distinction would seem to proceed from given and natural grounds: from the distinction between (human) persons and (all other) things. But the distinction between persons and things does not come to Locke ready-made, as it might seem from the *Second Treatise* alone. Instead, Locke strives throughout his *First Treatise of Government* to constitute the kind of being on which his politics comes to depend: a being defined by its a capacity for speech and—more peculiarly—by the specter of cannibalism.

Locke constitutes this being—the human person—by working through the same territory of creatureliness and cannibalism that shapes *Robinson Crusoe*. He begins by attacking Robert Filmer for sanctioning anthropophagy: "If God made all Mankind slaves to *Adam* and his Heirs, by giving *Adam* dominion over *every living thing that moveth on the Earth, Chapt.* I. 28. as our *A—* would have it, methinks Sir *Robert* should have carried his Monarchical Power one step higher, and satisfied the World, that Princes might eat their Subjects too, since God gave as full Power to *Noah* and his Heirs, *Chap.* 9.2. to eat *every Living thing that moveth*, as he did to *Adam* to have Dominion over them, the *Hebrew* words in both places being the same" (160). In this passage, Locke's move against Filmer seems sensationalist and somewhat slight: he shocks his readers by literalizing a common figure of speech, that of a sovereign consuming his subjects. But as Locke proceeds, the charge of cannibalism becomes a serious first step in an extended exegetical discussion of our God-given right to eat. The first passage to which Locke refers is God's donation to Adam at creation: "*And God Blessed them, and God said unto them, be Fruitful and Multiply and Replenish the Earth and subdue it, and have Dominion over the Fish of the Sea, and over the Fowl of the Air, and over every living thing that moveth upon the Earth"* (Gen 1:28, qtd. in Locke 156). On the basis of this passage, Filmer insists that there is only one kind of dominion, which is granted by God and wielded by the monarch over the earth and every living thing (fish, fowl, or human): *"Adam, having here Dominion given him over all Creatures, was thereby the Monarch of the whole World"* (Filmer, *Patriarcha*, qtd. in Locke 157). By contrast, Locke argues that there are various types of dominion, not all of which are divinely instituted. To support this claim, Locke looks to God's second covenant, with Noah. As with Adam, Locke points out, God grants Noah "dominion" over "every living thing that moveth." For Noah, however, this dominion includes the right to eat, while Adam's dominion did not even permit him, as Locke puts it, to "make bold with a Lark or a Rabbet to satisfie his hunger" (167).

For Locke, Noah's eating rights are crucial. First, the difference between Noah's right to eat "every living thing that moveth" and Adam's more limited dominion (he was granted, Locke notes, "the Herbs but in common with the Beasts" [167]) marks the difference between private property and property in common. Private property is not created until God's covenant with Noah. Only then, Locke explains, are Noah and his sons granted "the utmost Property Man is capable of, which is to have a right to destroy any thing by using it; *Every moving thing that Liveth,* saith God, *shall be Meat for you,* which was not allowed to *Adam* in his Charter" (167). This right to destroy moving, living things—to use them as food—is for Locke the original of private property. More importantly still, Locke argues, Noah's right to eat makes clear that God creates only property right, and not political authority. For if the category over which God granted dominion—the category of "every moving thing that liveth"—had included human beings, then God's covenant with Noah would permit cannibalism. Reasoning that property means the right to eat and that eating people is wrong, Locke asserts the basic distinction of his political society: between political authority, a dominion over human persons that is established by consent (synecdochally, speaking), and property right, a dominion over nonhuman things established by appropriation (synecdochally, eating). Finally, Locke concludes that because the dominion that God grants to Adam/Noah is not granted over (any) man, it must be granted to (every) man: that is, God does not grant Adam and Noah dominion as particular individuals but as representatives of man in general. There is no divine right of kings, but there is a divine right of kind.

Throughout the *First Treatise*, Locke aims to show that eating human beings is wrong and that eating other creatures is right. Locke's source for the term "creature" is Genesis (and Filmer's reading of it), but the centrality of "the Creatures" to Locke's *First Treatise* suggests that they present something of a problem, which Locke attempts to contain in his opening moves.[33] For creatures, which are sometimes human and not clearly things, threaten to confuse the categories that Locke would keep separate: property right and political authority, distinguished as the right to eat any*thing*, and the wrong of eating any*one*. This point is brought home if one sets Locke's political philosophy alongside his *Essay Concerning Human Understanding*. In the *Second Treatise of Government*, Locke grounds his account of the state of nature, of property, and of political society on the claim that God grants "the Dominion of the whole Species of Mankind, over the inferior Species of Creatures" (161). In the *Essay*, Locke depicts the "Species of Mankind" as a wholly unstable creature: "the *Idea* in our Minds, of which the Sound *Man* in our Mouths is the Sign, is nothing else but of an Animal of such a certain Form" (333). The *Essay* is in dialogue with Descartes's account of the human being rather than with Filmer's account of monarchical authority; there, Locke insists that if one inquires into "the precise and *unmovable Boundaries of* that *Species*," one learns that "there is *no* such thing *made by Nature*" (454). Describing case after case of "Creatures in the World" whose uncertain forms call into question the grounds and limits of species determination, Locke ultimately argues that species are general ideas that exist in our minds and in language: their "*real* and *nominal Essence* is the same" (450, 437). In the *Essay*, "human" is a human invention: "*the boundaries of the Species, whereby Men sort them, are made by Men*" (462).

The question that is raised by setting Locke's major works together is this: what happens to a political philosophy that asserts mankind's divine right of dominion over "the Creatures" if "man" is a variously composed complex idea, a "*Creature of the Understanding*" created not by God but by human beings themselves (430)? Crusoe raises a version of this same question at his conversion, when he asks "Lord, what a miserable Creature am I?" He follows this question with another, which asks about his identity in relation to others: "what am I, and all the other Creatures, wild and tame, humane and brutal, whence are we?" (72, 73). The difference that is revealed during Crusoe's conversion—the fact that Crusoe eats and God does not (or, only eats symbolically)—is crucial above all because it in turn reveals a relation of identity between creatures. This relation connects the question of creatureliness to that of cannibalism, construed not only as a figure for the various ways that one might exploit or appropriate the labor or land of other human beings, but also as a specific, material act. In *Robinson Crusoe*, cannibalism does not function as it does in the *Two Treatises*, to distinguish human beings from other creatures; instead, it signals the political question that arises from the instability of any such distinction. Crusoe defines cannibals—and would distinguish himself from them—by their "inhuman feastings on the bodies of their fellow-Creatures" (129). Yet against its would-be Lockean protagonist, *Robinson Crusoe* asks: if Crusoe does not know what kind of creature he is, then how does he know who his fellow creatures are, or, who is good to eat?

This is the threat posed by the "Society of . . . Fellow-Creatures" in which Crusoe finds himself: that all creatures are bound in relations not of potentially universal harmony (pace Thomson) but of cannibalistic consumption. Such a creaturely society is threatening, above all, because it extends outside of the novel. Crusoe's representative humanity—his direct representation of the abstraction "Man" or "Life"—insists that we are creatures too. To say this is to return to Gallagher, who argues, at the end of "The Rise of Fictionality," that what we experience when we read novels is "cathexis with ontological difference" (357). On Gallagher's view, readers come to novels secure in their "independent embodied selfhood" or "embodied immanence"; characters, by contrast, remain "forever tethered to the abstraction of type" (361). When we read fiction, Gallagher ventures, we are invited to imagine ourselves through the eyes of this tethered, incomplete character, and to experience the vicarious and "uncanny desire to be that which we already are": an independent, embodied, "ontologically plentiful" individual (361). Gallagher's sense of the individual's intrinsic significance and embodied independence aligns her, in this respect, with Watt, who likewise sets reality, materiality, and particularity together, and against fictionality, ideality, and generality. It is precisely the logic of these sets that Defoe disarticulates when he sets the real and the material (what Crusoe calls "historical") together with the general or abstract (what Crusoe calls "allegorical"). In *Robinson Crusoe*, finally, embodiment precludes both particularity and independence, because real living bodies are first and foremost the site of generality or species—not in the sense of taxonomic categories like human, parrot, or dog, but in the broadest sense of the creaturely identity shared by all living bodies, dependent and vulnerable creatures who must eat and might be eaten in turn.[34] For Gallagher, again, the readerly desire to experience "the contradictory sensations of *not being a character*" is a desire "to be that which we already are": an independent, embodied, "ontologically plentiful" person (361). For Defoe, by contrast, the readerly desire to not be a character is a desire to be that which we can never be: an author or Creator, an absolute monarch or an autonomous human being.[35] In this way, Defoe insists on the identity of literary characters and living creatures, both human and nonhuman. Crusoe is not a representative figure because he is immaterial, disembodied, and fictional—a "Nobody," in Gallagher's terms. Instead, he is the allegorical-historical "Representation of a Life" because he represents the abstract and dependent embodiment common to literary characters, human persons, and living animals. This is the general condition of creatureliness that the "universal man" Crusoe represents: a life necessarily composed of and by others, unable to confidently separate something to eat from "Some-Body to speak to." *The Life and Strange Surprizing Adventures of Robinson Crusoe* is the story of this condition, and of Crusoe's responses to it.

Sociable Creatures and the Figure of Personification

Throughout the *First Treatise of Government*, I have argued, Locke raises the specter of cannibalism in order to argue that there are different types of beings that call for different types of dominion. Throughout *Robinson Crusoe*, by contrast, Defoe raises the specter of cannibalism in order to dismantle Locke's categories of being and of dominion, or at least to reveal their construction. Defoe raises the specter of cannibalism most famously when, after Crusoe has been on the island for many years, he is "surpriz'd with the Print of a Man's naked Foot on the Shore" (121). Crusoe attributes the print to Satan, to himself, and finally to cannibals, and he responds, in his words, "like a Man perfectly confus'd and out of my self"—according to "the usual Practice of all Creatures in Fear," he fled like a "frighted Hare . . . to Cover, or Fox to Earth" (121). As this response indicates, the footprint unsettles Crusoe's sense of both who or what he is and of who or what surrounds him. Picturing himself in quick succession "like a Man," a hare, and a fox, Crusoe proceeds to see men in all kinds of things, to personify indiscriminately: "I came Home to my Fortification, not feeling, as we say, the Ground I went on, but terrify'd to the last Degree, looking behind me at every two or three Steps, mistaking every Bush and Tree, and fancying every Stump at a Distance to be a man" (121). Personification emerges in this scene as a figure for Crusoe's fear of cannibalism, registering Crusoe's apprehension of his own creaturely vulnerability by picturing bushes, trees, and stumps as persons-cum-predators.

At least, this is the way that Crusoe explains things. Crusoe claims that the footprint occasioned this response because it "frighted" him with the sudden possibility of other people: "I had liv'd here fifteen Years now; and had not met with the least Shadow or Figure of any People yet" (121, 126). But an earlier encounter between Crusoe and Poll suggests that Crusoe has already and repeatedly "met with the . . . Shadow or Figure of . . . People" on the island; that he does so, in fact, every time he addresses an animal. Crusoe's encounter with Poll—which occurs unexpectedly, during Crusoe's travels around the island—hints that Crusoe has been personifying animals since he arrived on the island, and this is why he is increasingly terrified by the possibility of (his own) cannibalism, a terror that culminates with the footprint and Crusoe's fancy that every bush, tree, and stump might be a man. In the scene with Poll, as in that of the footprint, Crusoe is once again "Surprize[d]" and "frighted" by the possibility of other people—this time, when he awakes thinking that "some Body spoke": "I was wak'd out of my Sleep by a Voice calling me by my Name several times, *Robin, Robin, Robin Crusoe*, poor *Robin Crusoe*, where are you *Robin Crusoe*? Where are you? Where have you been? . . . I thought I dream'd that some Body spoke to me: But as the Voice continu'd to repeat *Robin Crusoe, Robin Crusoe*, at last I began to wake more perfectly, and was at first dreadfully frighted, and started up in the utmost Consternation" (112). Critics like Marshall and Jager understand this scene as a dramatization and deflation of Crusoe's fear of the other, which dissolves when Crusoe realizes that the voice he hears is Poll's. Yet as Crusoe tells it, his "Consternation" at waking to hear the voice of another does not end when he opens his eyes and sees Poll: "even though I knew it was the Parrot, and that indeed it could be no body else, it was a good while before I could compose my self" (112). Crusoe struggles to "compose [him]self" because of a talking parrot here, just as later, the footprint will throw him "out of [him]self," making him act "according to the Practice of all Creatures." And in this scene, the "Shadow or Figure of . . . People" that frightens Crusoe is explicitly identified with the sociable animals (and the garrulous parrot, in particular) that populate the island.

Once again, Defoe's engagement with Locke indicates what is at stake in these scenes, and in the connection they draw between speaking and the company of animals, and ultimately, between personification and cannibalism. For both scenes (that of the footprint, and that of Poll's voice) draw on ideas that Locke introduces in the *Essay* about personhood, speech, and animation. These ideas pose potential challenges for a political philosophy committed to the right to eat "every living thing that moveth." Locke might worry that we "talk at random of *Man*," because man is a species of animal, and different people compose species differently, annexing the word "man" to a range of complex ideas (572). But he thinks that we speak more precisely about the "person," because it has a direct and particular referent in every one's experience: "This every intelligent Being, sensible of Happiness or Misery, must grant, that there is something that is *himself*" (345).[36] Locke defines this "something" as the "thinking thing" that "can consider itself as itself," which "it does only by that consciousness, which is inseparable from thinking, and as it seems to me essential to it" (335). One of the primary aims of Locke's account of personal identity is to create an ethical, juridical, and political category that rests on a more secure foundation than the unruly "*Man*."[37] Yet the "person" raises its own problems. Identifying personal identity with consciousness may set the person on firm epistemological ground, but it also makes this ground worryingly private. As Locke puts it, "What sort of outside is the certain sign that there is, or is not such an Inhabitant within?" (572).

This is Locke's version of the question of other minds, and it brings together questions of personhood—of the mental activities like memory and consciousness that constitute personal identity over time, and that ground ethical and legal notions of responsibility—with questions of species, in the sense of asking which sorts of bodies might house such mental activities. Locke's first answer to the question of other minds is speech: "Parrots, and several other Birds will be taught to make articulate Sounds distinct enough, which yet, by no means, are capable of Language. [For language] it was farther necessary, that he should be *able to use these Sounds, as Signs of internal Conceptions*; and to make them stand as marks for the *Ideas* within his own Mind, whereby they might be made known to others" (402). In this opening passage from his book "Of Words," Locke's "Parrots, and several other Birds" are machines of a recognizably Cartesian sort—articulate and living automata that, to borrow from Descartes's discussion of the animal-machine, "could never use words, or put together other signs, as we do in order to declare our thoughts to others" (1.140). Locke would seem to second Descartes's central claim: that while "we can certainly conceive of a machine so constructed that it utters words . . . it is not conceivable that such a machine should produce different arrangements of words so as to give an appropriately meaningful answer to whatever is said in its presence, as the dullest of men can do" (1.140). Speech is here a sign of mind, and the sole prerogative of human beings.

In his chapter on identity, however, Locke raises the very possibility that his discussion of language discounts: a parrot "that spoke, and asked, and answered common Questions like a reasonable Creature" (333). He does so chiefly to insist that there is no necessary connection between personhood and species: that "person" (consciousness) and "human" (an animal of a certain form) are wholly different types of identity. The parrot's "Body and Shape" unmistakably make it a parrot rather than a human being. On Locke's schema, its capacity to "discourse, reason, and philosophize" would seem, nonetheless, to make it a person (332, 333). To some extent, Locke raises the possibility of animal personhood as one thought experiment among others—one of the many suppositional scenarios Locke generates to explain his novel and perplexing proposition "that personal Identity reach[es] no further than consciousness reaches" (339). And yet Locke sets his account of the rational and discoursing parrot markedly apart from the imagined scenarios in this section (in which consciousness leaves the body of a prince to inform that of a cobbler, for example, or goes along with a severed finger). Locke quotes the "much credited Story" of the talking parrot at length from the memoirs of Sir William Temple ("an Author of great note"), who in turn gets the story from an eyewitness to the parrot's conversibility, one Prince Maurice, "in whom [Temple] acknowledges very great Honesty and Piety" (333, 334). Entering the *Essay* by way of testimony that is, in Locke's words, "sufficient to countenance the supposition of a rational *Parrot*" (333), Locke's parrot goes on to become an important figure in the period's literary imagination, around which writers gather questions of identity (what it is to be a life) and taxonomy (what it is to be alive, an animal rather than a thing).[38]

I return to Locke's parrot, and the larger discussion of personal identity, at some length in Chapter 4, in the context of *Tristram Shandy*. In the context of *Robinson Crusoe*, two things are crucial. First, the "much credited Story" of a parrot who speaks and responds "like a reasonable Creature" suggests that speech recapitulates rather than resolves the problem of other minds, recasting Locke's question of the "Inhabitant within" in this way: how can you know the difference between merely "articulate Sounds" and sounds that signal the "internal Conceptions of a mind"? Second, the story of the animal that speaks as if "to declare [its] thoughts to others" proposes an alternative answer to the question of other minds: that animation, as well as speech, might signal mind.[39] Locke hints at this answer at different moments in the *Essay*, as when he argues against the Cartesian claim to "certainly see" thinking in human beings and its absence in other creatures: "they must needs have a penetrating sight, who can certainly see, that I think, when I cannot perceive it my self, and when I declare, that I do not; and yet can see, that Dogs or Elephants do not think, when they give all the demonstration of it imaginable, except only telling us, that they do so" (115–16).

Locke elaborates the logic of this second and less explicit answer to the question of other minds in his chapter on power. There Locke argues that animation or "motivity"—the active power at work whenever a "Substance, or Agent, puts it self into *Action* by its own Power"—is an idea that we attach to mind: "The *Idea* of the beginning of motion, we have only from reflection on what passes in our selves, where we find by Experience, that barely by willing it, barely by a thought of the Mind, we can move the parts of our Bodies, which were before at rest" (285, 235). Locke contrasts motivity—this "active power" to begin motion from within, the idea of which comes from our experience of our selves—with mobility, the "passive power" to receive motion from without. Locke takes tennis and billiard balls as his primary examples of such passive power, as bodies with which we do not associate "any *Idea* of the beginning of motion": "A Tennis-ball, whether in motion by the stroke of a Racket, or lying still at rest, is not by any one taken to be a *free Agent*. If we enquire into the Reason, we shall find it is, because we conceive not a Tennis-ball to think, and consequently not to have any Volition, or preference of Motion to rest, or *vice versa*" (235, 238). Locke's discussion of power opposes the motivity of human beings to the mobility of tennis balls, and so passes over the more confounding case of animate and nonhuman beings. In doing so, he signals the possibility that the distinction between human being and tennis ball—or in Locke's terms, bodies with mind and those without, person and thing—in fact rests on the more fundamental divide between animate and inanimate.

In *Robinson Crusoe*, Defoe uses the Lockean figure of a parrot in ways that connect Locke's reflections on speech, animation, and personhood. Indeed, he takes them further, suggesting not only that one might demonstrate as well as declare mind, but that one *must* demonstrate mind in order for declaration to count as such, as a sign of mind rather than as merely articulate sound. To put the point this way is to come back, finally, to the scene of Poll's voice. Even if Poll speaks "just in such bemoaning Language [that Crusoe] had used to talk to him," Poll is not clearly Crusoe's projection or his echo—at least, not in the same way that Wilson is Noland's (112). Neither tennis ball nor volleyball, Poll is an animate creature, and his animation affects the context and the status of his speech. Recounting his fright at waking to Poll's voice, Crusoe makes clear that it is the parrot's capacity to move on his own that make his words seem the mark of mind: "First, I was amazed how the Creature got thither, and then, how he should just keep about the Place, and no where else: But as I was well satisfied it could be no body but honest *Poll*, I got it over; and holding out my Hand, and calling him by his Name *Poll*, the sociable Creature came to me, and sat upon my Thumb, as he used to do, and continu'd talking to me, *Poor* Robin Crusoe, and *how did I come here?* and *where had I been?* Just as if he had been overjoy'd to see me again; and so I carry'd him Home along with me" (112–13). Crusoe may have finally "got it over," but he is troubled by Poll's speech. Poll may speak in Crusoe's voice, but he does so of his own accord, surprising Crusoe with questions that their situation makes intelligible: "*how did I come here?* and *where had I been?*" Moreover, the situation that gives sense to Poll's questions—the encounter between Crusoe and Poll at Crusoe's home away from home—is affected by Poll's agency as much as Crusoe's, by Poll's capacity to "get thither" and "keep about the Place." As Crusoe shifts the voice of Poll's questions from the second person to the first (from "Where are you? Where have you been?" to "*how did I come here?* and *where had I been?*"), Defoe further underscores the sense that there are two people present at this encounter. Spoken in the first person, Poll's questions ask what Crusoe himself admits to wondering: how did *Poll* come here and where had *Poll* been? Moving himself and surprising Crusoe, Poll's self-motion generates the context that creates conversation as a sequence of questions asked and answered, the same sort of sequence that made Locke's parrot seem "a reasonable creature." Poll thus confronts Crusoe with the possibility that Locke himself points toward. Perhaps anything that moves of its own accord is mind, perhaps any animate body can be "Some-Body to speak to" (154).[40]

In the encounter between Crusoe and Poll, Defoe configures a relation between two animate creatures that suggests that the putatively human faculty of speech depends on the animal faculty of self-motion. For it is animation that gives rise to what Descartes calls the "arrangement of words"—the conversational and relational context—that makes "an appropriately meaningful answer" perceptible as such.[41] In this way, Defoe follows Locke in suggesting that motivity may be a sign of mind, even a necessary one. He also follows Locke in cautioning that another mind is never something one can certainly see. Ultimately, there simply is no outside that is "the certain sign that there is, or is not such an Inhabitant within" (572). Any outside—any body, or movement, or sound—requires a leap from empirical evidence to be taken as mark of mind. In Locke's "much credited Story" of a rational talking parrot, this leap is made by a chain of testimony and translation from sources of "acknowledge[d] . . . Honesty"—a chain that at once countenances this story and proliferates potential sources of doubt. (The parrot's words are verified by two Brasilian-Dutch interpreters, set down in French by Temple "just as Prince Maurice said them to [him]," and then quoted by Locke, accompanied by an English translation.) In *Robinson Crusoe* as in *The Seasons*, this leap from empirical evidence is construed as personification, though in *Robinson Crusoe*, once again, personification is not the propitious mechanism for expanding and denaturalizing a Shaftesburian social system that it is in Thomson's poem. Instead, it is the operation by which Crusoe speaks to animate creatures like Poll, and which finally generates the footprint, the sign of Crusoe's fear that his own imagination might or even must create the people that populate his world.

The scope of this fear is sweeping, for it hints that personification is the process by which Crusoe speaks not only with Poll, but also with Friday. When Friday arrives on the island, Crusoe does not tour him around in good Lockean fashion, pointing out objects and teaching him their names. He launches immediately into conversation. Crusoe imagines that Friday "was at first perhaps as much frighted" by Crusoe, a stranger with two guns, as he was by his captors. Crusoe attempts to reassure Friday and feels sure of success:

> I hollow'd again to him, and made Signs to come forward, which he easily understood, and came a little way. . . . [I] gave him all the Signs of Encouragement that I could think of, and he came nearer and nearer, kneeling down every Ten or Twelve steps in token of acknowledgement for my saving his Life: I smil'd at him, and look'd pleasantly, and beckon'd to him to come still nearer; at length he came close to me, and then he kneel'd down again, kiss'd the Ground, and laid his Head upon the Ground, and taking me by the Foot, set my Foot upon his Head; this it seems was in token of swearing to be my Slave for ever; I took him up, and made much of him, and encourag'd him all I could. (159)

Throughout this exchange, Crusoe does not describe his signs "of Encouragement," or those that mean "come forward" or that "made much" of Friday. Crusoe does not explain how Friday "easily understood" these signs, or how Crusoe knows that he did; nor does Crusoe explain how he knows that kneeling, for Friday, is a "token of acknowledgement for my saving his Life," or that setting Crusoe's foot on his head is a "token of swearing to be my Slave for ever." Nor, in the exchanges that follow, does Crusoe detail how he recognizes "all the possible Signs of an humble thankful Disposition," or "all the Signs . . . of Subjection, Servitude, and Submission imaginable" that Friday makes (161). Yet without shared words for things, conversation between Crusoe and Friday proceeds with remarkable ease: "he made Signs to me to let him go to him, so I bad him go, as well as I could. . . . I turn'd to go away, and beckon'd to him to follow me, making Signs to him, that more might come after them. Upon this he sign'd to me, that he should bury them with Sand, that they might not be seen by the rest if they follow'd; And so I made Signs again to him to do so" (160). In such swift and complex exchanges, it is not clear how Crusoe knows that Friday uses articulate sounds or meaningful signs to make "ideas within his own mind" known to Crusoe, as Locke would have it, or that Friday's signs mark the same "internal conceptions" in Friday's mind as they do in Crusoe's. Nevertheless, Crusoe proclaims that he was "easily understood" by Friday, and that in turn, "I understood him in many Things" (161).

Crusoe does not wonder how he knows that Friday means what Crusoe takes him to mean because Crusoe's conversation is not the kind of activity that Locke describes in book 3 of the *Essay*, in which a chain of representation between word, idea, and thing (at least ideally) connects persons together by connecting them to the same objects and ideas. Locke imagines conversation as a means to communicate ideas from one mind to another; in its simplest form, this model of mind and of language is the epistemological basis of his account of consent. Defoe, by contrast, imagines conversation as a sequence of animate responses, and he suggests that this sort of sequence involves personification at every step, attributing mind and meaning to actions, gestures, or sounds because of their position or arrangement. If we follow Crusoe's logic, Crusoe claims mutual understanding with Friday because their words and actions accord. Crusoe says come; Friday comes. Friday says he will be Crusoe's slave; Crusoe takes Friday as his slave. One might wonder about the potentially retrospective logic of this accord; Crusoe does not. For the understanding Crusoe claims with Friday does not require that Crusoe know exactly what Friday's words or actions mean. It requires only that Crusoe respond to Friday as one who means (that is, as a mind or person): "I took him up, and made much of him, and encourag'd him all I could." This response is not an act of personification in the sense of a "change of things to persons" performed by the power of a projective imagination—the process by which Chuck Noland talks to a volleyball, or Crusoe fancies a tree or a bush as a man. But it is personification in the sense of the leap from empirical evidence that occurs every time one responds to another, untroubled by the skeptical question of other minds.[42] This sort of personification emerges in the context of conversation—indeed, constitutes conversation as such—and it has everything to do with the animation of both parties. Personification in this sense is itself a response to the motions of another.

This account of conversation—as a sequence of responses, and as an effect of animation—underwrites the sort of understanding Crusoe claims with Friday. It also extends quite widely the society of fellow creatures with whom Crusoe might speak. Defoe signals this by structuring Crusoe's exchanges with different creatures in similar ways. Crusoe experiences a similar accord between words and actions in his encounter with Poll as he does in his first conversation with Friday: Poll calls to Crusoe, Crusoe wakes. Crusoe calls to Poll, and "the social Creature came to me . . . and continu'd talking." Poll talks "as if . . . overjoy'd" to see Crusoe, "and so I carry'd him Home" (112–13). The same kind of accord arises between Crusoe and the dog he finds on the wrecked ship, the "living Creature" that Crusoe lamented was not "Some-Body to speak to" (154). When Crusoe approached the ship, he relates, "a Dog appear'd upon her, who seeing me coming, yelp'd, and cry'd; and as soon as I call'd him, jump'd into the sea, to come to me, and I took him into the Boat" (149). The dog sees Crusoe and sounds his presence and distress; Crusoe calls to him, and he comes. Finally, these exchanges with Friday, Poll, and the dog all recall Crusoe's first encounter on the island, with "a Creature like a wild Cat," who "sat very compos'd, and unconcern'd, and look'd full in my Face, as if she had a Mind to be acquainted with me" (45). In response to her look, Crusoe tosses the cat "a bit of Bisket"; in response to his act, she comes and asks for more. Crusoe refuses, and so she leaves: "she went to it, smell'd of it, and ate it, and look'd (as pleas'd) for more, but I thanked her, and could spare no more; so she marched off" (45).

In these exchanges, Friday, Poll, and the dog all come in response to Crusoe's signal, just as Crusoe calls in response to the dog's cry and tosses or refuses biscuit in response to the cat's look. Arranged in this way, these responses seem to ratify the calls, signals, yelps, or cries that they follow as a kind of speech. A number of questions follow from the stripped-down, formal similarity of these different conversations. If Crusoe converses with a cat who looks "as if she had a Mind" and a parrot who talks "as if . . . overjoy'd," much as he converses with Friday, does Crusoe make human beings "Some-Body to speak to" just as he does parrots, by means of the everyday leap from empirical evidence that conversation entails, and which Defoe construes as a mode of personification?

Conversely, if it is this sort of personification that constitutes Friday as mind (rather than "as if" mind), could other creatures occasion a similar response?

The Creaturely Politics of Domestication

I have been arguing that *Robinson Crusoe* is everywhere alert to the twin possibilities that arise from the connections it draws between animation and speech: that persons might in some sense be personifications and that every (animate) body might be "Some-Body to speak to." These possibilities have significant stakes for the social and political imaginary of the novel, which ultimately develops a vision of society that is not grounded in solely human speech, on the model of social contract. The society of *Robinson Crusoe* is composed instead according to the more creaturely model of domestication, by means of relations of call and response, as well as eating, feeding, and being eaten.[43] These creaturely relations come together most memorably in Crusoe's portrait of his "little Family" at dinner:

> It would have made a Stoick smile to have seen, me and my little Family sit down to dinner; there was my Majesty the Prince and Lord of the whole Island; I had the Lives of all my Subjects at my absolute Command. I could hang, draw, give Liberty, and take it away, and no Rebels among all my Subjects. Then to see how like a King I din'd too all alone, attended by my Servants; *Poll*, as if he had been my Favourite, was the only Person permitted to talk to me. My dog, who was now grown very old and crazy, and had found no Species to multiply his Kind upon, sat always at my right Hand, and two Cats, one on one Side of the Table, and one on the other, expecting now and then a Bit from my Hand, as a Mark of Special Favour. (116)

Michael McKeon is one of the few critics who takes Crusoe's political rhetoric seriously here—even though, as Manuel Schonhorn also points out, Crusoe does not ridicule the scene in any wholly straightforward way: "Stoics may smile, we may smile, though Crusoe does not."[44] He also takes Crusoe at his word: when Crusoe declares his absolute command over his subjects, McKeon sees absolute command. As a result, McKeon takes Crusoe to stand for the "devolution of absolutism" that he sees as the paradigmatic move of modernity, which shifts absolutism from the political to the domestic domain, from the sovereign monarch to the sovereign self. In this respect at least, McKeon joins Schonhorn in reconceiving *Robinson Crusoe* along Hobbesian lines.

There are good reasons to substitute or at least supplement a Lockean *Crusoe* with a Hobbesian one, as Schonhorn and others have shown. But here I want to call attention to the ways in which Defoe cuts across both of these familiar political paradigms—as when he juxtaposes playful personification and absolutist political rhetoric to picture Crusoe's little family at dinner, or when he raises the question, after Locke of the *Essay*, of whether parrots, dogs, and cats might in some sense speak, and thus belong inside the bounds of civil society. I have been arguing that in such moments, Defoe pictures a society that is not Locke's. Crusoe's domestic relations do not follow on the free consent of discrete and autonomous individuals. He also pictures a society that is not Hobbes's. Despite the rhetoric that Crusoe sometimes invokes, his domestic relations are not imposed by an omnipotent and external force. Instead, *Robinson Crusoe* presents a domestic society composed by relations in which agency is much less clear—by conversations both within and across species that involve eating as well as speaking, and which serve to minimize the distance between these activities.

The contours of this domestic and creaturely society emerge most clearly in Crusoe's relations with his goats, and it is with these relations that I bring this chapter to a close. Crusoe's domestication of goats has often been viewed as an exercise in sovereign rule, the template or training ground for Crusoe's later rule over human beings.[45] Virginia Woolf found the matter more complicated, however, singling out Crusoe's goats, along with his cats, as one of the few knots or "inconsistencies" in the novel: "Why," she wonders, "if the wild cats are so very tame are the goats so very shy?"[46] Woolf's remark points to two central aspects of Defoe's domestic society. First, this society is not based on given distinctions between different sorts of being, not even the stable if malleable distinction between wild and tame. (Crusoe records his "Astonishment" that the "*European* Cats" he keeps as family are indistinguishable from the wild cats that he "kill[s] . . . like Vermine" [82].) Second, Woolf's remark about the goats' "shyness" indicates that, in Defoe's novel, domestication is never an act of sovereignty. Crusoe himself acknowledges as much when he complains early on that the goats are "so shy, so subtile, and so swift of Foot, that it was the difficultest thing in the World to come at them" (50). Realistically, goats are "shy" because they are prey animals, the fearful subjects of Crusoe's dominion (and of predation more generally). But Crusoe's complaints about the goats' shyness also signal their resistance to that dominion—their capacity to repeatedly upend the power dynamic we might expect between predator and prey, human and animal.

A brief run through of Crusoe's encounters with goats makes plain just how strange and insecure are Crusoe's relations with these creatures. Though his compressed narration can obscure just how long he takes to "come at" the goats, Crusoe really does have a good deal of difficulty, which is not easily explained in wholly practical terms. He contemplates breeding goats periodically for at least eleven years, over the course of what often seem accidental encounters rather than calculated experiments in domestication. These encounters begin during his first weeks on the island, with Crusoe's "first shot . . . among these Creatures" (50). This first shot, Crusoe relates, "kill'd a She-Goat which had a little Kid by her when [*sic*] she gave Suck to" (50). The kid follows him home and Crusoe brings it inside his walls, as he says, "in the hopes to have bred it up tame" (50). But, Crusoe reports, "it would not eat, so I was forc'd to kill it myself" (50). Two months later, Crusoe comes across another goat, which he lames and then brings home. Crusoe does not explain whether he intends to injure the goat, or why he then brings it home and nurses it back to health. He simply remarks, as if he did not anticipate the effect of his care, that "by nursing it so long it grew tame" (61). He then comments that "*This* was the first Time that I entertain'd a Thought of breeding up some tame Creatures, that I might have Food when my Powder and Shot was all spent" (61, my emphasis). Some three years pass before Crusoe next raises the subject of taming goats. Once again, he mentions the idea as if it were new: "I had often been musing, Whether it might not be possible to get a Kid or two, and so raise a breed of tame Goats, which might supply me when my Powder and Shot should be all spent" (88). This time, he is inspired to the thought by a third goat, whom Crusoe "sav'd . . . alive from the Dog" (88). Crusoe rescues the kid goat only to immediately leave her without food, enclosed in his bower: simply because, as Crusoe tells it, he "was very impatient to be at Home" (88). Crusoe returns some days later to discover the goat has become "tame with being hungry" (89).

This third goat provides Crusoe with a clear lesson in the domesticating effects of starvation—another technique, like all those Crusoe uses with the goats on the island, realistically grounded in the animal husbandry of his day. But again his account of his activities exceeds realist explanations of his efforts. For once again, the lesson of starvation seems lost on Crusoe when, eight years on, he at last sets out expressly to catch some goats. This time, Crusoe's actions seem deliberate rather than accidental; once again, they are prefaced by Crusoe's remark that he now "*began* seriously to consider what I must do when I should have no more Powder; that is to say, how I should do to kill any goat" (114, my emphasis). In this fourth and final episode, Crusoe traps four goats but then sets the largest one free, explaining that he "had forgot then what I learn'd *afterwards*, that Hunger will tame a Lyon" (114, my emphasis). My point in detailing each of these episodes is this: Crusoe is sometimes considered a model initiate of the new experimental method, but he has a blind spot when it comes to goats. In his various caprine encounters, Crusoe not only fails to learn from previous experiences; he seems even to forget that they have occurred. Crusoe's success at capturing three kid goats and breeding them into a herd of forty-three appears a less impressive display of dominion when one considers that this process takes fourteen years and at least three false starts to complete, and that it is characterized throughout by a striking absence of conscious agency, or even memory.

The goats do not provide Crusoe with an opportunity to exercise absolute dominion, on the model of Hobbes or anyone else. Instead, they condense the anti-Lockean argument Defoe puts forward in the novel, often against his own protagonist (and often, I have argued, in line with aspects of Locke's own thought). Crusoe finds goats "the difficultest thing in the World to come at," finally, because Crusoe's encounters with goats blatantly muddy distinctions between different types of beings and different types of dominion, distinctions that would either differentiate or secure Crusoe from the cannibals.[47] With his "first shot . . . among these Creatures," for example, Crusoe interrupts a domestic scene, killing a mother who gives suck to her kid. Crusoe is "griev'd . . . heartily" by this first casualty, and then finds himself a surrogate parent to the orphaned goat who follows him home (50). Yet when Crusoe discovers that he cannot make the kid feed, he concludes that he must feed on the kid, abruptly shifting the animal's status from family to food. With the third goat he takes into his home, Crusoe encounters a different problem: this time, he "could not by any Means bring it to pass" to breed her, to make her produce her family and his food (114). Yet Crusoe does not therefore make this goat his meal, for he "could never find it [in his] Heart to kill" her (114). Instead, she becomes family: "the Creature became so loving, so gentle, and so fond, that it became from that Time one of my Domesticks also, and would never leave me afterwards" (89). In Crusoe's interactions with goats, food and family are everywhere mixed together: creatures pass between these positions, or occupy both at once.

If Crusoe's relations with goats reveal that food is a means to make something family, and that making something family is a means to make it food, they also insist, contra Locke, that neither food nor family can be neatly divided from political forms of relation. The kid who will not eat and the kid who will not breed demonstrate that both food and family are means of frustrating the terms of Crusoe's society. Conversely, the kid whom Crusoe leaves to starve demonstrates that food can also be a means to bring society into being—as Crusoe relates, the goat "was so tame with being hungry," that it "follow'd me like a Dog; and as I continually fed it, the Creature became so loving, so gentle, and so fond, that it became from that Time one of my Domesticks also" (89). Crusoe goes on to apply the lesson he learns from the goat who is "like a Dog" to "a Dog" he finds on board the shipwreck, with whom he establishes society in an exchange of words, actions, and bread: "a Dog appear'd upon her, who seeing me coming, yelp'd, and cry'd; and as soon as I call'd him, jumped into sea, to come to me, and I took him into the Boat; but found him almost dead for Hunger and Thirst: I gave him a Cake of my Bread, and he eat it like a ravenous Wolf, that had been starving a Fortnight in the Snow: I then gave the poor Creature some fresh Water, with which, if I would have let him he would have burst himself" (149). This exchange, in which Crusoe rescues a solitary creature and takes him into service, in turn becomes the model for the kind of exchange by which Friday "consents" to Crusoe's society:

> [He] made all the Signs to me of Subjection, Servitude, and Submission imaginable, to let me know, how he would serve me as long as he liv'd. I understood him in many things, and let him know, I was very well pleas'd with him; in a little Time I began to speak to him, and teach him to speak to me; and first I made him know his Name should be *Friday*, which was the Day I sav'd his Life; I call'd him so for the Memory of the Time; I likewise taught him to say *Master*, and then let him know that was to be my Name; I likewise taught him to say, YES, and NO, and to know the Meaning of them; I gave him some Milk, in an earthen Pot, and let him see me Drink it before him, and sop my Bread in it; and I gave him a Cake of Bread, to do the like, which he quickly comply'd with, and made Signs that it was very good for him. (161)

In this passage, the syntax of Crusoe's parallel phrases, separated by semicolons, composes a list of equivalent acts: "I made him know his Name"; "I likewise taught him to say *Master*"; "I likewise taught him to say, YES, and NO";

"I gave him some Milk"; "and I gave him a Cake of Bread." Friday's "Signs . . . of Subjection" are here constituted as much by his repetition of Crusoe's acts of eating—"which he quickly comply'd with, and made Signs that it was very good for him"—as they are by his repetition of Crusoe's words: "Friday," "Master," "YES, and NO." This scene brings speaking and eating into close proximity, configuring both words and foods as signs to which one responds. In doing so, it formulates a number of discomfiting possibilities: that political relations may not be clearly distinguished from other types of relation, or reserved only for human beings; that much as Friday consents to his own subjection by eating Crusoe's bread, a goat may do the same; or conversely, that such activities (eating bread, drinking milk, saying yes and no) do not signal consent at all.

Two conversations suggest that this last possibility remains a crucial and unresolved problem in Defoe's novel. The first is Crusoe's initial encounter on the island, with the cat who looked "as if she had a Mind": "I presented my gun at her, but as she did not understand it, she was perfectly unconcern'd at it, nor did she offer to stir away; upon which I toss'd her a Bit of Bisket, tho' by the Way I was not very free of it, for my Store was not great: However, I spar'd her a Bit, I say, and she went to it, smell'd of it, and ate it, and look'd (as pleas'd) for more, but I thanked her, and could spare no more; so she march'd off" (45). In this scene, food is depicted as a more intelligible substitute for a gun, the sign with which Crusoe initiates conversation, but which the cat "did not understand." This exchange aligns eating (or feeding) with both speaking and presenting a gun. Something similar occurs at the end of the novel, when Crusoe and Friday encounter a bear on their voyage over the Pyrenees. Friday proposes to "*shakee the Hand with him*," dismissing Crusoe's cautions that "*he will eat you up*": "*Eatee me up! Eatee me up!* Says Friday, twice over again; *Me eatee him up*" (228). For Friday, the notion of eating up a bear seems equally to imply throwing stones, shooting a gun, and speaking. He begins with speech: "The Bear was walking softly on, and offer'd to meddle with no Body, till *Friday* coming pretty near, calls to him, as if the Bear could understand him; *Hark ye, hark ye*, says Friday, *me speakee wit you*" (228). Friday continues the conversation by shifting from speech to stones—following his call, he "takes up a great Stone, and throws at him, and hit him just on the Head"—and back to speech: "when he sees him stand still, he calls out to him again, as if he had suppos'd the Bear could speak *English*; *What you no come farther, pray you come farther*; so he left jumping and shaking the Bough; and the Bear, just as if he had understood what he said, did come a little further" (228, 229).

The exchange continues, bringing speech and action together in a series of responses until Friday "stept up close to [the Bear], clapt the Muzzle of his Piece into his Ear, and shot him dead as a Stone" (230). Friday might imagine that by shooting the bear, he could extract himself from creaturely conversation and acquire the status of a sovereign human subject. But by the end of the novel, this status has been utterly undone. In this closing scene, then, Friday is repeatedly figured as the bear himself, dancing for Crusoe and the company.

In Friday's encounter with the bear, Defoe cautions once again that there is no reliable way to isolate consent from force, speaking from eating (or, from shooting a gun). He also cautions that the domestic society organized around such creaturely activities and relations is not confined to Crusoe's island. Creaturely relations also characterize the Europe that Crusoe had tried to leave behind, when he began his adventures by refusing his father's offer of "daily Bread" (6). Crusoe leaves home because he imagines that he might escape domestic relations, or the creaturely subjection of being fed. He imagines, in other words, the possibility of sovereignty. But he ends up in a society much like the one he left, a table in the wilderness on and around which sit all kinds of creatures.

In the model of domestication that Defoe develops in *Robinson Crusoe*, then, society comes together neither through voluntary consent nor forced enslavement, but by means of activities like eating and breeding, as well as speaking reconfigured as an effect of animation. All these activities are instances of the creaturely agency that Julia Lupton describes as "actively passive, or, better, *passionate,* perpetually becoming-created."[48] It is this same sort of agency that, at the level of the narrative, shapes Defoe's novel as the "*Life and Strange Surprising Adventures*" of its central character. Despite his omnipresent narrating voice, Crusoe is emphatically not the author of his own story. He is a character embedded in adventures that are effected from without as much as from within—brought about by "Decree" as much as by "inclination" (14, 1); by other creatures (a parrot who comes hither, goats that are difficult to come at) as much as by Crusoe himself; by something that often looks simply like motivity, a creaturely principle of animation that keeps Crusoe perpetually on the move. Serial, episodic, without development or end, Crusoe's "strange, surprising adventures" surprise no one more than Crusoe himself, as they do when he awakes "dreadfully frighted" by the sense that "some Body spoke," or when he is "surpriz'd with the Print of a Man's naked Foot on the Shore" (112, 121).

Crusoe is "Surprize[d]" and "frighted" by his adventures—and by the domestic and creaturely relations from which they arise—three times during his stay on the island (112). The first time occurs with his encounter with Poll, and the second, with his discovery of the footprint. The third time comes shortly after he finds the footprint, in an episode that similarly interrupts Crusoe's sense of his own isolation. On this occasion, Crusoe enters a cave that he is certain is empty, reasoning that "no Savage, had he been at the Mouth of it, would be so hardy as to venture in, nor indeed, would any Man else; but one who like me, wanted nothing so much as a safe Retreat" (138). Yet once again, Crusoe detects presence where he had thought none possible, "I saw two broad shining Eyes of some Creature, whether Devil or Man I knew not" (139). Telling himself that there could be "nothing in this Cave that was more frightful than my self," Crusoe proceeds forward: "I had not gone three Steps in, but I was almost as much frighted as I was before: for I heard a very loud Sigh, like that of a Man in some Pain, and it was follow'd by a broken Noise, *as if* of Words half express'd, and then a deep Sigh again" (139). In a variation on his scene with Poll, Crusoe finally locates these sounds—guided, with some irony, by the light of one of his "very good Candles . . . of Goat's Tallow"—in a "monstrous frightful old He-goat . . . gasping for Life, and dying indeed of meer old Age" (139). The irony of the scene is one that Swift will exploit, when Gulliver dresses himself in Yahoo-skins and uses Yahoo-tallow to shore up his canoe.[49]

Crusoe reports that he "recover'd" from his fright at the goat who makes noises "like . . . a Man," "*as if* of Words." But as with Poll and the footprint, his fright does not wholly disappear. Crusoe returns to the goat in the subsequent scene, when he imagines himself living on the island, "till I had laid me down and dy'd, like the old Goat in the Cave" (141). Crusoe's twinning of himself and the goat suggests that what frightens Crusoe about his encounter in the cave is not only the possibility that a goat might be a "Man . . . like me"; nor is it that every creature might be a person, or "every Stump . . . a man" (139). Crusoe is also "frighted" by the possibility that a man might be (like) a goat, a creature subject to domestication rather than secured in his sovereignty by speech and social contract. Crusoe's own self-portrait sets this possibility in strikingly literal form:

> I had a great high shapeless Cap, made of a Goat's Skin, with a Flap hanging down behind. . . . I had a short Jacket of Goat-Skin, the Skirts coming down to about the middle of my Thighs; and a Pair of open-knee'd Breeches of the same, the Breeches were made of the Skin of an old He-goat, whose Hair hung down such a Length on either Side, that like *Pantaloons* it reach'd to the middle of my

Legs. . . . I had on a broad Belt of Goat's-Skin dry'd, which I drew
together with two Thongs of the same, instead of Buckles. . . . Under
my left Arm, hung two Pouches, both made of Goat's-Skin too . . .
and over my Head a great clumsy ugly Goat-Skin Umbrella, but
which, after all, was the most necessary Thing I had about me, next
to my Gun. (117–18)

This is one of the most frequently illustrated images of Crusoe's character,
and it presents a jarring picture of what it means to be a "representative of
Man in general." It might appear that in imagining a goat "like a Man" and a
man like a goat, Crusoe constructs a figurative relation between two different
kinds. But as Crusoe repeats "Goat's-skin" again and again, Defoe once again
insists on the materiality of this relation. With Crusoe's portrait of, as he puts
it, "such a Man as I was" (a self-portrait, that is, as goat), Defoe recasts once
more Locke's question of human identity: "What sort of outside is the certain
sign that there is, or is not such an Inhabitant within?" Or better, he tosses
out this question of inside and outside, of men and goats. If Crusoe wears the
skin of a goat or the clothes of a man, he is what he always is, which is what a
goat also is: a creature.[50] Stumbling on the image of himself as goat by a light
(made) of goat, Crusoe senses the precariousness of his status in a creaturely
world in which human sovereignty is neither possible nor justified—a world
in which persons are personified creatures, and "Some-body to speak to" can
also be something to eat.

Chapter 3

The Human

Satire and the Naturalization of the Person

Midway through his *Enquiry Concerning Political Justice*, William Godwin concludes that the precepts of political justice entail the dissolution of government. This conclusion, he remarks, was anticipated by an unlikely precursor: "Such is the idea of the author of *Gulliver's Travels* (Part IV), a man who appears to have had a more profound insight into the true principles of political justice, than any preceding or contemporary author." Godwin continues: "It was unfortunate, that a work of such inestimable wisdom failed, at the period of its publication, from the mere playfulness of its form, in communicating adequate instruction to mankind. Posterity only will be able to estimate it as it deserves."[1] Just as puzzled as Swift's contemporaries were by the playfulness of his form, posterity has not estimated *Gulliver's Travels* quite as Godwin imagined, as a political treatise advocating the Houyhnhnm society that Gulliver so longs to join. Instead, readers have divided over the status of this society, into what came to be known the "hard" and "soft" schools of criticism. The hard school reading—which, like Godwin, understands the Houyhnhnms to be an ideal to which Swift holds us up and finds us wanting—largely dominated the nineteenth-century reception of the book. By contrast, the twentieth century went mainly to the soft critics, who take a different view: that, as Edward Said put it, "the crucial thing about the Houyhnhnms is not whether they are supposed to be an ideal, but that they are animals."[2] As such, in the words of another critic, the Houyhnhnms are "a kind of life with which humanity has nothing to do."[3] On this view, we cannot be faulted for failing to live up to this alien, Houyhnhnm example; the target of Swift's satire is not humankind but Gulliver, the individual who thinks he might cast off his species, escape from humanity to live a more perfect form of life.

The point of this chapter is not to revive the debate between hard and soft readings of the *Travels* (nor to explore Godwin's intellectual or literary debts to Swift). Instead, my aim is to reconsider what Godwin calls the "playful form" that has generated these readings, and made it seem impossible to decide between them. Some time ago, Ian Watt identified the stakes of this debate. Assuring his readers that he would not propose "yet another solution to the problems offered by the Fourth Part," Watt ventures that any such solution will turn on Gulliver, and must take account "not only of the inherent contradictions between the functions of the ironic *personae* and the fully developed literary character, but also of the philosophical problem that underlies it—how to handle the individual-class dichotomy."[4] This chapter thus asks about Swift's playful form what I asked about *Robinson Crusoe*: what does it mean to represent man in general, and what does that have to do with animals? I share Watt's sense that Gulliver's "ontological state" is indeed the key problem of the *Travels*, one that reframes questions about humans and animals in terms of both literary genre and the logic of generality.[5] At the same time, I think that Swift's approach to each of these issues is more complicated than Watt envisions.

Watt centers his discussion of the *Travels* on Swift's oft-quoted letter to Pope, from September 1725:

> I have ever hated all Nations professions and Communityes and all my love is towards individualls for instance I hate the tribe of Lawyers, but I love Councellor such a one, Judge such a one for so with Physicians (I will not speak of my own Trade) Soldiers, English, Scotch, French; and the rest but principally I hate and detest that animal called man, although I hartily love John, Peter, Thomas and so forth. this is the system upon which I have governed my self many years (but do not tell) and so I shall go on till I have done with them I have got Materials Towards a Treatis proving the falsity of that Definition *animal rationale*; and to show it should be only *rationis capax*. Upon this great foundation of Misanthropy (though not in Timons manner) The whole building of my Travells is erected.[6]

Here are Watt's comments on this letter:

I must confess that, as commentary of *Gulliver's Travels*, I do not find this by any means self-explanatory or unambiguous. . . . Briefly, Swift seems to be qualifying the blank misanthropy . . . by explaining that his reaction to man in his collective aspect is the complete opposite of his reaction to man in his individual aspect. But since the common qualities of "John, Peter, and Thomas, and so forth," constitute whatever may be denoted by the collective term "man," it is surely to invert the fallacy of the class to assume that there can actually be any total contradiction between them.[7]

In terms that recall his discussion of *Robinson Crusoe* and the rise of the novel, Watt reasons that "John" and "man" are "two opposite ways of looking at what is ultimately the same thing."[8] Whether the sum total of individual instances or their lowest common denominator, the species "Man" is composed by collecting particular men ("John, Peter, Thomas, and so forth"). On Watt's view, the satirical persona and the novelistic character are the literary instantiations of this basic opposition between Man and men, the generic term and the individual instance: "mainly, and most of the time, [Gulliver] is an ironical *persona*, essentially a general representative of man collectively considered, but in the Fourth Part he becomes a man individually considered"—which means, for Watt, the bearer of "psychological reality."[9] At once a novelistic character and a satirical persona, Gulliver figures the two opposing aspects of man: he is man both individually and collectively considered. As such, he evokes in the reader the same conflicting feelings that Swift reports to Pope: we both love and hate him.

Watt is rightly skeptical of those who would read Swift's letter to Pope to be a self-evident commentary on the *Travels*: Swift loves individual men but hates the class; he satirizes "that animal called man" but saves a few men from censure, like Lord Munodi, the King of Brobdingnag, or the Portuguese captain. Watt argues that this position entails a logical contradiction, loving and hating what is "ultimately the same thing." To my mind, there is a still more basic problem with Swift's claim to "hartily love" individuals but to "hate and detest that animal called man": it is not clear that Swift loves individuals at all. Alongside the Swift of individual exemplars like Lord Munodi and the Portuguese captain, there is the Swift of *A Tale of a Tub* and its "Digression on Madness," which holds "the influence of single men" responsible for empires, new philosophy, and new religions—all terrible effects of an exaggeration of that "something individual in human minds" that "departs from the natural state or course of thinking."[10] The *Tub*'s modern Author embodies just as he diagnoses this sort of individualism-as-madness, and Gulliver too can seem stricken, imagining that he can move between species or even constitute a species all on his own.[11] Swift's attitude toward his own narrators is notoriously difficult to pin down. But the exaggerated individualism of figures like Gulliver or the tale-teller indicates, at the very least, that much that Watt takes as given are genuine questions for Swift. What is the proper way to conceive of the relation between the individual and the species? Is it the same for humans as for animals? What resources do different literary genres bring to bear on our experience of this relation, or what constraints do they impose? In focusing on Gulliver's "ontological state" Watt gets the crux of the *Travels* right, but by identifying the satirical persona with "Man" and conceiving the species as a collection of individual men, he makes literary and philosophical assumptions that Swift does not.

Gulliver is a famously shape-shifting figure—at different moments in the *Travels*, he is an insect, a kitten, a clock, a pet, a man-mountain, a *lusus naturae*. He is also and by turns a novelistic character, a figure in an animal fable (at least in aspiration), and a satirical persona, the first-person narrator of the *Travels*. Put somewhat schematically, the argument of this chapter is that Swift experiments, in books 2 and 4 in particular, with these different living and literary forms, each of which configures the relationship between the individual and the species differently. To live in Brobdingnag is to live in the world of the novel as conceived by *Robinson Crusoe*, a world of creaturely indistinction in which, Swift insists, identity can take the form only of the individual exception, conferred from without. To live in Houyhnhnmland, by contrast, is to live inside the animal fable, where distinctions are essential and fixed rather than conferred from outside. In this fabulous realm, the individual is not exceptional but synecdochal—a part that can stand for the whole because it is an embodiment of the species, identical to every other individual of its kind. Gulliver is drawn to this Houyhnhnm mode of identity, and to the social and psychological accord it promises. But ultimately, Swift concludes that both the novel and the fable configure human persons on forms of animal life (the pet and the natural-historical species, respectively), and so disregard important features of what it is to be human.

To put the point this way is to set Swift to the side of the tradition otherwise charted in this book. Swift may engage extensively with literary figures of animal life, and with beastly genres like fable. He may be suspicious of claims on behalf of human reason, or celebrations of "that animal called man." But he is committed, like no other writer in this book, to identifying and cultivating a mode of being that is exclusive to human beings. For Swift, this is personhood understood as a matter of grammar and point of view, in the minimal and also inalienable sense of the first-person perspective. This point is crucial: whatever else Gulliver is or becomes, he is the "I" that narrates the story. This is crucial for Swift in part because the first person is a mode of identity that remains constant amid whatever transformations take place. It is crucial, as well, because an individual conceived in fundamentally first-person terms is not simply opposed to the species, or a different quantity of an identical term. Contra Watt, the individual and the class are not, for Swift, "ultimately the same thing." Instead, Swift identifies the first person as the basis of a uniquely human logic of generality, a mode of individuation that is simultaneously a mode of speciation. Swift gets this sense of the first person from Hobbes, and he elaborates in literary terms the sort of reading practices Hobbes identifies as constitutive of the solely human practice of politics. Ultimately, Swift conceives satire as a literary version of Hobbes's Leviathan: a representational mechanism that incorporates the first person with humankind.

The Domestication of Lemuel Gulliver

For readers of *Robinson Crusoe*, Gulliver's arrival on the shore of Brobdingnag sounds a number of familiar notes.[12] Recall Crusoe, sailing with Xury toward "the truly *Barbarian* Coast": "[we] came to an Anchor in the Mouth of a little River, I knew not what, or where; neither what Latitude, what Country, what Nations, or what River" (21). Here is Gulliver, his ship forced off course by a storm at sea: "we came in full View of a great Island or Continent, (for we knew not whether) [*sic*] . . . [and] cast Anchor within a League of [a] Creek" (71). When the captain sends Gulliver and "a dozen of his Men" to shore in search of water, they encounter the same indeterminate creatures that so unsettled Crusoe: in Crusoe's words, "vast great Creatures" "mighty Creatures," "a dreadful Monster," and finally, "People" (23, 25, 26); in Gulliver's, "a huge Creature" and a "Monster"; followed by "seven Monsters" that Gulliver also calls "People" and "Barbarians" (71–72). As these creatures/monsters/ people chase the sailors toward the boat, Gulliver is stranded alone on a strange shore, separated—like Crusoe—from the company of "our Men" (71).

Gulliver comes to shore as a Crusoevian figure, but when he encounters its native inhabitants he shifts into the person of Friday. Tiny in a land of giants, Gulliver lies in a field as a gargantuan reaper approaches. In a scathing rejoinder to Friday's gesture of placing Crusoe's foot on his head—his token, according to Crusoe, "of swearing to be my Slave for ever" (Defoe, 172)—Gulliver "apprehend[s] that with the next Step I should be squashed to Death under his Foot" (73). Gulliver screams, and this scream initiates his first conversation in Brobdingnag, which reformulates Friday's first encounter with Crusoe from Friday's point of view:

> He [the Brobdingnagian] considered a while with the Caution of one who endeavours to lay hold on a small dangerous Animal in such a manner that it shall not be able either to scratch or to bite him, as I my self have sometimes done a *Weasel* in *England*. At length he ventured to take me up behind by the middle between his Forefinger and Thumb, and brought me within three Yards of his Eyes, that he might behold my Shape more perfectly. I guessed his Meaning, and my good Fortune gave me so much Presence of Mind, that I resolved not to struggle in the least. . . . All I ventured was to raise my Eyes towards the Sun, and place my Hands together in a supplicating Posture, and to speak some Words in a humble melancholy Tone, suitable to the Condition I was then in. For I apprehended every Moment that he would dash me against the Ground as we usually do any little hateful Animal which we have a mind to destroy. But my good Star would have it, that he appeared pleased with my Voice and Gestures, and began to look upon me as a Curiosity, much wondering to hear me pronounce articulate Words, although he could not understand them. In the mean time I was not able to forbear groaning and shedding Tears, and turning my Head towards my Sides; letting him know, as well as I could, how cruelly I was hurt by the Pressure of his Thumb and Finger. He seemed to apprehend my Meaning; for, lifting up the Lappet of his Coat, he put me gently into it. (73)

Casting Gulliver as Friday, Swift sends up the idea that Friday's gestural conversation with Crusoe constituted anything like consent, let alone consent to his own enslavement. What Swift pictures is not consent but a plea for one's life—a mind trying to make itself visible in order to persuade someone more powerful not to "dash him on the ground."

Swift's rewriting of *Robinson Crusoe* in book 2 of the *Travels* is remarkable for moments like this one, which explicitly refuse Crusoe's side of things by providing the first-person account that Defoe does not. It is remarkable, above all, for the way that it proceeds, swiftly and silently, to collapse into one first-person narrator all the positions that *Crusoe* includes. Much has been written, and rightly so, about Defoe's experiments with different forms of first-person narration in *Robinson Crusoe*, and the strain these show in the effort to compose one continuous narrative self.[13] Swift turns Defoe's experiments on their head, using first-person narration as a technique not for composing narrative identity (nor for exposing its troubling gaps) but for bringing out the creaturely logic of Crusoe's representative character, the substitutability of one person for any and every other. In the course of two pages, Swift's narrating persona shifts from Crusoe to Friday. For much of the chapter, in which Gulliver performs as a companion animal with a wonderful capacity for speech, it is Poll. With these unmarked shifts between persons, Swift formally instantiates the point that repeatedly frightens Crusoe: that any difference—of person or of species—is merely a matter of position. Differences between positions are not negligible; indeed, they can mean life or death. But they are not essential. One is moved between positions without warning, and from without.

Gulliver's way of putting the point is this: "Undoubtedly Philosophers are in the right when they tell us, that nothing is great or little otherwise than by Comparison" (72–73). Gulliver comes to realize that in Brobdingnag, nothing is *anything* otherwise than by comparison. Great or little, Crusoe or Friday, human being or parrot—size, person, and species all become relative positions, without any fixed or essential content. Gulliver begins to appreciate this fact during that first encounter when he (as Friday) is picked up by the (Crusoevian) giant reaper like "a small dangerous Animal . . . as I my self have sometimes done with a *Weasel* in England"; he fears he will be dashed against the ground, "as we usually do any hateful Animal which we have a mind to destroy" (73). From here, comparisons proliferate from different points of view. The farmer's wife reacts to Gulliver "as Women in *England* do at the Sight of a Toad or a Spider"; her son is as "mischievous [to Gulliver as] all Children among us naturally are to Sparrows, Rabbits, young Kittens, and Puppy Dogs" (75). Brobdingnagian natives are likewise reconfigured: to Gulliver, his Mistress's cat "seemed to be three times larger than an Ox" and the farmer's dog was "equal in bulk to four Elephants" (76); he does battle with two rats "the size of a large Mastiff," is tormented by flies "as big as a *Dunstable* Lark," and fights off wasps "as large as Partridges" (78, 91, 92).

These Brobdingnagian comparisons of size and species sound like similes: cats like oxen, dogs like elephants, flies as big as larks. But simile does not work in Brobdingnag as one might expect, as a stabilizing figure that cements existing categories in the face of a strange individual. The play with perspectives means that comparison gives way to identity, simile to metamorphosis. To Gulliver in Brobdingnag, a rat simply *is* a mastiff, a dog an elephant. The logic of this collapse becomes visible in moments like the following, when Gulliver explains how the native population tried to understand his arrival: "It now began to be known . . . that my Master had found a strange Animal in the Fields about the bigness of a *Splacknuck*, but exactly shaped in every part like a human Creature; which it likewise imitated in all its Actions" (80). A few things are going on in passages like this one. First, by knocking Gulliver out of species because he is missing a requisite attribute—splacknuck except for shape, human except for size—this passage configures species as collections: of requisite attributes, and of the individuals who bear them. Second, by zeroing in on size, a quality that is patently a matter of position and point of view, Swift identifies attributes as a matter of attribution. The attributes that set one inside this species or that depend on the perspective of others. As such, they might be missing or simply missed, moving an individual between species or leaving him outside species categories altogether.

This is what befalls Gulliver. To liken Gulliver to a splacknuck except for shape and a human being except for size is to identify Gulliver as neither splacknuck nor human but an exceptional individual—which means, here, nothing more than "a strange Animal." The "strange Animal" in Brobdingnag resembles the "fellow-Creature" on Crusoe's island. It is another indeterminate and capacious category ("Animal") and an adjective ("strange") accorded by some observing subject, the position from which one is familiar or strange, a fellow or food. But while Defoe conceives of the creature as a potential alternative to modes of generality arrived at by empirical induction, Swift presents the animal as induction's logical inverse: it is an effect of subtraction rather than addition, what remains when all attributes are stripped away. Other than this basic and base animality, all modes of identity—both who and what one is—become a matter of size, of relative position or power.

In a realm where there is no intrinsic identity but only relative positions—great or little, insect or bird, cat or cattle—the tiny Gulliver is everywhere subject to subtraction, an exception to every species. (Indeed, it is in this book that Gulliver is classified as an individual exception, as a "*Lusus Naturae*" or freak of nature [87].) At least, this is how he begins: as an individual without a category, merely a strange animal. He undergoes his own sort of metamorphosis when a young Brobdingnagian girl, Glumdalclitch ("little Nurse"), takes him into her home and makes him her pet, calling him *Grildrig* or "little man." This would seem a positive transformation—better a family pet than "a strange Animal in the Fields."[14] But throughout book 2, Gulliver experiences pethood as a profoundly precarious mode of being. His first sense of this comes when Glumdalclitch's parents send him to perform at a market town, transforming her pet into a "monster" (and, into profit), much as they had done "when they pretended to give her a Lamb, and yet, as soon as it was fat, sold it to a Butcher" (81). The perils of pethood persist in the household of the King and Queen of Brobdingnag, where one might expect Gulliver's status to be more secure. Instead, it is in the royal household that Gulliver meets with what he calls "the greatest Danger I ever underwent in that Kingdom," when a monkey claims Gulliver as kin, or a kitten: "After some time spent peeping, grinning, and chattering, he at last espied me, and reaching one of his Paws in at the Door, as a Cat does when she plays with a Mouse . . . he at length caught hold of the Lappet of my Coat. . . . He took me up in his right fore-foot and held me as a Nurse does a Child she is going to suckle, just as I have seen the same sort of Creature do with a Kitten in *Europe*. . . . I have good reason to believe that he took me for a young one of his own Species, by his often stroking my Face very gently with his other Paw" (101). It is not immediately clear why Gulliver considers this the greatest danger he has faced. His near-death experiences in Brobdingnag are legion: Gulliver is threatened by rats, wasps, and a frog, by hail stones, drowning, and a forty-foot fall. The monkey, by contrast, strokes Gulliver's face "very gently" and takes him for "one of his own Species."

This is precisely the problem. Gulliver experiences this incident as the greatest of dangers because it exposes the utter vulnerability of his identity rather than his body—his capacity to be taken for (and so, to be or become) one thing or another: a man, a monkey, a kitten. Swift emphasizes this point with a curious set of echoes that connect the monkey with a number of other figures in book 2. First, the monkey mimics Glumdalclitch, Gulliver's "little Nurse"; the monkey too, as Gulliver tells it, "held me *as a Nurse does*." These two figures in turn recall the nurse who enters the dining room with Glumdalclitch's younger brother, who screams until he is given Gulliver "for a Play-thing" (76). Gulliver recounts what happened next: the child "seized me by the Middle, and got my Head in his Mouth" (76). Gulliver screams so loudly that the frightened infant drops him, and the nurse tries to calm the child. This is the context of Gulliver's much discussed disgust at "the sight of her monstrous Breast," described in horrified and gargantuan detail as the infant begins to suck (76). Gulliver's disgust at the nurse's breast is typically read as disgust at women—either a misogynist response or a parody of it. This is surely the case, but it is worth noting that Gulliver's disgust is aimed at the figure of the nurse in particular. This is a gendered figure to be sure, but it is also a more specific figure for Gulliver's creaturely vulnerability in Brobdingnag, where what he is depends on where he is, and on what is done to him. In the households of Glumdalclitch and the King, Gulliver is a "little man" because and so long as he is treated as such, just as Crusoe's kids are family—quasi-persons who cannot be eaten—because and so long as Crusoe makes them so. Gulliver experiences the volatility of this sort of identity as he moves from sitting around the table to sitting on it, almost becoming food for a one-year old child. Pethood might protect Gulliver from the usual fate of "any little hateful Animal which we have a mind to destroy" (73). But this protection is fragile; it comes at the hands of others and can always be taken away.

Gulliver's vulnerability in book 2 is not restricted to his relations with women, children, and animals. The whole of Brobdingnag operates on this same domestic and creaturely logic. Swift makes this point by setting much of this book in the domestic-political domain of the sovereign, and by linking the figure of the nurse to the King of Brobdingnag himself. He does this by echoing the monkey-nurse's gesture of "stroaking my Face very gently" a few pages later, when Gulliver recounts for the King the political, economic, and legal systems of his native land. Gulliver begins by reasoning "That among other Animals, Bees and Ants had the Reputation of more Industry, Art, and Sagacity than many of the larger kinds. And that, as inconsiderable as he took me to be, I hoped I might live to do his Majesty some signal Service" (106). To Gulliver's dismay, the King is appalled by his account. "Taking me into his Hands, and stroaking me gently," Gulliver relates, the King delivers the words that Gulliver says he will never forget: "As for yourself . . . who have spent the greatest part of your Life in travelling, I am well disposed to hope you may hitherto have escaped many Vices of your Country. But, by what I have gathered from your own Relation . . . I cannot but conclude the Bulk of your Natives, to be the most pernicious Race of little odious Vermin that Nature ever suffered to crawl upon the Surface of the Earth" (111). The King repeats the monkey's gesture—"stroaking me gently"—as he simultaneously literalizes Gulliver's insect figure and shields Gulliver from its force, excepting Gulliver from that "most pernicious Race of little odious Vermin." Readers sometimes view the King of Brobdingnag as a benevolent and exemplary figure, one of the few individuals in the *Travels* that Swift seems to stand behind. But there is violence in the King's gentle stroking: the violence of the label "Vermin," and the exception that the monarch has the power to deny as well as to grant.[15] In this moment, Swift identifies the little Nurse, the monkey, and the King as variations on one and the same figure: the arbiter of a domestic-political society that gives rise to the individual as pet—a contingent and wholly unstable form of identity, because it is conferred from without.

I have been describing the world of Brobdingnag as Swift's spin on the world of *Robinson Crusoe*, a world in which species distinctions give way to animal identity and exceptions are granted from without—singling out Gulliver just as Crusoe singles out Friday or Poll, and protects both from the common creaturely fate of being shot (or eaten).[16] But there are important differences between Defoe's domestic vision and Swift's. For one thing, while Defoe's domestic relations defy neat resolution into a model either of contract or of absolutism, Swift more firmly aligns domestication with clear-cut force, calling it what Crusoe calls it only once, in the scene of Friday's imputed consent: slavery. Swift worries that the domestic relations that Defoe pictures can too easily be rendered comforting and sentimental, as if the problems of domestication could be resolved by a good nurse, or a benevolent master. For Swift, this is to suggest that slavery might be mitigated by affection—a suggestion he will not countenance. Swift places Gulliver in a variety of different domestic settings precisely to insist on their identity. Gulliver is not only enslaved by the farmer who subjects him to a "Life . . . laborious enough to kill an Animal of ten times [his] Strength," living off Gulliver's labor and selling him when the farmer saw that "[he] soon must dye" (85, 84). Gulliver is also enslaved when he goes to live with the good King of Brobdingnag—indeed, it is there that he refers to himself as "my Master's Slave," which is an epithet of courtly etiquette, but not only that (84). Even though he is "treated with much Kindness" by the King, Gulliver cannot fathom reproducing under such conditions: "I think I should rather have dyed than undergone the Disgrace of leaving a Posterity to be kept in Cages like tame Canary Birds, and perhaps in time sold about the Kingdom to Persons of Quality for Curiosities" (116). In a society in which one's identity depends on others, it does not matter whether one's master is kind or cruel, whether he makes you a pet or a monster—one lives "upon such a foot as ill became the Dignity of Human Kind" (116).

Such is Swift's diagnosis of the domestic and creaturely world of *Robinson Crusoe*, a world in which the individual is either a strange animal or a familiar one—a man made (and potentially unmade) by the power of someone else. Lacking fixed and intrinsic forms of identity, nothing holds one together as the person one is, or distinguishes one species from another. Or, almost nothing. Whether a freak of nature, a strange animal, or an exception to a race of vermin, whether Crusoe or Friday or Poll, Gulliver is consistently and most basically a first-person narrator, an "I." For Swift, this is a crucial because inalienable form of identity, the ontological state that remains constant amid all the transformations and exceptions that Gulliver undergoes. Unattached to any continuous self or stable species, however, this "I" is undifferentiated and vulnerable: "I was immediately by the force of it [hail] struck to the Ground. And when I was down, the Hail-stones gave me such cruel Bangs all over the Body, as if I had been pelted with Tennis-balls; however I made a shift to creep on all four, and shelter my self by lying flat on my Face on the Lee-side of a Border of Lemon Thyme" (96). This moment condenses Gulliver's condition throughout book 2: an "I" exposed to the elements, looking for shelter. Indeed, it is in Brobdingnag that Gulliver longs for home for one of the only times during his travels: "I could never forget those domestick Pledges I had left behind me. I wanted to be among People with whom I could converse upon even Terms, and walk about the Streets and Fields without fear of being trod to Death like a Frog or a young Puppy" (116–17). In a world in which species distinctions have come unhinged, Gulliver is a fundamentally homeless first-person perspective creeping about "like a Frog or a . . . Puppy," a merely animal "Body" subject to force. He longs for home, for kin, and for kind, "People with whom I could converse upon even Terms." He longs for the shelter of species.

The First Person and the Animal Fable

Approached in this way, book 4 appears to offer a solution to the problems presented in book 2, in the shape of a society built wholly on species—a term that appears twenty-eight times in *Gulliver's Travels*, twenty-three of them in its final book. The Houyhnhnm—which "in their Tongue, signifies a *Horse*, and in its Etymology, *the Perfection of Nature*"—is essentially a species-being, which means, here, a fixed and natural kind, an identity that is constant and logically prior to any insignificant and merely individual variation. Even the ranks of Houyhnhnm society are species in this sense. Just as no differences of opinion interrupt the Houyhnhnms' rational and immediate consensus, no personal preference interrupts their attitude of universal friendship—"a Stranger from the remotest Part is equally treated with the nearest Neighbour, and wherever he goes, looks upon himself as at home" (226). In contrast to Gulliver in book 2, to be a Houyhnhnm is to be at home everywhere in nature—to be essentially and inviolably what one is.

The story of book 4 is the story of Gulliver's efforts to "gain Admittance" to this Houyhnhnm order, and in particular to the Houyhnhnm household (194). He makes it part way: he is provided "a Place . . . to lodge in," he boasts, "but Six Yards from the House, and separated from the Stable of the *Yahoos*" (197–98). But Gulliver's betwixt and between position does not last. At home neither with the Houyhnhnms nor in the stable with the Yahoos, Gulliver is expelled from Houyhnhnmland—and, violently so, as Claude Rawson reminds us.[17] The reason for this turns on Gulliver's "ontological state," and what he wants it to be. What Gulliver wants is not to be a Houyhnhnm (as he knows he is not), nor even that the Houyhnhnms recognize that he is not a Yahoo (as he comes reluctantly to conclude that he is). What he wants, as he puts it, is for the Houyhnhnms to "condescend to distinguish me from the rest of my Species" (234). Gulliver's Master does distinguish him in this way, and it is for this as much as anything that the General Assembly sends Gulliver away: "the Representatives had taken Offence at his keeping a *Yahoo* (meaning myself) in his Family more like a *Houyhnhnm*, than a Brute Animal. . . . That such a Practice was not agreeable to Reason or Nature, nor a thing ever heard of before among them" (235). Condescending to distinguish Gulliver from his species, the Master Horse brings him into his home in the manner of a Houyhnhnm rather than a Yahoo, keeping him as a domestic companion rather than as cattle.

It is not so surprising that Gulliver is cast off the island: the exceptional and unnatural status of the pet seems altogether out of place in the natural and species order of Houyhnhnm society. What is more surprising is that Gulliver wants to be a pet in the first place. After all, this is the same sort of identity that Gulliver experienced in Brobdingnag as terrifying and ignoble enslavement. Something significant has changed between book 2, where pethood looked like a problem, and book 4, where Gulliver wants nothing more. What has changed is genre. To live in Houyhnhnmland is to live inside fable, where distinctions are natural rather than conferred. To Gulliver, this means that Houyhnhnmland promises a kind of pethood—or more simply, of individuation—that is not granted by the benevolence or power of others (as in Brobdingnag), but which is a natural and even species status. Gulliver's

desire that the Houyhnhnms "condescend to distinguish me from the rest of
my Species" is a desire that they recognize him as the logic of their society
would seem to require: as his own natural kind. This is to say, finally, that Gulliver wants a form of identity that is not conferred from without but which is
tied closely to his own sense of self.

To put things this way makes it sound like Gulliver is after recognition
that there is, to borrow Locke's phrase, an Inhabitant within. Whatever the
outward signs of species, this is his true kind: he is what Locke would call
a person. There is something to this. But the way that Gulliver is a person
has nothing to do with Locke's notion of personal identity, in the sense
of a narrative identity composed by consciousness and memory over time.
Gulliver's "sense of self" is simply the first-person perspective that remains
constant throughout the book; he is a person in this minimal and formal
sense of grammar and point of view. This is the sort of identity Gulliver
looks to house in Houyhnhnmland, and it is this that Houyhnhnmland—
and fable—cannot accommodate. What it is about fable that cannot accommodate the first person—or, what it is about first personhood that disrupts
the animal fable—are not simple questions. Swift's answers are still less so. I
approach them here by way of Swift's most extended poetic foray into fable,
"The Beasts' Confession to a Priest, on Observing how most Men mistake
their own Talents," a poem that one critic refers to as "a veritable thesaurus
of Swiftian preoccupations," and that, in its original 1738 publication, closes
with a footnote: "*vide* Gulliver in his account of the Houyhnhnms."[18] Far
less frequently read than *Gulliver's Travels*, "The Beasts' Confession" gets to
the heart of the debate over book 4 of the *Travels*, over Gulliver's "ontological state" and the status of the Houyhnhnm society. "The Beasts' Confession" shows that ultimately, the question of whether the Houyhnhnms are
an ideal or an alien form of life turns on Swift's sense of the incompatibility
between the fable and the first person.

"The Beasts' Confession" is Swift's version of the Aesopian fable, "The
Animals Sick of the Plague," which had been retold in the seventeenth century
by La Fontaine, L'Estrange, and others. In La Fontaine's version of the fable,
a series of animals gather to confess their sins, in hopes of easing the plague
they understand to be visited on them as punishment. The lion begins by con-
fessing to living on the lives of the innocent—sheep, and even the occasional
shepherd. He is followed by an equally sanguinary fox, tiger, boar, and bear,
who all insist that the lion's sins, like their own, are in fact acts of grace, or
honor, or justice. Finally, an ass comes forward and confesses that he has eaten

grass from a field without permission. The other beasts condemn the ass's tres-
pass as the most heinous of their crimes, and they sacrifice the ass to expiate
the sins of all. The plot of the fable concludes as the beasts offer up the weakest
and least vicious animal, giving rise to a moral about the pretense of justice,
the coincidence of might and right: "Thus human courts acquit the strong, /
And doom the weak, as therefore wrong."

Swift's version works differently. He takes from the traditional fable the
procession of beast confessors and their bad faith confessions—his animals
all "confess" to vices that are in fact excessive virtues. But in Swift's fable, the
virtues to which the beasts confess are conspicuously uncharacteristic: the
ass confesses to wit, the goat to chastity, the swine to pride or vanity. Furthermore, in Swift's poem there is no action from which to draw a concluding moral. The procession of animal figures and their confessions does not
build into narrative as it does in La Fontaine, culminating in the expiation
of crimes by the most innocent and a moral lesson drawn in conclusion: justice equates weakness and wrongdoing, might and right. Instead, the poem
remains in the form of a list or a catalogue. This is true even when Swift
marks the transition to the moral or "application" about a third of the way
into the poem, when the speaker directs the reader to "Apply the tale, and
you shall find / How just it suits with humankind" (73–74). Rather than
move to the expected moral lesson, the speaker simply continues the list, with
a series of human professions that come forward much in the same way as the
animal species had before them, to instantiate the indictment announced at
the outset: "how most men mistake their talents." Swift begins the catalogue
with "the pious wolf":

> "Good father, I must own with shame,
> That often I have been to blame:
> I must confess, on Friday last,
> Wretch that I was, I broke my fast:
> But, I defy the basest tongue
> To prove I did my neighbour wrong;
> Or ever went to seek my food
> By rapine, theft, or thirst of blood." (13–20)

As soon as the wolf comes forward, he seeks to identify himself as an exceptional case. Wolves may be guilty of rapine and theft, he implies; *I* am not.
Defying the definite article to proclaim his own difference, "*the* pious wolf"

insists that he is actually *this* pious wolf, a particular and exceptional specimen. This same logic continues as the poem moves to human beings. "The doctor" admits that he is not very good at turning medicine into profit—exempting himself from the schemes that "others, whom he will not name, / Have often practiced to their shame" (139–40). "The statesman" cites his atypical integrity and uses italics to likewise set himself apart from his kind: "Though some had spread a thousand lies / 'Twas *he* defeated the Excise" (149–50). Each figure in Swift's fable comes forward to disavow the logic of the species or type.

If there is a lesson to be drawn from the poem as a whole, it comes in two parts. The first concerns the logic of the list itself—something Swift underscores with the serial form of his poem, a potentially endless catalogue of individual aberrations composed at once by addition (one species after another) and subtraction (each individual excepting himself from his kind). At stake here is the right (or wrong) relationship between the individual and the species, and the error of exception. The repeated claim to exceptionality is presented as conceptually confused and morally culpable ("men mistake their talents")—and the form of Swift's poem presents this mistake as the pernicious consequence of conceiving of species as a class or collection, and individuals as exceptions. Swift insists that one cannot subtract attributes from an individual any more than one can subtract an individual from a species, by way of the sort of equation "the pious wolf" attempts: Wolf – rapine – theft + piety = me. There is no exceptional, pious wolf because animal species are not collectives of similar individuals, classed as such because each individual is itself a collection of similar attributes. As the genre of fable has long understood, species simply are fixed and essential characters: Wolf *is* rapine, Lion is courage. Each wolf is an embodiment of its essential species character and so is identical to all others—*this* wolf, like every other wolf, is always and necessarily Wolf. This is the proper logic of fable, Swift suggests, and of animal species.

This point leads to the second lesson of "The Beasts' Confession." Just as he affirms the species logic of fable, Swift critiques one way of viewing its figurative logic, which rests its injunction to "Apply the tale" on the resemblance between humans and animals. Swift stresses that the tale "suits to humankind" not because a conscientious lawyer resembles a pious wolf, but because the pious wolf is already a conscientious lawyer in animal dress. The poem concludes on precisely this point. Anyone who would disavow its species in this way—a pious wolf, or a goat that confesses to chastity—is patently not an animal but a figure for a human being:

I own, the moral not exact;
Besides, the tale is false in fact;
And, so absurd, that I could raise up
From fields Elysian, fabling Aesop;
I would accuse him to his face
For libeling the four-foot race.
Creatures of every kind but ours
Well comprehend their natural powers;
While we, whom reason ought to sway,
Mistake our talents every day:
The ass was never known so stupid
To act the part of Tray, or Cupid;
Nor leaps upon his master's lap,
There to be stroked and fed with pap;
As Aesop would the world persuade;
Our author's meaning, I presume, is
A creature *bipes et implumis*;
Wherein the moralist designed
A compliment to humankind:
For, here he owns, that now and then
Beasts may *degenerate* into men. (197–220)

Against the putatively comparative premise of the genre (look at animals and see yourselves), Swift's exceptional beasts flaunt the fact that they are not animals at all.[19] Like Mandeville's infamous bees—"Insects [that] liv'd like Men"—Swift's beasts expose the logic of the fable as tautology, not similitude. The speaker thus revises the charge he levels at "Our author" Aesop—that he is guilty of "libeling the four-foot race" by depicting it as it never was in nature—by turning the lesson out to readers: "Our author's meaning, I presume, is / A creature *bipes et implumis*." In its conclusion, Swift's fable links its lesson about the wrong way of conceiving species (the error of exception) to another, about the wrong way of reading fable (the error of comparison). Putting these lessons together, the final line of the fable—"Beasts may *degenerate* into men"—laments a move from animal to human (the real subjects of fable) and from species to individual (from beast to *men*).[20] Indeed, it identifies these moves with one another. The lone species that would disclaim its own identity, Man always degenerates into men.

In his discussion of the "autocritical fable," Frank Palmeri reads "The Beasts' Confession" along such lines, as a poem that concludes by renouncing its own genre with a familiar theriophilic refrain: an assertion of difference between humans and animals that rests on the superiority (and the species identity) of animals.[21] This is certainly the ostensible lesson of Swift's fable. But it is subject to considerable irony, on at least two fronts. First, the poem identifies human beings as exceptional because they alone make the error of exception. Second, in order to apprehend this first lesson, one has to read the speaker's concession, "Our author's meaning, I presume, is / A creature *bipes et implumis*," to refer to humankind. And when one reads these lines in this way, one identifies humankind as a featherless, two-footed creature—an identification that curiously echoes the speaker's accusation that Aesop libels "the four-foot race." In other words, just as he insists that there are no animals in this poem, the speaker identifies humankind *as* a class of animal—as a physical form of life defined by two feet and a lack of feathers.

The speaker's identification of humankind as a two-foot race—and thus as a kind of animal—may seem insignificant, a momentary turn of phrase. But the phrase has a notable and peculiar philosophical pedigree, and it is one that joins together Swift's twin ironies about human exceptionality and human animality. The phrase comes to Swift from Plato's *Statesman*, by way of Diogenes' infamous rejoinder—recounted here in Ephraim Chambers's 1728 *Cyclopædia*, which includes Plato's definition in the entry not for "man" but for "definition," as an example of a bad one: "The joke put upon him on that account is famous: Plato, it seems, had *defined* man, *animal bipes & implume, a two-footed animal without feathers.* Upon which, Diogenes the Cynic, a great derider of the Academics, threw a cock stripped of his feathers, and quite naked, into the middle of Plato's school: crying, 'Here is Plato's man.'"[22] Plato's definition (and attacks against it) took on new force in the wake of Linnaeus's 1735 *Systema Naturae*, with its controversial inclusion of human beings in the order of quadrupeds, one animal among others, classed according to a set of visible characters. To define man "by the Number of his Feet, and the Smoothness of his Skin," Reverend John Steffe wrote in 1757, was to give "the Definition of a *meer Animal*; such as a Naturalist would have given of a Frog, a Fly, or some other contemptible Insect."[23] For Steffe, Plato's definition (and undoubtedly, Linnaeus's as well) did not so much make it difficult to distinguish "man" from some other species of animal (like Diogenes' stripped bird). It made "man" an animal, full stop.

Like many of his contemporaries, Swift seems to side with Diogenes. In his original notes to "The Beasts' Confession," Swift glosses the notion of the featherless two-foot race as "a definition of man, disapproved by all logicians."

It recalls the base animality of Brobdingnag, the effect of stripping away all attributes until Gulliver is nothing but "a strange Animal in the Fields"; it recalls the brutishly physical Yahoos in Houyhnhnmland. But Swift's invocation of "Plato's man" in "The Beasts' Confession" is complicated by its original context in the *Statesman*. In the course of Plato's dialogue, the definition of man as a two-footed and featherless creature emerges to correct exactly the philosophical error that preoccupies Swift in "The Beasts' Confession" as well as in *Gulliver's Travels*: mistaking an exception for a category. The dialogue opens with "a Visitor from Elea," who reasons that to define the statesman one must define his subjects, the creatures that he governs or maintains. The Visitor then proceeds toward this definition, in a lesson on philosophical method, by division: the statesman is he who maintains living rather than nonliving creatures, a collective or herd rather than a single individual, tame rather than wild, gregarious rather than solitary, and so on. Continuing in this manner, the Visitor arrives at the definition of "human being" as a herd of tame, gregarious, two-footed, featherless creatures, and politics as "the art of herding human beings."[24]

This is the definition derided by Diogenes, so notorious in the eighteenth-century imagination, and apparently dismissed by Swift. But the alternative advanced by the Visitor's interlocutor, Young Socrates, seems equally unappealing. Midway through the dialogue, after dividing creatures into living and nonliving, collective and individual, the Visitor invites Young Socrates to make the next move. Young Socrates proposes the division of living herds into "human" and "beast," but the Visitor says no. The Visitor offers two— notably Swiftian—scenarios to illustrate why the division of human and beast mistakes an individual instance for a class or category, excepting an individual from a whole rather than dividing the whole properly into two. The first is the Greek practice of dividing humankind into "Greek" and "barbarian": "they use the single term 'barbarian' for all the other categories of people, despite the fact that there are countless races who never communicated and are incompatible with one another, and then expect there to be a single category too, just because they've used a single term."[25] The second scenario is the imagined practice of an intelligent animal species: "Imagine another species which is endowed with intelligence, as cranes are supposed to be (or you can imagine some other species, if you prefer), and imagine them undertaking the same task of distributing names as you; they might exaggerate the importance of their own species by making cranes into a single class to contrast with all other species, and they might lump together all other creatures, including humans—and what else would they call them but 'beasts'?"[26] It is difficult to isolate Plato's view throughout this remarkably slippery dialogue.[27] But Swift's view would seem clear. On the one hand, there is the featherless two-footed creature, a taxonomical class or set of Linnaean characters, the base animality of the strange animal in Brobdingnag, or the Yahoo in Houyhnhnmland. On the other hand, there is the human being as the exception to this base animality, derived by the same exceptionalist logic that Swift so often and explicitly rejects, enacted here at the level of the species rather than the individual. Neither is a viable way of conceiving of human being.

Swift's beast fable would thus seem to arrive at a dilemma, in the shape of two unsatisfactory definitions and two self-ironizing lessons. But I think it also hints at a way out of this dilemma—a way of conceiving of the human not as or opposed to animality, and of the individual not as or opposed to the species. This is not a path explicitly taken in the poem, but it is one that the poem points toward in the moves it makes from animal species to human professions, and from first-person speech to third-person account—as well as in its insistent refusal to mark these as moves. Paradoxically, the formal identity of each scenario and stanza—the relentless seriality that adds another species, the same as the last, and subtracts another individual, the same as the last—underscores the places where difference might emerge. This is most obvious with the "application" from animal species to human professions. The logic of the list moves swiftly past this shift, in a way that ought well give us pause, as professions are conspicuously not natural kinds. Unlike animal species, professions are simply and properly classes or aggregates: collections of similar individuals, which are themselves collections of similar attributes. The problem here is not that the conscientious lawyer is a logical impossibility, in the manner of the pious wolf, mistakenly trying to except himself from his kind. The problem is that men adhere to type when they need not, claiming exceptionality but in fact conforming wholly to type. By collapsing animal species and human professions into one and the same repetitive, serial catalogue—acknowledging no difference between the social and the natural order, the class and the species—Swift reminds us that these are different kinds of kinds.

The same is true of the move from the first to the third person. The wolf's opening first-person speech stands out from the rest of the poem, which otherwise proceeds as a catalogue of figures described in the third person. But it stands out most of all in its utter assimilation, as the first item in a catalogue that registers no difference between the first and the third person, any more than it does between the animal species and the human profession. Once again, Swift uses formal likeness to underscore substantive difference. Beginning from the first person, he intimates, we should end up with a different form than a list of like figures. Palmeri's account of the animal fable is helpful, I think, in explaining why we do not. In most of the poems Palmeri classes as autocritical (or "anti-metaphorical") fables, lions and wolves defy the usual figurative logic of the genre to comment directly on the plight of animals.[28] In such fables, Palmeri argues, lion and wolf do not stand for human qualities or beings but simply for Lion or Wolf. The logic of the autocritical fable, on Palmeri's account, is that of synecdoche rather than metaphor: animals function as "figure[s] for the literal animals" and "speak from the subject position of their species."[29] In "The Beasts' Confession," Swift is not concerned with the plight of animals in Palmeri's sense of their material and metaphorical use by human beings. But he is concerned with the generic logic of animals, and the generic limits of fable. Swift's point might be put this way: synecdoche is the proper logic of *all* fables, though we may mistakenly read for metaphor (for resemblance between humans and animals) instead. The synecdochal and species logic of fable—in which this wolf (and every wolf) is always and only Wolf, an embodiment of an essential species character—means that if a wolf could speak, it could speak *only* from the subject position of its species. When a wolf says "I" instead of "Wolf," we know he is mistaken, or lying—or human, which amounts to the same thing. In the animal fable, in other words, the first person is visible only as an error of individuation-as-exception.

This is the ultimate lesson of Swift's fable. Synecdoche is the proper logic of fable, and of the fabulous animal. But it is not the proper logic of human being. Indeed, the human is the one thing missing from the catalogue of kinds enumerated in "The Beasts' Confession." There is no properly human species in this poem: there is animality (beasts, and humankind as a class of beast) and there are men (all the conspicuously nonnatural varieties like lawyer and doctor, or the putatively individual exceptions.) Swift is after a mode of speciation—and of individuation—that is proper to human being, and he suggests that we might start to conceive such a thing in the first-person speech that cannot quite take shape in fable. To my mind, it is this that constitutes the autocritique of "The Beasts' Confession." It leaves us with a question that fable generates but cannot answer: what would it mean to speak from the subject position of *our* species? To say "I" and not claim to except ourselves from humankind, nor to simply speak for it, as one essential and identical Man? Swift looks for an answer to this question—for a way of representing humankind that starts from the first person—not in Plato, or in fable, but in

Hobbes. For Hobbes, as for Swift, starting from first personhood means that human beings are not identical species beings, nor a collection of similar (or exceptional) individuals. Hobbes insists that human beings are neither identical nor similar—we are equal, though it requires a particular sort of (fabulous) reading to acknowledge this. Swift thus looks to Hobbes for a model of the way that each of us might "apply the tale" and find that it "suits to human-kind" in the first person—in me.

Politics in the First Person

Hobbes opens the second book of the *Leviathan* by arguing, against Plato's Visitor and more directly (in Hobbes's view) against Aristotle, that humans are distinguished from animals as the sole subjects of politics: "It is true, that certain living creatures, as Bees, and Ants, live sociably with another, (which are therefore by *Aristotle* numbered amongst Politicall creatures;) and yet have no other direction, than their particular judgements and appetites . . . and therefore some man may perhaps desire to know, why Man-kind cannot do the same" (225). Hobbes lists no less than six reasons that men are not (like) bees and that bees are not political, which chiefly have to do with a difference in the relationship between the individual and the species: "amongst these creatures, the Common good differeth not from the Private; and being by nature enclined to their private, they procure thereby the common benefit" (225). Unlike bees and ants, "men are continually in competition"; their "Joy consisteth in comparing [themselves] with other men" and coming out on top (225, 226). Human beings are individuated in a way that animals are not, and because of this, they naturally incline toward envy, hatred, and war. Animals— at least social animals, like bees—live together in a naturally peaceful order. On Hobbes's view, they are essentially the synecdochal and species creatures of fabular convention. As a result, Hobbes concludes, "the agreement of these creatures is Naturall; that of men, is by Covenant only, which is Artificiall" (225). This artificial agreement—the social contract, as Hobbes conceives it— is a response to human individuation, conceived not as a matter of number (the one and the many) but as point of view.

Put differently, human beings need politics because unlike bees, they are not identical but equal. In Hobbes's formulation, "Nature hath made men so equall, in the faculties of body, and mind"; because of this, the state of nature is "a condition of Warre of every one against every one" (183, 189). The link

Hobbes draws between equality and war rests on a number of psychological and economic assumptions, not least about the scarcity of resources. But in the context of Swift, what is most striking is what Hobbes actually means by equality. Hobbes admits that observable differences between human beings "may perhaps make such equality incredible" (183), but he goes on to tie natural equality to the first-person point of view: "For such is the nature of man, that howsoever they may acknowledge many others to be more witty, or more eloquent, or more learned; Yet they will hardly believe there be many so wise as themselves: For they see their own wit at hand, and other mens at a distance. But this proveth rather that men are in that point equall, than unequall. For there is not ordinarily a greater signe of the equall distribution of any thing, than that every man is contented with his share" (184). Hobbes directs his argument about natural equality against a position he associates with Aristotle, which holds that some men are designed by nature to be servants or philosophers, according to the unequal distribution of physical or mental strength. But Hobbes does not make this argument as one might expect, by contesting the link he takes Aristotle to make between natural and political inequality. Instead, he contests the notion of natural inequality itself, repeatedly insisting that equality is a fact of nature and, remarkably, identifying this natural fact with the view "at hand" rather than "at a distance." The first-person perspective that each of us bears becomes the basis of Hobbes's ninth law of nature— "*That every man acknowledge other for his Equall by Nature*"—because, Hobbes reasons, "if Nature therefore have made men equall, that equalitie is to be acknowledged: or if Nature have made men unequall; yet because men that think themselves equall . . . such equalitie must be admitted" (211).

Insisting that "because men think themselves equall . . . such equalitie must be admitted," Hobbes can seem to make a point about the delusions and danger of vainglory—"the imaginative activity of comparing ourselves to others" and seeing likeness where none exists.[30] As Victoria Kahn argues, Hobbes diagnoses vainglory as the most human of errors, a form of self-aggrandizement—"comparison as emulation," or "metaphorical usurpation," in Kahn's words—that occurs whenever "'a man compoundeth the image of his own person, with the image of the actions of an other man; as when a man imagins himself a *Hercules,* or an *Alexander.*'"[31] Measured from some external or third-person perspective, one's sense of one's equality with everyone else would indeed be a version of vainglory, an obvious error of the imagination. But Hobbes insists that it is altogether irrelevant whether nature made men equal or unequal, considered from some objective

or third-person perspective. In the most elemental and formal sense of equality, there is no such objective stance; there are only relative positions. What
Hobbes calls natural equality is fundamentally a matter of first-person—and
of every first-person—point of view. Any "conditions of Peace"—that is, any
politics—must start from this point: from the law of nature that is individuation conceived in first-personal and formal terms, from every one's sense of
himself and the subsequent imperative that "every man acknowledge [every]
other for his Equall" (211).[32]

By making human individuation a matter of point of view, Hobbes configures a relationship between individual and species that is not a matter of
number, of logical or temporal priority, or of straightforward opposition.
Conceived in first-person terms, the Hobbesian individual is a distinct order
of being that also and by the same token tends to incorporation. Indeed, this
is the task of politics, on Hobbes's view: to incorporate "A Multitude of men"
but not override individuals conceived in irreducibly first-person terms—to
constitute the commonwealth as a form of "Unity . . . in Multitude" effected
by "every one of that Multitude in particular" (220), and to insist equally on
both "Unity" and "every one of that Multitude." Hobbes's effort to construct
a collective that begins from and also preserves individuation understood in
first-person terms is not something that accounts of a straightforwardly absolutist Hobbes tend to register. But it is something that I think interested Swift,
not least because it turns on a set of ideas and activities about which he cared
a good deal, which cross political with expressly literary concerns: authorship,
personation, representation, reading.[33] For Hobbes, these literary activities
enter political life most patently in the figure of the person—a figure that
serves to simultaneously unite and preserve so many particular points of view.

Hobbes's most extended discussion of personhood comes at the end of
the first book of the *Leviathan,* in the riddled and much-discussed chapter
that serves as a bridge between the natural-philosophical book 1, "Of Man,"
and the political-philosophical book 2, "Of Commonwealth." He starts with
a definition: "A PERSON, is he *whose words or actions are considered, either as
his own, or as representing the words or actions of an other man, or of any other
thing to whom they are attributed, whether Truly or by Fiction*" (217). From the
outset, Hobbes's conception of personhood is hard to hold onto, and its terms
become increasingly difficult to track as the chapter continues.[34] Hobbes
begins by distinguishing what he calls "a *Naturall Person,*" whose words or
actions are considered as his own, from "a *Feigned or Artificiall person,*" whose
words or actions are considered as those of another. But he also emphasizes

that "person" itself is a term that comes from theater and the tribunal, a term that belongs to the domain of fiction or representation. The full title of Hobbes's chapter is "Of Persons, Authors, and Things Personated," but the distinction between "person" and "thing personated" wears thin as Hobbes proliferates all manner of persons: the Commonwealth, provincial assemblies, and trade corporations; pagan idols and the Christian God; inanimate objects like churches, bridges, and hospitals; and humans beings like children, mad-men, and fools. Characterizing personhood as something that can attach to all sorts of things, Hobbes suggests that persons are personifications in a strong and straightforward sense: a status superadded to some things in order to grant them, as Sharon Cameron puts it, "intelligibility within a political and legal system."[35] Brought into being by the representational mechanism that is polit-ical society—and by the pleasure of the sovereign—Hobbesian personhood looks a good deal like pethood as Swift understands it in book 2 of the *Travels*.

This is often how Hobbesian personhood is understood, and for good reason. But there is more to Hobbes's account. For Hobbes, all kinds of things can be "persons," but only some can be what he calls "authors."[36] As he puts it, "There are few things, that are uncapable of being represented by Fiction" or, in a different formulation of the same point, "of which there cannot be a person."[37] But "things Inanimate, cannot be Authors"; "Likewise Children, Fooles, and Mad-men that have no use of Reason, may be Personated . . . but can be no Authors" (219). An author, for Hobbes, is only "he whose words or actions are considered . . . as his own"—the kind of being Hobbes calls a "natural person" and implicitly identifies as rational, adult, and human. The notion of a "natural person" can seem something of a logical contradiction in Hobbes's discussion, where "person" everywhere is aligned with represen-tation, with the artificial realm of politics rather than with any natural state. At the same time, Hobbes's notion of the natural person is an important one, because it signals his effort to articulate the ways in which some person(ifi-cation)s are different from others. Some persons—those whom Hobbes calls natural persons or authors—are both object and subject of the process of personification that Hobbes identifies as fundamental to political life.[38] He describes this process in some detail: "To appoint one man, or Assembly of men, to beare their Person; and every one to owne, and acknowledge himself to be Author of whatsoever he that so beareth their Person, shall Act. . . . This is more than Consent, or Concord; it is a reall Unitie of them all, in one and the same Person, made by Covenant of every man with every man. . . . The Multitude so united in one person, is called a COMMON-WEALTH, in latine,

CIVITAS. This is the Generation of that great LEVIATHAN" (227). The product and the bearer of this act of personation is the sovereign, the "*One Person, of whose acts a great Multitude, by mutuall Covenants one with another, have made themselves every one the Author*" (228).

Hobbes's conception of authorship—as a mechanism that both sustains natural multiplicity and establishes political unity—can seem like a trick of language or an outright lie, an elaborate and perplexing fiction of consent that makes it appear as if every man agrees to his own subjection. Certainly, Hobbesian authorship does not mitigate the force of his absolutism in any simple way, serving as it does to bind his whole all the more tightly. At the same time, his notion of authorship does affect the composition of his political society, and the agency that holds it together. For Hobbes, to author means to create or cause but also to acknowledge or own; authorship, in this sense, has as much to do with reading as with origination.[39] To acknowledge the sovereign as one's person or personation is to encounter it as a figure to be read, a form of representation that unites oneself with a multitude of men, and with "every one of that Multitude in particular" (220).[40] To read in this way is to effect a uniquely human form of speciation, the "reall Unitie" of humankind.

In the introduction to the *Leviathan*, Hobbes outlines what it looks like to do this. He begins from the commonplace that wisdom comes "not by reading of *Books*, but of *Men*," and he argues that most men read poorly. The problem, as Hobbes sees it, is that they look only to others, and "shew what they think they have read in men, by uncharitable censures of one another behind their backs" (82). Hobbes proposes a different way of reading: "But there is another saying not of late understood, by which they might learn truly to read one another, if they would take the pains; and that is, *Nosce teipsum, Read thy self*" (82). This again sounds like something of a commonplace, the moral injunction to consider oneself rather than cast judgment on others. But Hobbes's formulation suggests something more unusual. To begin with, as Tracy Strong has pointed out, Hobbes's translation of *nosce teipsum* makes a striking and unmarked substitution of "read" for "know."[41] And Hobbes proceeds to explain that the injunction to "read thyself" is less an imperative to focus on oneself than it is a more effective method "by which [men] might learn truly to read one another" (83). He puts the point this way: "though by mens actions wee do discover their designe sometimes; yet to do it without comparing them with our own, and distinguishing all circumstances, by which the case may come to be altered, is to decypher without a key" (83). Hobbes does not suggest that the problem with reading others is that we are not in the optimal position, with access only to men's "actions" and not to the "designes" that lie behind them. The central problem is not one of access but of method. Reading men without using the self as a "key," we proceed by induction, accumulating knowledge of particulars until we can make a claim about man in general. Hobbes insists that this does not work. Even if it were possible for "one man [to] read another by his actions . . . perfectly, it serves him onley with his acquaintance, which are but few. He that is to govern a whole Nation, must read in himself, not this, or that particular man; but Man-kind" (83). It is not only the sovereign who reads in this way; Hobbes identifies his own book as both the effect and the cause of a similar reading practice. (The point of *Leviathan*, he writes, is to "set down my own reading orderly, and perspicuously" so that another need "only to consider, if he also find not the same in himself" [83].) Whether we are sovereign or subject, Hobbes maintains that we never reach mankind by collecting individual men. The only way to proceed is directly from self to species: identifying one's actions with those of others, "read[ing] in himself . . . Man-kind."

This kind of reading might bring to mind Swift's madman from the *Tale of a Tub*, who "conceive[s] it in his power to reduce the notions of all mankind exactly to the same length, and breadth, and height of his own."[42] But Hobbes explicitly cautions against the habit men have of "measur[ing], not onely other men, but all other things, by themselves" (87). "From hence it is," Hobbes writes, "that the Schooles say, Heavy bodies fall downwards, out of an appetite to rest, and to conserve their nature in that place which is most proper for them; ascribing appetite, and Knowledge of what is good for their conservation, (which is more than man has) to things inanimate absurdly" (87). Faulting human beings for "measur[ing] not onely other men but all other things by themselves," and yet enjoining his reader to "read in himself . . . Man-kind," Hobbes begins to envision a method of reading that brings together self and species without collapsing them into identity—or that understands identification to be a matter of form rather than content, of point of view rather than a substantive set of shared features.[43] This is not the species identity of animals, nor is it a matter of resemblance, a relation between similar individuals, all bearing similar attributes. It is a "reall Unitie" of "every one of that Multitude in particular," which is no less real for being the result of an explicitly figurative reading practice that takes the self as the key to the kind. This is ultimately where I think Hobbes gets traction for Swift: with a uniquely human way of uniting individual and species that begins from the formal identity of first personhood to effect a nonnatural but nonetheless real unity between the first person and the human species.[44] For Hobbes, the representational mechanism that enables (indeed requires) one to read in this way is political society. For Swift, it is satire—which is to say, a practice of reading fable in the first person.

Reading Fable After Hobbes; or, Satire

To Gulliver, Houyhnhnmland looks a good deal like the world of Hobbes's bees and ants, in which there is no individual distinction and thus no politics, in Hobbes's sense of the word. What there is, to recall Plato's Visitor, is herd maintenance: as Margaret Doody points out in slightly different terms, the Houyhnhnms "practice animal husbandry, soberly and thoroughly, upon themselves. [They] treat themselves as objects, as a breed."[45] The Houyhnhnms are certain that their animal husbandry—practiced on themselves, or on their Yahoo cattle—operates according to the natural and species order that organizes all Houyhnhnm society, and dictates all Houyhnhnm actions. But the violence of the Houyhnhnms' treatment of the Yahoos sits uncomfortably alongside this conviction, and Gulliver's presence begins to make this visible. As he aspires to have his pethood ratified as its own natural kind, Gulliver threatens to expose the exceptionalist logic that already organizes Houyhnhnm society. "A wonderful *Yahoo*, that could speak like a *Houyhnhnm*," who wears clothes "to conceal what Nature had given" (199, 200), Gulliver threatens to expose that the Houyhnhnms are not a natural category distinct from any other but simply, in the words of Plato's Visitor, "another species . . . endowed with intelligence" that exaggerates its own importance by "lump[ing] together all other creatures, including humans—and what else would they call them but 'beasts.'"[46] At the same time, the world of the Houyhnhnms is the world of fable, which configures all activities and relations as part of an animal and species order. It is the work of the genre to present social distinctions and political relations in animal dress—to picture politics as nothing other than the order of nature.

Gulliver's most potent threat to the fabulous logic of Houyhnhnmland emerges at the meeting of the General Assembly, when the Master Houyhnhnm turns the members' attention to Gulliver in order to propose a new solution to the interminable question of Yahoo extermination. He explains "that in [Gulliver's] own and other Countries the *Yahoos* acted as the governing, Rational Animal, and held the *Houyhnhnms* in Servitude," and that they achieved this in part by means of the "Custom we [Gulliver's people] had of *Castrating Houyhnhnms* when they were young, in order to render them tame" (229). Gulliver first detailed this practice to his Master in the following terms: "the Males, designed for common Use of Riding or Draught, were generally *castrated* about two Years after their Birth, to take down their Spirits, and make them more tame and gentle" (204). Gulliver's use of the passive "designed," here, at once obscures and underscores the significant shift in meaning he enacts. For the Houyhnhnms, "design" is always in some sense without agent, the work of Nature or an omnipotent Creator, a kind of intelligent design. In Gulliver's phrase, by contrast, the horses "designed for common Use" are explicitly shaped by the designs or even machinations of human beings, clearly operating outside and against any natural order. This is what the Master presents to the General Assembly for consideration: that the Houyhnhnms treat Yahoos as Houyhnhnms are treated where Yahoos are in charge, with a technique of domestication or herd maintenance that is clearly not based in any natural design. Ultimately, this is Gulliver's lesson to the Houyhnhnms. Governing and rationality can be "acted"; domestication is a customary practice and not the work of nature; servitude is not the order of things but a matter of power. Gulliver's lesson is the inverse of Derrida's remark that "Politics supposes livestock."[47] Gulliver teaches that livestock supposes politics.

Much ink has been spilled over what Gulliver learns from the Houyhnhnms, and whether for good or ill. But what the Houyhnhnms learn from Gulliver—and simply that they might learn from Gulliver at all—is equally striking. So too, is the form that lesson takes. The Master Houyhnhnm presents Gulliver's lesson in the form of an incipient animal fable, reasoning "that it was no Shame to learn Wisdom from Brutes, as Industry is taught by the Ant, and Building by the Swallow" (230). Invoking the animal fable (and the industrious ant in particular) to teach a patently nonnatural technology for domesticating animals, the Master Houyhnhnm echoes the moment from book 2 when Gulliver offers the model of human society to the King of Brobdingnag. In that earlier moment, Gulliver reasoned similarly, "That among other Animals, Bees and Ants had the Reputation of more Industry, Art, and Sagacity than many of the larger kinds. And that, as inconsiderable as he took me to be, I hoped I might live to do his Majesty some signal Service" (106). The Master Houyhnhnm's echo of Gulliver's animal fable introduces the politico-domestic logic of book 2 into book 4, and in doing so shakes the natural ground of the Houyhnhnm order. (Something similar takes place when Gulliver's Houyhnhnm Master sees Gulliver without his clothes and uses the key phrase of book 2 to both identify him as animal and except him from that identity: "he then stroaked my Body very gently, and . . . said it was plain I must be a perfect *Yahoo*; but that I differed very much from the rest of my Species" [201].)

When the Master Houyhnhnm introduces his own Gulliveranian animal fable and assures the General Assembly "that it was no Shame to learn Wisdom from Brutes," he seeks to contain a problem that does not primarily have to do with the particular source of learning (lowly brutes or beastly Yahoos). Instead, it has to do with what it means to learn from animals—from nature—at all. To learn from nature implies that one is somehow outside of it, like Gulliver and especially like Gulliver in Brobdingnag; it implies that there is nothing fixed or essential about who or what one is. In generic terms, to learn from nature is to become a reader of fable rather than a figure within it, a reader who recognizes the nature represented in fable *as* representation. Which is also to say, in the most basic and also Hobbesian sense, as politics. In other words, Gulliver disturbs the putatively natural order of the Houyhnhnms less because he is or would be excepted from his species than because he is an outsider to the world of fable—because he is a reader, for whom the logic of fable is not a fact of nature but a literary convention. And he threatens to transform the Houyhnhnms into readers in turn, by presenting a lesson on the domestication of animals. Ultimately, this is not a transformation that the Houyhnhnms will permit. It is not a transformation that is possible, as it were, inside fable—inside Houynhnmland, a land famously without reading and writing.[48] But if Gulliver does not transform the Houyhnhnms into readers, his embedded animal fable does explicitly turn the tale out to us, the readers of the *Travels*. In so doing, it transforms the animal fable into a satire on mankind.

As many critics observe, Swift seeks a satirical mode from which there is no escape—a satire on mankind that necessarily implicates "me." Again and again, Swift voices frustration with the capacity of satire to allow the sort of exceptionalist logic he critiques in "The Beasts' Confession" and in the early books of *Gulliver's Travels*, as well as in the person of Gulliver himself. In *Battle of the Books*, for example, the "Author" famously laments that "Satire is a sort of glass, wherein beholders do generally discover everybody's face but their own"; the same complaint recurs in *A Tale of a Tub*, when the tale-teller observes that "satire being leveled at all is never resented for an offence by any."[49] Drawing a contrast with classical satire and perhaps with its readers, the tale-teller remarks that in present-day England, censures aimed at "the People in general" somehow permit "every Individual Person" to escape: "you may securely display your utmost *rhetoric* against mankind, in the face of the world; tell them, 'That all are gone astray, that there is none that doth good, no not one; that we live in the very dregs of time . . .' and when you have done, the whole audience, far from being offended, shall return you thanks as a deliverer of precious and useful truths. . . . 'Tis but a *ball* bandied to and fro, and every man carries a *racket* about him to strike it from himself among the rest of the company."[50] Swift looks for a way to make any such strike fail, or at least rebound.

There are different ways to describe how he goes about this in *Gulliver's Travels*, but on most accounts, the effort has little to do with the moral lessons of his satire—in paraphrase, Swift's satire of mankind sounds commonplaces about pride or avarice or hypocrisy. Instead, what is remarkable about Swift's satire has to do with its form, and the effects of that form on its readers. Ernest Tuveson thus suggests that we remember Swift because he "uniquely succeeded in doing what many had essayed. The satire on man sought to bring home to the individual in his inner being . . . to force the reader to include himself in the satiric reflection."[51] For Tuveson, as for many readers, Swift does this chiefly in book 4 of *Gulliver's Travels*. In what remains one of the most interesting elaborations of such a reading, W. B. Carnochan suggests that the first three books of the *Travels* proceed according to an inductive or empirical logic, collecting individual portraits toward one general satire on man. Carnochan argues that this approach reaches a dead end in book 3, which exaggerates and finally concedes the inductive argument: "So particular is the satire that we can from time to time correctly say: That is not us."[52] Having demonstrated that one cannot reach mankind by adding together individual men, Swift takes an entirely different approach in book 4, one epitomized in "Gulliver's intuition, enforced by the authority of the Houyhnhnms and by something like biological evidence, that man *is* a Yahoo."[53] Carnochan contends that no one escapes this argument by intuition or definition. "Until we get to Houyhnhnmland, we always have a decent chance of eluding Swift's satiric reach," he writes; but no man is beyond the reach of the natural, quasi-biological fact that "man *is* a Yahoo."[54] This point seems difficult to dispute, and yet the debate between hard and soft critics signals that we can indeed elude the reach of a satire that rests on such a formulation. This is not only because we might dispute definitions of man. Above all, it is because even as Gulliver intuits that *man* is a Yahoo, he never experiences *himself* as such—as a creature *bipes et implumis*, say. To the end, he persists in his sense that he does not wholly coincide with any species. No man may be beyond the reach of the fact that "man is a Yahoo," but each and every person is. What this means for Swift's satire is that in order to ensure that we cannot say, "That is not us," the intuition or definition that "man is a Yahoo" is not enough. It must be accompanied by the intuition that "I am a man."

This too may seem a logical enough proposition, even an undeniable one. But it is one that I think Swift calls into question—as both Descartes and Locke did before him, in different ways. There is some sense in which Swift thinks we can readily say, "I am not a man"—thinks, in fact, that this is all too easy to say whenever we speak in the first person and, like the various figures of "The Beast's Confession," declare ourselves exceptions from any kind. For Swift, then, the task of satire is to get each of us to speak from the subject position of the species—to say "I am a man." Or better, after Hobbes, the task of satire is to get each of us to read from such a position. Swift knows that satire does not always or easily achieve such reading—that satires aimed at "the People in general," as the tale-teller puts it, too often leave "every Individual Person" untouched.[55] Gerald Bruns identifies this as the effect of an "allegorical" tendency in satire, which "distances the terror of satire by generalizing its object"—targeting abstract general ideas like "liar" or even "man" and leaving individual persons safely outside.[56] Swift works to combat this sort of allegorical tendency by configuring a form of generality that does not admit of exception.

Critics of Swift often understand Swift to do this most powerfully in the animal fable of book 4, when the reader recognizes the degraded Yahoo as a just figure for humankind. By contrast, I am suggesting that "I" can always elude the force of this figure. I may recognize that man is a Yahoo but still, like Gulliver, not feel myself to be "that animal called man." It is not only in book 4 but in the text as a whole, and in the satirical persona of Gulliver in particular, that Swift succeeds in affecting the application he is after, as the reader identifies in the person of Gulliver both "mankind" and "me." This does not work because Gulliver is an everyman figure, or even a Crusoevian representative of man in general. He is, rather, a person that is at once and by turns every person (his shifts in book 2, from Crusoe to Friday to Poll, are one local example of this). As a result, Gulliver simultaneously and successively invites and repudiates identification in a characterological or substantive sense. Speaking from and as so many different and often contradictory positions, there is something in Gulliver for (and of) everyone. In part, this means that Gulliver is bound to say something with which one agrees, some sentiment or idea that one would acknowledge or own: that is me. It also means that in the next breath, Gulliver is bound to say something that produces the opposite reaction, jarring one's sense of identification into hostile refusal. This repudiation is all the more violent for the identification it overturns, for the suddenness with which acknowledgement turns to disavowal: that is not me.

Described in this way, the person of Gulliver might seem to produce the sort of reaction Swift seeks to avoid: the bandying of the satirical ball. But the identification with Gulliver is ultimately formal rather than characterological; it is an identity that I come to acknowledge because of Swift's constitution of the satirical first person, rather than the particular persons that Gulliver or I may be. Swift's satirical personae are notoriously difficult to distinguish from the authorial voice of Swift himself, as well as from the object of Swift's satirical scorn.[57] This is certainly true of Gulliver, a satirical persona named in the text only as "The Author," and who seems to be a central object of satire—though when and for what is something over which readers disagree. Collapsing both satirical positions (between author, persona, and object) and characterological distinctions (say, between Crusoe, Friday, and Poll), Swift gives the reader no settled place to stand, no safe position beyond the satire's reach.[58] Claude Rawson's formulation, from *Gulliver and the Gentle Reader*, is suggestive in this regard: "Swift's wider and more damaging comprehensiveness implicates both himself and his reader, and permits neither to stand outside; in this way, as well as through the tense intimacies of style, Swift's satire is so general that it becomes personal—and of the second and first, not only of the third, person."[59] On Swift's view, it may be possible to say, "I am not man." But it is not possible to say, "I am not Gulliver." For when one reads Gulliver's "I" and insists that that is not me, one enacts the same logic of exception that Gulliver himself embodies. By constructing his satire around the figure of the individual exception, Swift's satire ensures that there is no position that is not implicated in or as Gulliver's "I." Each of us is Gulliver in the most basic sense of sharing the same first-person form, a form of being that comes into view even or especially as it insists on its own exception from any sense of species.

To read oneself in Swift's satire, then—and Swift makes it impossible to read in any other way—is not to imagine a form of identity in which individual and class are "ultimately the same thing." The specifically human form of identity that emerges when one acknowledges Gulliver's "I" as one's own and so "read[s] in himself . . . Mankind" is not that of synecdoche or fable, the natural identity between individual and species enjoyed by Hobbes's bees and

Swift's Houyhnhnms. Indeed, the human form of identity that Hobbes and Swift elaborate is not something that is enjoyed at all. Swift may have rejected the political absolutism that made Hobbesian authorship seem a kind of trick—an experience of subjection, a feeling of being forced. But in the realm of letters, he is after something similar: a way of effecting "real Unitie" across the difference and discord that human individuation necessarily involves. For Swift, satire is a mechanism, like the Leviathan, that makes me read in myself my species, and so brings me into what Hobbes calls "agreement" with other men and with mankind. What it looks like to read in this way is for Swift, as for Hobbes, quite thin. Swift's word for this is "application," in the limited and formal sense of the instructions of "The Beasts' Confession": "Apply the Tale, and you shall find / How just it suits with human Kind" (73–74). In "The Beasts' Confession," once again, to "apply the tale" does not involve drawing a substantive moral lesson from a recounted narrative action (the sort of action that is wholly absent from the poem). So too, in *Gulliver's Travels*, to "leave the Judicious Reader to his own Remarks and Applications" (246) is not to leave the reader to his own "reading" in the sense of an interpretation of the narrative's moral lesson, definition of human being, or ideal form of society. Instead, to apply the tale is simply to read in the satirical mode that generates a species logic proper to human being because it follows the Hobbesian injunction to "read in himself . . . Mankind," and say what Gulliver will not: "I am man."

To the end, this is an injunction that Gulliver resists. Cast out of the world of fable, Gulliver nonetheless repudiates reading—along with the human and political forms of association it generates—and aspires instead to animal forms of being and relation, which Swift pictures as the simplicity of synecdoche, of essential species identity. This is one way to characterize Gulliver's mistaken sense of the kind of creature he is: he is a reader of fable who wants to be a figure within it. He thus concludes the *Travels* by turning away from reading and from human being, to talk to animals: "My Horses understand me tolerably well, I converse with them at least four Hours every Day" (244). The debate between hard and soft interpretations of the *Travels* often turns on this concluding scene of Gulliver back in England and talking to horses, disputing whether it is the object of Swift's sympathy or scorn. But it is not quite the end of the story: the *Travels* continues for one more chapter, in which, in the words of the chapter heading, *"the Author takes his leave of the Reader"* (245).[60] This final chapter presents an alternative ending to Gulliver's animal conversation: a turn to "the Reader," who is aligned in the *Travels* not with the oral Houyhnhnms nor with the mute Yahoos but with "the Women and the Vulgar," who esteem the "little old Treatise" Gulliver peruses in Brobdingnag, and who, in Laputa, defend representation against the projectors' "Scheme for abolishing all Words" (114, 157). Swift's move away from horses and toward the reader, away from animals and toward the women and the vulgar, is not simply a salutary or comforting alternative to Gulliver's delusion of animal conversation and identity. In their own way, Swift's readers are as terrible as the female Yahoo that confronts Gulliver with the biological fact of his animal Yahoo nature. Swift's readers, like Hobbes's, are also bearers of the species—in the sense not of a given natural identity but of naturalization, the becoming natural of representation that occurs, to recall Tuveson, when the reader brings the "satire on man . . . home to the individual in his inner being."[61] Gulliver might well choose the "great Amity" of horses over any such agreement with human beings (244). The same choice is not open to his reader. For this sort of interspecies amity, readers will have to wait for Sterne, who recasts Gulliver's animal conversation in a sentimental and quasi-georgic mode, and renders the first person as a vitalist rather than exclusively human form.

Chapter 4

The Animal

The Life Narrative as a Form of Life

Foucault memorably claimed that "life" did not exist until the end of the eighteenth century.[1] Before this time, he argued, there was no concept that united humans and cats and oysters and oak trees as one form of being, a form that called, in its distinctiveness, for its own form of knowledge. Foucault's characterization of the eighteenth-century emergence of "life" echoes, in a rather different key, a remark made by Francis Coventry, author of the popular and curiously pathbreaking *History of Pompey the Little; or, The Life and Adventures of a Lapdog* (1751). In the preface to his life narrative of a lapdog, Coventry identifies his era as "this *Life-writing Age.*"[2] By "life" Coventry means something different from Foucault: roughly, life in the sense of biography rather than biology. But in the eighteenth century, as Coventry's life narrative of a living animal suggests, these two kinds of "life" come together in curious ways.[3] The "life" was a prominent and protean genre throughout the century: from Boswell's *Life of Johnson* and Johnson's *Lives of the Poets* to the autobiographical lives of Cibber, Hume, or Gibbon; from the popular first-person "lives and adventures" of actual outlaw figures to Defoe's "allegorical-historical" versions of the same; from the exemplary novelistic lives of Richardson and Fielding to the lives of all sorts of creatures (coins, cats, lice, spinning tops) published largely in the wake of Coventry's canine life narrative. In this chapter, I consider how this proliferation of literary experiments with the form of the "life" might be related to emerging and uncertain ideas of "life" as a distinct form of being. To do this, I set one of the period's most well known lives, Laurence Sterne's *The Life and Opinions of Tristram Shandy*, alongside two of the era's most prominent philosophers:

Georges-Louis Leclerc, Comte de Buffon, the naturalist sometimes credited with revolutionizing eighteenth-century ideas of the living world, and John Locke, a figure to whom readers do not typically turn for a philosophy of life.[4] The first person is once again crucial. But it is no longer the exclusively human mode of individuation and speciation that it is for Swift and for Hobbes. Instead, the first person now appears as a form of life—a vitalist mode of agency and generality associated with the living animal.

The Life and Opinions of Tristram Shandy is conspicuously constructed around Tristram's twin lives: his third-person biological or animal life, which begins in the middle of volume 3 and threatens to end at the start of volume 7, and his first-person biographical *Life*, which is coextensive with the text as a whole. Critics have tended to consider these two lives as separate and antagonistic terms, and to set the novel on the side of the latter: for biographical writing and against biological life; for art and against nature; for the singular human imagination and against the specific and animal body.[5] Understood along such lines, *Tristram Shandy* is another novelization of Lockean philosophy—this time, of the distinction between the person (the unique first-person consciousness, life experienced from within) and the human (the generic animal body, life viewed from without) that Locke elaborates in the *Essay*'s chapter on identity. On this view, Sterne follows Locke in arguing for the priority of personal identity over the animal body and its associates: the family and the species, birth and death.

In many ways, this familiar Lockean reading makes sense.[6] From the moment that Walter declares that Tristram "should neither think nor act like any other man's child," the singularity of Tristram's biographical *Life* is its most frequently celebrated quality.[7] Tristram introduces his dedication by boasting "its singularity in the three great essentials of matter, form, and place"; he concludes his first volume by defying any reader to guess what follows: "I am of so nice and singular a humour, that if I thought you was able to form the least judgment or probable conjecture to yourself, of what was to come in the next page—I would tear it out of my book" (13, 63). When Tristram remarks that his life proceeds "364 times faster" than his *Life*, he declares this "an observation never applicable before to any one biographical writer since the creation of the world, but to myself" (228). Throughout his narrative, Tristram continues to call attention to the difference between his generic biological life and his singular biographical *Life*. Noting that it has taken nearly four volumes of his *Life* (and one year of his life) to write his "first day's life," Tristram declares: "I shall never overtake myself" (228). He continues, "was it not that my OPINIONS will be the death of me, I perceive I shall lead a fine life of it out of this self-same life of mine; or, in other words, shall lead a couple of fine lives together" (228). In such moments, Tristram does invoke a roughly Lockean schema of separate and separable lives. And yet Tristram also frustrates readers' efforts to separate his different lives, or even to distinguish which is which. He positions his author's preface in the middle of volume 3, for example, announcing the start of his biographical *Life* at the moment when his biological life begins. Reveling in his play on different senses of "life," Tristram does little to clarify the significance of these senses, or the nature of the relation between them.

The argument of this chapter is that *Tristram Shandy* does not recapitulate a familiar Lockean picture of life split in two, a picture that has become commonplace in critical accounts of the novel. Instead, Sterne unites first-person biographical *Life* and generic biological life as one form of "self-same life." Like Swift, then, Sterne is interested in the right relation between the individual and the species, and he too takes the first person to be essential to this relation. But unlike Swift, Sterne identifies first personhood as a properly animal rather than human form of being and relation. In doing so, he draws on an alternative (and tentative) tendency in Locke's thought, which identifies personhood with rather than against animality (as in Swift, Hobbes, and much of Locke himself). This is a tendency that appears most pointedly, and most puzzlingly, in Locke's strikingly Shandean story of the conversible parrot.

In the context of *Robinson Crusoe*, I emphasized that Locke uses the story of the parrot to advance his argument that the person and the human are distinct sorts of identity: a rational and conversible parrot is not human, for all that it might be a person. In the context of *Tristram Shandy*, the parrot is a paradigmatic Lockean person less because it is not a human being, than because it is a living animal—which means, here, both a first-person form of being and relation, and an effect of representation. The details of the story, and of Locke's discussion, are relevant to this point. Locke begins by asserting an essential accord between human beings about what counts as human, remarking that both Prince Maurice (a Dutch colonial administrator who had met the parrot) and William Temple (an English diplomat who had met Prince Maurice) believed that the parrot spoke rather than simply parroted, and that, nevertheless, "both of them call this Talker a *Parrot*" (334). With this claim, Locke glosses over key details of the original tale from Temple's *Memoirs*, which he nevertheless quotes in full:

"I had a mind to know from *Prince Maurice*'s own Mouth, the account of a common, but much credited Story, that I had heard so often from many others, of an old *Parrot* he had in *Brasil*, during his Government there, that spoke, and asked, and answered common Questions like a reasonable Creature. . . . He told me short and coldly, that he had heard of such an old *Parrot* when he came to *Brasil*, and though he believed nothing of it, and 'twas a good way off, yet he had so much Curiosity as to send for it, that 'twas a very great and a very old one; and when it came first into the Room where the Prince was, with a great many *Dutch-men* about him, it said presently, *What a company of white Men are here?* They asked it what he thought that Man was, pointing at the Prince? It answered, *Some General or other*; when they brought it close to him, he asked it, *D'ou venes vous?* It answered, *De Marinnan*, The Prince, *A qui estes vous?* The Parrot, *A un Portugais.* Prince, *Que fais tu la?* Parrot, *Je gard les poulles.* The Prince laughed and said, *Vous gardez les poulles?* The Parrot answered, *Ouy, moy et je scay bien faire*; and made the Chuck four or five times that People use to make to Chickens when they call them." (333–34)

On Temple's account, there is no agreement between human beings about the boundaries of their kind. Instead, Temple sets out to mock Prince Maurice by making him speak a fantastic tale from his "own Mouth," distinguishing himself as a properly modern Englishman by identifying the Dutch prince with the primitive Brazilians who tell (and believe) stories about talking animals. For his part, Prince Maurice resists this identification, assuring Temple "short and coldly" that "he had heard of such an old *Parrot*" but "he believed nothing of it." In the wider context of Temple's story, the parrot serves to upset both men's efforts to elevate themselves over others—parodically recasting human distinctions of nation and rank as the dominion of parrot over chicken, and asserting the formal equality of the first person over any such form of distinction.

Taken seriously, this scene might be understood as a parable about the priority of individual identity, which privileges the formally identical first person over any sort of species distinction (English or Dutch, colonizer or colonized, human or parrot). At the same time, the parrot's leveling first-person speech is a patently mediated, even fabricated, effect of representation and rhetorical figuration—"a common, but much credited Story" associated equally with a primitive and personifying imagination and the artifice of colonial and courtly culture. Locke does not comment on most of the details of this perplexing scene, but he does "tak[e] care that the Reader should have the Story at large in the Authors own Words" (334). In taking such care, Locke signals something important about the form of identity manifest, most plainly, when one says "I": persons may not be human, but they do need other people to come into being. For all its putative independence, the Lockean person emerges here in conversation with others: as both a first-person speaker and a figure of speech, a generic figure that "speaks, as it were, by the Mouths of others."[8] This is true of Prince Maurice and Temple no less than the parrot. It is certainly true of Tristram Shandy and of the many people who make up his *Life*.

In *Tristram Shandy*, Sterne picks up on the strain of Locke's thought that brings together the (first) person and the animal, living bodies and rhetorical figures—a strain that is most visible in the figure of the talking parrot, but which runs throughout Locke's discussion of personal identity. Sterne develops this strain of Lockean thought, I argue, both within and alongside new mid-century notions of life, species, and representation, best described as Buffonian and vitalist notions. Reading Sterne, Locke, and Buffon together in this way results in a different picture than the one made familiar by Foucault, in which a new order of things emerges toward the close of the eighteenth century. On Foucault's account, this is an order centered on the enigma of life and the hidden "form of animality"; its emergence is evidenced by the rise of the life sciences and the consolidation of literature as a separate domain—the refuge, as Foucault puts it, of the life or "raw being" of language.[9] In the writings on which I focus in this chapter, both life and literature take the different and distinctly eighteenth-century form embodied by Locke's parrot—a first-person life manifest in speech that is patently, if perhaps only partly, an effect of representation, a common story and a rhetorical figure. In these writings, life is thus characterized not by rawness but by composition, interrelation, and mediation. And the role of literature is not to shelter the raw being of language, but to make visible the irreducibly rhetorical aspect of both persons and animals—the role of representation in composing all the lives that make up this living world.

The Picker-Up Model of Personhood
and the First-Person Form of Life

Before Temple's conversible and confounding parrot comes on the scene, Locke begins his chapter "Of Identity and Diversity" by drawing distinctions. He starts by differentiating the identity of living creatures from that of matter, locating the former in the continuity not of material particles but of "life": "such an Organization of Parts in one coherent Body, partaking of one Common Life." This "animal Identity," he explains, continues "as long as it partakes of the same Life, though that Life be communicated to new Particles of Matter vitally united to [it]" (331). From here, Locke outlines a third type of identity, which becomes the chapter's primary focus and its major philosophical innovation: "that conscious thinking thing" that Locke calls the person or self (341). "*Person*," Locke writes, is that which "can consider itself as it self, the same thinking thing in different times and places; which it does only by that consciousness, which is inseparable from thinking, and as it seems to me essential to it: It being impossible for any one to perceive, without perceiving, that he does perceive. . . . And by this every one is to himself, that which he calls self" (335). Locke aims here at precision. But as he proliferates terms that he appears to use as synonyms (consciousness, thinking, perceiving), or simply repeats the same words (perceive, perceiving, perceive), Locke's efforts to define the "person" can seem to move in circles. Since its publication, readers of Locke's *Essay* have puzzled over exactly what this "person" is.

As I have suggested, Locke is clearer about what this "person" is not. He asserts first, that "person" is not "man," which is nothing else but "an Animal of such a certain form," and second, that person is not substance, neither matter nor spirit (333). Both of these points are crucial to one of the fundamental aims of Locke's chapter: to establish a form of identity free from all possibility for doubt or error, to liberate the person from anything of "which it cannot be sure" (345). For Locke, this includes both substance (a metaphysical idea that we can never empirically know) and species (a general idea that we can never know for sure). Yet Locke's insistence that "person" can be identified neither with a distinct substance nor with human being leads him into strange territory. Along with the much credited and at least semiplausible story of a reasonable and voluble parrot, Locke presents a number of patently incredible scenarios. In these, he moves personhood or consciousness between bodies and historical epochs, imagining that different men (Socrates and the "present Mayor of *Quinborough*") might be same person, that the same man (Socrates waking and sleeping) might be different persons, that the person of a prince might transmigrate into (the man of) a cobbler, that personhood or consciousness might go off with a severed finger (342). Dizzying as they can be, Locke's thought experiments all aim to make the same basic point: once again, the person is not human (an animal of such a certain form); the person is nothing other than consciousness.

This has become a routine point in readings of Locke, and it is one that I emphasize in my second chapter, on Defoe. But I think it is worth pausing over. For exactly what it means for Locke to equate personhood and consciousness is not immediately clear. To begin with, Locke works hard in this section to redefine familiar terms—in some cases, by inventing new ones. The most famous of Locke's linguistic innovations is "self-consciousness," a term that he uses interchangeably with both person and consciousness in his effort to explain the new form of identity that he seeks to articulate. A central task of this chapter is to argue that Sterne is onto something crucial about the form that "self-consciousness"—and so, personhood—takes for Locke: that the person is a fundamentally first-person form, which means in turn a living and vital form.[10]

Before going into detail about what it means for the person to be a first-person and so living form, it is worth noting that most readers understand the Lockean person differently: as a hybrid of the first and the third person, of consciousness and its objects. On Charles Taylor's account of Locke's "punctual self," for example, Locke follows Descartes in making the modern self a cross between two essentially distinct and separate orders: "radical subjectivity" and "radical objectivity," a "first person stance" and "a picture of the human being from a completely third person perspective."[11] On this picture, "I" (the person or consciousness) am essentially separate from "me" (the man or living—thinking, acting, embodied—being), and "I" relate to my "properties"—my thoughts, my actions, and my body—as a proprietor to his possessions, as separate or separable things. Taylor thus depicts Locke's notion of personal identity as a formulation that merges the *Essay Concerning Human Understanding* with the *Second Treatise of Government* to articulate one unified property model of personhood—what C. B. Macpherson calls "possessive individualism."[12] Such a reading does find a good deal of support in the *Essay*, where Locke frequently uses the language of ownership to explain his concept of "person": "That with which the *consciousness* of this present thinking thing can join it self, makes the same *Person*, and is one *self* with it, and with nothing else; and so attributes to it *self*, and owns all the Actions of that thing, as its own, as far as that consciousness reaches, and no farther" (341).[13] At times, moreover, this property logic is elaborated in strange ways, as when Locke depicts the person undergoing something like subtraction: "Thus any part of our Bodies vitally united to that, which is conscious in us, makes a part of our *selves*: But upon separation from the vital union, by which that consciousness is communicated, that, which a moment since was part of our *selves*, is no more so, than a part of another Man's *self* is a part of me; and 'tis not impossible, but in a little time may become a real part of another Person" (346). It is not entirely clear what process Locke pictures in this passage, as he imagines a part to separate from oneself and become part of another person. He might describe reproduction, excretion, even amputation—in this moment at least, it seems that these are distinctions without a difference. Even without reading the *Essay* through the *Second Treatise*, the person that emerges in such moments often does look much like Taylor's punctual self or Macpherson's possessive individual—what Locke elsewhere calls the "Inhabitant within."

This familiar version of Lockean personhood certainly appears throughout *Tristram Shandy*, most conspicuously and most often in the person of Walter Shandy. "An excellent natural philosopher" who was "originally a *Turky* merchant," Walter is the novel's principal mouthpiece for a property model of personal identity made up of opinions that, as Walter often boasts, belong to him alone (7). Tristram describes the process by which Walter acquires these opinions and so composes his unique person: "He pick'd up an opinion, Sir, as a man in a state of nature picks up an apple.—It becomes his own—and if he is a man of spirit, he would lose his life rather than give it up.—" (176). Tristram imagines that readers might wonder about a property or "picking-up" model of personhood that establishes property equally in opinions and in apples. To begin with, they might wonder just how "a man in a state of nature picks up an apple" and so makes it his own: "how did it begin to be his? was it, when he set his heart upon it? or when he gather'd it? or when he chew'd it? or when he roasted it? or when he peel'd? or when he brought it home? or when he digested?—or when he—?" (176). And Tristram—channeling Walter, channeling Locke—explains:

> the sweat of a man's brows, and the exsudations of a man's brains, are as much a man's own property, as the breeches upon his backside;—which said exsudations, &c. being dropp'd upon the said apple by the labour of finding it, and picking it up; and being moreover indissolubly wasted, and as indissolubly annex'd by the picker up, to the thing pick'd up, carried home, roasted, peel'd, eaten, digested, and so on;—'tis evident that the gatherer of the apple, in so doing, has mixed up something which was his own, with the apple which was not his own, by which means he has acquired a property;—or, in other words, the apple is *John's* apple. (177)

Like so much of Sterne's humor, this passage seems to ridicule the "learned chain of reasoning" that would prove a self-evident point: the apple is John's apple. But the self-evidence of this point becomes less certain as Tristram insists on the analogy between John and his apple and Walter and his opinions, which become "his" in exactly the same way: "he had spared no pains in picking them up, and . . . they had cost him moreover as much labour in cooking and digesting as in the case above, so that they might well and truly be said to be his own goods and chattels" (177). Sterne takes aim, here, at Walter's Lockean notion that an opinion can be "his" in the same way as an apple, that consciousness—and so persons—are composed of simple ideas that are picked up and put together like bits of matter. But Sterne does something more. He suggests that this "picking-up" model of property is as inadequate for apples as it is for ideas—for the component parts of living bodies as it is for the parts of minds. Apples are not simply "pick'd up," Sterne reminds us. They are also eaten.

In his *Second Treatise*, Locke works hard to render this a distinction without a difference. This is Locke, in the passage that supplies Tristram the source of his parody: "He that is nourished by the Acorns he pickt up under an Oak, or the Apples he gathered from the Trees in the Wood, has certainly appropriated them to himself. No Body can deny but the nourishment is his. I ask then, When did they begin to be his? When he digested? Or when he eat? Or when he boiled? Or when he brought them home? Or when he pickt them up? And 'tis plain, if the first gathering made them not his, nothing else could" (288). It is this account of labor—which identifies all kinds of activities as forms of picking something up—that grounds what is often thought of as Locke's property model of personhood. Locke explains: "The Fruit, or Venison, which nourishes the wild *Indian*, who knows no Inclosure, and is still a Tenant in common, must be his, and so his, *i.e.* a part of him, that another can no longer have any right to it, before it can do him any good for the support of his Life" (287). Many commentators have noted that Locke works to identify appropriation with eating in order to make unlimited private property as natural—and as proper—as nourishment.[14] Sterne points out that Locke does this by first identifying eating with appropriation: a move that effectively transforms the person from a living creature into a collection of goods, a mechanical assortment of the things he picks up. By equating the act of gathering by which "the wild *Indian*" makes fruit "his" with the act of eating by which he makes fruit "a part of him," that is, Locke elides the distinction between "his" and "him," possession and person.[15] Or, he refashions aspects of persons *as* possessions: thoughts and actions can be one's property in the same way as an apple in a basket, or in one's belly.

With Walter, Sterne isolates and critiques Locke's tendency to mark no fundamental difference between thinking, eating, and stocking one's pantry— to conceive of all forms of being and action as variations on the relation between "the picker up," "the thing pick'd up," and the act of "picking them up." This tendency can be seen clearly in Locke's sequence from the *Second Treatise*, which begins with digestion and ends with picking up, implying the logical reduction of various activities to this last form of labor, of "picking up": "When he digested? Or when he eat? Or when he boiled? Or when he brought them home? Or when he pickt them up?" In his send up of this passage, Tristram undoes Locke's logic by adding extra terms to his sequence and, crucially, by reversing its order. Beginning with picking up and proceeding through actions like carrying home, chewing, roasting, peeling, eating, and digesting, Tristram calls attention to the material specificity of each type of activity, and so emphasizes the differences between them. Finally, Tristram extends Locke's list, moving past digestion to suggest what comes next: "when he brought it home? Or when he digested?—or when he—?" With his concluding dash, Tristram indulges in a characteristic moment of deflationary and excremental humor. He also makes a serious point: that eating implies not only a putting together of the person, but also a coming apart.[16] Eating is unlike "picking up," that is, because not everything that one eats becomes either "his" or "him"; digestion is always accompanied by excretion, incorporation by loss. Tristram reminds us that in a manner wholly unlike property or things, persons are perishable.

With this reminder, Sterne counters Locke's more conspicuous property model of personhood with an alternative that he also gets from Locke: a first-person form of "vital union" that incorporates actions and ideas—and apples—in a wholly different manner than one picks something up. This countermodel can be seen most clearly in passages where Locke shifts away from terms like "consciousness," "person," or "self" altogether, moving from nouns to a repetition of the first-person pronoun. For example: "whatever has the consciousness of present and past Actions, is the same Person to whom they both belong. Had I the same consciousness, that I saw the Ark and *Noah*'s Flood, as that I saw an overflowing of the *Thames* last Winter, or as that I write now, I could no more doubt that I, that write this now, that saw the *Thames* overflow'd last Winter, and that view'd the Flood at the general Deluge, was the same *self*" (340–41). Between "the consciousness" and the "Person" with which this passage begins, and the "*self*" with which it ends, Locke resorts to a repeated use of the first person to explain what it means to be "the same Person" or "the same *self.*" This move adds little in the way of content to these terms, and it produces some of the *Essay's* more difficult, knotty prose. But Locke's repetition of the first person shifts here from the stylistic register of the philosophical treatise into that of a germinal life narrative: "I saw . . . I saw . . . I write; I, that write . . . that saw . . . that viewed." And this generic shift signals that Locke's person does not easily or entirely fit into the kinds of doubled forms with which we are familiar: subject and object, proprietor and possessions, the picker-up and the things picked up. Rather than a possessive subject constituted by the actions, ideas, or objects that it owns, the Lockean "I" appears here as a term that expresses a particular mode of acting and perceiving, and generates a particular form of life.

In order to elaborate this point, I want to turn for a moment to consider Locke's person by way of Elizabeth Anscombe's essay "The First Person." Anscombe might seem an unlikely lens for Locke, but there are good reasons to bring them together: Anscombe and Locke both write against Descartes, and Anscombe focuses her account on the idea of "self-consciousness," the term that Locke first coined. Anscombe begins by calling attention to "the first-person character of Descartes' argument": specifically, to his claim that "I could suppose I had no body . . . but not that I was not," and his subsequent inference that "'this I' is not a body."[17] Anscombe thinks that Descartes is onto something about the peculiarity of the first-person form, but that he goes wrong when he considers the first person in terms of the question, "what does 'I' stand for?" (50). On Anscombe's view, this question leads Descartes to suppose the existence of the cogito, a thing or substance that thinks. Against Descartes, Anscombe argues that "I" does not "stand for" anything; it is not the name for a human being apprehended from a particular point of view. For Anscombe, "I" is not a subject at all, but a word used to express "'unmediated agent-or-patient conceptions of actions, happenings, and states.'" Anscombe calls this type of use the "expression of self-consciousness," and she associates it with the living body (64). To illustrate the use of "I" she is after, Anscombe cites the example of a man who has lost his memory and no longer knows that he is "Smith, a man of such-and-such a background" (59). Anscombe points out that he may not know that he is such-and-such a man, but "he has neither lost the use of 'I,' nor is he usually at a loss what to point to as his body, or as the person he is" (59). Aligning "his body" with "the person he is," Anscombe notes that "person" does not mean simply "body" in the sense of a corpse;

it means "a living human body" (60). For Anscombe, "I" does not refer to "Smith" (or to "Descartes") from another point of view. Instead, it is a wholly different use of language: one that composes a "life" in the sense of a living body and its unmediated conceptions of actions, happenings, and states, all the events of which one might say, "I saw, . . . I saw, . . . I write." One might lose the facts of one's life, but not its form: the first-person form of (at once, and roughly) biographical and biological life.

Locke explicitly poses the question about reference that Anscombe rejects: in his words, "what *Person* stands for" (335). But it is not clear that Locke's sense of "self-consciousness" always takes the conventional subject-object form that Anscombe would overturn. For one thing, in Locke's moment, no conventional sense of "self-consciousness" exists. Locke invents the term in an effort to articulate a notion of personhood that is neither some "man," like Descartes or Smith, nor some "thing," like the substantial soul.[18] Here is the passage in which, according to the *OED*, Locke coins the term: "it matters not whether this present *self* be made up of the same or other Substances, I being as much concern'd, and as justly accountable for any Action that was done a thousand Years since, appropriated to me now by this self-consciousness, as I am, for what I did the last moment" (341). Following Anscombe, one might read Locke's coinage in two different ways. The hyphen might serve to split "self" and "consciousness" as object and subject, as it is most often taken to do. But it also might indicate that Locke is working to express something outside of the usual logic of language.[19] I have cited examples of this kind of linguistic strain: moments when Locke repeats the same word ("It being impossible for any one to perceive, without perceiving, that he does perceive"), or repeatedly uses the first person ("I saw, . . . I saw, . . . I write"). The "thing" in Locke's frequent phrase, "that thinking thing," works similarly, as a syntactical placeholder that calls attention to its own lack of referent. These different types of repetition suggest that we might pause before resolving Lockean self-consciousness into familiar or stable forms of thought. Certainly, Locke's sense of self-consciousness frequently seems to work as Anscombe says it does—to mean "consciousness of a self. A self will be something that some things either have or are. . . . [The self] is what he calls 'I'" (49). But at times, Locke hints at a different logic: a logic in which self-consciousness, the form of the (first) person, is modeled not on the opposition between subject and object but rather, as in Anscombe, on the form of the living body.

The suggestion that Locke at least sometimes models the person on the living body might well strike readers of the *Essay* as strange, as Locke opens his discussion of identity and diversity by explicitly distinguishing personal from such bodily identity (animal or human). At different points in the discussion, however, he brings these different sorts of identity back together. He does first by means of analogy: "Different Substances, by the same consciousness (where they do partake in it) being united into one Person; as well as different Bodies, by the same Life are united into one Animal, whose *Identity* is preserved, in that change of Substances, by the unity of one continued Life" (336). At other moments Locke goes further still, depicting "consciousness" and "life" less as two separate and analogous terms than as one form of what he calls "vital union." He writes: "our very Bodies, all whose Particles, whilst vitally united to this same thinking conscious self, so that we feel when they are touch'd, and are affected by, and conscious of good or harm that happens to them, are a part of our *selves: i.e.* of our thinking conscious *self*" (336).[20] Despite his own spatial metaphors, then, Locke often insists that consciousness is not lodged inside the body like an inhabitant within. It is spread through every particle of our "very Bodies," throughout every part of the vital union that is "this same thinking conscious self." It is not altogether clear how far Locke takes the analogy or identity between consciousness and the living, vitally united body, but the connection he draws between these terms is suggestive. If consciousness is (like) life, then the Lockean first person is not the form of radical subjectivity that Taylor terms "Locke's punctual self," an agent that stands apart from the various objects and properties that it calls its own. The Lockean person is neither subject nor object, but a different sort of being and acting altogether: the first-person form of "vitally uniting" that composes actions, thoughts, and matter into "one continued Life."[21]

To talk about the first person in this way is to say very little about the actual form this life takes: the notion of "one continued Life" does not imply narrative in the sense of a coherent or shapely plot. To characterize the first person as a form of life is simply to identify the first person with the potential for form that emerges from all the actions, happenings, and states of which one might say "I saw, . . . I saw, . . . I write." It is this potential that so often makes Tristram's narrative sound like the jumbled form generated by Locke's "I"—the I that "write this now, that saw the *Thames* overflow'd last Winter, and that view'd the Flood at the general Deluge" (341)—as in this oft-quoted passage from the end of volume 7: "I am at this moment walking across the market-place of Auxerre . . . I am this moment also entering Lyons . . . and I am moreover this moment in a handsome pavilion built by Pringello. . . . Let me collect myself, and pursue my journey" (414). In such moments, Sterne both undercuts and follows Locke in making a mockery of this notion of "collecting" oneself despite dispersal across different places, times, species, and men. He also follows Locke in his assurance that however many times, places, or men I may be, I can never be elsewhere. Thus when Tristram announces that he will take leave of all the characters of his story in order to "enter upon a new scene of events," he finds that there is one departure that he cannot make: "Let us leave, if possible, *myself:*—But 'tis impossible,—I must go along with you to the end of the work" (355). To say this is to return to the question of Tristram's separate or separable lives, and to his riddled formulation: "I perceive I shall lead a fine life of it out of this self-same life of mine; or, in other words, shall lead a couple of fine lives together" (228). Locke and Anscombe help us to read these lines so that their stress falls not on "a couple of fine lives" but on the concluding "together." Viewed in this way, Tristram's narrative does not seek to replace life with *Life*, or to affirm the latter at the expense of the former. Instead, it demonstrates that the two are fundamentally one vitally united form, the union that Tristram refers to as "this self-same life of mine." This self-same life is not "mine" as Walter wants his opinions to be "his," or "him." It is mine in the sense of the immediacy of first-person consciousness that both Locke and Anscombe articulate, one tied to the capacity of the living body to generate the happenings of which one says, "I saw, . . . I saw, . . . I write."

Throughout *Tristram Shandy*, Sterne sets the vital and generative form of Tristram's "I" against Walter's mechanical process of picking things up, a mode of "collecting myself" that elides distinctions between persons and things, the living and the nonliving. Just as Walter does not recognize any important difference between eating, thinking, and picking up, he sees no significant distinction between ratiocination and reproduction, a hypothesis and a human being. "Engendered in the womb of speculation," Walter's hypotheses are like offspring of which he must be "safely deliver'd"; Bobby and Tristram are, in turn, the products of Walter's mind (83). And just as he identifies delivering an opinion and delivering a child, Walter equates cultivating persons with cultivating land. When he inherits a legacy of a thousand pounds, Walter debates whether he should enclose the "undrained, unimproved common" or educate Bobby by sending him to Europe—alternatives rendered commensurate by the comparison. When Bobby dies (and so ends Walter's debate between "the two old projects, the OX-MOOR and my BROTHER" [266]), Walter turns his attention to the cultivation of Tristram, composing the *Tristrapaedia* as a means for stocking his son's person with his

own, proper opinions. Convinced that the auxiliary verb is a "great engine
. . . [by which] every idea engender[s] millions," "how barren soever" a child's
brain might be, Walter vows that Tristram "shall be made to conjugate every
word in the dictionary" until he has "increase[d] his knowledge to such a
prodigious stock" (323–24, 329–30). In all these moments, Walter gives voice
to the mechanical, associationist logic that underwrites a putatively Lockean
property model of personhood, a logic that understands minds and bodies
to be composed like matter, of simple entities—ideas or apples—that can be
put together or taken apart. Without any sense of the specificity of the living
creature, Walter's picker-up model of personhood construes all relations as
the effects of association or its dissolution, of the addition or subtraction of
separate or separable parts.

There is nothing surprising about the claim that *Tristram Shandy* is
opposed to mechanism; Tristram himself asserts as much: "Now, of all things
in the world, I understand the least of mechanism" (416). Most often, however, Tristram is understood to oppose mechanism with "life" in the form of
an individual human consciousness or singular imagination. But in *Tristram
Shandy*, Walter is a figure for both mechanism and individualism, both impotence and the unique imagination. In part, the problem with Walter's proposal
to educate his son by way of auxiliary verbs is that it pictures the mind as
an engine and a product of manufacture, and ideas as furnishings or stock.
Another problem with Walter's proposal is that this mechanism for making
ideas is an engine of self-generation, "the soul a going by herself upon the
materials as they are brought her" (322). Throughout *Tristram Shandy*, Walter
champions a form of property personhood in which one's individual biographical life is cut off from specific or animal life, and composed like a collection of
goods. And repeatedly, Walter's ideas about persons are linked to bodily harm,
to instances of impotence and injury. Walter insists on childbirth by forceps
for the sake of Tristram's soul; Tristram ends up losing his nose. Walter writes
an educational manual to stock his son's mind with ideas; Tristram is circum-
cised by a falling window. Walter wonders whether to cultivate his son Bobby
or his land; Bobby dies before he can decide. In all these moments, Sterne
insists that there is something wrong with a form of generation modeled on
the mechanics of grammar, and with a form of unique or proper personhood
constituted by picking things up. He insists, that is, that Walter's mechanical
and individualist form of *Life* is a threat to life itself. This is why Tristram looks
to perpetuate his first-person *Life* elsewhere: in the reproductive and species
world of Buffon's animated nature.

Buffon, Species, and the Reproduction of Life

I have been arguing that Locke's discussion of personal identity at times moves toward a vital (because first-personal) logic, and that Sterne sets this aspect of Locke's thought against the more familiar possessive and mechanical model of the Lockean person, embodied in *Tristram Shandy* by Walter. In this section, I elaborate Sterne's sense of personhood as a vital and first-personal form—the form of Tristram's *Life and Opinions*—by turning to the natural-historical writings of Buffon. Sterne may have known Buffon, as they traveled in similar circles in Paris (both were friends of Diderot, and frequent visitors at d'Holbach's salon). He would surely have known of him, as Buffon enjoyed the same overnight fame with the first volumes of the *Natural History* as Sterne did a decade later, with *Tristram Shandy*.[22] Intellectually, the two writers share a good deal: a significant if uncertain debt to Locke; a preoccupation with reproduction, sterility, and hybridity; hostility toward mechanism and mathesis; and an explicit interest in the intersection of writing and life. What's more, Buffon develops many of the significant aspects of his vitalist vision in his natural-historical descriptions of characteristically Shandean animals: the horse, the ox, the goat, the mule, and the ass, as well as the human being. Buffon is the "iconic figure" of Peter Hans Reill's account of a specifically eighteenth-century or Enlightenment tradition of vitalism; on many accounts, his thirty-six-volume *Natural History, General and Particular* marked "the turning point" in eighteenth-century notions of life.[23]

Historian of science Philip Sloan argues that Buffon's enduring significance lies with what he calls "Buffon's fundamental question," which is a question that Sloan argues first emerges in the eighteenth century: "what *is* a species, and more specifically, what is a *biological* species?"[24] Buffon answers this question most famously and most extensively in his 1753 entry on the ass, first published in the third volume of his *Natural History*. Put simply, his answer is reproduction: "All the similar individuals which exist on the surface of the earth, are regarded as composing the species of these individuals. It is neither, however, the number, nor the collection, of similar individuals, but the constant succession and renovation of these individuals, which constitutes the species. . . . The ass resembles the horse more than the spaniel does the grayhound; and yet the latter are of the same species, because they produce fertile individuals; but, as the horse and ass produce only unfertile and vitiated individuals, they are evidently of different species" (3.405–6). In itself, the reproductive criterion is not new: it is there in the seventeenth-century English naturalist John Ray, as it is in Gulliver's encounter with the female Yahoo. What is novel in Buffon is that a previously epistemological test becomes an ontological fact. For Buffon, reproduction is not only a means of determining who or what belongs to which species; it is what species *are*. As Buffon puts it in his entry on the goat: "[to] produce fertile individuals: This is the only character which constitutes the reality of what is called *species* both in the animal and vegetable kingdoms" (3.491). Buffon is clear about the consequence of this claim: "Species being thus confined to a constant succession of individuals endowed with the power of reproduction, it is obvious that this term ought never to be extended beyond animals and vegetables, and that those nomenclators who have employed it to distinguish the different kinds of minerals have abused terms and confounded ideas" (3.407). In the *Essay*, Locke uses "species" and "general ideas" as two ways of saying the same thing, and cites "man" and "gold" as his two main and interchangeable examples. In the *Natural History*, Buffon throws out this longstanding usage, arguing that living creatures are not collected together in the manner of things (as a class or collection of similar individuals), and that "species" are always and only biological species. For Buffon, reproduction gives the living world its own unique form of relation, its own peculiar logic of generality. [25]

Sterne announces his interest in the reproduction of life on the first page of *Tristram Shandy*, with a scene of a father, a mother, and a clock. In one of the few readings of *Tristram Shandy* to think in some detail about Sterne's engagement with the eighteenth-century life sciences, Louis Landa argues that this opening scene launches Sterne into contemporary debates about animal generation.[26] As Landa pictures it, this debate pitted ovists (those who located the germ of life in the egg) against animalculists (those who locate it in the sperm); its stakes concerned the reproductive roles of men and women, as well as their social, economic, and legal consequences. This is a useful frame for the question that so interests Walter, and that "the best lawyers and civilians in this land" answer in the negative: "*Whether the mother be of kin to her child*" (262). At the same time, Landa's account of the animalculist/ovist debate overshadows all that these positions share. Both are preformationist theories that aim to square the fact of animal generation with theological and natural-philosophical orthodoxy about the original act of creation and the clockwork universe that it brought into being. Animal generation was a source of some perplexity for this orthodox view, as the analogy of the clock does little to explain how new animals come into being. Preformation solves this difficulty by insisting that they do not: everything and everyone is there from the beginning. The first seed, as Buffon glosses this preformationist point, contains "all the individuals which would successively arise, till the final destruction of the species" (2.24). As Buffon and others remark, this means that there is no such thing as reproduction or generation but only the unfolding of what is always already there, every individual germ a man in miniature simply waiting to make his way in the world.

Landa is certainly right that in the later seventeenth and early eighteenth centuries, the main debate in embryology turned on the question of whether these tiny preformed germs were contained in the female (the ovists) or the male (the animalculists). But this debate was already dated by the time that Sterne pictured an act of generation both prompted and interrupted by the winding of a clock, as well as a homunculus complete with "skin, hair, fat, flesh, veins, arteries, ligaments, nerves, cartileges, bones, marrow, brains, glands, genitals, humours, and articulations . . . a Being of as much activity,—and, in all senses of the word, as much and as truly our fellow-creature as my Lord Chancellor of England" (6). The belatedness of *Tristram Shandy* to the preformationist debate suggests that its commitments rest elsewhere altogether: on the side of an emerging vitalist position, of which Buffon was not the first but was one of the most prominent voices. Indeed, *Tristram Shandy* invokes many of the central points of this midcentury critique of mechanism: preformation's difficulty in explaining hybrids or mules (crosses between distinct species, which bear resemblance to both), or the fact that *every* individual is a hybrid, bearing features of both father and mother; its difficulty accounting for deformation, accidents, variation, and novelty. But for Buffon and I think also for Sterne, there is a more elemental dispute with the fundamental premises of preformation: the idea that the individual is primary and simple and that species are collections of these separate and separable simple entities, as well as with the mechanical worldview within which such ideas make sense.[27] Both seek to overturn this mechanical worldview with a vitalism centered on reproduction, which is to say on specifically living modes of being and relation.

Sterne does this most strikingly at the start of the *Tristrapaedia*, the educational treatise Walter writes for Tristram alone, which presents and in many ways instantiates his singular—and both relentlessly mechanist and excessively individualist—opinions about the reproduction of persons and the cultivation of their minds. The *Tristrapaedia* opens with an introductory preface "upon political or civil government; the foundation of which being laid in the first conjunction betwixt male and female, for procreation of the species" (312).

There, Sterne pictures the contours and consequences of Walter's mechanist worldview in especially acute and Buffonian terms. Walter begins, here, by echoing a commonplace of political philosophers from Puffendorf and Grotius to Filmer and Locke, who all locate the origin of civil society in the domestic sphere. But Walter does not continue as eighteenth-century ears might expect, with a declaration like Locke's, "The *first Society* was between Man and Wife, which gave beginning to that between Parents and Children" (319). Instead, Walter asserts, "the original of society [is] . . . nothing more than the getting together of . . . a man,—a woman—and a bull" (312). Strange as it may sound, Walter does not invent this formulation: as he tells Yorick and Toby, it comes from Hesiod's georgic *Works and Days*, by way of the Florentine humanist Poliziano. As Yorick points out, however, Walter gets Hesiod wrong: "I believe 'tis an ox, quoth *Yorick*, quoting the passage—A bull must have given more trouble than his head was worth" (312). Walter agrees, proffering yet "a better reason still": "the ox being the most patient of animals, and the most useful withal in tilling the ground for their nourishment,—was the properest instrument, and emblem too, for the joined couple, that the creation could have associated with them" (312). Toby adds his assent, and Walter "strik[es] out the bull, and put[s] the ox in his place" (312).

Like the trio of man, woman, and bull/ox, the pairing of Hesiod and Poliziano is not Walter's invention. They are linked by way of Aristotle, who uses the same line from Hesiod in the first book of the *Politics*: "Out of these two relationships between man and woman, master and slave, the first thing to arise is the family, and Hesiod is right when he says—'First house and wife and an ox for the plough,' for the ox is the poor man's slave."[28] Poliziano enters the picture with a commentary on this passage, which, as historian Peter Godman tells it, begins with a correction of Aristotle that sounds much like Yorick's correction of Walter.[29] For Hesiod's full line reads somewhat differently: "First of all, get a house, and a woman and an ox for the plough—*a slave woman and not a wife*, to follow the oxen as well."[30] Poliziano contends that Aristotle would not have made such an error of sense, simply missing the distinction Hesiod makes between slave woman and wife. Poliziano thus concludes—with "mock solemnity," on Godman's view—that Hesiod's text must be corrupted, speculating that "a learned man, with a sense of humor but without taste for marriage . . . had interpolated the offending line as a joke. In the margin of his manuscript of Hesiod, he had written: 'A bought, not a married woman, to follow the oxen,' and posterity, delighted or deluded by his impishness, had transmitted the result."[31] It is not hard to imagine Sterne's delight at this scenario of a learned chain of reasoning that originates in an error or a joke. But Sterne does more in this scene than poke fun at philology. He also makes a point about the specificity of living creatures, and the reproduction of life.

First, by having Walter cite Hesiod instead of the more likely passage from Locke (or Grotius, or Puffendorf), Sterne inserts an animal into a political discourse that typically focuses on persons and things, underscoring this move with an extended discussion of which animal to insert. Furthermore, as Walter and Aristotle move from Hesiod's georgic advice to a farmer to an explicitly political genre, both shift from property relations (the trio of house, slave, and ox) to relations that include kinship (the trio of man, woman, and bull/ox), but neither marks this as a shift. Hesiod's trio of house, slave woman, and ox constitutes a domestic sphere that is not obviously organized around distinctions between different types of being: a thing, a person, and an animal make up its original unit. And when Aristotle moves from slave woman to wife, collapsing or ignoring the distinction Hesiod draws between them, he would seem to go Hesiod one better, depicting a domestic economy that elides any difference between the labor of women and the labor of oxen, the production of family and the production of food.[32] Walter repeats this elision when he strikes out the bull and puts an ox in its place. In doing so, he recalls something of the logic that we see in the second book of the *Georgics*, where Virgil applies the terms of child rearing to the cultivation of vines: in Dryden's translation, the husbandman should teach young plants how to "lift their Infant Head[s]"; use stakes as crutches to help them "learn to walk"; show tenderness to his "Nurseling[s]" in their "Nonage," and "Indulge their Child-hood."[33] When Thomson invokes and inverts the logic of such moments in *The Seasons*, he counsels parents to rear children like plants, as another living element in the whole "Earth animated" that Thomson pictures (*Su*, 296). When Walter inverts Virgil's georgic logic in *Tristram Shandy*, he does so in the service of an utterly un-Thomsonian worldview: proposing to cultivate both children and crops like one would make any thing, by means of the abstract and uniform picker-up model of labor that he associates with Locke.

At the start of the *Tristrapaedia*, Walter repeats Aristotle's citation of Hesiod in this Lockean spirit; and like Aristotle, he gets one term of Hesiod's trio wrong. But Walter's is a repetition with a difference. For while a "woman" might, in fact, serve to produce both children and crops, the ox is capable of production but not of reproduction. By replacing a fertile animal with a sterile one, Walter replaces reproductive with productive capacity, a living creature with an instrument of labor. This is an antigeorgic move, and with it, Walter unwittingly reveals the difference that Tristram worked to expose in his riff on Walter's "picker-up" model of personhood: the difference between the reproduction of life and the production of goods, or between persons and things. In other words, despite the pun on "labor" that Aristotle/Hesiod underscore with the pun on "woman" (wife/slave), Sterne insists that living bodies are not composed like things, by putting together separate and separable simple parts. In a life narrative haunted by the specter of impotence, Sterne cautions that there is something unsustainable about a society that sees nothing special about life. The ox might well be "the properest instrument," but it is hardly a sound "emblem," for the conjugal couple. Put in Lockean terms, the ox is instead an emblem for a property model of personhood, a living creature turned into a thing as its body is made useful—and sterile—by removing an extra, alienable part.[34]

The ox is one emblem for the barrenness and inanimacy that results from eliding the distinction between the living body and the machine or thing. Another is the mule, a creature set outside of species and the logic of reproduction—and one that, Tristram declares, "Philosophers, with all of their ethics, have never considered rightly" (406). Tristram turns to the mule most pointedly in his story of the abbess of Andoüillets, where he pictures the animal in conspicuously Lockean terms, possessed of both articulate speech and the power to consent. When two mules realize that they are no longer forced forward by a muleteer and his whip, they confer and come to a decision: "By my fig! said she, swearing, I'll go no further—And if I do, replied the other—they shall make a drum of my hide.—And so with one consent they stopp'd thus—" (407). If consent is often associated with the power that comes from having property in one's own person, here it is associated with sterility and standstill. The power the mules exercise is the power to stop, and this is a power that Tristram, fleeing Death in France, finds suspect: "so much of motion, is so much of life, and so much of joy—and that to stand still, or get on but slowly, is death and the devil" (396). In contrast with Tristram's sense of life as motion, the immobility of inanimate objects and the standstill of self-possessed persons appear more alike than different. Picturing Locke's autonomous, self-possessed individual as a mule with the capacity to consent, Sterne insists that this is a figure not of power but of impotence, a form not of life but of death. Against Walter and Walter's Locke, the ox and the mule—against figures of individual persons that look very much like inanimate things—Sterne looks to the reproductive logic of Buffon's vitalism to compose *The Life and*

Opinions of Tristram Shandy out of the vital union of the individual and the species, and of living creatures with others.

What I am calling Buffon's "reproductive vitalism" centers on a term that is, in this moment, relatively new. "Reproduction" enters both French and English around the turn of the eighteenth century and, even in the 1780 English edition of Buffon's *Natural History*, it was still unusual enough to call for comment.[35] As historian and Buffon biographer Jacques Roger suggests, Buffon surely turns to this new term at least in part to mark the novelty of his ideas.[36] "Generation" had in large part become the preformationists' word, connoting development or unfolding as much as creation or production. On Roger's view, Buffon uses "reproduction" to signal his turn away from the mechanistic explanations of preformation, and to designate instead the vital activity of renovating life in all its forms, including those that preformation had difficulty explaining. As Buffon uses it, then, "reproduction" occurs when one worm is cut in half to make two, when a male and a female come together and make three, when a dead body decomposes and new living beings are generated, when one eats and so renovates oneself. The variety of processes Buffon includes under the umbrella of "reproduction" might seem curious, but this signals two significant features of Buffon's—and Sterne's—vitalism, which are implied in the term "reproduction" itself.

To begin with, "reproduction" enters both French and English with the two primary senses it still carries: in the first, reproduction is the action by which living things perpetuate the species; in the second, it is the act of making a copy or exact equivalent, usually in works of art or representation.[37] This means that if Buffon turns to "reproduction" for the reason Roger suggests—in order to develop a newly vitalist account of how life comes to be—he centers this account on a term that has a distinctly mechanist ring. More significantly still, "reproduction" brings together species and individual in perplexing ways. To say that one "generates" another is to assert a causal connection between two individuals that may otherwise have nothing in common. To say that one "reproduces" oneself in another is to say something quite different—something implied in the self-reflexive logic on which the term itself insists (one "generates" another, but "reproduces" oneself). On the one hand, then, reproduction in Buffon designates a mode of relation that tends toward identity rather than causation or even resemblance, and this serves to strengthen his species concept—the (much discussed and still disputed) sense that species is, for Buffon, the fundamental unit of nature. On the other hand, the notion of reproduction itself privileges the individual as its primary unit, the form that

is renovated or perhaps simply copied over time. We might think of reproduction as Buffon's (other) fundamental question, which is most basically a
question not about the nature of species or of individuals but about the relationship between them.

The vagaries of Buffon's notion of reproduction and so of his strain of
vitalism more broadly are fully on display in two key moments in the *Natural
History*, which together configure the relationship between species and individual in ways that are particularly complicated, and resonant in the context
of *Tristram Shandy*. The first moment comes in Buffon's "Second View of
Nature," a set of philosophical reflections on nature and natural history that
begins by "suppos[ing] the species to change places with the individual" and
considering how Nature "would appear to a being who represented the whole
human species" (7.91). From the "sublime and general" view of this "being
whom we have substituted for the species," Buffon marvels, there is no birth
and no death. The "thousandth animal, in the order of generation, is the same
to him as the first" (7.91). This is a world without time, without succession,
without individuals: "In this alternate destruction and renovation, in all these
successive vicissitudes, he perceives only permanence and duration. The season of one year is to him the same as that of the preceding, the same as that
of millions of ages. The thousandth animal, in the order of generation, is the
same to him as the first. In fine, if man lived for ever, if all the beings which
surround him existed in the same manner as they do at present, the idea of
time would vanish, and the individual would become the species" (7.90–91).
This passage is often cited as evidence that Buffon sees species as the basic unit
of nature, and indeed, he seems to say as much: "Individuals, whatever their
kind or number may be, are of no value in the universe. Species are the only
existences in Nature; for they are equally antient and permanent with herself"
(7.89). This is Buffon's vitalism at its apparently most idealist, in the sense
of affirming the form or template of the Species over its instantiation in any
material body.

At a different moment in the *Natural History*, Buffon offers another
sublime view of Nature's indifference to individuals, which begins similarly:
"[Death] is unable to injure Nature; his strokes, on the contrary, make her
shine with additional lustre. She permits him not to annihilate the species,
but allows him, successively, to mow down individuals, with a view to demonstrate her independence both of Death and of Time" (3.425). This sublime
view does not appear in an entry on Buffon's philosophy of nature. Instead
and curiously, it serves to open his 1753 entry on the ox. Buffon goes on to

celebrate the ox for producing more food than it takes in, a capacity in which, he writes, "the ox is superior to that of any other creature; for he restores to the earth as much as he takes from it" (3.432). Here, Buffon's natural history of the ox anticipates Walter Shandy, celebrating the sterile ox for its reproductive capacity—as the source of food and so of life: "Without the aid of this useful animal, both the poor and the opulent would find great difficulty in procuring subsistence; the earth would remain uncultivated; our fields and gardens would become parched and barren. All the labour of the country depends upon him. He is the most advantageous domestic of the farmer. He is the very source and support of agriculture" (3.432–33). If reproduction is effected equally by nutrition as it is by propagation, Buffon seems to say, the ox is indeed the most fertile of animals, responsible for the production of so many lives and so much life—if not of any other oxen.

I bring together these two moments from the *Natural History* because their different ways of configuring the relationship between individual lives, animal species, and Life get at one of the most distinctive features of Buffon's vitalism—which Sterne both draws on and departs from in *Tristram Shandy*, as he elaborates a similarly vitalist vision in the more explicitly literary form of the life narrative. Buffon's "Second View of Nature" would seem to affirm the species as the fundamental unit of nature. By contrast, "The Ox" appears largely indifferent to species, its sublime view coming to focus either above or below, on the individual living bodies that are fed (the bodies of the farmer, the poor, the opulent) or on the whole food chain: "Nature always equally animated, the earth equally peopled, . . . the total quantity of life remains always the same" (3.425). One of the most remarkable features of Buffon's strain of vitalism is its oscillation between these prospects, as well as the repeated return from either—as in the "Second View of Nature," when Buffon descends from the sublime view of the species to ask: "From whence proceed those alterations of life and death, those laws of growth and decay, all those individual vicissitudes, and all those reiterated representations of one and the same thing?" (7.93). In such moments, Buffon makes clear that a vitalism centered on reproduction is neither an idealist vitalism of the Species over any individual instantiation, nor a materialist vitalism of living matter over any specific form or any particular life. It is instead a vitalism of composition that seeks to hold species and individuals together without privileging either—without fixing on the sublime and species view that renders individuals "of no value in the universe," or presenting the individual as a discrete and elemental unit of nature.

To put things this way is to echo Reill's account of Enlightenment vitalism, which centers on Buffon precisely because he emphasizes "the elemental nature of conjunction."[38] As Reill points out, Buffon argues that the "abstract" and the "simple" may be the most elemental forms of our own thought, and so appropriate to the method of mathematics or physics. But the same is not true of the life sciences or natural history, because "in nature, no abstract exists; nothing is simple; every object is compounded [composé]" (2.21). The most elemental unit of nature is not simple or inert but composite and active, formed and also forming. Buffon again aims this point at defenders of preformation: "There are . . . no pre-existing germs, or germs infinitely contained within each other. But there is an organic matter diffused through all animated nature, which is always active, always tending to form, to assimilate [toujours prête à se mouler, à s'assimiler], and to produce beings similar to those which receive it" (2.352). In Buffon's animated nature, reproduction is the way of matter itself, and relation its elemental, irreducible form. It is this emphasis on composition, animation, and relation that secures animal life pride of place in Buffon's natural history: "what a number of relations . . . ! [que de rapports]" Buffon exclaims, referring to the animal body (2.2). Like many naturalists before and after him, Buffon grants the animal first rank in the order of nature. For Buffon, more unusually, this ranking results from the animal's abundance of relations: "In the animal, the whole powers of nature are united; . . . his body is a world in miniature, a central point to which every thing in the universe is connected. These are his peculiar relations" [L'animal réunit toutes les puissances de la nature . . . son individu est un centre où tout se rapporte, un point où l'univers entire se réfléchit, un monde en raccourci: voilà les rapports qui lui sont propres] (2.6). The animal's abundance of relations is, for Buffon, the form that individuation takes. Translated literally, the passage reads: "Its individual is a center where everything relates, a point where the entire universe is reflected, a world in miniature."

Buffon's description of the animal could serve as a decent description of the form of *Tristram Shandy*: an individual that is irreducibly composite, life as an abundance of relations. Even if Tristram celebrates singularity throughout his *Life and Opinions*, he makes clear that singularity does not take the form that Walter imagines: Tristram's singular *Life* is not properly his own. From its opening parody of the autonomous individual in the figure of a homunculus "guarded and circumscribed with rights," Tristram's *Life* is occupied more with the Shandy family than with Tristram (who shares even his proper name with Parson Yorick—itself a family name that is conspicuously not Yorick's "own") (6). In this life narrative, even singularity is a "family-likeness," which Tristram shares with Toby and with Walter ("all the SHANDY FAMILY were of an original character throughout") (53). And ultimately, singularity comes to look like a trait common to the entire nation ("this strange irregularity in our climate producing so strange an irregularity in our characters") if not to the whole species—as the ubiquitous figure of "A man and his HOBBY-HORSE" suggests (52, 61). Throughout the novel, Tristram's singular and first-person *Life* is located firmly on the side of the species and of life—what Tristram calls "True *Shandeism*," which "opens the heart and lungs, and . . . forces the blood and other vital fluids of the body to run freely thro' its channels, and makes the wheel of life run long and cheerfully round" (270). For the sake of this vital movement, Sterne repeatedly strikes out emblems of self-possession and thinghood: Walter and his patient ox, or the two mules who effect nothing but standstill. In their place, he puts figures of speciation, of social and sexual intercourse—a Jack Asse and Jenny, Tristram and an ass, even "A COCK and a BULL"—which produce Tristram's *Life* not as a kind of one (like the mule, or Walter), but, as Yorick exclaims in the work's final lines, as "one of the best of its kind" (539).[39]

In this concluding pun on being "one of a kind," we can hear the central question of Buffon's reproductive vitalism, which is a question about how to hold the individual and the species simultaneously in view: "whence . . . all those individual vicissitudes, and all those reiterated representations of one and the same thing?" This is also Sterne's central question, registered in *Tristram Shandy* by the black page that mourns the loss of individual life, and the Shandeism that delights in "the wheel of life run[ning] long and cheerfully round" (270). It is a question, moreover, that Buffon seems at times to close down, coming down on the side of the Species or of living matter, the sublime view of Man or of Life that is everywhere and always the same. Buffon's frequent tendency to overshadow the individual vicissitudes on which his own reproductive logic insists is, I think, a literary or historiographical as much as a philosophical problem, an effect of writing the natural history of "Man" or "The Ox" in ways that seem necessarily to obscure individual men, or oxen.[40] We might thus think of *Tristram Shandy* as a response to this problem of natural-historical representation, the problem of representing life. While Buffon writes a natural history of "Man" that sometimes renders individual men (not to mention women) invisible, Sterne develops a form of life-writing more adequate to Buffonian vitalism, and to the challenge of holding individual and species simultaneously in view.[41] He does this by presenting

Buffon's reproductive and species logic in the first person, and by composing life in and as conversation with others, as an effect of rhetorical artifice and a cause of real sentiment.

The Natural History of Tristram Shandy

Two related moments in volume 5 help to bring this last claim into focus, by revealing the reproductive and species logic of *Tristram Shandy*'s first-person form. In each of these moments, Walter quotes from the first-person prose of another person, and each time, his first-person quotation is mistaken for his own proper speech. Both instances occur on the occasion of Bobby's death, which prompts Walter to philosophical reflections on the subject. In the first instance, Walter starts out talking to Toby in his own person ("do not, I beseech thee, interrupt me at this crisis"), and then he shifts, without indication, into the voice of another. The quotation marks do not indicate that Walter is quoting, here, but simply that he speaks out loud:

> "Returning out of *Asia*, when I sailed from *Aegina* towards *Megara*," *(when can this have been? thought my uncle Toby)* "I began to view the country round about. *Aegina* was behind me, *Megara* was before, *Pyraeus* on the right hand, *Corinth* on the left.—What flourishing towns now prostrate upon the earth! Alas! Alas! said I to myself, that man should disturb his soul for the loss of a child, when so much as this lies awfully buried in his presence—Remember, said I to myself again—remember thou art a man." (284)

Only when Walter has finished speaking does Sterne clue the reader in to the meaning of Toby's interjection. Toby did not know (nor, necessarily, did the reader) that "this last paragraph was an extract of *Servius Sulpicius's* consolatory letter to *Tully*" (284). Unaware of this, Toby tried to fit Walter's first-person speech into Walter's own biographical narrative. Since Walter had once been involved in trade to the Levant, "my uncle *Toby* naturally concluded, that in some one of these periods he had taken a trip across the *Archipelago* into *Asia*; and that all this sailing affair . . . was nothing more than the true course of my father's voyage and reflections" (284).

The second instance of such confusion comes at the end of the same conversation. Walter now reads from the section of Socrates' trial oration that,

roughly speaking, asserts the value of *Life* (one's personal or biographical identity) over life (one's physical life): on Plato's formulation, "I shall never alter
my ways, not even if I have to die many times"; on Sterne's, "*That we and our
children were born to die,—but neither of us born to be slaves*" (295).[42] This time,
both the reader and Toby know that Walter is quoting Socrates. But Elizabeth,
who stands listening in the doorway, does not. Tristram explains to the reader
that Walter often expressed the same sentiment as Socrates: "My father, I say,
had a way, when things went extremely wrong with him . . . of wondering why
he was begot,—wishing himself dead;—sometimes worse"; in such moments,
Tristram writes, "you scarce could have distinguished him from *Socrates* himself" (296). Elizabeth illustrates Tristram's point. Overhearing a speech whose
content "was not altogether new to her," she assumes that Walter speaks in his
own person—until he comes to something that she does not recognize. Here,
Sterne uses quotation marks and Socrates' name to ensure that the reader
avoids Elizabeth's error:

> "I have friends—I have relations,—I have three desolate children,"—
> says *Socrates*.—
> —Then, cried my mother, opening the door,—you have one
> more, Mr. *Shandy*, than I know of.
> By heaven! I have one less,—said my father, getting up and walk-
> ing out of the room. (297)

Thinking that she has heard Walter confess to fathering a child outside of
marriage, Elizabeth discovers that her own son Bobby has died.

I am interested in these moments because in both, listeners go wrong by
interpreting Walter's "I" as his own, taking his first person to stand for Walter
himself, his own travels, and his own children. They get this wrong, in each
case, because Walter's use of the first person does not point to the facts of
his own life but rather expresses his sentiments—something to which, Sterne
insists, the Lockean property logic of "one's own" is not appropriate. Tristram underscores this point by wondering how Socrates' sentiment—which,
Tristram notes, in fact did not belong to Socrates but to Eleazor, who in turn
"had it from the philosophers of India"—had come into Walter's possession.
He imagines that "*Alexander* the Great, in his irruption into *India*, . . . [had],
amongst the many things he stole,—stole that sentiment also"; after which
Alexander or his men likely carried it from Greece to Rome to France to
England: "So things come round" (295–96). Poking fun at the idea that a

sentiment might "come round" like a thing, that it might be stolen and carried
from nation to nation, Sterne hints that some "things"—sentiments, opinions,
ideas—are both more and less than one's own. More, in the sense that sentiments or ideas cannot simply be separated from oneself, like external goods
and chattels: they are "him" rather than "his." And less, in the sense that one's
sentiments or ideas can also be somebody else's.

The content of Walter's quotations furthers this lesson about the logic of
both sentiments and the persons they affect. The consolatory letter to Cicero
concludes, in Sterne's paraphrase, "Remember, said I to myself again—remember thou art a man" (284). And in the section leading to Walter's quotation,
Socrates' oration says something similar: in Plato's words, "My friend, I am a
man, and like other men, a creature of flesh and blood, and not 'of wood or
stone,' as Homer says."[43] Both passages speak in the first person about "man,"
and Sterne highlights the link between the first person and this common species form by having Toby and Elizabeth miss it, taking "I" to refer to Walter alone. Despite his claims to possess a life uniquely his own, then, Walter
speaks his sentiments by a different logic, undercutting his claims to singularity by shifting into a sort of prosopopoeia: speaking, as Quintilian has it, "by
the Mouth of others."[44] Sterne's point about the first person here is not exactly
the familiar thought that "I" can be spoken by anyone, a sense of dispossess-
ion recuperated by the properly human power, as Derrida puts it in a gloss of
Kant, to appropriate this generic form and make it one's own, to "possess the
representation of an 'I.'"[45] Sterne's point is rather that the problem of human
individuation that so preoccupies Hobbes and Swift—the problem of taking
seriously both one's sense of self and the fact of human speciation—is not such
a problem. As Sterne sees it, there are alternative forms of unity and relation
available to us than those proposed by Hobbes or Swift: the Leviathan held
together by the force of the sovereign, or the lash of Swiftian satire. Indeed,
Sterne suggests that simply by representing myself in the first person, I set
myself under the sign of the species. Pitting Walter's claims to self-possession
against the form of his speech, Sterne presents the first person as an implicitly
general or species form.

Philosopher Michael Thompson's recent work on the "representation of
life" helps to explain what it means to conceive of the first person as a generic
or species form, as I think Sterne does here.[46] Thompson begins by arguing, in
a Buffonian spirit, that a living thing is not simply one kind of thing among
others, something that could be designated by a particular set of properties or
attributes. Instead, Thompson contends, life has a logical form of its own: a

special form of agency and of generality, of unity between being, action, and kind. We designate the peculiar logic of living things by a form of description that Thompson calls "natural-historical": a form familiar from nature television or field guides about "*the* bobcat," or from Buffon's history of "the ass" or "the ox."[47]

Thompson develops his account of this natural-historical form from an insight that also informs James Thomson's *The Seasons*. In my first chapter, I suggested that Thomson thinks that at least some types of actions cannot be perceived simply by looking at the scene before us, at what we see happening here and now. In *The Seasons*, actions that are not apprehended by empirical observation call for a special form of representation, which is simultaneously personification and natural description. Thompson makes a related point. On his view, empirical observation is not sufficient to apprehend some types of actions or happenings; these take the form of description that Thompson calls "natural-historical." Whenever we describe something as the subject of such actions—actions like walking, eating, breeding, and thinking—Thompson argues that we give a "natural-historical," "vital," or "'anti-individualistic' account of the thing."[48] In Thompson's words: "the characterization of an individual organism here and now as thinking or speaking, like the characterization of it as eating or breathing or leafing out, is a life form-dependent description: take away the life form and we have a pile of electrochemical connections; put it back in and we have hunger and pain and breathing and walking . . . [and] in suitable cases, self-conscious thought and discourse as well. The life form *underwrites* the applicability of these diverse state- and process- types in individual cases."[49] Thompson inverts Buffon's point that we cannot think of species outside of life to argue that we cannot think of life outside of species (more precisely, outside of the uniquely generic logic of the life form). In the representation of life, our descriptions of actions or happenings always draw on a "wider context," something more than that which we see happening here and now.[50] This wider context is composed of two elements. The first is the logical concept of the life form itself, the notion that some individuals are not exactly individuals, as any description of what they do is shot through with form. The second element is our empirical knowledge about any particular life form, like the jellyfish or the bobcat, which leads us to describe what we observe as, say, eating or walking.

Unlike the logical notion of the life form, then, Thompson thinks that our ideas about any particular life form are acquired and amended by means of empirical observation. But there is one exception: "the life form that I bear."

Thompson argues that I apprehend *this* form of life not through empirical observation but immediately, "through the first person, or through the I-concept."[51] At the same time, Thompson insists that consciousness or thinking— even or especially my own consciousness or thinking—is apprehended much like eating or breeding, by referring to the "wider context" of a life form. Thompson puts the point this way: "In the self-conscious representation of myself as thinking, as in all my self-conscious self-representation, I implicitly represent myself as alive, as falling under life-manifesting types. And in bringing myself under such types I bring myself under a life form. . . . Self-consciousness is thus always implicitly form-consciousness."[52] Thus for Thompson, "I" is as much an "anti-individualistic" form of representation as "the bobcat." It is the form in which I represent myself as a living creature of a certain kind.

I have introduced Thompson's work here because of what it reveals about the first-person form of life in Sterne—a form of life at once first personal and specific, which is also to say both individualist and anti-individualist. I have also introduced Thompson because of his insistence that the "life form" is not a biological or empirical species concept. Thompson cautions that, thought philosophically rather than biologically, the life form is a very "thin category," which "leave[s] many questions of sameness and difference of life-form unsettled.'"[53] Thompson's point is that when I say "I," I do not say anything about the content of my particular life form, or those with whom I might share it: "I might now engage in the skeptical doubt whether this life form of mine has any *other* bearers, and I might not know much about how to fill in the blanks [of its content]—but I bring the basic duality of life form and individual bearer into the picture."[54] When I say "I" and so bring myself under a life form, I do not identify with any biological species but simply represent myself as a specific form of generality and of agency—what Locke calls "vital union." This point is important because for Thompson, the "life form I bear" is the human form of life, but this is not the same thing as any empirically designated category of "human being." And crucially, both Sterne and Tristram would extend "the life form I bear" beyond humankind, by way of a reproductive process that operates in the domain both of living bodies and of literary representation.

It is this sort of reproductive process that begets Walter's speech from Socrates' oration, a sentimental and species version of prosopopoeia that reconfigures citation as conversation, parroting as first personhood. *Tristram Shandy*'s paradigmatic instance of this sort of reproduction comes in volume 7, when

Tristram stops to talk with an ass who blocks his path. Tristram's sentimental encounter with the ass reconfigures Toby's famous encounter with the fly,
replacing an animal who goes his own way ("get thee gone," says Toby) with
another who stays to eat.[55] In good Buffonian fashion, eating is presented
here as an explicitly reproductive activity, a sentimental, sociable, and vitalist
alternative to Walter's efforts at self-possession. As Tristram tells it, the ass
"was eating the stem of an artichoke as this discourse went on, and in the little
peevish contentions of nature betwixt hunger and unsavouriness, had dropt
it out of his mouth half a dozen times" (420). For Tristram—who notes that
he "keep[s] neither man or boy, or horse, or cow, or dog, or cat, or anything
that can eat or drink" (511)—it is the animal's act of eating (and, of dropping
his artichoke to the ground and then picking it up) that somehow generates
sympathy, making it possible for Tristram to "fling my own heart into his, and
[see] what is natural for an ass to think—as well as a man, upon the occasion"
(420). As he watches the animal with the artichoke, Tristram begins to construct a life narrative: "God help thee, Jack! said I, thou hadst a bitter breakfast
on't—and many a bitter day's labour—and many a bitter blow, I fear, for its
wages—'tis all—all bitterness to thee, whatever life is to others.—And now
thy mouth, if one knew the truth of it, is as bitter, I dare say, as soot—(for he
had cast aside the stem) and thou hast not a friend perhaps in all this world,
that will give the a macaroon" (420). Tristram gives the ass a macaroon and
then tries to make it move. The halter breaks in his hand, and their "com-
mun[ion]" shifts into conversation, as Tristram records the ass's first-person
speech: "'Don't thrash me with it—but if you will, you may'—If I do, said I,
I'll be d—d" (419, 421).

   In this scene, Sterne suggests that the ass is "the only creature of all the
classes of beings below [him]" with which Tristram "can commune for ever,"
because the ass and Tristram share a common form of life (419). This form is
not that of the mule with articulate speech and the capacity to consent. It is
the vital, first-person, and explicitly embodied form of activities like eating,
feeling, thinking, and finally speaking, a form that is both cause and effect of
conjunction or coupling, of the reproduction of life. This is not reproduction
as usual, certainly—the capaciousness of Sterne's notion of reproduction is
perhaps rivaled only by Buffon's. As Sterne pictures it here, the reproductive
process generates life in the biological and also biographical sense, making
animals from artichokes, producing persons from others. These persons are in
some sense figurative—the ass's first-person speech is patently an effect of Tristram's projective and personifying imagination. At the same time, Tristram's

ass is an animate living body, a creature, like Crusoe's Poll, with the capacity to say "I" outside of language but in conversation, as it responds to Tristram and elicits Tristram's response in turn.

In picturing a sentimental conversation that proceeds from nutrition and animal motion to interpersonal and cross-species dialogue, Sterne operates in what I think is a Buffonian vitalist mode, reproducing life and species as a constant succession and renovation of individuals. Put in somewhat different as well as literary terms, Tristram's sentimental conversation with the ass operates in what we might think of as a georgic mode. By this, I mean in part to recall Walter's invocation of Hesiod's georgic at the start of the *Tristrapaedia*, which he overwrites when he resolves the specificity of different forms of labor (and life) into one abstract and unified process of picking things up. I also mean to emphasize the highly rhetorical aspect of Tristram's sentimental conversation with the ass, a characteristically Shandean variation on the sort of poetic labor that Addison celebrates when he praises Virgil's "most laboured" language: a labor of linguistic and rhetorical mediation that functions, as Dryden's translation of Virgil puts it, "to embellish" its theme "with the Magnificence of words."[56] One of the georgic's characteristic rhetorical figures is the trope of animation that Walter inverts when he would cultivate his children and crops like things: the figure that Virgil uses to depict vines as children, or, to take examples from the first book of the *Georgics*, the land as thirsty, soil as barren, the earth as a womb that takes nourishment and gives birth. Hesiod uses the same figure to depict the year as something that grows old and dies. This figure often gets labeled "personification," but this makes sense only if personification is understood much as Thomson understands it in *The Seasons*, as animation. This figure is metaphorical but it is not only that. The georgic earth really is, to borrow a phrase from Poliziano, a "Life-giving earth."[57]

In the life-giving earth in which Tristram lives and writes, even mules are fertile, as Buffon so hoped they might be. A short while after he stops to talk with an ass, Tristram joins with a mule to cross the plains of Languedoc. He describes their travels this way: "by stopping and talking to every soul I met who was not in a full trot . . . by seizing every handle, of what size or shape soever, which chance held out to me in this journey—I turned my *plain* into a *city*—I was always in company, and with great variety too; and as my mule loved society as much as myself, and had some proposals always on his part to offer to every beast he met—I am confident we could have passed through Pall-Mall or St. James's-Street for a month together, with fewer adventures—and seen less of human nature" (430). This is Tristram's reprisal of the scene of the mules of Andoüillets, recast as a scene not of impotence, isolation, and stasis but of reproduction, sociability, and animal motion. Somewhere "in the road betwixt Nismes and Lunel," Tristram's mule does come to a stop, apparently at the sounds of a fife and drum: "I'm frighten'd to death, quoth he" (430). "Making the same resolution [as] with the abbesse of Andoüillets," the mule resolves to stand still, and he tells Tristram so: "I'll not go a step further—'Tis very well, sir, said I—I will never argue a point with one of your family, as long as I live; so leaping off his back, and kicking off one boot into this ditch, and t'other into that—I'll take a dance, said I—so stay you here" (430). Unlike the abbess and novice who try to force their mules forward, Tristram transforms the mule's standstill into dialogue, and into dance.

In this scene with the mule, as when he stops to talk with the ass, Tristram's capacity to recuperate standstill as motion is presented as an explicitly reproductive capacity, a capacity to generate life in its various senses—leading Tristram to the "sun-burnt daughter of Labour" with whom he imagines spending the rest of his days, and also "into Perdrillo's pavilion" where he now writes his life narrative, "pulling a paper of black lines, that I might go on . . . in my uncle Toby's amours" (431). In *A Sentimental Journey*, Sterne imagines extending this reproductive capacity further still: "I pity the man who can travel from *Dan* to *Beersheeba*, and cry, 'Tis all barren—and so it is; and so is all the world to him who will not cultivate the fruits it offers. I declare, said I, clapping my hands chearily together, that was I in a desart, I would find out wherewith in it to call forth my affections—If I could not do better, I would fasten them upon some sweet myrtle, or seek some melancholy cypress to connect myself to—I would court their shade, and greet them kindly for their protection."[58] The sentimental travels of Tristram and Yorick emerge as a clear counter to Walter's system of auxiliary verbs, "the soul a going by herself on the materials" (323). The movements or "affections" that Sterne calls sentimental are not generated out of oneself alone but are "called forth" in response to others—making conversation with an ass, generating a city from a plain, cultivating connections with even a sweet myrtle or a melancholy cypress. This sort of reproductive operation may look to some like solipsism or stasis, but the logic of Sternian sentiment does not clearly distinguish between solitude and sociality, and between moving, being moved, or even standing still.[59] These are distinctions that arise from the mechanical "combinations of matter and motion," Sterne insists.[60] They are not the stuff of life.

To characterize *Tristram Shandy* as reproductive in this way is to strain against the specter of impotence that hangs over the narrative—over Tristram and Jenny, as much as Toby, Walter, the mule, or the ox. In doing so, my point is not to argue that impotence is a value rather than a problem in *Tristram Shandy*, in the manner of readers like Georg Lukács and Carol Kay, who see Sterne's project as one of cordoning off the purposeless play of literature from the instrumental logic of life in the world.[61] Certainly there is something to the sense that Sterne rejoices in the useless and the purposeless. But I think Sterne holds utility and productivity somewhat further apart, celebrating uselessness as well as productivity in the domain of both art and life. As Jesse Molesworth points out in a different context, the flip side of Sterne's anxiety about impotence is its impossibility. In *Tristram Shandy*, there is no way not to produce or to reproduce: if not life then *Life*, if not motion then emotion, if not sex then sentiment.[62] In a world in which singularity is a species trait, the first person a form of life, and animation the site of an expansive sociality, productivity is as relentless as it is useless. This may look like delusion or magical thinking (as it does to Molesworth), but I think Sterne is committed to this sort of productivity as the principle of both life and writing: the sort of productivity that does not make any thing, but that does reproduce life in all its forms.

I have been working to suggest that Tristram's sentimental, sometimes sexual, and frequently cross-species conversations represent Sterne at his most Buffonian, laboring to generate a form of vital and reproductive life. I want to close with a moment from the *Natural History* in which Buffon is at his most Sternian. This comes in the midst of Buffon's extended discussion of experiments in animal generation: "From the experiments and observations formerly made, it is apparent, that all animated beings contain an amazing quantity of living organic particles. The life of an animal or vegetable seems to be nothing else than a result of all the particular *lives* (if the expression be admissible) of each of these active particles, whose life is primitive, and perhaps indestructible" (2.282). We might think of Buffon's description of all the "little particular lives" that compose the life of an animal or vegetable as a twin scene to Tristram's conversation with the ass, out of which emerges another particular life. Like Sterne's representation of the ass's first-person life, Buffon's "little lives" are markedly rhetorical, a kind of personification. But Buffon registers discomfort with this personification in a way that Tristram does not, emphasizing that these "little particular lives" are conspicuously figurative, an almost inadmissible expression in the pages of his *Natural History*.

Buffon voices a similar discomfort with figuration—at least, with figuration presented as empirical observation—elsewhere in his discussion of animal generation, in another description of the moving bodies that the microscope makes visible in the seminal fluid of animals. Here Buffon maintains—at some length, and with some defensiveness—that while he might personify living particles as "little particular lives," he will not call them "animals." He admits that everyone else does: "It will be demanded of me, why I deny these moving bodies to be animals, after they have uniformly been recognized as such by every man who has examined them? It may likewise be asked, How is it possible to conceive the nature of living organic particles, unless we allow them to be real animals?" (2.215). Buffon does not answer either of these questions directly, but he does hint at a response when he goes on to insist that he will not even call living particles "animalcules, and thus suppose an animal is composed of little animals."[63] In part, Buffon suggests that to call a living particle "an animal" is in some sense to return to preformation, with its "small animals, or organized living *homunculi*, included in each other in endless succession, and which, to render them men, or perfect animals, require[s] nothing but expansion, and a transformation similar to that of winged insects" (2.137). But Buffon does not draw an explicit connection between the label "animal" and the theory of preformation. Instead, he launches into a long discussion of "the word *animal*, in common acceptation," which makes a similar point. The problem with "the word *animal*," Buffon argues, is that it seems to designate some elemental or given thing in nature: "when the word is once received, we imagine it to be a line drawn between the different productions of nature; that every thing above this line is an *animal*, and every thing below it a vegetable. . . . But, as has already been remarked these lines of separation have no existence in nature" (2.217). Buffon suggests that "an animal" is not a production of nature but something more like "a life": an effect of representation, or a figure of speech.

Like the sublime view of nature that opens "The Ox," Buffon's discussion of "the word *animal*" is peculiarly placed, a philosophical and also literary reflection buried amid the detailed technical results of scientific experiment and observation. Once again, though, this placement is telling. For Buffon's point has to do with the incongruity between empirical, experimental observation and the idea of the animal—and more broadly, with the effort of science to cut its ties with literature, to present as direct observation what is irreducibly a rhetorical figure. In other words, to look in the microscope and see an animal is in part to recall the logic of preformation, and so to deny the active form in and as which all animals are composed. It is also to mistake where and how such composition takes place—to get the domain of animality wrong. Buffon makes this point most clearly in his "Initial Discourse," the methodological manifesto in which he counters Linnaean taxonomy with his own practice of description and history. Buffon begins by urging readers to "imagine a man who . . . has forgotten everything, or who wakens to completely strange surroundings" and sets this man "in a field where animals, birds, fishes, plants, and stones appear successively to his eyes."[64] After an initial period of confusion, Buffon writes, "he will naturally arrive at that first great division, *Animal, Vegetable,* and *Mineral*"—the first step in "com[ing] to judge the objects of natural history by the connections which they have with his own life," and thus in establishing a domestic order of nature that begins with the most familiar of animals, with the horse, the ass, the dog, the ox.[65] The difference here is striking. In his discussion of laboratory experiments on animal generation, Buffon worries that one might mistake "the animal" for a given or natural kind; in the "Initial Discourse," he identifies the animal as "that first great division" in the order of nature. Reading Buffon's "Initial Discourse" alongside his personification of microscopic particles and his reflections on the word "animal," a claim emerges that we might call Shandean. The claim is this: animals are not generated under a microscope but in the countryside. They are products of the sort of personification that constitutes a living particle as "a life," or that represents an ass—or a parrot—as the subject of first-person speech. In other words, "animal" is a term of the plain and the city, of the living world and of living together. In his discomfort with sliding what it is to have or be a life down to the microscopic level (and into the laboratory), Buffon signals something that Sterne and at times Locke also signal. Like a person and like an animal, a life is not composed of little lives housed inside and apprehended by the instruments of experimental science. A life is composed of and by the many lives that people the plain or city, and the conversation that is both cause and effect of their vital first-person form. The labor of such personification, in other words, is not solitary—which is why the homunculus is not our fellow creature, and the ass is.

Chapter 5

The Child

The Fabulous Animal and the Family Pet

The previous chapter concluded with the vitalist and georgic vision shared by Sterne and Buffon, composed of broadly reproductive relations between animals and other people. This final chapter closes in around the narrowly reproductive unit of the familiar household to focus on the figures of the child and the family pet, and on literature written for children. Toward the end of the eighteenth century, writers and booksellers began to produce a body of literature specifically for juvenile readers, and very quickly, children's literature became the most conspicuous literary home of animal life. Writing her *Thoughts on the Education of Daughters* at an early moment in this development, Mary Wollstonecraft offers this recommendation: "Animals are the first objects which catch [children's] attention; and I think little stories about them would not only amuse but instruct at the same time, and have the best effect in forming the temper and cultivating the good dispositions of the heart."[1] After more than two centuries of children's literature largely dominated by animal stories, Wollstonecraft's recommendation resonates with the familiarity of common sense. Even at this initial moment in the history of writing for children, Wollstonecraft delivers her proposition as though the connection between children and animals needs no explanation. In what follows, I step back from this assumption of self-evidence to consider why animals enjoy such prominence in a body of writing concerned with introducing children to language and to literature.

The story of the rise of English children's literature is not as well known as the story of the rise of the English novel, or even the fall of the rhetorical figure of personification.[2] But it follows a familiar narrative of modernization. Critics typically chart a progressive development from the domestic and domesticating genre of the moral fable to the wild mode of fantasy and play, from the Enlightenment to Romanticism, from Locke to Rousseau.[3] This story is an old one, the basic elements of which can be traced at least to Charles Lamb's 1802 letter to Coleridge:

> Mrs Barbauld['s] stuff has banished all the old classics of the nursery; & and the Shopman at Newbery's hardly deign'd to reach them off an old exploded corner of a shelf, when Mary ask'd for them. Mrs B's & Mrs Trimmer's nonsense lay in piles about. Knowledge, insignificant & vapid as Mrs B's books convey, it seems, must come to the child in the *shape of knowledge*, & his empty noddle must be turned with conceit of its own power, when he has learned that a Horse is an Animal, & Billy is better than a Horse, & such like: instead of that beautiful Interest in wild tales, which made the child a man, while all the time he suspected himself to be no bigger than a child. . . . Damn them. I mean the cursed Barbauld Crew, those Blights and Blasts of all that is Human in man & child.[4]

Lamb's remarks may have licensed generations of later critics to dismiss much of early children's writing as "nonsense."[5] But Lamb's own dismissal carries a curiously hyperbolic charge. Lamb indicts writers like Anna Letitia Barbauld and Sarah Trimmer for threatening "all that is Human in man & child" by presenting "insignificant & vapid" truisms—especially, that "a Horse is an Animal, & Billy is better than a Horse"—in the "shape of knowledge." Reading the didactic animal stories of early children's writers, Lamb suggests, somehow shapes the species itself, forming (or deforming, on Lamb's view) the persons that children are or become.

Some time before Lamb blasted the "Barbauld Crew" for trafficking in taxonomic "knowledge" that undermined the very essence of human being, Samuel Johnson also singled out Barbauld (née Aikin) for derision, characterizing her writing for children as a facile effort to shore up species boundaries: "'Miss Aikin was an instance of early cultivation, but in what did it terminate? In marrying a little Presbyterian parson, who keeps an infant boarding-school, so that all her employment now is, 'To suckle fools, and chronicle small-beer.' She tells the children, 'This is a cat, and that is a dog, with four legs and a tail; see there! you are much better than a cat or a dog, for you can speak.'"[6] Barbauld's *Lessons for Children* (1778–79) is published in four volumes, each aimed at a different age group (between two and four years old), and narrated by a mother to her son Charles. This age-graded design was a major innovation in the history of reading.[7] At the level of content, however, Barbauld's *Lessons* can seem altogether familiar, instilling humanist lessons about speech and species in much the way that Johnson charges. The first volume opens with a lesson about Charles and his cat: "You cannot catch puss," Charles's mother begins. "Do not pull her by the tail, you hurt her."[8] This lesson links Puss's sentience to her ethical standing; her capacity to be hurt makes her an exemplary object of kindness. But when Charles's mother directs a similar set of instructions to Puss (do not do that, you hurt her), the lesson proceeds differently: "But puss, why did you kill the rabbit? You must catch mice; you must not kill rabbits. Well, what do you say, did you kill the rabbit? Why do you not speak, puss? Puss cannot speak" (1.7–8). As the *Lessons* continues, Charles learns that he is "better than a cat or a dog," on Johnson's formulation, because unlike Puss, he can answer for his actions: "Do you know why you are better than Puss? Puss can play as well as you; and Puss can drink milk, and lie upon the carpet; and she can run as fast as you. . . . But can Puss talk? No. Can Puss read? No. Then that is the reason why you are better that [*sic*] Puss—because you can talk and read. . . . I never saw a little dog or cat learn to read. But little boys can learn. If you do not learn, Charles, you are not good for half as much as a Puss. You had better be drowned" (3.4–7). Johnson and Lamb ridicule Barbauld's lessons about speech and species, but she insists that the stakes of this teaching are high. Language—here, talking and reading—is a capacity on which the child's life and humanity both depend.

In order to teach the stakes of speech, however, Barbauld does something strange. She shifts from the realist scenario of a mother, child, and a pet that cannot speak to an allegorical animal fable about two sheep who can. Charles's mother warns him not to go into the field alone, because "perhaps you would die, and that would be a sad tale to tell" (3.40). She then segues into such a tale, which takes the form of a fable—"a story about a lamb" who thinks it "very hard" to be "shut up" every night in a sheepfold (3.41). The fable centers on a dialogue between the lamb and her mother: "She came to her mother, who was a wise old sheep, and said to her, I wonder why we are shut up so every night! the dogs are not shut up, and why shou'd we be shut up? I think it is very hard, and I will get away if I can, I am resolved, for I like to run about where I please, and I think it is very pleasant in the woods by moonlight—Then the old sheep said to her, you are very silly, you little lamb, you had better stay in the fold. . . . if you wander about by yourself, I dare say you will come to some harm. I dare say not, said the little lamb" (3.43–45). The lamb does not heed her mother's warning to stay in the fold, and the story ends as she is seized by a wolf and fed to its cubs: "Here, I have brought you a young fat lamb—and so the cubs took her, and growled over her a little while, and then tore her to pieces, and ate her up" (3.52). Throughout Barbauld's text, the moral of the stories told by both ovine and human mothers is that speech—including, here, the capacity to read, or to understand stories and their lessons—is the means to safeguard against death as drowning or being eaten by wolves. In a version of the familiar Lockean lesson that speech makes one human, and being human secures one from being eaten, Charles learns that he is better than Puss because he can speak, and that his life depends on this advantage. What, then, is he to make of a "story about a lamb" that features garrulous sheep and wolves?

Most broadly, this is a question about why and how the difference between humans and animals is staked on the grounds of speech. More specifically, it is a question about why and how, at an early moment in the development of children's literature, writers take up the fable form, the literary genre of the talking animal.[9] The beginning of an answer is literary historical. Aesop's fables had long been used to teach children to read, and Locke had lately endorsed this practice in his *Some Thoughts Concerning Education*, singling out Aesop's fables as, in his words, "the only Book I know fit for Children."[10] Influenced by both this long-standing practice and this authoritative endorsement, eighteenth-century writers began to adapt animal fables specifically for children (Eleanor Fenn's *Fables in Monosyllables* or William Godwin's *Fables, Ancient and Modern*), to include fables in juvenile anthologies and periodicals (Barbauld and her brother John Aikin's *Evenings at Home*, John Newbery's *Lilliputian Magazine*, or, somewhat differently, Thomas Day's *Sandford and Merton*), or to mix features of the fable with other narrative forms like the novel or it-narrative (Joachim Henricke Campe's *New Robinson Crusoe*, Dorothy Kilner's *Life and Perambulation of a Mouse*, Sarah Trimmer's *Fabulous Histories*, or Mary Wollstonecraft's *Original Stories, from Real Life*). If the fact of literary influence helps to explain why early children's writers took up the fable form, though, it says little about why the fable took hold in this new type of writing, or how it took shape. In this chapter, I argue that the fable appeals to children's writers for quite different reasons than it appeals to Gulliver. In Swift, the fable promises a synecdochal and species identity in which each individual is identical to every other, because all embody an essential species character. For children's writers, the fable carries a different promise: of granting personhood even to those human beings who have not yet learned to talk, by identifying the motions and especially passions of animals as a mode of speech.

In detailing what children's writers did with the fable—how they bring children and animals together, and to what end—I adhere in some respects to familiar narratives about the history of writing for children. Like many others, I understand the development of children's literature to be linked to the educational philosophies of Locke and Rousseau, and to their remarks about what and why children should read. But I am less interested in the narrative of modernization and liberation with which these philosophers are often associated, than in the models of personhood and species that each elaborates, and the generic and formal experiments to which these give rise. On my view, Locke privileges the animal fable—conceived in curiously natural-historical terms—for its capacity to constitute children as persons, while Rousseau looks to *Robinson Crusoe* to make the child a man (or simply, "Man"). The dispute between their positions turns on differing notions of what it means to speak, to pity, and especially to read. In the first half of the chapter, I argue that writers in a Lockean tradition of juvenile fiction—including Sarah Trimmer, Dorothy Kilner, and Wollstonecraft—combine elements of fable, natural history, and the life narrative to compose a multispecies domestic sphere around a mode of speech widened to include the intelligible, suffering bodies of both children and animals. In this literature, all animals are persons, but it turns out that (almost) all persons are pets: individuals excepted from their species by someone more powerful, who interprets their motions and vocalizations as meaningful signs of mind or sentience. In the second half of the chapter, I read Barbauld's *Lessons for Children*, alongside Rousseau's critique of fable and his recommendation of *Robinson Crusoe*, as an explicit and formally inventive meditation on what it means to model persons on pets in this way. Barbauld learns a good deal from Lockean children's writers, much as Rousseau does from Locke. But ultimately, she is wary of the tendency of writers like Trimmer, Kilner, and Wollstonecraft to exempt their readers from the domestic and figurative economy their fiction depicts. In her *Lessons for Children*, Barbauld makes conspicuous and shifting use of the second person to counter this tendency, configuring reading as an activity that neither transforms animals into persons nor makes the child a man, but rather identifies every one of us with the creaturely vulnerability of the animal, or the Crusoevian character.

The Fabulous History of Lockean Childhood

> The dog barks. The hog grunts. The pig squeaks. The horse neighs.
> The cock crows. The ass brays. The cat purrs. The kitten mews. The
> bull bellows. The cow lows. The calf bleats. Sheep bleat. The lion
> roars. The wolf howls. The tyger growls. The fox barks. Mice squeak.
> The Frog croaks. The sparrow chirps. The swallow twitters. The rook
> caws. The bittern booms. The pigeon coos. The turkey gobbles. The
> peacock screams. The beetle hums. The grasshopper chirps. The
> duck quacks. The goose cackles. Monkeys chatter. The owl hoots.
> The screech-owl shrieks. The snake hisses. Charles talks.
> —Anna Letitia Barbauld, *Lessons for Children* (2.56)

This chapter began with two moments from Barbauld's *Lessons*: a domestic
scene between a boy and his cat that sets children above animals because of
their capacity for speech; and an animal fable that features talking sheep and
wolves. Despite the oddity of their juxtaposition, these moments operate
according to fairly clear-cut distinctions between different sorts of being and
different sorts of writing: human and animal, speech and nonspeech, the realist domestic tale and the allegorical animal fable. Not all of Barbauld's *Lessons*
work in this way. Take the following "story," for example, in which Barbauld
crosses the realist tale and the animal fable to link the moral lesson of kindness
toward animals to questions about animal speech. The story begins when a
"boy was walking by himself one day, and a pretty black dog came out of a
house, and said Bow wow bow wow; and came to the little boy, and jumped
upon him, and wanted to play with him; but the little boy ran away. The dog
ran after him, and cried louder, Bow, bow, wow; but he only meant to say,
Good-morrow, how do you do?" (3.90–92). Not understanding that the dog
would simply say hello, and fearing that "a dog [might] eat up a little boy," the
boy runs away from the dog and falls into a ditch (3.90). He is finally rescued
by the dog and the human beings who better understand animal discourse,
who know to follow when the dog "scratched at the door, and said, Bow wow;
for he could not speak any plainer" (3.93). This story—of a dog who "said Bow
wow bow wow" but "meant to say, Good-morrow, how do you do?"—brings
aspects of the animal fable into an everyday domestic scene, and it presents a
more peculiar lesson about kindness and animals than the one that Charles
learns in the opening scene with Puss. For here, Charles learns that animals,
like children, are creatures with a capacity for speech.

Barbauld's story of a dog who says "bow wow" condenses the formal strategies and interspecies imaginary of early English children's literature, by crossing the child reader with the fabulous animal, as well as the conventions of animal fable with the realism of the novel or life narrative. My sense that there is something significant at stake in this intersection has not been widely shared. Indeed, it cuts across a more widespread dismissal of the children's fable, and sometimes, of the animal fable more generally. Literary critics who are interested in the fable very often lament its passing, during the eighteenth century, from a complex genre of political commentary into a vehicle for the childish fantasy of talking to pets.[11] Scholars interested in children and children's fiction, by contrast, tend to follow Lamb in dismissing children's fables, deriding the form for replacing children and their interests with miniature adults and the mores of established society. Meanwhile, historians and philosophers who are interested in animals frequently dismiss fables altogether: insisting, with Harriet Ritvo, that fable has "little connection to real creatures"; or declaring, with Derrida, that "Above all, it would be necessary to avoid fables. . . . Always a discourse *of* man, on man, indeed on the animality of man, but for and as man."[12]

I note these objections because they seem to me telling. Pointing to a lack of some "real" (real politics, real children, real animals), all these critics locate the problem with children's fable—or with fable in general—in the relation between its literal and figurative levels of meaning. Yet each set of critics conceives of this relation quite differently. On the one hand, scholars of the fable protest that the figurative dimension—the political tenor behind the animal vehicle—has dropped out of children's fables, to leave only a literal, simple-minded fantasy about animals that talk. On the other hand, scholars interested in children and animals protest that the figurative dimension of the fable has taken over, turning children and animals into mere allegorical figures for adult human beings. The difference between these positions suggests that fabulous figuration may not be as straightforward as it is sometimes taken to be. Indeed, children's fables raise rhetorical questions about the relationship between vehicle and tenor that are at the same time social and species questions about the relationship between child and adult, animal and human.

This is particularly true in the wake of Locke, who characterizes the animal fable in terms that defy any clear separation of its figurative and literal dimensions. Locke begins by praising the fable for its capacity to delight children at the same time that it teaches them valuable moral lessons. He goes on to recommend that children's editions of Aesop include illustrations of the animals that they feature, arguing that this will increase children's store of knowledge by teaching them about actual animals: the wolf, the sheep, the dog, the crow.[13] In other words, Locke thinks that fable might serve to combine moral and natural-historical lessons, to instruct children about human society and also about different animal species. As readers of Locke have often noted, Locke's sense of this combination makes the fable form especially apposite to another of his most influential pedagogical ideas: that kindness to animals is one of the fundamental moral lessons of early childhood education. Identifying animals as both the ideal figurative subjects and the primary literal objects of moral lessons for children, Locke develops a model of the fable in which animals are allegorical figures for human beings and are also actual animals—a model in which the primary moral lesson of the animal fable concerns the perils not of vanity, idleness, or pride, but of cruelty to animals.

In the wake of Locke's endorsement of the Aesopian fable and his concerns about children's treatment of animals, a host of children's writers make a move much like Barbauld's: crossing the animal fable with novelistic realism to insist that their fabulous animals are really animals, from and toward whom children learn kindness. In doing so, they everywhere call attention to the status of animals' fabulous speech—at once maintaining that real animals do not really speak, and also hinting at some more complicated idea of what it might mean to "speak." Eleanor Fenn ("Mrs. Teachwell"), for example, opens her *Fables in Monosyllables* with a dialogue between aunt and nephew meant to clear up any confusion: "LADY. Can Ants speak? / BOY. No Aunt. / LADY. Can Flies talk? / BOY. No Aunt." The *Fables* "talk of what [animals] say" only because, as the aunt puts it, "I write in the way that I think will please a child."[14] Fenn then proceeds along straightforward Lockean lines with a fable about frogs that suffer torture at the hands of young boys, and complain about their suffering. The picture gets more complex when Fenn resumes the framing dialogue after her first fable. This time, the aunt suggests a slight but significant revision to her position on animals' capacity to speak: "LADY. How is this? Can Frogs speak? / BOY. They can croak, and make a noise, but they can not speak; can they, Aunt? / LADY. No, my dear; but this man says for the Frog, what we think the poor thing would say, if it could speak."[15] In her commentary on the frog's complaint, Fenn grounds her lesson against cruelty to animals on the notion that "the poor thing" is in some sense the source of its own speech: to "say for the Frog" is to express its own, proper feelings, to give words to what it "would say." William Godwin makes this point even more explicitly in the opening of his own collection of fables for children, *Fables,*

Ancient and Modern, which maintains that fables do not put words into the mouths of animals simply to please juvenile readers with a witty instance of prosopopoeia. Or at least, this is prosopopoiea grounded in natural-historical knowledge, which Godwin insists is simply translating what an animal says into another idiom: "I have one thing to mention to you for fear of mistakes. Beasts and birds do not talk English; but they have a way of talking that they understand among one another, better than we understand them; and you, if you attend to your dog, or your cat, or your horse, you may generally make out what he wants from his voice or his look. I am going sometimes to tell you what an animal says; that is, I am going to put his meaning into English words."[16] Writers like Fenn and Godwin acknowledge that they must invent speeches for animals, by means of figuration or fabulation. But they also claim to give voice to "what an animal says," by means of translation from one language into another.

This point becomes the guiding conceit of Sarah Trimmer's novel-length and hugely popular *Fabulous Histories: Designed for the Instruction of Children, Respecting their Treatment of Animals*. Trimmer's *Fabulous Histories* has been called "the most representative children's book of the period,"[17] and indeed, it brings together a number of the central conceptual concerns and formal strategies of late eighteenth-century writing for children, developing the animal fable along the more realist lines of the novel, life narrative, or natural history (all invoked in Trimmer's "history") into the new genre of writing that Trimmer calls "fabulous history." Trimmer begins by assuring readers that we are in the conventional genre of fable, where speaking animals are allegorical figures designed for the pleasure of children: "[They] used often to express a wish, that their Birds, Cats, Dogs, &c. could *talk*, that they might hold conversations with them. Their Mamma therefore, to amuse them, composed the following Fabulous Histories; in which the sentiments and affections of a good Father and Mother, and a Family of Children, are *supposed* to be possessed by a *Nest of Redbreasts*; and others of the feathered race are, by the force of imagination, endued with the same faculties."[18] Trimmer's reminder that "Birds, Cats, Dogs, &c." do not really talk is immediately followed by an aside that suggests that they do: children should be "taught to consider them [the *Fabulous Histories*], not as containing the real conversation of Birds, (for that it is impossible we should ever understand,) but as a series of FABLES, intended to convey moral instruction applicable to themselves" (x–xi).

Throughout the narrative, Trimmer elaborates on her parenthetical qualification, as well as the generic mix that yokes "fable" to "history." She uses animals as allegorical figures to convey moral lessons about human relations. She also mixes together different orders of being and of meaning, incorporating talking animals and moral lessons into what otherwise seems a realist narrative. In Trimmer's history of two families (one avian, one human), the robins are figures for human children, who learn moral lessons along with their avian stand-ins. But the education of Robin, Dicky, Flapsy, and Pecksy Redbreast both parallels and intersects with the education of their human counterparts, Harriet and Frederick Benson. (Indeed, while the robins are schooled in a variety of subjects—the dangers of pride, or excessive fear, or disobedience—Harriet and Frederick learn only one lesson, that of kindness toward animals.) In this way, the robins are both figures for and objects of the Benson children's education, and their presence in the same narrative field complicates any straightforward understanding of the text as either an allegorical or a realist narrative, either fable or history.

This makes Trimmer's text a peculiar generic hybrid, in ways that are somewhat difficult to parse. Like typical fabulous figures, Trimmer's birds speak (English) among themselves and before the reader, playing out a host of pedagogical scenarios as figurative human beings. But in a narrative world populated by both human and animal characters, the robins also communicate in specifically avian ways. Thus when the Redbreasts are reunited with their injured eldest son in the presence of the Benson children, the birds' English is replaced by a different sort of fabulous speech: they express their happiness in song and in touch; and "they twittered a thousand questions" (130). A similar play with the fable form and its use of prosopopoeia occurs when the robins visit an aviary: "The first bird that attracted their notice was a Dove, who sat cooing by himself in a corner in accents so gentle and sweet, that a stranger to his language would have listened to them with delight; but the Redbreasts, who understood their import, heard them with sympathetic concern. 'Oh, my dear, my beloved mate,' said he, 'am I then divided from you for ever?'" (195). In this scene, the robins function to translate various avian tongues for the reader who is "stranger to [the] language." After the dove, the robins turn to "attend to the notes" of a lark, for which they once again provide an English translation: "His eyes were turned up towards the sky, he fluttered his wings, he strained his throat, and would, to a human eye, have appeared in raptures of joy; but the Redbreast perceived that he was inflamed with rage. 'And am I to be constantly confined in this horrid place?' sang he" (196–97). There is something in this scene of Sterne's sentimental interspecies conversations, in which speaking proceeds from animal motions like eating or walking. But here, speaking is associated with animal motion in its passive and passionate mode, with the sentient (perceiving, feeling, suffering) animal body.[19] Trimmer's scene of translated speech brings together the "real conversation of Birds"—rendered in realist terms as twittering, cooing, and fluttering—together with its fabulous translation, which speaks almost invariably of suffering: of longing for love, or the desire for freedom.

Throughout the *Fabulous Histories*, it is the children's mother and tutor, Mrs. Benson, who most often serves in the role of translator, teaching children to apprehend sentience or suffering as speech. She begins her language lessons early on, admonishing Harriet and Frederick for failing to feed the Redbreasts at their usual hour: "I fear your birds would bring heavy complaints against you, were they able to talk our language" (17). In subsequent encounters with animals—in the Bensons' own fields, garden, and parlor, at a nearby farm, or at neighboring house with too many pets—Mrs. Benson works to teach children to translate the complaints of different species. To improve their translation skills, she recommends the study of natural history. Mrs. Benson recalls that her own childhood propensity for catching insects was cured by her father's "excellent microscope, in which he shewed me a number of different objects; by this means I learnt, that even the minutest creatures might be as susceptible of pain as myself; and I declare I cannot put anything to death, without fancying I hear its bones crack, and that I see its blood gushing from its veins and arteries" (157–58). Despite her praise of this "excellent microscope," Mrs. Benson does not give a visual description of the "different objects" that she saw through its lens: "I can fancy them appearing to me of the same magnitude a microscope would shew them, and one of them addressing me in this manner—'Step aside, I entreat you, and let me and my associates pass in safety, that we may repair the mischief you have done to our city. The magazine of corn is fallen in, and I fear my dear parents are buried in the ruins; I hear the lamentation of my mate for the danger of our little ones; and behold two of my dear friends, who you have trod upon, in the agonies of death'" (159). On Mrs. Benson's account of looking at ants, the microscope quickly shifts from a technology of vision into one of hearing and of speaking, or making speak.

Depicting her imagination as a microscope that grants voice to ants, Mrs. Benson suggests that to regard insects with "*microscopic eyes*" is less to observe or describe than it is to personify, to "mak[e] . . . ideal speeches" (162, 160). At

the same time, by closing the rhetorical and conceptual distance between figuration and translation, Mrs. Benson characterizes personification or making
speak *as* magnification, as a mode of observation or seeing. In other words,
Mrs. Benson underscores the mediation involved in figuring animal speech,
but she associates this mediation not with poetry so much as natural history, and with a technological apparatus that preserves a material relation to
its object. Mrs. Benson insists that one does not simply fabricate the "ideal
speeches" of animals whole cloth: "in order to have a proper notion of their
form, and to be capable of making these ideal speeches, you must study Natural History" (160–61). This mode of vision, which Mrs. Benson calls "justice," is a natural-historical form of personification that fashions the speech
of animals from "a proper notion of their form": from knowledge about their
bodies, relations, passions, suffering (160). Buffon's *Natural History* provides
an instructive point of comparison here, with its insistence that we cannot
see an animal or a life—and certainly not the significant animal movement
that might count as a mode of speech—by looking into a microscope. In
the *Fabulous Histories*, Trimmer moves the microscope out of the laboratory,
into the field and the popular natural-historical genre of stories for children,
where it becomes a privileged technology of personification, of making speech
out of one's observations of animal bodies and motions. As personification
collapses into magnification and fabrication into translation, conspicuous rhetorical mediation is twinned here with the sense that speech is something one
observes directly in animal forms and movements.

Locke's interest in fable helps to specify the logic of Mrs. Benson's practice
of fabulous-historical translation, and its stakes for the education of children.
As I discuss in Chapter 2, one of the central innovations of Locke's political philosophy was to assert, against defenders of absolutist government, that
there are different types of dominion that accord with different types of being:
most fundamentally, property right (a limitless dominion over nonhuman
beings that is constituted by appropriation) and political authority (a limited
dominion over human beings that is constituted by consent). In condensed
form, Locke figures these two modes of dominion as eating and speaking, and
he insists that they are utterly separate: that there are some kinds of beings
you speak to (human persons) and others that you eat (anything else). Even
if this insistence is troubled by the creatures of Genesis in the *First Treatise*,
or by a particularly eloquent parrot in the *Essay*, Locke repeatedly asserts that
the faculty of speech consolidates the category of the human person, and sets
other creatures outside of its bounds.

Locke's insistence that speech divides human persons from nonhuman things—and so, marks the bounds of a political society constituted by contract—makes children a more significant problem than either biblical creatures or Brazilian parrots. At least, it makes children a problem much closer to home. In both the *Essay* and *Some Thoughts Concerning Education*, Locke makes plain that, for a long while, children are like animals: animate creatures without speech or reason, wholly occupied with the perceptions, sensations, and motions that humans share with animals.[20] In the *Two Treatises of Government*, by contrast, Locke insists that even at birth children are not like animals: they cannot be subject to the unlimited type of dominion Locke calls property. This point is crucial for Locke, because someone like Filmer would defend absolutist government by citing the fact of childhood: the fact that, as Locke puts it, "no Man is Born free" (142). Children do indeed seem to trouble Locke's figure of the human person with a form of human being that looks clearly animal. But Locke works hard to find a place for the child in his political system, arguing, "Children . . . are not born in this full state of Equality, though they are born to it"; or again, that "we are *born Free*, as we are born Rational; not that we have actually the Exercise of either" (304, 308). In his political philosophy, then, Locke resolves all creatures into his two grand categories of (human) person and (nonhuman) thing and accords each its own proper mode of dominion. At the same time, he acknowledges that children are more properly in-between creatures. They cannot be owned, or eaten; nor can they enter into political society, a realm constituted by consent or speech.

At this point, it is worth recalling Lamb's ridicule of writers like Barbauld and Trimmer. What Lamb fails to take seriously is that for this "Crew," as for Locke, the lesson that "a Horse is an animal, & Billy is better than a Horse," is not an "insignificant & vapid" truism presented in the form of "Knowledge." Pairing children with animals, and speech with the sentient or suffering body, these writers repeatedly pose as an open question something that Lamb takes to be self-evident: what is it, in Lamb's words, that "made the child a man"? Much as it is for Locke, this is a real question for late eighteenth-century writers for children. And while this sounds like a developmental question, it is also, and perhaps more fundamentally, a political issue. According to a thesis forwarded most famously by historian Philippe Ariès, the developmental question of how to make the child a man only emerged as such during the seventeenth and eighteenth centuries, as childhood came to be understood as a unique stage of life.[21] Citing Locke in particular, Ala A. Alryyes transposes Ariès's thesis about the invention of childhood into a more explicitly political register, and proposes a shift in emphasis: "it is not the child who was missing before then, but rather the adult. The emergence of childhood . . . [is] inextricably intertwined with the modern citizen's desire to differentiate himself or herself from the dependent subject of absolutism, a subject long imaged as a child."[22] In Alryyes's adaptation of Ariès's thesis, Locke (and those political philosophers who followed him, like Rousseau) develops an account of childhood in order to develop an account of adulthood. On this view, "child" and "man" are primarily political categories, and only secondarily either biological or psychological stages. To make the child a man is thus to make him the kind of being that social contract theorists like Locke envision: an independent being whose political status is secured by speech.

Locke's recommendation of fable is linked to the peculiar status of the child in his political philosophy. The fable is the literary form of speaking animals. It is also, as Jayne Lewis puts it, "the only literary form in which the principal characters regularly devour one another."[23] The fable thus takes up at the level of form the set of relations on which Lockean politics are centered, as well as the aim that links these politics to his pedagogy: the aim of transforming eating into speaking, of making persons—in the sense of speakers—out of animals. In the *Essay*, Locke suggests that to make the child a man—to move from the sentient animal to the speaking person—is a matter of child development. In the *Two Treatises*, he insists that this development is in an important sense a matter of becoming what one already is. One cannot exactly make a child a man, because childhood is a mode of animal life that is always already personhood. Ultimately, this is the reason that Locke grants his naturalized version of fable a privileged place in his educational program: because its fabulous-historical logic identifies different orders—animal and human, child and adult, sentience and speech—without wholly pinning down the logic of this (quasi-figurative, quasi-literal) identification. This fabulous-historical logic enables Locke to bring children inside the political realm, but to leave this realm shaped around "speech." In doing so, however, this fabulous-historical logic opens Lockean childhood onto questions of kindness with as well as toward animals—questions of "kindness" in its ontological as well as its ethical sense. In other words, by the same logic that the fabulous history incorporates children into its social order, it would also seem to incorporate animals.

The Life of the Family Pet

The Lockean tradition of children's literature is everywhere shaped by the promise and the problems that emerge from its fabulous-historical identification of sentience and speech. In Trimmer's *Fabulous Histories*, for example, the expansive ideal of configuring every animal as a speaker—and so, as a person—comes up against the exigencies of animal life, and especially, the intractable relations of eating and being eaten. This occurs most acutely when the Benson children visit a neighboring farm, which houses not only humans and birds but also cows, chickens, turkeys, sheep, pigs, bees, butterflies, moths, caterpillars, fish, eels, frogs, and toads. The visit to the farm is the centerpiece of the *Fabulous Histories*—the longest section of the narrative by far, which embodies its ideal vision of kindness to animals in the figures of Mr. and Mrs. Wilson, farmers–cum–animal advocates: "As there are no Courts of Justice in which [beasts] can seek redress, I erect one for them in my own breast," Mr. Wilson explains (183). It is in the Wilsons' garden that Mrs. Benson calls on natural-historical knowledge to translate the cracking bones and gushing blood of ants into ideal speeches about perishing children, lost friends, and the destroyed fruits of labor.

In some respects, the Wilsons' farm epitomizes Trimmer's capacious domestic ideal, extending kindness in the shape of speech even to ants. At the same time, the farm is the site of considerable anxiety, as Mrs. Benson works hard to separate animals who speak from animals that are eaten: "Miss Harriet observed the innocent countenances of the sheep and lambs, and said she thought it was a thousand pities to kill them. It is so, my dear, said her mamma, but we must not indulge our feelings too far in respect to animals which are given us for food" (172). Mrs. Benson makes speeches for ants, then, but she stops short at sheep and lambs, and at caterpillars: "Caterpillars and snails, it is true, we are obliged frequently to destroy, on account of their devouring fruit and vegetables" (157). In Trimmer, who tries as hard as anyone to follow her own domestic vision to its logical limits, insects are both privileged speakers and figures for the specter of an all-encompassing consumption, lives that somehow present a threat to our own: "I often regret, said Mrs. Benson, that so many lives should be sacrificed to preserve ours; but we must eat animals, or they would at length eat us, at least all that would otherwise support us" (149). The domestic imperative to construe all relations in terms of speaking here morphs into its opposite: everyone and everything is eating and being eaten. As they tour the Wilson's farm, Mrs. Benson continues her uneasy effort to limit feeling—and speaking—when it comes to food. But Harriet understands the potential reach of her mother's fabulous-historical translation: "The speech you made for the ant, mamma, said Harriet, has scarcely ever been out of my head since: I should like to hear what you could say for every live creature we see. I had need to have strong lungs, my dear, to perform such a task as that, replied Mrs. Benson" (184). Taking up the task that overwhelms Mrs. Benson, Harriet comes to see speaking everywhere, even or perhaps especially at table: "I shall be ready to make speeches for every piece as it lies in a dish before me" (165).

The tension that surfaces at the Wilson's farm—between Harriet's desire to "say for every liv[ing] creature" and Mrs. Benson's sense that it is impossible to do so—is the central tension of the fabulous-historical tradition of children's literature more generally. Dorothy Kilner's *Life and Perambulation of a Mouse* plays out this tension at the level of form, and begins to indicate quite explicitly its consequences for children. Kilner's *Life of a Mouse* is significant as one of the first it-narratives written for children; it helped to speed the genre's migration into the emerging realm of children's literature.[24] Like *Tristram Shandy*, Kilner's *Life of a Mouse* is self-conscious about the link it draws between the living animal and the literary genre of the life narrative, and in Kilner, this self-consciousness focuses especially on animal speech. The tale opens with a human narrator who sojourns at a manor house, Meadow-Hall, trying to fulfill the task their host has assigned: to "relate the history of their own lives."[25] The narrator begins to despair at her task but then encounters a novel solution: "The adventures of my life (though deeply interesting to myself) will be insipid and unentertaining to others, especially to my young hearers: I cannot therefore attempt it;—Then write mine, which may be more diverting, said a little squeaking voice, which sounded as if close to me. . . . Will you write my history?" (1.xi). The voice comes from a mouse called Nimble. The narrator confesses to be "much surprised to be so addressed by such an animal" but agrees to serve as its amanuensis, and the text shifts from her framing narrative to Nimble's first-person narration of his life, ostensibly his transcribed first-person speech.

Kilner's autobiography of a mouse enacts the sort of fabulous-historical translation that Mrs. Benson teaches, rendering sentience as speech, the living animal as the literary form of a first-person *Life*. It also acknowledges that this translation is not available to all animals. On first view, Kilner's *Life and Perambulation of a Mouse* appears to depict generic or species life. This is the life narrative of "*a Mouse*" after all, and like a figure in an animal fable, Nimble in many respects seems to represent his kind (he moves, for example, "with all the nimbleness of its species" [xii]). But Nimble's narration serves to single him out from his species—to make this the story of an exceptional specimen rather than a generic figure, the *Life* of *this* particular mouse rather than simply of *a* mouse, or Mouse. This occurs within the narrative itself, as the events of the story separate Nimble from his siblings, who are killed one by one. After suffering all manner of pain and peril, Nimble alone is discovered by the woman who, in the framing conceit of the tale, hears and records his speech. He pleads with her for his life: "for pity sake, have compassion on me, and either put me out of my present misery by instantly killing me, or else giving me something to eat; for, if you knew my sufferings, I am sure it would grieve your heart" (2.x). The woman agrees to protect Nimble from cats and from people, to both save and write his life: "That most gladly . . . I will do; you shall live in this large, green-flowered tin canister, and run in and out when you please, and I will keep you supplied with food" (2.84). This scene condenses the fabulous-historical form of the narrative as a whole: a form of domestication that translates animal life into the exceptional figure of the family pet, and makes Nimble something more or at least other than "a Mouse."

Like Gulliver in Brobdingnag, Kilner is keenly aware of the limits of a domestic ideal centered on the figure of the family pet, which depends wholly on the translator who transforms mouse life—the undifferentiated and expendable life of "vermin and animals"—into the protected first-person *Life* of Nimble the mouse (1.47). The consequences of these limits for both animals and children become the centerpiece of the scene that Nimble witnesses between a young boy, Charles, Charles's father, and Nimble's brother Brighteyes. When the father finds Charles dangling the mouse by its tail, Nimble recalls: "*Brighteyes* then gave a fresh squeak from the violence of his pain. The gentleman then turning hastily round, exclaimed eagerly, What is it *alive?*" (1.43). In this moment, Charles's father apprehends Brighteyes's squeak as a sign of suffering and suffering as a mode of speech, as Charles himself fails to do. In doing so, the father begins to identify being alive and being a *Life*; he also, and more troublingly, begins to identify child and animal, on the grounds of their common susceptibility to pain. Demanding what right Charles has to torment another living creature, the father asserts an analogy between Charles and the mouse, as similarly sentient creatures: "If it is only because you are larger, and so have it in your power, I beg you will consider, how you would like, that either myself, or some great giant, as much larger than you as you are bigger than the mouse, should hurt and torment you?" (1.45). He quickly proceeds to literalize the identification he asks Charles to imagine, as he subjects his son to the same torment to which Charles had subjected the mouse:

> Since you think pain so very trifling an evil, try, *Charles*, how you like *that*, said he, giving him at the same time some severe strokes with his horse-whip. The boy then cried, and called out, I do not like it at all, I do not like it at all. Neither did the *mouse*, replied his father . . . he did not *like* it, and told you so in the language which you perfectly well understood; but *you* would not attend to his cries: *you* thought it pleasant to hear it squeak, because you were *bigger* and did not *feel* its torture. *I* now am bigger than *you*, and do not feel *your* pain, I therefore shall not yet leave off. (1.47–48)

While Trimmer translates the speech of animals in order that children see their suffering and treat them with kindness, Kilner's father begins with suffering, inflicting pain as a crucial step in teaching Charles to hear a mouse speak his own words, to translate its squeaks to mean "I do not like it at all." In this moment of painfully literalized identification between child and animal, the promise of the fabulous history—the promise of a mode of speech that is identical to the suffering animal body and thus given directly and immediately to vision—gives way to the wholly mediated notion of intelligibility, a mode of speech entirely at the mercy of other people to apprehend or attend to as such.

Wollstonecraft's contribution to children's literature, *Original Stories, from Real Life*, spells out the logic of animal intelligibility at work throughout Kilner's *Life and Perambulation of a Mouse*, and in the scene of Charles's beating in particular. Wollstonecraft is explicitly indebted to both Kilner and Trimmer—in her *Thoughts on the Education of Daughters*, Wollstonecraft singles out Kilner's *Life of a Mouse* for recommendation; in *Original Stories*, she uses Trimmer's subtitle as the heading for her first three chapters, and she has the governess, Mrs. Mason, give her pupils Trimmer's text to read. When the elder pupil, Caroline, asks if she might share the *Fabulous Histories* with a neighboring child, Mrs. Mason repeats Trimmer's caution: "Certainly, . . . if you can make her understand that birds never talk."[26] When actual animals appear on the scene, Mrs. Mason likewise echoes Trimmer's qualification of what it means to "talk": "The country people frequently say,—How can you treat a poor dumb beast ill; and a stress is very properly laid on the word dumb;—dumb they appear to those who do not observe" (11). Following Trimmer, Mrs. Mason insists that only "those who do not observe" take an ostensible lack of speech to imply an actual lack of speech.[27]

At the start of the *Original Stories*, Caroline and her sister, Mary, clearly belong in the class of "those who do not observe": "the children were regardless of the surrounding beauties, and ran eagerly after some insects to destroy them" (2). Their education gets underway as Mrs. Mason, like the father in Kilner's *Life of a Mouse*, puts the girls in their place: "You are often troublesome—I am stronger than you—yet I do not kill you" (4). Prompted by the analogy Mrs. Mason asserts between children and insects, Caroline and Mary begin "to observe," and to observe, in particular, the "speech" of the "dumb." Caroline and Mary first notice a lark singing: "The children watched it, and listened to its melody, They wondered what it was thinking of—of its young family, they concluded: it flew over the hedge, and drawing near, they heard the young ones chirp" (6). As the girls watch and listen to the bird, they begin to practice the sort of fabulous-historical observation that understands animal motions, sounds, and bodies to be intelligible forms, the signs of thought and feeling. Their lesson continues as "an idle boy" enters the scene and fires his shot at the lark and its mate. At this point, Mrs. Mason instructs the girls not only to identify animals as intelligible, but to identify this sort of intelligibility—the intelligibility of animal suffering—as their own: "the cock, had one leg broke, and both its wings shattered; and its little eyes seemed starting out of their sockets, it was in such exquisite pain. The children turned from it. Look at it, said Mrs. Mason; do you not see it suffers as much, and more than you did when you had small-pox?" (6–7). This lesson—to "look at it" and see "it" as "you," its suffering body as your own intelligible form—is continued in the next field: "they met another boy with a nest in his hand, and on a tree near him saw the mother, who, forgetting her natural timidity, followed the spoiler; and her intelligible tones of anguish reached the ears of the children, whose hearts now first felt the intelligible emotions of humanity" (8). As the children's "intelligible emotions" are awakened by the "intelligible tones" of other creatures, Caroline and Mary return the nest to its proper place, and at last ascend to their own: "give me your hands, my little girls," Mrs. Mason says to them, "you have done good this morning, you are my fellow-creatures" (9–10). In these opening scenes of the *Original Stories*, Wollstonecraft makes plain that it is children who start out "dumb" and proceed to speech, identifying sentient life as speaking *Life* in order to achieve their own fabulous-historical identity: that of "intelligible . . . humanity." In Wollstonecraft, in other words, children become persons much as Nimble becomes a pet—by becoming intelligible beings, legible to those more powerful than they.

Like Mrs. Benson with her microscope or Nimble's amanuensis with her green-flowered canister, Wollstonecraft's Mrs. Mason is the all-powerful arbiter of such intelligibility, the internal reader/translator who transfigures dumb animals into fellow-creatures. In story after story, she brings suffering to speech, putting into words a dog's "dumb anguish" when its master drowns its pups, or the "speechless anguish" and "inarticulate accents" of a man who likewise suffers the loss of his children (16–17, 22, 25). Mrs. Mason's term for her acts of personification or prosopopoeia is "pity." Sometimes, though, Mrs. Mason's "pity" does not serve to attribute speech or personhood, but to take it away. When Caroline and Mary fight over who will care for their new pet birds, for example, one bird falls to the ground and dies. Mrs. Mason replies with an admonition: "I pity you. You are now inferior to the animals that graze on the common" (28). She follows this remark with the story of Jane B., whose anger leads to the death of Jane's dog, the dog's litter of unborn pups, Jane's mother, and finally, Jane herself. Perhaps the most conspicuous effect of Jane's anger, throughout the story, is the way that it moves her down a chain of being until she is truly "inferior to . . . animals"—not simply speechless or unintelligible but altogether inanimate. In life, Mrs. Mason remarks, Jane "resembled a heap of combustible matter"; in death, her "lifeless countenance displayed the marks of convulsive anger" (33, 34). Wollstonecraft pictures Jane's loss of intelligibility (of personhood, animation, and finally life itself) as an abdication, a consequence of Jane's actions and uncontrolled passions. But there is a clear sense that Mrs. Mason holds sway, exercising the power of pity to deny as well as grant intelligibility, transforming children into fellow creatures or into heaps of lifeless matter, translating life into speech or bringing it to an end altogether.

By developing children's literature in its fabulous-historical mode, writers like Trimmer, Kilner, and Wollstonecraft elaborate the perplexing and precarious logic of Lockean childhood, which figures animals as persons but understands persons, finally, as pets. By identifying cooing, squeaking, barking, and speaking as different tongues that require nothing more than translation, these children's writers affirm that it is not a problem if children are (like) animals, because animals are also persons, sentience is also speech. At the same time, they make plain that this sort of identity is a matter of intelligibility or legibility, which means that it is also exceptional, contingent, and determined from without. As Trimmer's Mrs. Benson puts it: "Though they cannot speak our language, each kind has one of its own, which is perfectly understood by those of their own species; and so far intelligible to us, as to convince us they are susceptible of joy, grief, fear, anger, and resentment" (60). The fabulous history might incorporate children—and animals—into its social order by identifying the capacity to move and be moved, to feel and to suffer, as a sort of speech. But it does this, finally, by identifying "speaking" as being read, and by locating reading within a clear hierarchy of species. Intelligibility is always, in Trimmer's words, "intelligib[ility] to us."

In the fabulous-historical tradition of children's literature, then, children and animals are always already persons, as they are in Locke. But in this tradition, personhood is not the inviolable and autonomous form that Lockean politics would seem to require. Instead, it is pethood, the creaturely and dependent status that so troubled Swift.[28] To put the point this way is to recall the vulnerability of Gulliver in Brobdingnag. It is also and more directly to anticipate Rousseau, the great successor to and critic of Lockean education. In *Emile*, Rousseau takes pointed aim at Locke's commendation of fable, insisting that any literary genre that turns people into pets is singularly unsuited to making the child a man. Writing after and against Locke, Rousseau works to replace the figure of the family pet with the radically generic and species logic of identifying with or even as one's fellow creatures, a logic of identification that Rousseau designates by the term "pity." Remarkably, this is a sort of identification that Rousseau associates with reading *Robinson Crusoe*, and it underwrites, in turn, Barbauld's astonishing and innovative *Lessons for Children*—perhaps more of a blight on "all that is Human" than even Lamb realized.

To Make the Child a Man: Rousseau and the Suffering Animal

Part way through the second book of *Emile; or, On Education*, Rousseau declares the fable unfit for pedagogical purposes. He focuses his remarks on La Fontaine's "The Crow and the Fox," which begins when a fox spies a crow with a piece of cheese in his beak, and goads the crow to *show his fine voice* (114). The crow falls prey to the fox's flattery and opens his beak to speak (or sing); food rather than words fall from his mouth, and into the waiting jaws of the fox. In the course of his remarks on the fable, Rousseau turns to the problem of animal speech. Imagining a child's response to the line in which the fox "*Made to [the crow] a speech*," Rousseau writes: "A *speech*! Foxes speak, then? They speak, then, the same language as crows?" Rousseau counsels his imagined preceptor to take care: "Weigh your response well before making it. It is more important than you think" (112). Rousseau does not specify what is so important about this response, nor does he spell out exactly what he takes to be the problem with fable. But he suggests that it has to do with the relationship between the child reader and the speaking animal, and he puts his objection in terms of identification: "In the preceding fable children make fun of the crow, but they all take a fancy to the fox. In the fable which follows, you believe you are giving them the cicada as an example, and it is not at all so. It is the ant they will choose. One does not like being humiliated. They will always take the advantageous role. It is the choice of *amour-propre*; it is a very natural choice" (115). Reading fables, Rousseau cautions, children identify with the clever fox rather than the outwitted crow; instead of a lesson in the danger of vanity, they are schooled in the powers of speech.

On Frances Ferguson's reading of Rousseau, this sort of misidentification is the fault of the fable form. Just as fables depict contests of discursive power at the level of content (the fox who outwits the crow with the trickery of words), they replicate these contests at the level of form, separating readers who are "in" on the fable's meaning (the discursively powerful foxes, the "speakers") from those who are not (the crows who lose their cheese, the "eaten"). The form of the fable thus works against its ostensible lesson, compelling children—like everyone else—to identify "with the animal on the winning side."[29] Ferguson puts the point this way: "If the legend about the fable precisely holds it out as a means of outwitting tyrants, what Rousseau has to say about it suggests an important challenge to that view—namely, that the lore about the fable includes no stories about tyrants who were outraged by them, who, that is, did not feel themselves to be in on the joke. By this account, the fable itself represents flattery incarnate, as it plays upon the child's (or the tyrant's) desire for a knowledge that seems to separate the sheep from the goats, and in which the beholder is always a sheep."[30] On this view, Rousseau's objection to fable resembles Swift's concern about satire: that it operates as a ball bandied to and fro, which lets every individual escape. The reader of fable is necessarily a fox (or a sheep, in Ferguson's terms); the crow is always other people.

Put in the terms of early English children's literature, Ferguson's point is that the reader of fable is never in the position of Kilner's Charles or Wollstonecraft's Jane B., or even of Wollstonecraft's Caroline and Mary: the position of being or failing to be intelligible, of sentient animal life that might or might not be translated into speech. However precarious the position of the child and the animal within the fable or fabulous history, the position of the reader is altogether different. Set outside of the domestic economy that (sometimes) identifies sentience with speech, the reader is configured as the inviolable arbiter of identification and intelligibility, on the model of all-powerful readers like Mrs. Mason or Mrs. Benson—the foxes of the fabulous history. In this way, the fabulous history constitutes its reader as the sort of Lockean person that the children and animals within the texts can never be: a bearer of intrinsic meaning, the self-sufficient subject of speech.

This might sound like a good thing. But Rousseau warns that in the case of children, at least, it is also patently false. The child is not possibly "in" on the fable; she is not possessed of such facility with language. As a result, the sense of foxhood (that is, the sense of an independent or inviolable personhood) that children acquire in reading fables actually depends on others—a point that Rousseau illustrates with an anecdote about a child who reads the life of Alexander and receives the "tribute of praises" from adults, even though he "understood nothing at all of the story he had told so well" (110). Rousseau condemns fables, that is, because they beguile children with a feeling of mastery that is in fact not mastery but dependence. As Ferguson puts it, the fable functions as "a parable of inequality," inducting children into relations of domination/dependence by generating the sentiment of amour-propre that is both cause and consequence of such relations.[31] If Locke celebrates the fable for transforming the order of eating (the order of nature, animality, childhood, might) into the order of speaking (the order of society, humanity, personhood, right), Rousseau cautions that this transformation is illusory, because speech itself always resolves into reading—or more precisely, into being read. And being read is a matter of power, of the relations of domination and dependence that Rousseau, like the genre of the animal fable, routinely figures as eating and being eaten. Rousseau thus makes explicit a caution also sounded in children's literature by Trimmer, Kilner, and Wollstonecraft: forms of subjectivity grounded on the capacity for speech ultimately rest one's person on other people, on those with the power to grant or deny intelligibility. In the naked logic of fable, Rousseau insists, speaking is simply eating and being eaten; persons are nothing more than pets.[32]

The generic tendency to disguise might as right, creaturely dependence as voluntary and interpersonal relation, makes fable the literary epitome of civil society for Rousseau, a state that he memorably characterizes, near the end of

Emile, as one in which we "can no longer do without eating man" (454). In *Emile*, Rousseau's task is to conceive civil society differently, and he begins by decrying domestication in recognizably Swiftian terms, as an engine of degeneration that disfigures the human species into all kinds of unnatural, because monstrously individuated, creatures:

> Everything is good as it leaves the hand of the Author of things; everything degenerates in the hands of man. He forces one soil to nourish the products of another, one tree to bear the fruit of another. He mixes and confuses the climates, the elements, the seasons. He mutilates his dog, his horse, his slave. He turns everything upside down; he disfigures everything; he loves deformity, monsters. He wants nothing as nature made it, not even man; for him, man must be trained like a school horse; man must be fashioned in keeping with his fancy like a tree in his garden. (37)

In *Emile*, Rousseau sets out to do something he thinks has never before been done: to make the child a man rather than a pet, a monster, or something to eat.

The terms of this project are already sketched in Rousseau's "Discourse on the Origin and Foundations of Inequality Among Men" where, under the rubric of domestication, Rousseau denounces the sort of education that appears to lead to "the perfection of the individual, and in fact, [tends] toward the decrepitude of the species."[33] In the "Discourse on Inequality," Rousseau focuses his attention on the formal and political problem of the right relation between individual and species that so concerned Hobbes and Swift. And he addresses this problem in Buffon's natural-historical idiom, by making "man in general" the object of his explicit address: "Oh Man, from whatever country you come, whatever your opinions may be, listen: here is your history. . . . It is, so to speak, the life of your species that I am going to describe to you in accordance with the qualities which you received and which your education and habits could corrupt but not destroy."[34] In *Emile*, Rousseau takes up the project that he envisions in the "Discourse on Inequality," of developing an education that would not set the individual and the species at odds but would rather, in Rousseau's words, "Suit the education of man to man, not to what is not man" (194). He lauds Emile as "a young man . . . who has not received a particular form," and assures readers that this is how he will stay: "On leaving my hands he will, I admit, be neither magistrate nor soldier nor priest. He will, in the first place, be a man" (254, 41–42). *Emile* thus sets out to realize what remains in the "Discourse on Inequality" an absent and abstract figure. It sets out to materialize, in the person of Emile, the "Man" of Rousseau's apostrophe.[35]

There are some curious features of what it means, for Rousseau, to make the child a man (or simply, Man). Rousseau explains that the education of Man must start by eliminating all that belongs to a particular people, rank, or station, "regard[ing] as incontestably belonging to man only what was common to all, at whatever age, in whatever rank, in whatever nation" (254). What remains after such elimination, Rousseau suggests, may not be specifically human: "Men are not naturally kings, or lords, or courtiers, or rich men. All are born naked and poor; all are subject to the miseries of life, to sorrows, ills, needs, and pains of every kind. Finally, all are condemned to death. This is what truly belongs to man. This is what no mortal is exempt from" (222). Like Swift, Rousseau sets out to identify "what truly belongs to man," rather than to particular individuals, ranks, or professions. But as he argues that what is proper to man is proper to all who are susceptible to "sorrows, ills, needs, and pains," and ultimately, to suffering and death, Rousseau begins to suggest that what "truly belongs to man" might also belong to animals. At times, he approaches this point quite explicitly, as he does when he notes that animals fare no worse for their lack of medical care: "I will be told that animals, living in a way that conforms more to nature, ought to be subject to fewer ills than we are. Well, their way of life is precisely the one I want to give my pupil" (55). If the task of *Emile* is to make the child a man, Rousseau here seems to say that this means making him animal.[36]

The central role of animal identity in Rousseau's account of child development is most evident, and most perplexing, in the crucial Rousseauvian sentiment of pity. In *Emile*, Rousseau describes the onset of pity this way:

> Emile, having reflected little on sensitive beings, will know late what it is to suffer and die. He will begin to have gut reactions at the sounds of complaints and cries, the sight of blood flowing will make him avert his eyes; the convulsions of a dying animal will cause him an ineffable distress before he knows whence come these new movements within him. . . . Thus is born pity, the first relative sentiment which touches the human heart according to the order of nature. To become sensitive and pitying, the child must know that there are beings like him who suffer what he has suffered, who feel the pains

he has felt, and that there are others whom he ought to conceive of as able to feel them too. In fact, how do we let ourselves be moved by pity if not by transporting ourselves outside of ourselves and identifying with the suffering animal, by leaving, as it were, our own being to take on its being? We suffer only so much as we judge that it suffers. It is not in ourselves, it is in him that we suffer. Thus, no one becomes sensitive until his imagination is animated and begins to transport him out of himself. (222–23)

Rousseau's notion of pity is famously complex, and it has seemed to some readers to vary in significant ways from one text to the next.[37] But across Rousseau's different discussions of pity, one point recurs. The paradigmatic scene of pity, for Rousseau, involves being moved, transported, or animated by identifying with a suffering animal.

This striking fact about Rousseauvian pity opens onto to another. There are no suffering animals in *Emile*. Emile's imagined reactions to "the sight of blood flowing" and "the convulsions of a dying animal" sound very much like an introduction to the sort of scene that Trimmer's Mrs. Benson presents through her microscope ("I hear its bones crack, and . . . I see its blood gushing from its veins and arteries"), or that Wollstonecraft's Mrs. Mason pictures ("the cock, [with] one leg broke, and both its wings shattered; and its little eyes seemed starting out of their sockets, it was in such exquisite pain"). But nowhere does Emile's preceptor orchestrate an encounter between Emile and a suffering animal, as he orchestrates so much else. Nor does he subject Emile to the kind of suffering to which Trimmer and Wollstonecraft subject their pupils. In *Emile*, there are no beatings, no episodes of smallpox, no painful accidents or injuries—nothing of the physical, animal suffering that repeatedly serves to prepare children like Wollstonecraft's Caroline or Kilner's Charles for pity on the model of fabulous-historical translation. Instead, Rousseau offers only vague hints about how the sentiment of pity is to be cultivated: "To excite and nourish this nascent sensibility, to guide it or follow it in its natural inclination, what is there to do other than to offer the young man objects on which the expansive force of his heart can act—objects which swell the heart, which extend it to other beings, which make it find itself everywhere outside of itself—and carefully to keep away those which contract and concentrate the heart and tighten the spring of the human *I*?" (223). Despite the centrality of animals to Rousseau's account of pity, and despite the centrality of pity to Rousseau's account of education, Emile gets no magnified insects, mangled birds, or squeaking mice, the objects to which children's writers turn again and again to "swell the heart, [and] extend it to other beings." What he gets instead, I think, is *Robinson Crusoe*. This is the primary object Rousseau offers his pupil in order to "make [the heart] find itself everywhere outside of itself," to expand rather than contract "the human *I*."

Admittedly, this is an odd suggestion. But consider the oddity of Rousseau's recommendation of *Robinson Crusoe*:

> I hate books. They only teach one to talk about what one does not know. . . . Since we absolutely must have books, there exists one which, to my taste, provides the most felicitous treatise on natural education. This book will be the first that my Emile will read. For a long time it will alone compose his whole library, and it will always hold a distinguished place there. . . . What, then, is this marvelous book? Is it Aristotle? Is it Pliny? Is it Buffon? No. It is *Robinson Crusoe*. . . .
>
> This novel, disencumbered of all its rigmarole, beginning with Robinson's shipwreck near his island and ending with the arrival of the ship which comes to take him from it, will be both Emile's entertainment and instruction through the period which is dealt with here. I want to make him dizzy; I want him constantly to be busy with his mansions, his goats, his plantations; I want him to learn in detail, not from books but from things, all that must be known in such a situation; I want him to think he is Robinson himself. (184–85)

Rousseau says that he assigns *Robinson Crusoe*, "disencumbered of all its rigmarole," because he wants Emile to learn "not from books but from things" (185). Some commentators have tried to make sense of this remark by reading it in terms of the generic contrast one might draw between the realist *Crusoe* and a figurative form like fable.[38] On this reading, to "disencumber" *Crusoe* of its "rigmarole" is to remove any hint of political or religious allegory, in order to permit the kind of wholly literal reading of which a child is capable. Unlike La Fontaine's fables, the expurgated *Crusoe* would not teach Emile to talk about what he does not know (and so would not subject him to the dominion of others) because it is filled only with material things, the stuff of Emile's own experience.

This sort of reading certainly finds support in Rousseau's discussion of *Crusoe*, and of fable. But there is a good deal that remains puzzling about

Rousseau's recommendation of *Crusoe*—not least, the fact that Rousseau recommends learning "not from books but from things" in a book, while recommending another. So too, many of the "things" in Defoe's novel—mansions, goats, plantations—presumably take Emile well beyond anything he might know from personal experience. Finally, redacting *Crusoe* as Rousseau recommends does not necessarily put an end to allegory or figurative reading. Between Crusoe's shipwreck and the arrival of his eventual rescuers—the section of the novel that Rousseau characterizes as "Robinson Crusoe on his island, alone"—there is plenty of fodder for traditional allegorical readings, from religious conversion to colonial ambition (184). What there is not, in Rousseau's abridged *Crusoe*, is other people. This may sound like a simple point, but on my view it is crucial to understanding Rousseau's rejection of fable and his endorsement of Defoe's novel. If the foxes and crows of fable generate amour-propre, originating inequality and the civil regime of eating men, Rousseau insists that *Robinson Crusoe* works differently. Centered wholly on the character Crusoe, Rousseau understands Defoe's novel to operate according to—or simply as—the sentiment of pity.

Once again, this is a peculiar claim, and it rests on Rousseau's peculiar, and peculiarly intransitive, notion of pity, in which the object of pity matters less than the sort of subjectivity that it generates, and avoids generating. Rousseau presents pity as a salutary alternative to sentiments like envy: "the best-conceived sentiment that man can have about his species," he writes, is to "pity them and not want to resemble them" (236). At the same time, Rousseau registers the troubling possibility that pity might separate Emile from his species rather than to identify him with other men: "He will say to himself, 'I am wise, and men are mad.' In pitying them, he will despise them" (245). Rousseau worries, here, about the tendency of pity to shade into contempt, which is simply envy, turned on its head. He warns that this is "the error to be most feared" (245). It is the error of the philosopher in the "Discourse on Inequality," who regards the suffering of others and says: "Perish if you will, I am safe."[39] It is also the error of kings: "Why are kings without pity for their subjects? Because they count on never being mere men" (224). Rousseau insists that the sentiment of pity, properly conceived and felt, does not permit such sentences ("Perish if you will, I am safe"), because it does not admit of the opposition on which they depend, between myself and men, between "I" and "you." The first person may well be a species form, as Sterne suggests in *Tristram Shandy*. But for Rousseau, it is not enough to say "I" and so set myself under the sign of the species. It is not even enough to engage in the sort of reading practice that Hobbes envisions, in which the self is the key to the kind—and thus to say what Gulliver will not: "I am man." Rousseau counsels that the sentiment of pity must be cultivated with care because it asserts identity not just between mankind and me, but between me and you: "Do not, therefore, accustom your pupil to regard the sufferings of the unfortunate and the labors of the poor from the height of his glory; and do not hope to teach him to pity them if he considers them alien to him" (224). In short, Rousseau requires that one not only speak but also finish Gulliver's sentence: I am man, and so are you.

On Rousseau's account, pity is a delicate operation, and difficult to sustain, because like amour-propre, it is a relative sentiment that depends on a comparison between self and other, me and you. Pity would thus seem to do what it is meant avoid: to split I from you, myself from men. But while the emotions of amour-propre (like envy or contempt) assert a qualitative distinction between persons, judging oneself to be better or worse endowed in some attribute than some other person, pity asserts a purely formal distinction. The formal difference at play in pity ("the child must know . . . that there are others") thus rests on a more fundamental sort of identity—the identity of attributes that make each one of us the kind of being we all are, a being that suffers or feels ("who suffer what he has suffered, who feel the pains he has felt").[40] Pity at once apprehends that I am not you, we inhabit different positions; and that I am you, I suffer what you suffer. This is the sort of identity Emile is meant to embody in the common species form of "Man." Emile (or, simply, "Man") may feel "the best-conceived sentiment that man can have about his species," which is "to pity them and not want to resemble them" (236). But Rousseau is not after resemblance. Emile ("Man") may not resemble other men; he nonetheless and simply is identical to them. To recall Watt's remarks on Swift, we might conclude that for Rousseau, the individual and the species are indeed "ultimately the same thing." But this identity between individual and species proceeds by way of the second person, by way of the experience of pity that identifies me and you.

From here, we are in a position to return to Rousseau's critique of fable, to his comments on *Robinson Crusoe*, and to the issue of identification. Rousseau's problem with fable is not only that the child misidentifies with the fox. It is that in doing so, he necessarily does not identify with the crow. This is what makes the fable a parable of inequality and an engine of amour-propre, above all: not misidentification but nonidentification. By conceiving some men (crows) to be alien to himself, the fable deforms the Man that

Emile is meant to be, contracting "the human I" by setting some men out-side its bounds. The danger here is not that Emile will commit the error of exceptionality, disavowing his species by insisting, with Gulliver, that I am not man. It is that Emile will commit the error of exclusion, insisting that *you* are not man, or that I am not you. (These are, for Rousseau, two ways of saying the same thing.) One might understand *Robinson Crusoe* much as Rousseau understands fable: as a form that breeds contempt by contracting the spring of "the human I," splitting Man into foxes and crows in the persons, say, of Crusoe and Friday. But this is not how Rousseau reads *Crusoe*. For Rousseau, there are no foxes and crows in *Robinson Crusoe*. There is only "Robinson himself." In characterizing Defoe's novel this way, it may be that Rousseau overlooks Friday—and indeed, Rousseau mentions Friday only once, by way of dismissal, as "Friday, who now hardly concerns him" (185). It also may be that Rousseau recognizes something important about *Robinson Crusoe*, which extends the point Swift dramatizes when he silently shifts Gulliver's first-person narration from Crusoe to Friday to Poll. What Rousseau recognizes, I think, is that the allegorical-historical and creaturely logic of Defoe's novel col-lapses all persons into one—collapses, especially, the first- and second-person dyad of the reader and "Robinson himself."

The point I mean to emphasize here is that Rousseau does not admit *Robinson Crusoe* into Emile's education because it convincingly imitates the world, and thus prevents the child from overreaching his interpretive abili-ties. He admits *Crusoe* because Defoe's allegorical-historical novel collapses the difference between persons both inside and outside of the text, and thus collapses the difference between text and world, reading and acting. Rousseau insists that when Emile reads *Robinson Crusoe* and identifies with its central character, he is not so much reading about another as he is reading as—or simply being—another.[41] As "Robinson himself," Rousseau writes, Emile is "to be busy with his mansion, his goats, his plantations" (185). If realism matters to Rousseau's endorsement of *Crusoe*, it is in this allegorical-historical sense, which turns less on the fit between text and world than it does on the crea-turely logic of identity that gives rise to this fit: "I want him to think he is Robinson himself" (185).

In the end, Rousseau's insistence that *Crusoe* is not quite a book, and that Emile is not so much reading as acting, goes some way toward unraveling the opposition he otherwise draws between *Crusoe* and the fable. Rousseau anticipates this unraveling near the start of his pedagogical program, when he establishes a contrast between "fables" and "the words of fables": "Emile will never learn anything by heart, not even fables, not even those of La Fontaine, as naïve, as charming as they are, for the words of fables are no more fables than the words of history are history" (112). Rousseau might banish "the words of fables" from Emile's education because of their tendency to generate inequality. But he does present his pupil with something like fables themselves: well-shaped plots from which moral lessons emerge, like the contest between Emile and the gardener over beans and melons, or the contest between Emile and a magician over the motions of a magnetic duck. Like La Fontaine's fable of the fox and the crow, both are structured on discursive contests between two people, and both dislodge Emile from his first-person perspective as he learns that his garden, or his cleverness, is actually somebody else's. At the start of the fable of Emile and the magician, for example, Emile is (or thinks he is) the fox, and he humiliates the magician by revealing the mechanics of his magic trick, the magnet inside an apparently self-moving animal. But ultimately (and truthfully, all along), Emile is the crow, himself humiliated by the magician (and behind him, always, the preceptor), when he tries to cement his victory. The fable ends by confounding Emile's efforts to control the animal's motions and so to demonstrate his superiority over another human being, and by expropriating his person into the story of someone else. (The magician appears at Emile's door and asserts the priority of his own perspective, admonishing: "What did he do to us to make us want to discredit his game and take away his livelihood? . . . 'You should have believed that a man who has spent his life practicing this paltry trickery knows more about it than do you who have devoted only a few moments to it'" [174].) Rousseau is remarkably and densely self-conscious here, as he plays out a fable about a Cartesian animal-machine (the magnetic duck) that concludes by reducing Emile to a creature moved from without, presenting his ideal "Man" as a suffering animal in a way that defamiliarizes our sense of both "suffering" and "animal."

Rousseau underscores this point with a series of echoes that run throughout this section of Emile's education. First, there is Rousseau's description of the way Emile is affected by the fabulous scenario of the magician and the magnetic duck: "At the crowd's clapping and acclamation he gets dizzy; he is beside himself" (173). Then, there is Rousseau's account of reading *Crusoe*: "I want to make him dizzy. . . . I want him to think he is Robinson himself" (185). Rousseau recalls both of these occasions in which Emile is "dizzy" and "beside himself" when he characterizes pity as the sentiment "which make[s] [one] find itself everywhere outside of itself" (223). And finally, just a little further on, Rousseau explicitly links the fable of Emile and the magician to the cultivation of pity, and more precisely, to the effort to prevent pity from shading into contempt. He counsels: "Do not get lost in fine reasonings intended to prove to the adolescent that he is a man like others and subject to the same weaknesses. Make him feel it, or he will never know it. This is again a case of an exception to my own rules; it is the case in which my pupil is to be exposed voluntarily to all the accidents that can prove to him that he is no wiser than we are. The adventure with the magician would be repeated in countless ways" (245). Rousseau suggests that reading *Crusoe* and acting the adventure with the magician—a fable in deed rather than words—achieve one and the same thing: the dizzying, expropriating experience of identifying with or simply as a suffering animal, which is also the experience of living in the second person, apprehending the actions and happenings of my life as the actions and happenings of somebody else.

In fabulous-historical children's literature, Wollstonecraft, Kilner, and Trimmer ask their pupils (and their readers) to regard the suffering of animals, and to interpret such suffering as similar to their own—as meaningful or legible, a mode of nonlinguistic speech. This, in Lockean children's literature, is pity. On Rousseau's view, this sort of reading falsely promises to shore up the self as the source of intelligibility, secure in its own capacity to generate or arbitrate meaning. Because of this, he does not present Emile with a suffering animal, whose suffering Emile might learn to read as speech. He simply announces that at sixteen, Emile "knows what it is to suffer, for he has himself suffered" and he "begins to feel himself in his fellows . . . and to suffer from their pains" (222). I have been arguing that if Emile has suffered, and if this prepares him to feel himself in or as his fellows, this "suffering" occurs in the various dizzying lessons to which his preceptor subjects him, in which he finds himself beside or outside himself, in or as someone else. This is the case when Emile (thinks he) plants a garden and/but (actually) destroys another's property, or when he gives a natural-historical lesson about magnetism and/but learns a moral lesson about pride and humility. In these episodes, Emile suffers identification *as* rather than *with* a figure in a fable—as a character in a story scripted by someone else, in which Emile's actions, like his person, both are and are not his own. The same operation is at work when Emile reads *Robinson Crusoe* and gets dizzy, "busy with his mansions, his goats, his plantations," thinking that "he is Robinson himself." In all these instances, identification is not something Emile enacts but something he undergoes; it does not shore up his sense of self but makes it more difficult to distinguish from somebody else.

This is the sort of identification—or more simply, of identity—that counts, for Rousseau, as pity.

It is at this point in *Emile*—when acting in fable and reading *Crusoe* come to look like versions of the sentiment of pity—that Rousseau returns to La Fontaine. Once Emile has acted his part in the "adventure with the magician," and once this fable has been "repeated in countless ways," Emile is finally ready for the fox and the crow: "The time of mistakes is the time of fables. . . . The child who has never been deceived by praise understands nothing of the fable I examined earlier. But the giddy young man who has just been the dupe of a flatterer conceives marvelously that the crow was only a fool" (247–48). Rousseau reinstates "the words of fables"—along with reading more generally—at precisely this moment, after Emile has suffered the dizzying effects of acting in fable and of being Crusoe. Emile can now read fables because reading is no longer reading but acting, and because acting is not so much acting as suffering—being moved, animated, transported outside of oneself. This is the dizzying stuff of pity, of feeling oneself in or as one's fellows, in the second person. Put differently, Emile can now read fables because he knows that he, like everyone else, is actually and always a crow: not a reader of the Mrs. Mason variety, but a character in the creaturely and Crusoevian sense. He knows that I am man—a suffering, mortal animal—and so are you.

Reading Animals: Lessons for Children

To close this chapter I want to come back to Barbauld, the writer Frances Ferguson has called "the most gifted English interpreter of Rousseau,"[42] and to set her quite firmly apart from the "Crew" of fabulous-historical writers like Trimmer, Kilner, and Wollstonecraft, with whom she is very often grouped. Pity is everywhere in Barbauld's *Lessons for Children*, a text peopled with a host of pitiable objects (most often, suffering animals) that are marked as such, in the sparse idiom of the *Lessons*, with the moniker "poor": a cat whose tail is pulled ("poor puss"), a hungry child ("a poor little hungry boy"), lambs blown about in the March wind ("Poor things!"), little birds taken out of their nest ("Poor little birds!"), a partridge shot by a hunter ("Poor thing!"), a fish caught on a hook ("Poor little fish!"), a sparrow eaten by a cat ("Poor sparrow"), even a scratched arm ("Poor arm!") (1.7, 1.9, 2.13, 2.17, 2.30, 2.49, 2.53, 1.43). Notably, Barbauld's parental or preceptor figure is not set outside of this economy of pity—as she is in Trimmer, Kilner, and Wollstonecraft—but takes her place among lambs and limbs and fish: "Poor mamma!" (1.42) More significantly still, pity is more than a matter of narrative or thematic content in Barbauld. It is the abiding formal principle and rhetorical aim of the *Lessons* as a whole, in the sense of the radical and second-person species identity Rousseau outlines in *Emile*.

In spite of all the features meant to adapt the *Lessons* to the capacities of young readers—generous white space, large font, few and simple words—Barbauld's work is dizzying, to an extent unmatched by any of her contemporary writers for children. In part, this is because Barbauld mixes literary genres and forms to even more disorienting effect than Trimmer or Wollstonecraft. She sets largely conventional fables alongside realist domestic narratives as well as some blend between the two; she includes straightforward natural history lessons ("Copper is red. The kettle and pots are made of copper"; "The Lion lives in a den. He is very strong") along with first-person variations of the same: "The Swan says, My name is Swan: I am a large bird, larger than a goose. . . . I am very fierce to defend my young: and if you were to come take them away, I should beat you down with my strong pinion, and perhaps break your arm" (3.56, 3.84, 4.89, 4.94–95). Barbauld insists that "you are better than Puss— because you can talk and read," but everywhere she presents cats (and clocks, and swans, and the sun) talking, and far more eloquently than any child.

The most distinctive and, in Rousseau's sense of the word, most dizzying aspect of the *Lessons for Children* is its second-person address. Barbauld's reader does not read a story about a set of characters—Charles, Puss, Mamma, Papa—as she does in the works of Kilner, Trimmer, or Wollstonecraft. Instead, Barbauld begins her first volume by setting the scene that equates "Charles" and "you," the act of reading with the actions about which one reads: "Come hither Charles, come to mamma. Make haste. Sit in mamma's lap. Now read your book. Where is the pin to point with? Here is a pin." (1.5–6). On Ferguson's view, this aspect of the *Lessons* is part of Barbauld's response to Rousseau's critique of fable, an effort to "erase . . . the boundary dividing the book and the world of the actual child for whom Barbauld was writing, her adoptive son (and biological nephew) Charles. The deictics of the texts—the references to 'this' and 'that'—coordinated exactly with those of this child's actual world; and the textual references to the cat and the sewing kit were confirmed (for Charles and Anna Letitia Barbauld, at least) in references to the cat and the sewing kit with which they had direct acquaintance."[43] For Ferguson, Barbauld's coordination of text and world is the "major achievement of her age-graded readers," serving "continually to point to a shared world. . . . link[ing] adults and children, teachers and taught, by constantly referring to the world that they all occupied."[44] This is surely part of the point and the effect of Barbauld's formal innovations in the *Lessons*, its use of the second person, and its repeated deictic references. At the same time, Ferguson's remarks raise an intriguing question, as her parenthesis would seem to delimit a rather narrow scope for Barbauld's achievement—constricting the shared world to which the *Lessons* points to "Charles and Anna Letitia Barbauld, at least."

The question of what is happening for readers who are neither Charles nor Anna Barbauld becomes more pressing as the second-person scenarios of the *Lessons* become more elaborate. The fourth and final volume of the text, for example, begins in the everyday domestic realm of Charles ("you") and his mother but then moves far from home. "Little boy, come to me. Tell me how far from home have you been in your life? I think I should like to go a great long way with you, and see what we could see: for there are a great many places in the world besides home" (4.31–32). As Charles and his mamma ("we") set out, the deictic mode becomes increasingly pronounced, and wholly detached from the scene of reading: "Now we cannot see papa's house at all; and we can see only the top of the church steeple. Let us go a little farther. Now look back. Now we cannot see the church at all. . . . Did you see that pretty brown creature that ran across the path? Here is another! And look! There is another; there are a great many. . . . Now we are come amongst a great many trees. . . . Now we are upon the great sea. . . . Now we cannot see any green fields at all, nor any houses, nor any thing but the great deep water" (4.36–37, 44–45, 56–60). Throughout this volume, the text remains resolutely in the mode of description, keeping the reader in the realm of the visible, material world, much like Emile reading *Robinson Crusoe*. At the same time, the insistent deixis continually calls attention to the scene of reading, in a way that at once collapses text and world and exposes the conspicuous gap between them. If the *Lessons* presents reading as simply seeing what is before one's eyes, that is, then so much of what is in Barbauld's text is patently not there before the eyes of its readers, any more than Crusoe's plantation or goats were there before Emile. ("Look, there are black clouds," one reads, when presumably there are no such clouds to see [3.12].) As the disconnect between description and deixis is strained further and further, words like "here," "now," and perhaps especially "you" are increasingly unhinged from familiar modes of reference.

The second person and deictic mode of Barbauld's *Lessons* in some sense collapses text and world, then, but this does not obviously bring child and adult onto the same page by coordinating the text with the child's actual world (at least, not unless the child is Barbauld's adoptive son, Charles). Instead, Barbauld brings adult and child together by pointing less to a shared world than to a shared position, the "you" at the center of the *Lessons*. As with Rousseau's expurgated *Crusoe*, this serves to collapse text and world only insofar as it also collapses the distinction between persons (adult and child, reader and character, I and you), and so between reading and acting, acting and suffering, moving and being moved. This sort of collapse is signaled within the *Lessons* itself, where "you" is a quietly shifty figure. Its referent is usually and most explicitly Charles, the child/pupil addressed by the mother/tutor's first-person speech. But sometimes, these positions are inverted—as when the *Lessons* shifts into the voice of the child to offer a lesson to mothers both within and outside the text: "Lay by your work, mamma, and play with me" (1.33). At other times the subject of the second person is uncertain, as it is in the line, "Boil some milk for a poor little hungry boy," which might address either Charles or the maid, who is also present in the scene (1.9). The form of the *Lessons* functions to undercut the significance of such uncertainty, as "you" serves to identify everybody: it is Charles, and Anna Barbauld, and it is the reader, whoever you might be.

Most of the time, the *Lessons* seems altogether untroubled by its frequent and sometimes unmarked shifts between persons, happily moving child, mother, or maid into the position of first-person speaker, or of second-person address. But this interchangeability of persons—and in particular, the mobility of child and adult, character and reader, you and I—makes reading the *Lessons* a dizzying experience, something very much like reading *Crusoe* and thinking one is Robinson himself. This sort of reading impacts the lesson for which Barbauld comes to be known, that "you are much better than a cat or a dog, for you can speak." At the level of content, Barbauld's *Lessons* sometimes does school Charles ("you") in "talking and reading" in order to make him ("you") better than Puss, and thus to save him from being eaten or drowned—making the child a man on the model of a fox, or a not-crow. But the form of the *Lessons* works instead on the Rousseauvian logic in which its reader is constantly made to "find itself everywhere outside of itself," never sure where it will be next, or whom: swan, sheep, sun, moon, child.

Barbauld does not conclude her *Lessons* with the sort of confident claims about speech and species that both Johnson and Lamb deride, nor with the more complex identification of sentience and speech that I have attributed to the fabulous-historical tradition of children's writers. She closes, instead, with a scene attuned to what it means or feels like to live the dizzying form of

identity that the *Lessons* enacts, a creaturely "you" rather than a person possessed of the capacity to speak. This comes when Barbauld's overseas journey
lands Charles ("you") in France:

> Let us go and talk with those people. Here, you little girl! pray give
> us some of your nice fruit. Serviteur Monsieur. What do you say little
> girl? I do not understand you. I cannot help that. Here is an old man
> cutting the vines; we will speak to him. Pray old man, will you give
> us some of your fruit? We are come a great way to see you. Serviteur
> Monsieur. What do you say? We do not know what Serviteur Mon-
> sieur is, It is French. But we do not understand French. I cannot help
> that; you must go home and learn. And why do you speak French?
> Because this is France. Did not you know that everybody speaks
> French in France? Ha, ha, ha! He, he, he! Ho, ho, ho, ho! Here is a
> foolish little boy come a great way over the sea, and does not know
> that every body speaks French in France. Ha, ha, ha! He, he, he! Ho,
> ho, ho! Here is a foolish little boy come a great way over the sea, and
> does not know that every body speaks French in France. Ha, ha ha!
> He, he, he! Ho, ho, ho!—What shall we do, little boy? Every body
> laughs at us; and all the little birds twitter and chirp at us. (4.66–70)

It takes little more than an imagined voyage and another language to disrupt
any sense of Charles ("you") as a secure speaker who is "better than Puss." As
"Every body laughs" and "all the little birds twitter and chirp," Charles ("you")
becomes a dumb, incapable, and unintelligible creature, "a foolish little boy,"
so-called with a textual stutter that emphasizes his own linguistic failure (the
repetition of the nonsense refrain that begins, "Ha, ha, ha! He, he, he!"). "We
will go home again," somebody says, perhaps Charles, or his mother (4.70–71).
But at this point in the *Lessons*, it is not clear where or what home might be.

This scene suggests that the form of the *Lessons* works against the developmental program that Barbauld seems to promise, for it makes plain that
configuring reading on the model of Rousseauvian pity promises no clear
path beyond animal identity. To say this is to suggest that Barbauld interprets
Rousseau quite differently than does Lévi-Strauss, who famously characterizes
Rousseauvian pity as a mechanism for producing human persons, and human
society, out of animal species. In *Totemism*, Lévi-Strauss identifies Rousseau
as the first to understand how the "'specific' character" of animals enables
"the triple passage (which is really only one) from animality to humanity,

from nature to culture, and from affectivity to intellectuality"; he points to Rousseau's notion of pity as central to this understanding.[45] From the specific character of animals and the structure of pity, Lévi-Strauss argues, comes logic, language, and crucially, the individual human person: "It is because man originally felt himself identical to all those like him (among which, as Rousseau explicitly says, we must include animals) that he came to acquire the capacity to distinguish himself as he distinguishes them, i.e., to use the diversity of species as conceptual support for social differentiation."[46] From pity with animals, Lévi-Strauss argues, one comes to see oneself as a similarly "specific character," which means a particular individual, an essentially and qualitatively distinct being.

There is much that is compelling about Lévi-Strauss's reading of Rousseau. Above all, Lévi-Strauss never loses sight of the animal at the center of Rousseau's scene of pity, and he insists on thinking about the animal in formal as well as thematic terms (this is the crux of his distinction between "good to think" and "good to eat"). In characterizing pity as the source of what he elsewhere calls "personality," however, Lévi-Strauss pays little heed to one of Rousseau's central concerns: the fact that the origin of individuation is also the origin of inequality. Rousseau may be out to make the child a man, but he also aims to ensure that this man does not take the shape of the distinctive human person described by Lévi-Strauss. Indeed, Rousseau often seems out to make a man with precisely the sort of generic and species character that Lévi-Strauss attributes to animal life. This is what Barbauld picks up on in her *Lessons for Children*, and this, perhaps, is the threat to "all that is Human in man & child" that Lamb sensed in Barbauld, and worked, with aggressive mockery, to defuse. For the lesson that "Billy is better than a Horse" is not advanced with any conviction or consistency in the *Lessons*. Instead, it often appears to be just what Lamb suspects: an empty statement in the shape of knowledge. Rather than make the child a man, Barbauld's *Lessons* leaves its readers as it leaves Charles: in the time of pity and of creaturely animal identity. This may not be a positive vision—Barbauld's child ("you") suffers what Rousseau explicitly calls "humiliation." But Barbauld suggests that it is a vision we cannot simply leave behind, if we are to compose a world capable of housing all its people: animal as well as human, you as well as me.

Coda

Growing Human

Some three and a half decades after her *Lessons for Children*—and some three years after her vociferously antiwar "Eighteen Hundred and Eleven" received such hostile reviews that she ceased to publish her work—Anna Barbauld wrote a poem entitled "The Caterpillar."[1] The poem begins in a garden, with an encounter between poet and insect. It ends on a battlefield, with an imagined encounter between one human being and another. Both encounters begin when "a single sufferer" moves someone more powerful to stop what they are doing: "when thou / . . . Present'st thyself before me, I relent" (23, 28). Both encounters are characterized as interpersonal interruptions of enmity between species (human and caterpillar, my people and yours, fellow creature and vermin), occasions on which "I" am made to "feel and clearly recognise / Thine individual existence, life, / And fellowship of sense with all that breathes" (25–27). Perhaps most striking are the poem's closing lines, which turn from a tableau of the weeping war hero and the single sufferer at his feet to personification, or away from it:

> He is grown human, and capricious Pity,
> Which would not stir for thousands, melts for one
> With sympathy spontaneous:—'Tis not Virtue,
> Yet 'tis the weakness of a virtuous mind. (39–42)

As a way of bringing this book to a close, I want to think with Barbauld about what has become of personification as a poetic art of restoring animality, and what it might mean to "grow human."

In its opening lines, "The Caterpillar" rewrites any number of earlier interspecies encounters, from Tristram's communion with an ass to Trimmer's Mrs. Benson looking through her microscope at ants. Here is Barbauld's version of this sort of scenario:

No, helpless thing, I cannot harm thee now;
Depart in peace, thy little life is safe,
For I have scanned thy form with curious eye,
Noted the silver line that streaks thy back,
The azure and the orange that divide
Thy velvet sides; thee, houseless wanderer,
My garment has enfolded, and my arm
Felt the light pressure of thy hairy feet;
Thou hast curled round my finger; from its tip,
Precipitous descent! with stretched out neck,
Bending thy head in airy vacancy,
This way and that, inquiring, thou has seemed
To ask protection; now, I cannot kill thee. (1–13)

The "curious eye" that Barbauld pictures "scann[ing the] form" of the caterpillar—noting line, color, and movement—recalls the fantasy figured by Mrs. Benson's microscope: that natural-historical observation might provide a solid and perceptible ground for "justice." Once again, there is the sense that animal motion is a kind of speech, and that this speech is something that one can see: the insect's "inquiring," observed by way of a stretched neck and a bending head, a petition for protection made with light feet and curling body. So too, there is the sense that apprehending animal motion might serve to secure its person: "I cannot harm thee now." Barbauld may well have in mind Gulliver's arrival in Brobdingnag, as she too pictures a benevolent giant who singles out a "strange Animal in the Fields" for protection.[2] But Barbauld sets this scene in the tradition of sensibility rather than satire, her line, "thy little life is safe," echoing Cowper's assurance, in *The Task*, to his pet hare Tiny: "one at least is safe."[3] Notably, Barbauld distributes incapacity across animal and human—the caterpillar may be introduced as a "helpless thing," but it is the speaker who finally seems helpless, the subject of only three verbs in thirteen lines, two of them negative: "I cannot harm," "I cannot kill," "I have scanned." Somehow scanning the form of the caterpillar seems to disable the poet, much as Mrs. Benson's microscope managed to stop children's cruelty to animals in its tracks.

There is more to say about this opening section of the poem, not least about how self-consciously Barbauld at once invokes and also undercuts the fantasy of an ethical response that arises from the evidence of the senses, figuring the speaker's looking in terms of reading a poem (scanning its form,

even feeling the pressure of its feet). In this way, Barbauld joins so many of
the writers I have been discussing in insisting on the role of poetry—and of
linguistic mediation and rhetorical figuration more generally—in bringing a
"houseless wanderer" inside the shelter of recognizable and valuable "form." In
other respects, though, "The Caterpillar" seems to depart from the works on
which this book has focused. Throughout this book, I have been interested in
the way that literary form serves to incorporate individuals directly into some
species or kind—and more broadly, in a strain of thought that understands
animals to be specific in a way that things are not, a mode of being in which
the relationship between individual and species is one neither of aggregation
nor of opposition. Barbauld's poem, by contrast, sets the individual and the
species more clearly at odds—the individual on the side of life and right relation, the species on the side of slaughter and death. As the gardener/poet
continues to address the caterpillar—to address *this* particular caterpillar—she
emphasizes its good fortune to be so singled out from its species:

> Yet I have sworn perdition to thy race,
> And recent from the slaughter am I come
> Of tribes and embryo nations: I have sought
> With sharpened eye and persecuting zeal,
> Where, folded in their silken webs they lay
> Thriving and happy; swept them from the tree
> And crushed whole families beneath my foot;
> Or, sudden, poured on their devoted heads
> The vials of destruction.—This I've done
> Nor felt the touch of pity: but when thou,—
> A single wretch, escaped the general doom,
> Making me feel and clearly recognise
> Thine individual existence, life,
> And fellowship of sense with all that breathes,—
> Present'st thyself before me, I relent,
> And cannot hurt thy weakness.—(14–29)

Barbauld's language of the caterpillar "race," "tribes," "nations," and "families"
invokes Thomson's *The Seasons*; in particular, her scene of slaughter echoes
Thomson's condemnation of "the guilty Nations" of human beings for plun-
dering "the busy Nations" of bees (*Su*, 1711; *Sp*, 510). In *The Seasons*, Thomson
uses this vocabulary (of nations, tribes, and so on) to insist on the ethical

importance of the harm human beings inflict on other species. In "The Caterpillar," Barbauld implicates the same vocabulary in the perpetration of such
harm. Thomson's personifying and general terms—his many human and nonhuman people, tribes, and nations—no longer serve to compose the "social
Commerce" of a whole "Earth animated," or to envision a "full-adjusted Harmony of Things" (*A* 834; *Su* 292; *A*, 835). In Barbauld, they serve instead as
terms of division, exclusion, and enmity: my people rather than yours. To
except one from this sort of species, Barbauld would seem to say, is simply
to recognize what each of us most fundamentally is—what the poem calls an
"individual existence."

Characterized in this way, Barbauld's poem appears to signal the end of the
literature of animals and other people, or at least of its interest in the capacity
of rhetorical figures and generic forms to help us to apprehend the specificity
of living creatures. Aligning the "fellowship of sense" with "individual existence" and setting these against generic and species figures, "The Caterpillar"
sounds a note familiar from much of contemporary animal studies—antici-
pating its suspicion of species as the germ of speciesism, and of generic and
abstract figures as obstacles to recognizing the lives of animals, and to living
well with them. Some of Barbauld's best readers understand the poem along
such lines, to present a fairly straightforward thesis about the way that generic
figures enable indifference or violence, and a scene in which this is arrested by
the poet's "abrupt awareness of the individual caterpillar's physical presence."[4]
This logic seems so palpable that readers sometimes impute to the poem a real-
world origin (Barbauld in her garden, plagued by caterpillars), and then use
that origin to read the poem—to characterize it, for example, as "an observation, a meditation provoked by an incident" that prompts Barbauld to admit
that "she could be just as frenzied as any, till brought up against the individual
reality of her victim."[5] On this view, the poem records and recommends a
move from generic figures to actual individuals, from representation to presence, from poetry to the world outside—the garden or the fields of battle.

There is clearly something to this view, which makes good sense of the
scenes Barbauld stages in this poem. But to my mind, there are two significant
drawbacks to reading Barbauld's poem in this way. First, such a reading necessarily downplays the patent rhetorical artifice and generic conventionality
of the intimate encounters on which the poem centers—it wants them to
be more real, or at least more realist, than they are. As a result, it overlooks
how uncertain the poem can be about what individuals and species are. Second, it has trouble making sense of the poem's conclusion, which characterizes

the intimate interpersonal encounter as the work of "capricious Pity." As an ethical ideal, this seems considerably less promising than an abstract principle like Virtue—though it should be said that this principle appears in Barbauld's poem as an empty or at least unavailable abstraction, invoked only in negative terms: "'Tis not Virtue." I will come back to Barbauld's remarkable conclusion shortly. Here I want simply to note that it does not readily support the sense that Barbauld elaborates an ethics of the singular face-to-face encounter. Instead, the poem's conclusion urges us to keep in view the highly self-conscious, deliberate work of poetic composition, as well as the scene of reading.[6] When we do this—when we approach "The Caterpillar" by way of the eighteenth-century literature of animals and other people—it becomes something less familiar and I think quite powerful: a poem without ready figures for what it is after. Indeed, it becomes a poem about the exhaustion and renovation of figurative resources—a poem concerned with the regeneration of literary forms and the possibility of once again composing relations between humans and animals, individual and species, so that we might live together in less harmful ways.

In "The Caterpillar," as in the *Lessons for Children*, Barbauld's pronouns do a lot of work. Throughout its opening section, the poem's first-person voice courts readerly identification of a familiar sort—the identification with another whom one might wish to resemble (the benevolent speaker), rather than the sort of dizzying identity *as* another that one suffers on the model of Rousseauvian pity (and Barbauld's *Lessons*)—or, somewhat differently, in Swiftian satire. In the middle section of "The Caterpillar," however, the first sort of identification starts to shade into the second, as "I" proceed to slaughter, persecute, crush, and destroy "whole families beneath my foot." Here, the scene of benevolent protection shifts into one of zealous persecution, friendship into enmity, I and thou into us and them. The continuity of the first person across these transformations—and, the implication of the reader in that person—works against the sense that the intimate and individual encounter offers an "escape" from the "general doom" of species. Instead, the I-you couple appears a smaller scale version of the we-you figure that Barbauld associates with persecution and destruction—a potentially more salutary version maybe, but embodying essentially the same logic.[7]

Barbauld intensifies this point in the final third of the poem, as the subject position of the first person is taken over by the storm of war. This last section of the poem begins midline, as both scene and species shift suddenly, by means of a mere "So":

And cannot hurt thy weakness.—So the storm
Of horrid war, o'erwhelming cities, fields,
And peaceful villages, rolls dreadful on:
The victor shouts triumphant; he enjoys
The roar of cannon and the clang of arms,
And urges, by no soft relentings stopped,
The work of death and carnage. Yet should one,
A single sufferer from the field escaped,
Panting and pale, and bleeding at his feet,
Lift his imploring eyes,—the hero weeps;
He is grown human, and capricious Pity,
Which would not stir for thousands, melts for one
With sympathy spontaneous:—'Tis not Virtue
Yet 'tis the weakness of a virtuous mind. (29–42)

In its own way, "The Caterpillar" is as dizzying as Barbauld's *Lessons*, especially as its sudden shifts of scale, species, and setting are counterbalanced by a disconcerting consistency of person or at least of position. Over the course of the poem, "I" proceed from a benevolent protector to a merciless persecutor to a storm of war (and then to its hero). A good deal of the force of Barbauld's poem comes from the formal alignment of these figures, and the trouble this makes for any consolation the poem might promise. As the poem proceeds, the garden comes to resemble the field of war—another space that serves to enclose a domestic realm, and a site of the violence that comes from keeping people out. The problem, as Barbauld conceives it, is a Rousseauvian one. The I-you dyad might look like a positive relation in some of its incarnations (when "I" am a benevolent protector), but the form itself is a problem. So long as "I" am set apart from "you"—from the suffering animal, "panting and pale, and bleeding"—mine is not the "human *I*."[8] Instead, it is—or can always become—the inhuman logic of "the storm / Of horrid war." This is a point Barbauld might have taken from Thomson's hunted hare, for whom human beings are "the coming Storm" (*A* 417).

This account makes "The Caterpillar" sound bleak, and I think it is. The poem presents a powerful vision of what it would mean to live well with others, and then implicates that vision in the very logic from which it promises escape.[9] Something similar occurs at the end of the poem, when Barbauld figures competing ethical models as equally unappealing personified abstractions: the choice between capricious Pity and hollow Virtue. But there is more to the conclusion than this. In particular, Barbauld's final line brings together pity and virtue as the apparently positive attributes of a peculiar figure: "the weakness of a virtuous mind." It is a paradoxical phrase: virtue, in its older sense of power or efficacy, seems the direct opposite of weakness. At the same time, the poem depicts the caterpillar's weakness as virtuous in just this sense—as having the power to arrest the gardener's actions. The weakness of a "virtuous mind" recalls the paradoxical sort of agency associated, throughout this book, with animals: moving and being moved at once.

If the poem points a way forward from the problem it enacts—from its sense that existing forms and figures have been exhausted or put to undesirable ends—it comes in these closing lines, and in the figure with which this capacity to move and be moved is associated: "He" that "is grown human." Crucially, it is not entirely clear, in the poem, who "He" is. The immediate antecedent is "the hero"—a figure that occupies the position previously held by the first person, the "I" that is at once the speaker and the reader of the poem—who grows human by taking pity on the sufferer. But it equally makes sense to read "He" as the "single sufferer" ("thee") who grows human as he moves the hero—most obviously, in the sense that he is grown human in the hero's eyes, and perhaps in ours. I think the undecidability of referent is the point. Growing human, Barbauld suggests, involves incorporating the two persons around which the poem has been organized, in order to compose a form of agency that at once moves and is moved, and a form of generality from which there is no exception, and no outside.[10]

The figure of human being that is grown, here, is emphatically not a biological one. But the metaphor of growth does associate this figure with the living process of reproduction, in its broadest Buffonian sense. Here one does not create or invent a new figure so much as grow one out of the materials one has to hand: hollowed out personified abstractions, exhausted conventions of sensibility, a Thomsonian idiom too easily co-opted as a call to arms. We can see the initial encounter between human ("I") and caterpillar ("thee") as a scene of reproduction in this sense, which dramatizes the poetic labor that goes into composing a new figure. This process begins in the opening lines, which decompose the caterpillar into the basic material elements of color and line ("the silver line," "the azure and the orange") and then composes those elements into the parts of a living body, so that shapes like "back" and "sides" become visible as body parts alongside others: feet, neck, head, eye, arm, and finger. That some of those body parts belong to the gardener and some to the caterpillar is deemphasized by the fact that there are no repeated body parts between them. It is almost as if human and caterpillar together constitute one compound body. The work of this scene is thus to abstract from both species and individual identity, taking bodies apart in order to configure this new composite figure. (This abstraction occurs again in the conclusion, when the repetition of "his"—"his feet" and "his eyes"—obscures which body part belongs to the hero, which to the sufferer.)

Characterizing this scene as an interpersonal encounter goes only so far in apprehending the complicated work of composition Barbauld undertakes here, and the sort of figure she works to generate. This is neither an individual nor a species figure; it is composed of the first person and the second, human and animal. More specifically, it is composed of human and caterpillar. Barbauld takes as her paradigm for multispecies cohabitation not a useful or beloved companion animal but abhorred vermin—as Johnson has it in the *Dictionary*: "from *cates*, food, and *piller*, Fr. to rob; the animal that eats up the fruits of the earth."[11] In doing so, she urges us to focus on precisely those creatures who resist incorporation into "the fellowship of sense"—those creatures that Thomson would call wild, and that he has such trouble integrating into the great "social . . . Harmony of Things." Barbauld insists that the challenge of living with other animals, as with other people, cannot be met only by figures of harmony or sympathy. Living together requires figures of paradox and contradiction, forms capable of housing opposition and discord without coming apart.

This is what Barbauld is after in composing a figure of human being out of the first and second person, human and caterpillar, weakness and virtue. It is also what she is after with the perplexing personification with which she associates this figure: capricious Pity. This phrase seems a clear condemnation of pity, and a sudden reversal of much of the poem to this point. Caprice is, after all, rarely a good thing. "A sudden change or turn of the mind without apparent or adequate motive," it characterizes a way of acting associated most commonly with tyrants.[12] But Barbauld's jarring usage urges us to attend to alternative associations, and to imagine other possibilities. As Ephraim Chambers informs readers of the *Cyclopædia*, capriciousness has animal origins: "from the Lain *capra*, goat, to whose wantonness it is supposed to bear allusion" (in the *OED*'s formulation, "apparently < *capro* goat, as if 'the skip or frisk of a goat'").[13] If one lives in a time of tyranny—or simply, in a time in which human agency resembles nothing so much as an inhuman storm—a "sudden change or turn of the mind" may not be so bad. Under such circumstances, capricious animal motion might offer a model for acting otherwise—a model for arresting dominant forms of action, or for imagining the sorts of actions Barbauld's composite "human" figure might perform, somewhat loosed from the imperatives of self and species.

This is an appropriate figure with which to end a book about animals and other people: a personification that would reclaim caprice as animal motion, and identify such motion as the means of growing human. By concluding with this figure, I do not mean to propose caprice as an ethical model for living well with others, including other animals. If we are after ethical models, Barbauld provides a more straightforward one quite ready to hand: the sympathy made possible by singling an individual out from its species, sheltering it from our general indifference or animosity toward other kinds. It is easier to see what it would entail (and why it might be a good thing) to recognize the "individual existence" of another, than it is to envision what it would mean to pity like a goat (or, to conceive of the agency of a human-caterpillar compound). But I am arguing, as I have been throughout the book, that there are good reasons to read Barbauld's poem—and literature in general—for its perplexing, difficult figures, rather than for its stance on existing ethical models. What we stand to gain from reading in this way—for focusing on a peculiar personification like capricious Pity, and its provocation to think right relation from wanton or apparently unmotivated animal motion—is the possibility of conceiving forms of being and relation that do not yet exist, that we do not quite know how to imagine. In the reproduction and regeneration of old literary forms, we might glean new ways of living.

Notes

INTRODUCTION

1. James Thomson, *The Seasons*, ed. James Sambrook (Oxford: Oxford University Press, 1981), *Summer*, line 378; *Winter*, line 87. All references to this text are hereafter cited parenthetically by line number and abbreviated by season: *Sp, Su, W, A*. Sambrook's edition follows the 1746 edition of Thomson's much-revised poem.

2. Georges-Louis Leclerc de Buffon, *Natural History, General and Particular, by the Count de Buffon, translated into English. Illustrated with above 260 copper-plates, and occasional notes and observations by the translator,* 9 vols., trans. William Smellie (Edinburgh: William Creech, [1780–85]), 2.1; hereafter cited parenthetically in the text, by volume and page number.

3. In part, Buffon makes an epistemological point about the human situatedness from which any natural knowledge is produced: "Our divisions are based solely upon the relations which things seem to have with us," he writes in the "Initial Discourse" of his *Histoire Naturelle*, trans. John Lyon, *Journal of the History of Biology* 9.1 (1976): 164. At the same time, he makes an ontological point about what beings are, and about the priority of relation to being. For a similar sense of "the social" as "a trail of associations between heterogeneous elements"—not a type of being or material, but "a *type of connection* between things that are not themselves social," see Bruno Latour, *Reassembling the Social: An Introduction to Actor-Network-Theory* (Oxford: Oxford University Press, 2005), 5.

4. References from Pope's *Essay on Man* are from *Poetry and Prose of Alexander Pope*, ed. Aubrey Williams (Boston: Houghton Mifflin, 1969), epistle 3, lines 182–83; epistle 1, line 210. For these and other period examples of "the word 'people,' which looms so large in eighteenth-century poetic diction," see John Sitter's important discussion in *The Cambridge Introduction to Eighteenth-Century Poetry* (Cambridge: Cambridge University Press, 2011), 201–2.

5. "people, n." *OED Online*. Oxford University Press, June 2014. http://www.oed.com .proxy.uchicago.edu/view/Entry/140404?rskey=k97PQq&result=1#eid. See also Joanna Picciotto, "Reading People," which links Thomson's many animal "people" to Milton and to the literature of physico-theology more broadly, which she characterizes in terms congenial to my own. Physico-theology, Picciotto argues, is "interest[ed] in expanding, and thereby estranging, the category of personhood" by cultivating reading as "an exercise in sympathetic identification" with all sorts of "people"—a term that Picciotto understands, quite minimally, as nonparticularized "bodies that constituted other centers of experience" (3, 5, 30). Unpublished ms., cited by permission of the author.

6. Sitter, *Cambridge Introduction*, 201.

7. Daniel Defoe, *Robinson Crusoe*, ed. Michael Shinagel (New York: Norton, 1975), 116; hereafter cited parenthetically in the text.

8. Samuel Johnson, *A Dictionary of the English language: In which the words are deduced from their originals, and illustrated in their different significations by examples from the best writers. To which are prefixed, a history of the language, and an English grammar*, 2 vols. 2nd ed. (London: printed by W. Strahan, for J. and P. Knapton, T. and L. Longman et al., 1755–56), s.v. "Personification"; Erasmus Darwin, *The Botanic Garden, containing The Loves of the Plants* (Lichfield: J. Jackson, 1789), vi. Catherine Packham quotes this phrase from Darwin in her *Eighteenth-Century Vitalism: Bodies, Culture, Politics* (Houndmills: Palgrave Macmillan, 2012), to make the marvelous point that Darwin uses "personification throughout his verse . . . to further animate already visible, already living objects . . . [as] a means of enabling a vitalist nature to be brought to imaginative life" (155–56).

9. René Descartes, *Discourse on the Method*, in *The Philosophical Writings of Descartes*, 2 vols., trans. John Cottingham, Robert Stoothoff, Dugald Murdoch (Cambridge: Cambridge University Press, 1984–85), 1.140.

10. For useful discussions of Descartes's view of animals, see John Cottingham, "'A Brute to the Brutes?': Descartes' Treatment of Animals," *Philosophy* 53.206 (1978): 551–59; and Peter Harrison, "Descartes on Animals," *Philosophical Quarterly* 42.167 (1992): 219–27. Harrison urges us to situate Descartes's animal-machine within the context of his philosophical system more broadly and argues that when we do this, we see that the animal soul or mind—a principle of action apart from the structure of body parts and their response to external stimuli—is the one thing Descartes does not retrieve from skepticism, as he does God, other (human) minds, and the external world.

11. On this move in Descartes, see Jacques Derrida, *The Animal That Therefore I Am*, ed. Marie-Louise Mallet, trans. David Wills (New York: Fordham University Press, 2008), 172n1.

12. Julian Jaynes, "The Problem of Animate Motion in the Seventeenth Century," *Journal of the History of Ideas* 31.2 (1970): 225.

13. See Jaynes, "The Problem of Animate Motion," 225. In the third volume of his *Introduction to the Literature of Europe, in the Fifteenth, Sixteenth and Seventeenth Centuries* (London: John Murray, 1839), Henry Hallam translates Campanella's phrase as "The world is an animal, sentient as a whole" (148). In her introduction to the "Animal, All Too Animal" special issue of *Eighteenth Century* (52.1 [2011]: 1–10), Lucinda Cole locates the "collective disarticulation" of the ancient doctrine of *anima mundi* with natural philosophers like Bacon, Descartes, and Thomas Willis (4).

14. In *The Accommodated Animal: Cosmopolity in Shakespearean Locales* (Chicago: University of Chicago Press, 2013), Laurie Shannon makes a compelling case that modern dyads like person/thing, society/nature, subject/object did not so completely organize the early modern world—or at least, that they rested on the more fundamental (as well as relational and shifting) distinctions between animate and inanimate, eater and eaten. For a concentrated formulation of this point, see 225. With this argument, Shannon builds on Bruno Latour's *We Have Never Been Modern*, trans. Catherine Porter (Cambridge, Mass.: Harvard University Press, 1993), which offers a powerful account of the ways in which the birth of the modern figure of "humanity" entails "the simultaneous birth of 'nonhumanity'—things, or objects, or beasts," as well as of the intellectual, political and ecological consequences that attend these twin births (13). At the same time, by identifying animals as one variety of nonhumanity among others ("things, or objects, or beasts"), Latour curiously recapitulates the modern reduction of "the ontological varieties that matter to two" that he so forcefully critiques (79).

15. John Locke, *An Essay Concerning Human Understanding*, ed. Peter H. Nidditch (Oxford: Oxford University Press, 1975), 115–16; hereafter cited parenthetically in the text.

16. See Ian Watt, *The Rise of the Novel: Studies in Defoe, Richardson, and Fielding* (Berkeley: University of California Press, 2001), esp. 11–15.

17. Barbara Johnson, "Anthropomorphism in Lyric and Law," in *Persons and Things*, by Johnson (Cambridge, Mass.: Harvard University Press, 2010), 190. For a rather different sense of anthropomorphism, see Cora Diamond's discussion of the notion of "fellow creature," which she glosses as the "extension of a non-biological notion of what a human life is," in "Eating Meat and Eating People," *Philosophy* 53.206 (1978): 474. On the benefits of "a touch of anthropomorphism" (99), see Jane Bennett, *Vibrant Matter: A Political Ecology of Things* (Durham, N.C.: Duke University Press, 2010), 98–100, 119–22.

18. Barbara Johnson, "Anthropomorphism in Lyric and Law," 190.

19. Denis Diderot and Louis Jean-Marie Daubenton, "Animal," in *Encyclopédie ou Dictionnaire raisonné des sciences, des arts et des métiers, par une Société de Gens de lettres*, ed. Denis Diderot and Jean le Rond d'Alembert, accessed online at the ARTFL Encyclopédie Project, http://artflx.uchicago.edu/cgi-bin/philologic/getobject.pl?c.1:1101.encyclopedie0311. My translation.

20. For a related argument about the representation of nature in general (and vegetal nature in particular), see Deidre Lynch's call for a "greenhouse" rather than "green" romanticism—for "modes of inquiry that, disallowing the polarities between the organic and the cultural and between genuine Nature and figurative language that are sometimes assumed by romantic studies of an ecocritical bent and anti-rhetorical stance, would instead be mindful of how often, at the start of the nineteenth century, knowledge of Nature depended on practices of artifice and exhibition that rendered Nature a representation of itself" (693). See Lynch, "'Young Ladies Are Delicate Plants': Jane Austen and Greenhouse Romanticism," *ELH* 77 (2010): 689–729.

21. William Cowper, "Pairing Time Anticipated: A Fable," in *The Poems of William Cowper*, 3 vols., ed. John D. Baird and Charles Ryskamp (Oxford: Clarendon, 1980–95), 3.51, lines 1–4; hereafter cited parenthetically in the text, by line number.

22. Cowper, note to "Pairing Time," in *Poems of William Cowper*, 3.51. Baird and Ryskamp note that the poem was first published in William Enfield's 1790 anthology *The Speaker*, remarking that "the additional words in *The Speaker* may be Enfield's rather than Cowper's. Cowper mentions Rousseau's *Emile, ou de l'Education* in his letter to Unwin of 21 September 1779, but in another connection" (3.303n1).

23. Jean-Jacques Rousseau, *Emile; or, On Education*, trans. Allan Bloom (New York: Basic, 1979), 112; hereafter cited parenthetically in the text.

24. Cowper, note to "Pairing Time," 51.

25. Derrida, *Animal That Therefore I Am*, 32. In his essay, "Zoophilpsychosis: Why Animals Are What's Wrong with Sentimentality," *Symploke* 15.1–2 (2007), Tobias Menely summarizes Derrida's influence in literary animal studies this way: "Derrida provides a key theoretical resource for scholars turning to the question of the animal, most notably by exposing the inadequacy of the prevailing interpretive gesture that categorically consigns animals to symbolic labor, either as anthropomorphized substitutes for human beings or as the other against which the category of the human is constituted" (248). Menely calls for (and his own work amply demonstrates) "hermeneutic sensitivity to the ways animals rendered in literary texts . . . may engage readers' sympathies in a manner that would inform their lived relations with other sentient creatures" (248). Laurie Shannon makes a similar call in *The Accommodated Animal* and explicitly frames this as a counter-Enlightenment gesture: "In the aftermath of technoscience and the Enlightenment, we have preferred our textual animals 'fabulous and chimerical,' as fables, symbols, 'animal imagery,' or any other confinement we can think of to dematerialize their stakeholdership or participation" (53). This characterization of the Enlightenment is prominent in much recent

work in animal studies, a field that Kari Weil, for example, characterizes as committed to the "ongoing reassessment of Enlightenment ideals and a concurrent effort to give new definition to the human not as being opposed to animals, but as animal" (13). In Weil, *Thinking Animals: Why Animal Studies Now?* (New York: Columbia University Press, 2013).

26. Shannon, *Accommodated Animal*, 5.

27. Shannon, *Accommodated Animal*, 5. Shannon echoes Donna Haraway in particular, who protests against using animals as "an alibi" for human themes, insisting that "they are not just here to think with." In Haraway, *The Companion Species Manifesto: Dogs, People, and Significant Otherness* (Chicago: Prickly Paradigm, 2003), 5. Qtd. in Shannon, *Accommodated Animal*, 49. See also Frank Palmeri's introduction to *Humans and Other Animals in Eighteenth-Century British Culture: Representation, Hybridity, Ethics*, ed. Frank Palmeri (Aldershot: Ashgate, 2006), 3–4.

28. Shannon, *Accommodated Animal*, 5. See also David Perkins, *Romanticism and Animal Rights* (Cambridge: Cambridge University Press, 2007), x–xi.

29. Shannon, *Accommodated Animal*, 68.

30. Cowper depicts animals as examples of tyranny with what Tobias Menely refers to as "surprising directness": "I am recompensed, and deem the toils / Of poetry not lost, if verse of mine / May stand between an animal and woe, / And teach one tyrant pity for his drudge" (*The Task*, book 6, lines 725–28). The quotation from Menely comes from *The Animal Claim: Sensibility and the Creaturely Voice* (Chicago: University of Chicago Press, 2015), 153. At the same time, as I argue throughout this introduction, Cowper's animals are everywhere emblems or figures for human beings, virtues, and actions. So too, Cowper figures himself as an emblem of animal woe, in terms that are both formulaic and deeply felt: "I was a stricken deer" he writes in *The Task* (3.108); or, from his "Spiritual Diary" of 1795, "It is I who have been the hunted hare." References to *The Task* come from *The Poems of William Cowper*, vol. 2. Cowper's "Spiritual Diary" is in *The Letters and Prose Writings of William Cowper*, ed. James King and Charles Ryskamp, 5 vols. (Oxford: Clarendon, 1979–86), 4.467–71. On these moments in Cowper, see Menely, *Animal Claim*, 149–50, 153–54.

31. Shannon, *Accommodated Animal*, 53.

32. The list comes from Perkins, *Romanticism and Animal Rights*, 46.

33. In *Elephant Slaves and Pampered Parrots: Exotic Animals in Eighteenth-Century Paris* (Baltimore: Johns Hopkins University Press, 2002), Louise Robbins argues that seventeenth-century fabulists like La Fontaine brought a new degree of naturalism to the form, incorporating elements from natural history, travel narrative, and the new science. See esp. 158–63. See also Rachel Trickett, "Cowper, Wordsworth, and the Animal Fable," *Review of English Studies* 34.136 (1983): 471–80. Jane Spencer recounts a similar story of "the incomplete but significant shift in animal representation from the fabular, the allegorical and the satirical to the naturalistic, the empathetic and the inwardly focused" in her essay "Creating Animal Experience in Late Eighteenth-Century Narrative," *Journal for Eighteenth-Century Studies* 33.4 (2010): 470.

34. See Keith Thomas, *Man and the Natural World: Changing Attitudes in England 1500–1800* (New York: Penguin, 1983); Ingrid H. Tague, "Dead Pets: Satire and Sentiment in British Elegies and Epitaphs for Animals," *Eighteenth-Century Studies* 41.3 (2008): 289–306; Peter Singer, *Animal Liberation* (New York: Harper Collins, 1975); Perkins, *Romanticism and Animal Rights*; Christine Kenyon-Jones, *Kindred Brutes: Animals in Romantic Period Writing* (Aldershot: Ashgate, 2001); Kathryn Shevelow, *For the Love of Animals: The Rise of the Animal Protection Movement* (New York: Henry Holt, 2008). As Michael Trask points out, Singer cuts something of a strange figure in this company, because his individual is more of an abstract unit than a singular or particularized creature. See Trask, "The Ethical Animal: From Peter

Singer to Patricia Highsmith" *Post45* (2012), online at http://post45.research.yale.edu/2012/11
/the-ethical-animal-from-peter-singer-to-patricia-highsmith/. Singer is certainly less interested in the rise of affective attachments to particular domestic companions. But he too lauds
"the eighteenth century [as] an unusually fertile period for our ideas about animals, as it was
for the development of progressive ideas in general," in Peter Singer, Foreword, "Animals
in the Eighteenth Century," ed. Glynis Ridley, special issue, *Journal for Eighteenth-Century
Studies* 33.4 (2010): 427.

35. For an interesting variation on the association between individuation and life, see
Denise Gigante, *Life: Organic Form and Romanticism* (New Haven, Conn.: Yale University Press,
2009). Gigante charts a vitalist tradition from midcentury natural philosophers through poets
like Christopher Smart, Byron, and Keats, in which life means a "tendency toward individuation" that always "threatens to overwhelm formal containment"—the bounds of poetic genre,
of conceptual abstractions, or of natural-historical species (48). See also Richard Nash, "Joy
and Pity: Reading Animal Bodies in Late Eighteenth-Century Culture," *Eighteenth Century* 52.1
(2011): 47–67, which argues that "nowhere is the abyss separating Derrida and Descartes more
profound than in the starkly polarized ways in which the former pairs particularity with a potential for subjective interiority, while the latter pairs a mechanized understanding of embodiment
with an erasure of the individual subsumed into the larger category" (50). Under the sign of
Descartes, then, Nash aligns generality with deanimation; under the sign of Derrida, he lines up
particularity, subjective interiority, and animation. But he also identifies the challenge of ethics
as getting beyond any straightforward opposition between general and particular: "to disrupt the
totalizing label without recourse to an endless regress of particularizing exceptions of named (or
even anonymous individuals)" (51).

36. Frank Palmeri, "The Autocritique of Fables," in *Humans and Other Animals in
Eighteenth-Century British Culture*, ed. Frank Palmeri (Aldershot: Ashgate, 2006), 83–100;
Anne Milne, *"Lactilla Tends Her Fav'rite Cow": Ecocritical Readings of Animals and Women in
Eighteenth-Century British Labouring-Class Women's Poetry* (Lewisburg, Pa.: Bucknell University
Press, 2008); Tess Cosslett, *Talking Animals in British Children's Fiction: 1786–1914* (Aldershot:
Ashgate, 2006); Markman Ellis, "Suffering Things: Lapdogs, Slaves, and Counter-Sensibility,"
in *The Secret Life of Things: Animals, Objects, and It-Narratives in Eighteenth-Century England*,
ed. Mark Blackwell (Lewisburg, Pa.: Bucknell University Press, 2007), 92–116; Laura Brown,
*Homeless Dogs and Melancholy Apes: Humans and Other Animals in the Modern Literary Imagi-
nation* (Ithaca, N.Y.: Cornell University Press, 2010). A number of collections and special issues
provide a good introduction to work at the intersection of literary animal studies and eighteenth-
century studies, including Palmeri, *Humans and Other Animals in Eighteenth-Century British
Culture*; Mark Blackwell, ed., *The Secret Life of Things: Animals, Objects, and It-Narratives in
Eighteenth-Century England* (Lewisburg, Pa.: Bucknell University Press, 2007); Glynis Ridley,
ed., "Animals in the Eighteenth Century," special issue, *Journal for Eighteenth-Century Studies*
33.4 (2010); Lucinda Cole, ed., "Animal, All Too Animal," special issue, *Eighteenth Century* 52.1
(2011). There is also a good deal of work on particular animal species or kinds in this period,
which is wonderfully alert to the traffic between literal and figurative animals, including Ingrid
Tague on pets in *Animal Companions: Pets and Social Change in Eighteenth-Century Britain* (University Park: Pennsylvania State University Press, 2015); Donna Landry on eastern horses in
Noble Brutes: How Eastern Horses Transformed English Culture (Baltimore: Johns Hopkins University Press, 2009); Richard Nash on primates in *Wild Enlightenment: The Borders of Human
Identity in the Eighteenth Century* (Charlottesville: University of Virginia Press, 2003); Harriet
Ritvo on New Leicester or Dishley sheep in "Possessing Mother Nature: Genetic Capital in

Eighteenth-Century Britain" in *Early Modern Conceptions of Property*, ed. John Brewer and Susan Staves (London: Routledge, 1995), 413–26.

37. Menely, *Animal Claim*, 104.

38. Menely, *Animal Claim*, 153. Intriguingly, Menely closes his reading of Pope's *Windsor-Forest* by turning to the allegorical and also animal personification of "Peace descending . . . / [with] her Dove-like Wing," in which he locates the possibility of an abstract animal figure that cannot be fully reduced to the logic of sovereign violence. See 104–5.

39. Nash, "Joy and Pity," 57.

40. Menely, *Animal Claim*, 115, 8.

41. Menely, *Animal Claim*, 8.

42. In *The Animal That I Therefore Am*, Derrida insists on the singularity of his cat: "I must make it clear from the start, the cat I am talking about is a real cat, truly, believe me, *a little cat*. It isn't the *figure* of a cat. It doesn't silently enter the room as an allegory for all the cats on the earth, the felines that travers myths and religions, literature and fables. . . . The cat that looks at me naked and that is *truly a little cat, this* cat I am talking about . . . she and no other, the one *I am talking about here*" (6). Yet throughout this section, Derrida continues to foreground the complicated relationship between the generic and the singular, the literal and the figurative—framing his insistence on the singularity of his cat with an extended and masterful prolepsis that disclaims (and ensures) its connection to all sorts of feline literary figures: the cats of Kafka, Montaigne, Baudelaire, Rilke, Carroll, etc.

43. For other helpful readings of Cowper's animal poems that take seriously their formal and generic sophistication, see Conrad Brunström and Katherine Turner, "'I Shall Not Ask Jean-Jacques Rousseau': Anthropomorphism in the Cowperian Bestiary," *Journal for Eighteenth-Century Studies* 33.4 (2010): 453–68; and Richard Terry, "'Meaner Themes': Mock-Heroic and Providentialism in Cowper's Poetry," *Studies in English Literature, 1500–1900* 34.3 (1994): 617–34. On animals in *The Task* in particular, see Menely, *Animal Claim*, 147–63.

44. On the derivation of the word "fable" from the Latin root meaning "to talk," see John Heath, *The Talking Greeks: Speech, Animals, and the Other in Homer, Aeschylus, and Plato* (Cambridge: Cambridge University Press, 2005), 14, and Mark Loveridge, *A History of Augustan Fable* (Cambridge: Cambridge University Press, 1998), 4.

45. See Louis Marin, *Food for Thought*, trans. Mette Hjort (Baltimore: Johns Hopkins University Press, 1989), 74, and Jayne Lewis, *The English Fable: Aesop and Literary Culture, 1651–1740* (Cambridge: Cambridge University Press, 1996), 8.

46. Giorgio Agamben, *The Open: Man and Animal*, trans. Kevin Attell (Stanford, Calif.: Stanford University Press, 2004), 28.

47. Michel de Montaigne, "The Apologie for Raymond Sebond," in *The Essayes of Montaigne: John Florio's Translation*, ed. J. I. M. Stewart (New York: Modern Library, 1933), 400. Also qtd. in Shannon, *Accommodated Animal*, 85.

48. See Thomas Hobbes, *Leviathan* (London: Penguin, 1985), 197; hereafter cited parenthetically in the text.

49. See Jessica Riskin, "The Defecating Duck; or, The Ambiguous Origins of Artificial Life," *Critical Inquiry* 29.4 (2003): 599–633.

50. Michael Thompson, "Apprehending Human Form," in *Modern Moral Philosophy*, ed. Anthony O'Hear (Cambridge: Cambridge University Press, 2004), 67.

51. For another model for this sort of quasi-figurative operation and being, see Joseph Slaughter's characterization of the logic of twentieth-century human rights law (and its literary correlative, the Bildungsroman) as a particularly complex "figurative process of naturalization" that he calls

"incorporation"—a personifying operation that transforms the natural human into the artificial (and rights-bearing) person at the same time that it asserts the two to be identical—"presuppos[ing] the person *is* a person in order to effect the person *as* a person" (21). See Joseph R. Slaughter, *Human Rights, Inc.: The World Novel, Narrative Form, and International Law* (New York: Fordham University Press, 2007), esp. 1–44. See also Slaughter's fascinating discussion of the role played by *Robinson Crusoe* in the UN debates over the text of the Universal Declaration of Human Rights, 45–85.

52. The quotation comes from Henri Bergson, *Les Deux Sources de la morale et de la religion*, 88e édition (Paris: PUF, 1958), 192, my translation. This extract is quoted in Claude Lévi-Strauss, *Totemism*, trans. Rodney Needham (Boston: Beacon, 1963), where the final sentence reads: "'An animal lacks concreteness and individuality, it appears essentially as a quality, and thus essentially as a class'" (93). In Needham's translation, the relationship between individual concreteness and specificity is configured as one of mutually exclusive opposition, while Bergson's original formulation emphasizes the way an animal brings together individual concreteness and a generic or species character: "Un animal a donc beau être du concret et de l'individuel, il apparaît essentiellement comme une qualité, essentiellement aussi comme un genre."

53. This point is certainly behind much of Derrida's play with the generic and the singular throughout *The Animal That I Therefore Am*, and in his characterization of his encounter with his cat in particular.

54. Lévi-Strauss, *Totemism*, 99. Lévi-Strauss traces this thought to the eighteenth century and to Rousseau in particular—the first thinker, according to Lévi-Strauss, to understand the "'specific' character" of animals and to elaborate its significance for human intellection and human society.

55. Lévi-Strauss, *Totemism*, 93. William Godwin, *Enquiry Concerning Political Justice*, ed. Isaac Kramnick (Harmondsworth: Penguin, 1976), 756.

56. Samuel Johnson, "Thomson," in *Lives of the English Poets*, 3 vols. (Oxford: Clarendon, 1950), 3:300.

57. Throughout this book, the task of cohabitation sometimes centers on affective relationships with companionate animals—the sort of relationships that Michael Trask takes to be at the center of a good deal of contemporary animal studies (and which he associates with the dominance of Levinasian ethics in the field). But often, the project of cohabitation comes closer to the sense that Trask associates with Peter Singer, in which "the animal need not be our companion in any but the most unspecific sense (cohabitant of the planet)" ("Ethical Animal," par. 6). This more impersonal and even planetary sense of cohabitation is what is invoked in Thomson's use of "people" for all sorts of creatures, or in Buffon's depiction of "the numberless objects with which the surface of this globe is covered and peopled" (*Natural History*, 2.1).

58. On the domestic as a political-philosophical trope in eighteenth-century studies, see (among many others) Nancy Armstrong, *Desire and Domestic Fiction: A Political History of the Novel* (New York: Oxford University Press, 1987); Michael McKeon, *The Secret History of Domesticity: Public, Private, and the Division of Knowledge* (Baltimore: Johns Hopkins University Press, 2005); and Helen Thompson, *Ingenuous Subjection: Compliance and Power in the Eighteenth-Century Domestic Novel* (Philadelphia: University of Pennsylvania Press, 2005). On the domestic realm as a multispecies domain in this era, see esp. Thomas, *Man and the Natural World*; Brown, *Homeless Dogs and Melancholy Apes*; Tague, *Animals Companions*; and Harriet Ritvo, *The Animal Estate: The English and Other Creatures in the Victorian Age* (Cambridge, Mass.: Harvard University Press, 1987), and "Possessing Mother Nature."

59. Menely, *Animal Claim*, 9. For a different sense of social contract, see Stanley Cavell's remarks on Locke and Rousseau in *The Claim of Reason: Wittgenstein, Skepticism, Morality, and*

Tragedy (Oxford: Oxford University Press, 1999), 22–28, and on Locke in *Cities of Words: Pedagogical Letters on a Register of the Moral Life* (Cambridge, Mass.: Belknap Press of Harvard University Press, 2004), 49–69. Cavell associates the politics of social contract with speech in the sense of what he calls "conversation": "my speaking for others and my being spoken for by others, not alone speaking to and being spoken to by others" (*Cities*, 51). In doing so, he transforms Quintilian's definition of prosopopoeia (the figure by which we "speak, as it were, by the Mouth of others") into a fundamental ethico-political question: "How do you know you are speaking for anyone and being spoken for by someone?" (51); or, as he puts it in *The Claim of Reason*, "how [do] I know with whom I am in community"? (25). References to Quintilian are from the 1756 English edition of Quintilian, *Institutes: M. Fabius Quinctilianus his Institutes of eloquence: or, the art of speaking in public, . . . Translated into English, . . . with notes, critical and explanatory, by William Guthrie, Esq; in two volumes* (London: printed for T. Waller, 1756), 2:415.

    60. Henry Home, Lord Kames, *Elements of Criticism*, 3 vols. (Edinburgh: printed for A. Millar, A. Kincaid and J. Bell, 1762), 3:70. Kames argues that "figures of speech" simply compare two entities that remain entirely distinct, while in "figures of thought" like personification, we really believe, or actually suppose, the personified entity to have life, sense, or intelligence.

CHAPTER 1. THE PERSON

    1. In the preface to *Lyrical Ballads*, Wordsworth singles out "personifications of abstract ideas" for censure. William Wordsworth, "Wordsworth's Prefaces of 1800 and 1802," in *Lyrical Ballads*, ed. R. L. Brett and A. R. Jones (New York: Routledge, 1991), 250. As M. H. Abrams points out, Wordsworth is also critical of personifications of natural objects that are insufficiently supported by a poet's feeling. Abrams, *The Mirror and the Lamp: Romantic Theory and the Critical Tradition* (New York: Oxford University Press, 1953), 291–92.

    2. See Auguste Comte, "Cinquante-Deuxième Leçon," in *Cours de philosophie positive*, in *Oeuvres d'Auguste Comte*, 12 vols. (Paris: Éditions Anthropos, 1968–71), 5.1–91; Edward Tylor, *Primitive Culture: Researches into the Development of Mythology, Philosophy, Religion, Language, Art, and Custom*, 7th ed., 2 vols. (New York: Brentano, [1924]), 2.287, 467–96; Karl Marx, "The Fetishism of the Commodity and Its Secret," in *Capital: A Critique of Political Economy*, 3 vols. (Oxford: Oxford University Press, 1976–81), 1.163–77; Oliver Wendell Holmes, "Lecture 1: Early Forms of Liability," in *The Common Law* (New York: Dover, 1991), 1–38; Sigmund Freud, "Animism, Magic and the Omnipotence of Thought," in *Totem and Taboo: Some Points of Agreement Between the Mental Lives of Savages and Neurotics*, in *The Standard Edition of the Complete Psychological Works of Sigmund Freud*, ed. James Strachey, 24 vols. (London: Hogarth, 1953–74), 13.75–99. In different ways, each of these texts grounds modernity and its own claim to knowledge on two related sets of distinctions: first, between persons and things, and second, between moderns and primitives.

    3. *The New Princeton Encyclopedia of Poetry and Poetics*, ed. Alex Preminger and T. V. F. Brogan (Princeton, N.J.: Princeton University Press, 1993), 902. A number of critics also draw a line between primitive and modern around the (especially eighteenth-century) figure of personification. See Chester Chapin, *Personification in Eighteenth-Century English Poetry* (New York: King's Crown, 1955), 128; Patricia Meyer Spacks, *The Insistence of Horror: Aspects of the Supernatural in Eighteenth-Century Poetry* (Cambridge, Mass.: Harvard University Press, 1962), 144; Stephen Knapp, *Personification and the Sublime: Milton to Coleridge* (Cambridge, Mass.: Harvard University Press, 1985), 139–41.

4. See Bruno Latour, *We Have Never Been Modern*, 13–48.

5. Samuel Johnson, *Dictionary of the English language*, s.v. "Personification."

6. On personification in eighteenth-century poetry, see esp. John Sitter, *Cambridge Introduction to Eighteenth-Century Poetry*, 157–77.

7. For a related argument, see Lynn Festa's essay "Person, Animal, Thing: The 1796 Dog Tax and the Right to Superfluous Things," *Eighteenth-Century Life* 33.2 (2009), which pays splendid attention to "the rhetorical erosion of seemingly categorical distinctions between humans and animals, between animate and inanimate, between persons and things" in verbal and visual responses to the effort to introduce a tax on dogs (2).

8. William Wordsworth, "Essay, Supplementary to the Preface," in *The Prose Works of William Wordsworth*, ed. W. J. B. Owen and Jane Worthington Smyser, 3 vols. (Oxford: Clarendon, 1974), 3.73. For a more recent example, see Lawrence Buell, *The Environmental Imagination: Thoreau, Nature Writing, and the Formation of American Culture* (Cambridge, Mass.: Harvard University Press, 1995), 221–26.

9. William Hazlitt, "Thomson and Cowper," in *Lectures on English Poets and The Spirit of the Age* (London: J. M. Dent, 1910), 86. For a survey of critical responses to Thomson's use of personification, see Ralph Cohen, *The Art of Discrimination: Thomson's "The Seasons" and the Language of Criticism* (Berkeley: University of California Press, 1964), 315–80.

10. William Wordsworth, "Essay, Supplementary to the Preface," in *Wordsworth's Literary Criticism*, ed. W. J. B. Owen (London: Routledge, 1974), 204; Samuel Johnson, "Thomson," in *Lives of the English Poets*, 3:300.

11. Quintilian, *Institutes*, 2.258, 415.

12. Quintilian, *Institutes*, 2.258–60, 416.

13. Quintilian, *Institutes*, 2.225.

14. Quintilian, *Institutes*, 2.225, 223.

15. In some contexts, prosopopoeia, personation, and personification designate different figures or objects of figuration. But eighteenth-century writers tend to follow Johnson in taking "personification"—and less frequently, personation—to be the lay English translation of the technical Latin "prosopopoeia." See James J. Paxson, *The Poetics of Personification* (Cambridge: Cambridge University Press, 1994), 27.

16. Kames, *Elements of Criticism*, 3.55.

17. James Beattie, *Essays: On poetry and music, as they affect the mind; on laughter, and ludicrous composition; on the usefulness of classical learning*, 3rd ed. (London: printed for E. and C. Dilly, 1779), 256.

18. Hugh Blair, *Lectures on Rhetoric and Belles Lettres*, 3 vols. (Dublin: Whitestone, Colles, Burnet et al., 1783), 3.383–84.

19. Joseph Priestley, *A Course of Lectures on Oratory and Criticism* (London: printed for J. Johnson, 1777), 247.

20. The same question emerges in discussions of personification from Comte to Holmes, in which the figure of personification functions both to assert and to complicate claims to modernity. In each of these works, personification is identified with some variety of animism, a term in which the crucial distinction often falls not between human person and nonhuman thing but along the potentially quite different axis of animate and inanimate. In his *Cours de philosophie positive*, for example, Comte defines fetishism as "our primitive tendency" to conceive of all bodies to be "animated by a life essentially analogous to our own" (24). He goes on to call this animation "personification," just as he insists that this tendency to "animate" or "personify" is shared by both animals and human beings (see 29–30, 36–37; my translation). Comte's concept

of fetishism as animation/personification influences Edward Tylor's idea of primitive "animism," which in turn informs Holmes's notion of primitive "personification." Yet in Holmes's most common example of this primitive personification, the act of *personi*fication turns a tree into an *animal* (*The Common Law*, 11).

21. *New Princeton Encyclopedia*, 902.

22. Frances Ferguson, *Wordsworth: Language as Counter-Spirit* (New Haven, Conn.: Yale University Press, 1977), 26.

23. Adela Pinch, *Strange Fits of Passion: Epistemologies of Emotion, Hume to Austen* (Stanford, Calif.: Stanford University Press, 1996), 48. Lynn Festa makes a similar point, discussing object narratives, in *Sentimental Figures of Empire in Eighteenth-Century Britain and France* (Baltimore: John Hopkins University Press, 2006), 131–32.

24. On this, see Hugh Blair's discussion of personification in the *Lectures on Rhetoric and Belles Lettres*, which begins this way: "One of the greatest pleasure we receive from poetry, is, to find ourselves always in the midst of our fellows; and to see every thing thinking, feeling, and acting, as we ourselves do. This is, perhaps, the principal charm of this sort of figured style, that it introduces us into society with all nature" (3.391). The "society with all nature" composed by way of personification in Blair, as in Thomson, ultimately looks less like Latour's modern constitution than it does the reassembled sociality that he calls for in its stead. See Latour, *Reassembling the Social*. There, Latour urges us to begin our accounts of sociality not with human subjects (and the objects they act on), but with animation itself—with the very thin fact of action or doing. He urges us, too, to take seriously the work of figuration in resolving action into actors and looks to the literary domain to remind us of the diversity of figures available to us—"there exist many more figures than anthropomorphic ones," he writes (53).

25. Jonathan Swift to Charles Wogan, 2 August 1732, in *Correspondence of Jonathan Swift*, 5 vols., ed. Harold Williams (Oxford: Clarendon, 1963–65), 4.53, also qtd. by Sambrook, in the introduction to Thomson's *The Seasons*, xxix.

26. James Sambrook introduces his 1981 edition of *The Seasons* along such lines: "The poet is his own subject. Standing alone, he finds in the shapes and sounds of unconscious external nature the self-conscious life of his own thought," xxxii. On Thomson's animated descriptions, see also Alan Dugald McKillop, *The Background of Thomson's "Seasons"* (Minneapolis: University of Minnesota Press, 1942), 70; W. B. Hutchings, "'Can Pure Description Hold the Place of Sense?': Thomson's Landscape Poetry," in *James Thomson: Essays for the Tercentenary*, ed. Richard Terry (Liverpool: Liverpool University Press, 2000), 48.

27. Hazlitt, *Lectures on English Poets*, 87.

28. John Barrell, *The Idea of Landscape and the Sense of Place 1730–1840: An Approach to the Poetry of John Clare* (Cambridge: Cambridge University Press, 1972), 41.

29. Barrell, *Idea of Landscape*, 5.

30. Kevis Goodman, *Georgic Modernity and British Romanticism: Poetry and the Mediation of History* (Cambridge: Cambridge University Press, 2004), 38.

31. Barrell, *Idea of Landscape*, 26.

32. Kames, *Elements of Criticism*, 1.317. Qtd. in Barrell, *Idea of Landscape*, 3.

33. See Barrell, *Idea of Landscape*, 22, 23, 39, 44, 50.

34. Kenneth Clark, *Landscape into Art* (London: John Murray, 1949), 63. Qtd. in Barrell, *Idea of Landscape*, 11.

35. Barrell, *Idea of Landscape*, 59.

36. Barrell, *Idea of Landscape*, 59.

37. Barrell, *Idea of Landscape*, 59.

38. Ralph Cohen, *The Unfolding of "The Seasons"* (Baltimore: Johns Hopkins University Press, 1970), 23.

39. For an important exception to this tendency to see Thomson's "people" as preserving boundaries between humans and animals, see John Sitter, *Cambridge Introduction to Eighteenth-Century Poetry*, 199–202.

40. In her brilliant reading of Thomson, Kevis Goodman suggests that Thomson's periphrases, and particularly the paradigmatic "nameless nations," register ambivalence about the imperial order that he otherwise celebrates. While I agree that *The Seasons* registers anxieties about as well as support for imperialism, my sense is that Thomson's notion of empire extends well beyond human nations. See Goodman, *Georgic Modernity*, 60–62. Thomson's description of "nameless nations" appears in *Su*, 287–317.

41. Claude Lévi-Strauss, *The Savage Mind* (Chicago: University of Chicago Press, 1962), 149, 136.

42. Lévi-Strauss, *Savage Mind*, 151–53.

43. Lévi-Strauss, *Savage Mind*, 175.

44. In a related discussion of *The Savage Mind*, Frances Ferguson argues that Lévi-Strauss, unlike Foucault and like Jeremy Bentham in this regard, "treats individuality as an artifact of a group relation" (1157). See Ferguson, "Canons, Poetics, and Social Value: Jeremy Bentham and How to Do Things with People," *MLN* 100.5 (1995): 1148–64.

45. Cohen, *Unfolding*, 102. For Barrell's account of Thomson's poet-aristocrat's "eye," see *English Literature in History 1730–80: An Equal, Wide Survey* (New York: St. Martin's, 1983), 73–78; see also Barrell, *Idea of Landscape*, 22. In her reading of *The Seasons*, G. Gabrielle Starr helpfully shifts the organizing perspective of the poem from a "self" to a "system." In contrast to the argument I am making, however, she understands the multiple I/eyes in Thomson's poem to be human and connected via sympathy into something like a general point of view. See Starr, *Lyric Generations: Poetry and the Novel in the Long Eighteenth Century* (Baltimore: Johns Hopkins University Press, 2004), 75–84. See also Goodman's discussion of Thomson's "microscopic eye" in *Georgic Modernity*, 38–66.

46. As these examples suggest, and contrary to readings like Barrell's, Thomson's eyes generally do not gaze, fix, or compose. Instead, they are very often not acting but acted on. When they are described as acting, Thomson's eyes are modified by adjectives more often than verbs, and they move with aimless rather than directed or deliberate motion. See *Sp*, 88–89, 518–20, 542–43; *Su*, 692–93.

47. Ralph Cohen classifies Thomson's various personifications into four distinct categories: periphrasis, allegorical personification, pictorial or figural personification, and mere metaphoric personification (*Unfolding*, 25). Cohen's categories helpfully point to the diversity of Thomson's personifying practices, but they can also obscure the uncertain status of Thomson's descriptions.

48. Virgil, *Georgics*, in *The Works of Virgil: Containing his pastorals, Georgics and Æneis. Translated into English verse by Mr. Dryden. In three volumes*, vol. 1 (London: J. and R. Tonson, 1763), book 2, lines 498, 493, 500, 497, on pages 258–59.

49. Thomson, *Liberty*, part 2, lines 11–12; *The Castle of Indolence*, canto 2, lines 568–76. In James Thomson, *Liberty, The Castle of Indolence, and Other Poems*, ed. James Sambrook (Oxford: Clarendon, 1986). All references hereafter cited parenthetically by part/canto and line number.

50. Samuel Taylor Coleridge, *Biographia Literaria; or, Biographical Sketches of My Literary Life and Opinions*, in *The Collected Works of Samuel Taylor Coleridge*, 16 vols. (Princeton, N.J.: Princeton University Press, 1969–), 7.201, qtd. in Knapp, *Personification and the Sublime*, 32.

51. Knapp, *Personification and the Sublime*, 2; see also 59–65.

52. On passion as a mode of agency or "power," see Locke, *Essay Concerning Human Understanding*, 285–86; 294. The sense of passion as motive force informs the whole of Hume's *A Treatise of Human Nature*, ed. P. H. Nidditch (Oxford: Oxford University Press, 1978), and book 2 in particular. In terms relevant to my own discussion, Adela Pinch points out that the central Humean passion, sympathy, is an attempt to "overcome the passivity of mind of the empiricist account as it is usually understood" (*Strange Fits of Passion*, 34).

53. Virgil, *Georgics*, book 3, lines 375, 380.

54. Virgil, *Georgics*, book 3, lines 381–82, 387–88.

55. See Suvir Kaul, *Poems of Nation, Anthems of Empire: English Verse in the Long Eighteenth Century* (Charlottesville: University of Virginia Press, 2000), 131–82.

56. Anthony Ashley Cooper, third Earl of Shaftesbury, "An Inquiry Concerning Virtue or Merit," in *Characteristics of Men, Manners, Opinions, Times*, ed. Lawrence E. Klein (Cambridge: Cambridge University Press, 1999), 192, 230. On the connection of Thomson and Shaftesburian philosophy, see Robert Inglesfield, "Thomson and Shaftesbury," in *James Thomson: Essays for the Tercentenary*, ed. Richard Terry (Liverpool: Liverpool University Press, 2000), 67–91.

57. Shaftesbury, "Inquiry," 230.

58. See Shaftesbury, "Inquiry," 169, 171, 173, 192, 198, 205, 206.

59. Shaftesbury, "Inquiry," 168–69.

60. "Species" is also Lévi-Strauss's term. Thus, while the logic of Thomson's personification anticipates that of Lévi-Strauss's totemic operation—producing peoples and persons as totemism does species and individuals—the difference in their terminology is worth noting. For Lévi-Strauss, "species" is a term that enables the passage from nonhuman nature to human culture and society; it both creates and cements the divide between these realms. Thomson's "people," by contrast, denies any such divide.

61. Thomson surely has in view a similar moment in Shaftesbury's "The Moralists," in which Theocles leads Philocles on a flight of fancy "through different climates, from pole to pole and from the frigid to the torrid zone" (313). See "The Moralists, a Philosophical Rhapsody, Being a Recital of Certain Conversations on Natural and Moral Subjects," in *Characteristics of Men, Manners, Opinions, Times*, ed. Lawrence E. Klein (Cambridge: Cambridge University Press, 1999), 313–15.

62. Goodman, *Georgic Modernity*, 60.

63. On this sort of composition, see Joanna Picciotto's "Reading People," which links Thomson to the Royal Society ideal of an undifferentiated and fungible observer, "an eye that belongs to no one in particular" (16). Picciotto goes on to suggest that "the speaker of [*The Seasons*] is the collectivized eye, and I, of [the] public" (16)—but closer to my own sense of Thomson is her notion of serially inhabiting individual but undifferentiated perspectives, which she characterizes as an ideal not of an impartial but of "a consecutively partial" spectator (20).

64. I am grateful to Neil Chudgar for his conversation about this passage. For a related discussion of personification, see Samuel Levin's illuminating "Allegorical Language," in *Allegory, Myth Symbol*, ed. Morton W. Bloomfield (Cambridge, Mass.: Harvard University Press, 1981), 23–38. Levin argues that personification establishes an incongruity between noun and predicate that requires resolution: either (and most often) by conforming the noun to the usual meaning of the predicate—"the rock was merry" becomes "the human being was merry"—or, less frequently, by conforming the predicate to the usual meaning of the noun—"the rock was merry" becomes "the rock was glistening." Levin also identifies something he calls "*radical dispersonification*" (30). This figure calls for the resolution not of a semantic but of a conceptual incongruity: called to read both noun and predicate literally, "we try to conceive of merriment

as something that might be experienced by a rock" (29). Thomson's personifications operate much as Levin's radical dispersonification does, except that the conceptual shift comes not in the meaning of "merriment" but of "rock." That is, Thomson would conceive of a rock (or Amelia or a pine tree) as something that experiences merriment (or, strickenness): that is, as a person.

65. Lévi-Strauss, *Savage Mind*, 214.

66. See Ferguson, "Canons, Poetics, and Social Value," 1158. Ferguson makes a case for the ethical importance of this version of personification, "the moment in which the progression from genus to species to individual ceases to feel formal and comes to feel like 'personality' itself—the fount and end-product of emotion" (1159).

67. Lévi-Strauss, *Savage Mind*, 166.

68. This back-and-forth movement between personifications and persons illuminates a characteristic feature of Thomson's poetry: his interest in what Alan McKillop calls "the statuesque": Thomson's "sweeping descriptions of natural phenomena are full of movement . . . [but] in the midst of his scenes he often puts stationary figures, used in an elaborately decorative way. . . . He was always fascinated by the idea of human figures frozen or petrified in natural postures" (*Background of Thomson's "Seasons,"* 70–71). As McKillop's formulation indicates, critics often take this combination of animated natural phenomena and frozen human figures to be inversely related. Yet Thomson's statues are not wholly static figures; at least, their stasis is never permanent. As often as he imagines human beings petrified by lightning or love or snow or surprise, he also depicts statues, as in *Liberty*, "Sprung into Motion; soften'd into Flesh; / . . . fir'd to Passion, or refin'd to Soul" (2.311–12). For Thomson, a statue is not a petrified form but a motive force, a mold that can be animated again and again. Like allegorical personifications, statues fix persons in order to keep others in motion.

69. On Thomson's critique of hunting, see Tobias Menely, "Animal Signs and Ethical Significance: Expressive Creatures in the British Georgic," *Mosaic* 39.4 (2006): 120–23; and *Animal Claim*, 114–23.

70. See for example Barrell, *English Literature in History*, 65–74.

CHAPTER 2. THE CREATURE

1. *Cast Away*, dir. Robert Zemeckis, 20th Century Fox, 2000.

2. Tom Hanks, interview with Charlie Rose, DVD special feature, *Cast Away*.

3. Margy Rochlin, "Marooned on an Island, Out on a Limb," *New York Times* 5 November 2000, late ed.: 2A.1.

4. Rochlin, "Marooned," 2A.1.

5. Rochlin, "Marooned," 2A.1.

6. Irene Basey Beesemeyer, "Crusoe the *ISOLATO*: Daniel Defoe Wrestles with Solitude," *1650–1850: Ideas, Aesthetics, and Inquiries in the Early Modern Era* 10 (2004): 89.

7. David Marshall, "Autobiographical Acts in *Robinson Crusoe*," *ELH* 71 (2004): 908; Eric Jager, "The Parrot's Voice: Language and the Self in Robinson Crusoe," *Eighteenth-Century Studies* 21.3 (1988): 327.

8. Jager, "Parrot's Voice," 325.

9. Jager, "Parrot's Voice," 325, 326.

10. Samuel Taylor Coleridge, *Coleridge's Miscellaneous Criticism*, ed. Thomas Middleton Raysor (London: Constable, 1936), 194, 293. Reprinted as "[Crusoe as a Representative

of Humanity]," in Daniel Defoe, *Robinson Crusoe*, ed. Michael Shinagel (New York: Norton, 1975), 268.

11. I discuss Rousseau's view of *Robinson Crusoe* in Chapter 5. For Joyce's account of Crusoe as "the true prototype of the British colonist" and the embodiment of "the whole Anglo-Saxon spirit," see James Joyce, "Daniel Defoe," in Daniel Defoe, *Robinson Crusoe* (New York: Norton, 1975), 356.

12. Watt, *Rise of the Novel*, 62.

13. Watt, *Rise of the Novel*, 64. Watt reads Coleridge in much this additive, inductive way, to make a sociological and perhaps also psychological point about Crusoe's universality, in which "universality" means "average" or "middling." See *Rise of the Novel*, 78.

14. Daniel Defoe, "Robinson Crusoe's Preface," in *Serious Reflections During the Life and Surprising Adventures of Robinson Crusoe with His Vision of the Angelick World. Written by Himself* (London: W. Taylor, 1720), unpaginated.

15. Michael McKeon is a significant exception, suggesting in *The Secret History of Domesticity* that we might understand Defoe's allegorical-historical narrative in a variety of ways: as an autobiographical secret history; as the secret history of the private life of a public figure; as a more general political allegory of Stuart absolutism; or as a literalized allegory in which "hermeneutic signifying system seems to assume a life of its own" (623).

16. See Charles Gildon, *The Life and Strange Surprizing Adventures of Mr. D—— De F——* (London, 1719); and Catherine Gallagher, "The Rise of Fictionality," in *The Novel*, vol. 1, *History Geography, and Culture*, ed. Franco Moretti (Princeton, N.J.: Princeton University Press, 2006), 339–41; hereafter cited parenthetically in the text.

17. Gallagher joins a number of critics who in different ways have begun to decouple novelistic character from narratives about the rise of individualism, by turning their attention to flat, typical, or abstract figures. See for example Aaron Kunin, "Characters Lounge" *Modern Language Quarterly* 70.3 (2009): 291–317; Deidre Shauna Lynch, *The Economy of Character: Novels, Market Culture and the Business of Inner Meaning* (Chicago: University of Chicago Press, 1998); Sandra Macpherson, *Harm's Way: Tragic Responsibility and the Novel Form* (Baltimore: Johns Hopkins University Press, 2010); Alex Woloch, *The One vs. the Many: Minor Characters and the Space of the Protagonist in the Novel* (Princeton, N.J.: Princeton University Press, 2003).

18. Watt, *Rise of the Novel*, 31.

19. Catherine Gallagher, *Nobody's Story: The Vanishing Acts of Women Writers in the Marketplace, 1670–1820* (Berkeley: University of California Press, 1995), xv. See also McKeon's evocative notion of the "concrete virtuality" of fictional character, which he introduces in *Secret History of Domesticity* (see esp. 109). Ultimately, McKeon remains committed to the idea that I am arguing against: that the only sort of generalization available in the modern eighteenth century is the product of an empiricist or inductive logic, which collects discrete individuals into groups. McKeon thinks that only in a traditional (premodern and pre-eighteenth-century) social imaginary do we see something different: a worldview in which people are taken "to be first of all not creative individuals but created parts of a totality that pre-exists individuality: creatures created by a collectivizing force beyond their own agency" (108). For McKeon, this is what constitutes "traditional ontology as such": that individuals are creatures rather than creators of collectives (108).

20. For a related sense of what it means to be representative in this capacious and creaturely way, see Picciotto's discussion of the affinity between the creatures of physico-theology and the characters of the early novel. In this discussion, Picciotto makes brief but very suggestive reference to Crusoe, as a "highly generalized subject position" that resembles the Adam of Bacon and the physico-theological tradition: "both Adamic man and the creatures he contemplated are

. . . linked by a common feature, or featurelessness; as candidates for identification, they don't exclude anyone in particular" ("Reading People," 13–14; see also 22–23).

21. In *Harm's Way*, Sandra Macpherson also suggests that the eighteenth-century novel understands the person (and with it, the literary character) as a "material abstraction" (21). My thinking throughout this section owes a good deal to hers. But I am interested, here, in the animate rather than the obdurately material body. Macpherson's focus on the brute (inanimate, insensible) materiality of the body is tied to her interest in the way that novels like *Journal of the Plague Year* and *Roxana* understand human beings to cause harm much as things (and animals) cause harm, by virtue of being matter in motion. I take Defoe in *Robinson Crusoe* to be interested not only in the intentionality often ascribed to human beings or the sheer mobility of inanimate things, but in the creaturely agency that Locke calls motivity and that I am calling animation or self-motion.

22. R. John Williams also understands *Robinson Crusoe* as a novel concerned with creature-liness, shrewdly pointing out, of the scene with Xury and the lion, that "we have a lion not with a snout, paws, and claws, but with a 'head,' a 'nose,' a 'leg,' and a 'knee,' a lion not referred to as 'it' but as 'him,' a lion whose hideous roaring and 'struggling for life' seems hauntingly human" (340). I share Williams's sense that "in the violence of the moment, one cannot explicitly gauge the traditional dichotomy between human and 'beast,'" but not the conclusion that he then draws: that "it is out of this narrative confusion that Crusoe consistently emerges as sovereign" (342). See R. John Williams, "Naked Creatures: *Robinson Crusoe*, the Beast, and the Sovereign," *Comparative Critical Studies* 2.3 (2005): 337–48.

23. On the epistemological and aesthetic considerations around depicting the unfamiliar, see J. Paul Hunter, *Before Novels: The Cultural Contexts of Eighteenth-Century English Fiction* (New York: Norton, 1990), 212–44, esp. 227–37; and G. Gabrielle Starr, "Objects, Imaginings, and Facts: Going Beyond Genre in Behn and Defoe," *Eighteenth-Century Fiction* 16.4 (2004): 499–518.

24. Julia Reinhard Lupton, *Citizen Saints: Shakespeare and Political Theology* (Chicago: University of Chicago Press, 2005), 161. In *On Creaturely Life: Rilke, Benjamin, Sebald* (Chicago: University of Chicago Press, 2006), Eric Santner also writes beautifully about the politico-theological category of the creaturely, though for Santner and the writers he discusses (Rilke, Benjamin, Sebald), "the 'creaturely' pertains not primarily to a sense of a shared animality or a shared animal suffering but to a biopolitical animation that distinguishes the human from the animal" (38–39). See also Anat Pick's *Creaturely Poetics: Animality and Vulnerability in Literature and Film* (New York: Columbia University Press, 2011), which understands the creature much as I do—as "first and foremost a living body—material, temporal, and vulnerable" (5), and which sets this sort of creaturely embodiment against both species and personal identity (see esp. 6–7, 17). Like both Lupton and Santner (and following Simone Weil), Pick also emphasizes the religious dimension of creatureliness—the "rapprochement between the material and the sacred" it attempts (17).

25. I am grateful to Abigail Zitin for suggesting to me the significance of Crusoe's own astonishment or incapacitation.

26. For readings of *Robinson Crusoe* as an empty shell of Puritan allegory, in which the material supplants the spiritual dimension entirely, see Watt, *Rise of the Novel*, 73–85; Michael McKeon, *Origins of the English Novel, 1600–1740* (Baltimore: Johns Hopkins University Press, 2002), 315–37; John Richetti, "Secular Crusoe: The Reluctant Pilgrim Re-Visited," *Eighteenth-Century Genre and Culture: Serious Reflections on Occasional Forms*, ed. Dennis Todd and Cynthia Wall (Newark: University of Delaware Press, 2001), 58–78. Critics who argue that the spiritual

dimension of Crusoe's adventures is paramount, and presented according to Puritan convention, include J. Paul Hunter, *The Reluctant Pilgrim: Defoe's Emblematic Method and the Quest for Form in "Robinson Crusoe"* (Baltimore: Johns Hopkins University Press, 1966); and G. A. Starr, *Defoe and Spiritual Autobiography* (Princeton, N.J.: Princeton University Press, 1965).

27. Critics who view Crusoe's illness and conversion as an experience of submission that precipitates an ever-greater mastery—one now securely underwritten by God—include John Richetti, *Defoe's Narratives: Situations and Structures* (Oxford: Clarendon, 1975), 41–46; G. A. Starr, *Defoe and Spiritual Autobiography*, 122–23; Hunter, *The Reluctant Pilgrim* 171–74; and Ilse Vickers, *Defoe and the New Sciences* (Cambridge: Cambridge University Press, 1996), 118.

28. Julia Reinhard Lupton, *Citizen Saints*, 161.

29. A wide range of critics discuss *Robinson Crusoe* in terms of the political and economic symbolics of cannibalism. See, for example, Everett Zimmerman, "Robinson Crusoe and No Man's Land," *Journal of English and Germanic Philology* 102 (2003): 506–29; and Wolfram Schmidgen, *Eighteenth-Century Fiction and the Law of Property* (Cambridge: Cambridge University Press, 2002), 32–62. Both pose useful challenges to the common understanding of *Robinson Crusoe* as a straightforward defense of colonialism. For thoughtful interpretations that do take *Robinson Crusoe* to champion the colonial project, see Peter Hulme, *Colonial Encounters: Europe and the Native Caribbean 1492–1797* (London: Methuen, 1986); and Roxann Wheeler, "'My Savage,' 'My Man': Racial Multiplicity in *Robinson Crusoe*," *ELH* 62.4 (1995): 821–61. For an interpretation that argues that Defoe ultimately seeks to defend a mercantile and colonial economic system but is also troubled by its costs, see Carol Houlihan Flynn, *The Body in Swift and Defoe* (Cambridge: Cambridge University Press, 1990), 149–76.

30. At times Carol Houlihan Flynn emphasizes the literal dimension of Crusoe's concern with cannibalism, remarking Defoe's interest in the whole of the "physical economy": his concern that the mere fact of living may mean that "to survive we may find ourselves consuming each other" (*Body in Swift and Defoe*, 149).

31. John Locke, *Two Treatises of Government* (1690; Cambridge: Cambridge University Press, 1988) 287; hereafter cited parenthetically in the text.

32. Schmidgen, *Eighteenth-Century Fiction and the Law of Property*, 60.

33. In an important discussion of early modern commentaries of Genesis, Laurie Shannon identifies "the creature" as a political and juridical category that included both humans and animals as stakeholders in a "zootopian constitution"—"a multikinded domain whose diverse parties are governed by shared rules" (43). I am characterizing Locke as working both within and against the tradition that Shannon charts. See Shannon, *Accommodated Animal*, esp. 40–47.

34. See J. M. Coetzee's *Elizabeth Costello* (New York: Penguin, 2003) for an extended meditation on this sort of undifferentiated creaturely identity. As Costello says of Kafka's "Report to an Academy"—with a nod to Crusoe's Poll—"We don't know and will never know . . . whether it is about a man speaking to men or an ape speaking to apes or an ape speaking to men or a man speaking to apes . . . or even just a parrot speaking to parrots" (19). Crusoe discovers something similar on the island, where species distinctions like human and parrot come to seem little more than empirically derived class distinctions, aggregates that might decompose, or be composed differently. By contrast, an allegorical and creaturely logic cannot be taken apart, because it is the formal and material logic of what Costello calls "a body-soul" (78). Throughout *Elizabeth Costello*, Coetzee repeatedly suggests that novelistic characters share this same basic form of identity with animals. He puts this point a number of ways: the animal and the novelistic character both are "a living soul," "an embodied soul," and "a body-soul"—the last of these formulations stressing the hyphen against the implicit Cartesian plus sign, and all of them invoking, with

"soul," a set of terms that includes idea, form, mind, and species. See also Coetzee's remarks on Defoe in the chapter of *Elizabeth Costello* entitled "Realism," and in his acceptance speech for the 2003 Nobel Prize in Literature, "He and His Man," online at http://www.nobelprize.org /nobel_prizes/literature/laureates/2003/coetzee-lecture-e.html.

35. On this desire, see Nancy Yousef, *Isolated Cases: The Anxieties of Autonomy in Enlightenment Philosophy and Romantic Literature* (Ithaca, N.Y.: Cornell University Press, 2004). In her reading of Rousseau, in particular, Yousef associates the fantasy of autonomy with the animal (see 63–95). In Defoe, it is more readily associated with God.

36. I understand Locke to use the terms "person" and "self" interchangeably (if not always clearly or consistently) in the *Essay*. For example, he launches his argument against the "ordinary way of speaking" that takes "the same Person, and the same Man, [to] stand for one and the same thing" with a scenario of a "self" that remains constant across different men: "Had I the same consciousness, that I saw the Ark and *Noah*'s Flood, as that I saw an overflowing of the *Thames* last Winter, or as that I write now, I could no more doubt that I . . . was the same *self*, place that *self* in what Substance you please, than that I write this am the same *my self* now whilst I write . . . that I was Yesterday" (340–41). For a reading of Locke's *Essay* that takes the "person" and "self" to be quite different terms, see Jonathan Lamb, *The Things Things Say* (Princeton, N.J.: Princeton University Press, 2011), esp. 138–43.

37. Locke makes clear in the *Essay* that personhood is his primary ethical and juridical category (see for example 230, 341). The vocabulary used throughout Locke's *Two Treatises* makes clear that "person" is also his primary political category, though I think that there it largely coincides with "human." For an argument that contends that "person" remains clearly distinct from "human" even in Locke's political philosophy, see John W. and Jean S. Yolton's introduction to Locke's *Some Thoughts Concerning Education* (Oxford: Clarendon, 1989), esp. 1–2, 14–22.

38. Recently, too, Giorgio Agamben takes Locke's account seriously, writing in *The Open: Man and Animal*, that "a witness as credible as John Locke refers to the story of the Prince of Nassau's parrot—which was able to hold a conversation and respond to questions 'like a reasonable creature'—more or less as a certainty" (24).

39. Descartes, *Discourse on the Method*, 1.140.

40. In *Why Do We Care About Literary Characters* (Baltimore: Johns Hopkins University Press, 2011), Blakey Vermeule refers to Defoe's novels as "autistic" for the way that they "almost pathologically avoid[] mind reading" (129, 100). By this, she means that Defoe's novels attend to bodies rather than minds; they are characterized by "mind blindness," something Vermeule associates with representing humans as animals (and thus as mere bodies) (see esp. 193–214). I am suggesting something like the inverse. On my view, Crusoe does not fail to attach minds to some bodies (human ones); rather, he begins to attach minds to all bodies—or simply to see moving (or apparently self-moving) bodies as minds. It is not that he is unable to see mind, but that he is increasingly unable to see anything but.

41. Descartes, *Discourse on the Method*, 1.140.

42. As I am characterizing them, Crusoe's conversations operate on a model closer to Stanley Cavell's notion of "acknowledgement" than Locke's account of language. In explaining this mode of apprehending others, Cavell can sometimes seem to invoke a fairly straightforward model of personification—as when he suggests that we might think of acknowledgement as "empathic projection" (*Claim of Reason*, 421). But Cavell's notion of projection is not straightforward. It is not an action performed by an active subject upon a passive object, but the effect of a relationship between two persons—an activity that one does not so much perform as undergo. See 329–496, esp. 395–98, 420–25.

43. For a reading that emphasizes the comfort that Crusoe derives from his domestic companions rather than the fear that they generate, see Cynthia Wall, *The Prose of Things: Transformations of Description in the Eighteenth Century* (Chicago: University of Chicago Press, 2006), 108–14. Wall urges us to "reinvest Defoean things . . . with some *pleasure* that reaches beyond use value or profit," and so to attend to what we too often overlook: that "Crusoe's pleasure in his raisins, in his 'little family' of cats and dogs and goats, in his umbrella, in his orderly shelves, is a sort of obverse to the Footprint" (109, 112). Wall argues convincingly that Crusoe takes great pleasure in the capacity of everyday things to constitute reality and so shore up Crusoe's sense of self; this argument is echoed in Susan Fraiman's sense that Crusoe is the first in a tradition of outcast figures for whom domesticity means "neither propriety and status nor captivity and drudgery but rather safety, sanity, and self-expression—survival in the most basic sense" (341). I find both arguments compelling accounts of Crusoe's domestic activities, though I wonder whether the cats and dogs fit so neatly with the other "things" in which Crusoe takes comfort. At least, I take Defoe (like Brontë, for Fraiman) to be alert to the "gothic aspects" of the domestic, as well as to its capacity to shelter or secure the self. In Fraiman, "Shelter Writing: Desperate Housekeeping from Crusoe to Queer Eye," *New Literary History* 37.2 (2006): 341–59.

44. Manuel Schonhorn, *Defoe's Politics: Parliament, Power, Kingship, and "Robinson Crusoe"* (Cambridge: Cambridge University Press, 1991), 147. For McKeon's reading of this scene, see *Secret History of Domesticity*, 625–26; and *Origins of the English Novel*, 327–28. On Crusoe's exercise of absolute sovereignty over his territory, see McKeon's *Origins of the English Novel*, 333–34.

45. McKeon, for example, identifies Crusoe's domestication of goats with his later domestication of Friday and aligns both acts with God's domestication of Crusoe: "Robinson has learned to internalize this principle of divine cultivation to some degree, for he has trapped, 'penn'd,' and domesticated the wild beasts of his island, most notably its goats" (*Origins of the English Novel*, 329).

46. Virginia Woolf, "Robinson Crusoe," in *Robinson Crusoe*, by Daniel Defoe, ed. Michael Shinagel (New York: Norton, 1975), 310.

47. In *Wild Enlightenment*, Richard Nash also argues that common interpretations of *Robinson Crusoe* are troubled by the goats, and by Crusoe's relation to them. There is a good deal of affinity between Nash's fascinating discussion of *Robinson Crusoe* and my own. Nash notes that, in eighteenth-century natural history, the goat is "something of a puzzle": "In an emerging discourse of species, the identity of goats was as vexed as the identity of the wild man—perhaps a degenerated production of an originally domestic species; perhaps a primitive original from which, by cultivation, the domestic sheep had been improved; perhaps a hybrid production, half-wild, half-domesticated" (87). At the same time, Nash takes the puzzling status of goats to be an inadvertent rather than deliberate element of Defoe's novel: "the virtual ecology of *Robinson Crusoe* enables a reading of problematic human identity in the narrative that undermines the conventional reading of *Crusoe* as a heroic novel of the triumph of 'economic individualism.' This is not to say that the novel does not assert such a doctrine . . . but rather that . . . it also (inadvertently as it were) compromises its own doctrine by calling into question the very wild/civilized dualism it seeks to establish in a clear economic relation" (100).

48. Julia Reinhard Lupton, *Citizen Saints*, 161.

49. Carol Houlihan Flynn also notes this moment, and Swift's (in her view more self-conscious) recasting of it, in *The Body in Swift and Defoe*, 159.

50. Relevant here are Laurie Shannon's reflections on the human negative exceptionalism envisioned in *King Lear*, in which "the 'coveredness' of animals—their not really being 'naked'—figures their self-completeness or natural sufficiency." "Poor, Bare, Forked: Animal Sovereignty,

Human Negative Exceptionalism, and the Natural History of King Lear," *Shakespeare Quarterly* 60.2 (2009): 186. Shannon argues that in the tradition to which *Lear* belongs—a tradition of thinking about animal rather than human sovereignty—clothing characterizes the human in the sort of negative terms usually (or later) associated with animal life: our "layering-on of a second skin, a more adequate one that originally belonged to another creature, spells out the radical insufficiency of man" (191). See also Shannon, *Accommodated Animal*, 127–73.

CHAPTER 3. THE HUMAN

1. Godwin, *Enquiry Concerning Political Justice*, 552.
2. Edward Said, "Swift as Intellectual," in *The World, the Text, and the Critic* (Cambridge, Mass.: Harvard University Press, 1984), 89.
3. Kathleen M. Williams, "Gulliver's Voyage to the Houyhnhnms," *ELH* 18.4 (1951): 280.
4. Ian Watt, "The Ironic Tradition in Augustan Prose from Swift to Johnson," in *The Character of Swift's Satire: A Revised Focus*, ed. Claude Rawson (Newark: University of Delaware Press, 1983), 315.
5. J. Paul Hunter, "*Gulliver's Travels* and the Later Writings," in *Cambridge Companion to Jonathan Swift*, ed. Christopher Fox (Cambridge: Cambridge University Press, 2003), 226. While critics chiefly interested in Swift's rational horses or humanoid beasts think largely in terms of fable, those who ask about Gulliver, like Watt and Hunter, look most often to the novel. Hunter concludes that Gulliver is not a character in any traditional novelistic sense, as do Claude Rawson and Ronald Paulson. See Rawson, *Gulliver and the Gentle Reader* (London: Routledge, 1973), 30; Rawson, "Gulliver and Others: Reflections on Swift's 'I' Narrators," in *Gulliver's Travels*, by Jonathan Swift, ed. Albert J. Rivero (New York: Norton, 2002), 487; and Paulson, *The Fictions of Satire* (Baltimore: Johns Hopkins University Press, 1967), 171. Critics who argue that we are at least partly encouraged to consider Gulliver as (or in relation to) a novelistic character include Dennis Todd, *Imagining Monsters: Miscreations of the Self in Eighteenth-Century England* (Chicago: University of Chicago Press, 1995), 171; and Clement Hawes, "Three Times Round the Globe: Gulliver and Colonial Discourse," *Cultural Critique* 18 (1991): 187–88; 207–210.
6. Jonathan Swift to Alexander Pope, 29 September 1725, in *Gulliver's Travels*, ed. Albert J. Rivero (New York: Norton, 2002), 262.
7. Watt, "Ironic Tradition," 316.
8. Watt, "Ironic Tradition," 316.
9. Watt, "Ironic Tradition," 316–17, 315.
10. Jonathan Swift, *A Tale of a Tub and Other Works*, ed. Angus Ross and David Woolley (Oxford: Oxford University Press, 1986), 78, 80.
11. For this argument, see Allen Michie, "Gulliver the Houyahoo: Swift, Locke, and the Ethics of Excessive Individualism," in *Humans and Other Animals in Eighteenth-Century British Culture*, ed. Frank Palmeri (Aldershot: Ashgate, 2006), 67–82.
12. The connections between *Robinson Crusoe* and *Gulliver's Travels* are not limited to book 2. For a powerful reading that focuses instead on book 1, see J. Paul Hunter's "*Gulliver's Travels* and the Novel," in *The Genres of* Gulliver's Travels, ed. Frederik N. Smith (Newark: University of Delaware Press, 1990), 56–74.
13. See, for example, Homer O. Brown, "The Displaced Self in the Novels of Daniel Defoe," *ELH* 38.4 (1971): 562–90; Jager, "Parrot's Voice"; Marshall, "Autobiographical Acts in *Robinson Crusoe*"; and Richetti, *Defoe's Narratives*.

14. See Ann Cline Kelly, "Gulliver as Pet and Pet Owner: Conversations with Animals in Book 4," *ELH* 74.2 (2007): 323–29.

15. For a different reading of this moment, see Neil Chudgar, "Swift's Gentleness," *ELH* 78.1 (Spring 2011): 137–61.

16. For a related discussion of the status of the pet, see Srinivas Aravamudan, *Tropicopolitans: Colonialism and Agency, 1688–1804* (Durham, N.C.: Duke University Press, 1999), 29–70.

17. Esp. in Claude Rawson, *God, Gulliver, and Genocide: Barbarism and the European Imagination, 1492–1945* (Oxford: Oxford University Press, 2001).

18. Brean Hammond, "Swift's Reading," in *Cambridge Companion to Jonathan Swift*, ed. Christopher Fox (Cambridge: Cambridge University Press, 2003), 80. Swift's note to "The Beasts' Confession" is cited in *Jonathan Swift: The Complete Poems*, ed. Pat Rogers (New Haven: Yale University Press, 1983), 866n220. All quotations from "The Beasts' Confession" are taken from this edition and are cited parenthetically in the text by line number.

19. Bernard Mandeville "The Grumbling Hive; or, Knaves Turn'd Honest," in *The Fable of the Bees; or, Private Vices, Public Benefits* (Indianapolis: Liberty Fund, 1988), line 13.

20. On the uniquely human "capacity to swerve, or fall, from type," see Shannon, "Poor, Bare, Forked," 176.

21. See Palmeri, "Autocritique of Fables."

22. Ephraim Chambers, "Definition," in *Cyclopædia: Or, an universal dictionary of arts and sciences; . . . In two volumes* (London: James and John Knapton et al., 1728), 1.177.

23. John Steffe, *Five Letters: Containing . . . for religious knowledge, piety, and devotion* (London: printed for J. Buckland, at the Buck in Pater-noster Row; T. Toft in Chelmsford, 1757), 47.

24. Plato, *Statesman*, ed. Julia Annas and Robin Waterfield, trans. Robin Waterfield (Cambridge: Cambridge University Press, 1995), 18.

25. Plato, *Statesman*, 11.

26. Plato, *Statesman*, 13.

27. In his 1978 lectures on governmentality, for example, Michel Foucault characterizes the *Statesman* as one of the few Greek texts to elaborate a pastoral vision of politics, with its statesman-shepherd governing human beings as a population of living creatures. Foucault argues that Plato elaborates this account of politics-as-shepherding in order to subject it to critique and advance an alternative, unfolded by the Visitor in the story he tells of an original state of nature in which every species of living creature had a divine herdsman to supply its needs, so there was neither interspecies predation nor intraspecies conflict. On Foucault's reading of Plato, the point of this story is that this world is not ours: its rule was not political, and our rulers are not shepherds. Eventually, the universe changed course, and this golden age came to an end. This is the beginning of politics. *Security, Territory, Population: Lectures at the Collège de France, 1977–78*, ed. Michel Senellart, trans. Graham Burchell (Houndmills: Palgrave Macmillan, 2007), 140–47.

28. Palmeri, "Autocritique," 83.

29. Palmeri, "Autocritique," 84.

30. Victoria Kahn, *Wayward Contracts: The Crisis of Political Obligation in England, 1640–1674* (Princeton, N.J.: Princeton University Press, 2004), 145.

31. Kahn, *Wayward Contracts*, 150; Hobbes, *Leviathan*, 89; qtd. in Kahn, *Wayward Contracts*, 145.

32. On the sweeping (and shocking) achievement of Hobbes's discussion of natural law—"his artificial production of the laws of nature"—see Kahn, *Wayward Contracts*, 154–66, quote on 163. Kahn argues that Hobbes effectively overturned the nature of natural law by deducing

(which is to say, artificially producing) the laws of nature from the natural desires of every individual.

33. For an important and different approach to Swift's concerns about political and literary representation, see Carole Fabricant, "Speaking for the Irish Nation: The Drapier, the Bishop, and the Problems of Colonial Representation," *ELH* 66.2 (1999): 337–72.

34. There are a number of excellent and extended accounts of Hobbesian personhood, to which my discussion is very much indebted. See esp. Hannah Pitkin, "Hobbes's Concept of Representation," parts 1 and 2, *American Political Science Review* 58 (1964): 328–40, 902–18; Quentin Skinner, "Hobbes and the Purely Artificial Person of the State," in *Visions of Politics*, vol. 3, *Hobbes and Civil Science* (Cambridge: Cambridge University Press, 2002), 177–208; Samantha Frost, *Lessons from a Materialist Thinker: Hobbesian Reflections on Ethics and Politics* (Stanford, Calif.: Stanford University Press, 2008); and in literary studies, Jonathan Lamb's *The Things Things Say*, esp. 78–86, 150–60. Though the focus of his reading of Hobbes lies elsewhere, Tracy Strong also has important things to say about personhood and representation in "How to Write Scripture: Words, Authority, and Politics in Thomas Hobbes," *Critical Inquiry* 20.1 (1993): 128–59.

35. Sharon Cameron, *Impersonality: Seven Essays* (Chicago: University of Chicago Press, 2007), viii. She continues, "For Hobbes, the definition of a person (or agent) is what we agree to treat as a person. . . . To be a person or agent, according to Hobbes, it is not sufficient to consider yourself a person; you must also be considered as [such]" (viii). For a similar account of personhood (which does not cite Hobbes as a source), see Miguel Tamen, *Friends of Interpretable Objects* (Cambridge, Mass.: Harvard University Press, 2001), esp. 77, 107, 137.

36. In *The Things Things Say*, Jonathan Lamb characterizes the Hobbesian author differently, as a figure of "isolation and unpredictability" that is fundamentally alien and so hostile to the domain of representation, delegation, and artificial personation that constitutes civil society (130). Lamb also associates the Hobbesian figure of the author with Swift, among others. See also xiv–xv, 8–12, 175–200.

37. The first phrase, "There are few things that are incapable of being represented by fiction," comes from the 1651 English edition of *Leviathan*. In the 1668 Latin edition (part or all of which may have been composed earlier than 1651), this phrase reads, "There are few things of which there cannot be a person. For although a person is by nature something which understands, still, that whose person is borne is not always necessarily so." See Hobbes, *Leviathan, with Selected Variants from the Latin Edition of 1668*, ed. Edwin Curley (Indianapolis: Hackett, 1994), 102n5.

38. The notion that we are somehow the subjects of our own personification is central to Samantha Frost's recent work on Hobbes, which makes an interesting case for seeing Hobbes as an ethical as much as a political theorist. Frost argues that "in his theory of ethics, Hobbes shows that our participation in practices of reading and being read is a condition of our political subjectivity" ("Faking It: Hobbes's Thinking-Bodies and the Ethics of Dissimulation," *Political Theory* 29.1 [2001]: 32). In order to be read, Frost contends, Hobbes insists that an individual must present herself as legible, and she does this by "acting in accordance with—or quite literally, impersonating—the laws of nature [by which] individuals make themselves legible to one another" (43). See also Frost, *Lessons from a Materialist Thinker*.

39. On this sense of authoring as owning in the sense of claiming or acknowledging, see Lamb, *Things Things Say*, 139.

40. In emphasizing Hobbes's interest in the political operations of representation and of reading, I have in mind the Hobbes that Kahn describes in *Wayward Contracts*, who "emphasized the fictional dimension of contract to a greater degree than before," and thus construed "politics

as a realm of poetics, even fabrication" (6, 16). My understanding of Hobbesian reading is influenced throughout by Tracy Strong's "How to Write Scripture."

41. Strong, "How to Write Scripture," 143.

42. Swift, *Tale of a Tub and Other Works*, 80.

43. Kahn makes a similar point in *Wayward Contracts*, when she notes that Hobbes seeks to replace the dangerous "metaphorical activity of comparison as emulation"—in which one vaingloriously imagines oneself to bear attributes that in fact belong to someone else—with "metaphor conceived of as a stable contract between individuals who agree to ignore their differences" (150). Kahn argues that Hobbes is after this second and essentially formal "process of metaphorical identification . . . that achieve[s] the proper combination of imaginative identification and distance" between individuals—allowing us to see "that we are alike in wanting what we individually desire and in disliking the frustration of those desires," however different the content of those desires may be (150–51).

44. References to Hobbes are scattered throughout Swift's work, and most depict the Hobbesian order in ways that miss much of what is crucial about Hobbes's system: the distinction between the political and the natural, the commonwealth and the crowd, the first person and the animal species, the one and the many. Critics often attribute these passages directly to Swift and conclude that he is resolutely anti-Hobbesian (and often antimodern and anti-individualist). The strongest version of this argument I know is Warren Montag's *The Unthinkable Swift: The Spontaneous Philosophy of a Church of England Man* (London: Verso, 1994). For readings that argue that Swift was hostile to Hobbes's politics but shared many of his views about materialism, the causes of civil discord, or authorship, see (respectively) Frank Palmeri, *Satire in Narrative: Petronius, Swift, Gibbon, Melville, and Pynchon* (Austin: University of Texas Press, 1990); Everett Zimmerman, *Swift's Narrative Satires: Author and Authority* (Ithaca, N.Y.: Cornell University Press, 1983); and Jonathan Lamb, "Swift, *Leviathan*, and the Persons of Authors," in *Swift's Travels: Eighteenth-Century Satire and Its Legacies*, ed. Nicholas Hudson and Aaron Santesso (Cambridge: Cambridge University Press, 2008), 25–38; as well as Lamb, *Things Things Say*, 175–200.

45. Margaret Anne Doody, "Insects, Vermin, and Horses: *Gulliver's Travels* and Virgil's *Georgics*," in *Augustan Studies: Essays in Honor of Irvin Ehrenpreis*, ed. Douglas Lane Patey and Timothy Keegan (Cranbury, N.J.: Associated University Presses, 1985), 162.

46. Read in light of Young Socrates' division of "human" and "beast," the Houyhnhnms are guilty of what Fredric Bogel identifies as the Augustan notion of pride: "the tendency to treat a part as though it were a whole—a fantasy not simply of superiority but of distinctness and self-sufficiency. 'Synecdoche as symptom' might describe this mechanism" (225). Fredric V. Bogel, *The Difference Satire Makes: Rhetoric and Reading from Jonson to Byron* (Ithaca, N.Y.: Cornell University Press, 2001).

47. Derrida, *Animal That I Therefore Am*, 96.

48. See Terry Castle, "Why the Houyhnhnms Don't Write: Swift, Satire, and the Fear of the Text," *Essays in Literature* 7 (1980): 31–44.

49. Swift, *The Battle of the Books*, 104; *A Tale of a Tub*, 23; both in *Tale of a Tub and Other Works*.

50. Swift, *Tale of a Tub*, 24.

51. Ernest Tuveson, "Swift: The View from Within the Satire," in *The Satirist's Art*, ed. H. James Jensen and Malvin R. Zirker (Bloomington: Indiana University Press, 1972), 77, 82.

52. W. B. Carnochan, *Lemuel Gulliver's Mirror for Man* (Berkeley: University of California Press, 1968), 64.

53. Carnochan, *Lemuel Gulliver's Mirror for Man*, 65.

54. Carnochan, *Lemuel Gulliver's Mirror for Man*, 64.

55. Swift, *Tale of a Tub*, 24.

56. Gerald Bruns, "Allegory and Satire: A Rhetorical Mediation," *New Literary History* 11.1 (1979): 128.

57. Many critics have remarked what Rawson calls "the traffic between Swift and his fictional speakers, his 'I' narrators." Rawson argues, for example, that "the important issue is not the character of Swift's personae or I's but the perpetual though elusive interplay with a central authorial energy operating behind them" ("Gulliver and Others," 495). Referring to *A Tale of A Tub* in particular, Ernest Tuveson writes, "Is the author really a fully realized *persona*? I come more and more to think he is rather a voice, an alter ego of Swift himself" ("Swift" 56). In *The Literary Persona* (Chicago: University of Chicago Press, 1982), Robert C. Elliot focuses his discussion on Swift and remarks that "the notorious instability of Swift's personae in their relation to the author makes the relation author-spokesman-reader often painfully confused, the definition of the situation ambiguous" (116).

58. In *The Difference Satire Makes*, Fredric Bogel argues that conventional satire is structured around three stable and separate positions: the persona, the reader, and the object against which the first two are united. Looking in particular at Swift's poetry, Bogel argues that Swift's satires long for but consistently fail to produce such stable positions, generating instead an "authorial uncertainty [and] an equivalently unauthoritative reader position" (125).

59. Rawson, *Gulliver and the Gentle Reader*, 46.

60. This is in part to echo Everett Zimmerman's characterization of *Gulliver's Travels* as "a book not about a man who undergoes certain experiences but about a man who writes a book about experiences that he has undergone" (*Swift's Narrative Satires*, 116–17). Richard H. Rodino cites this as a "pioneering description of the *Travels*" in the very helpful "Authors, Characters, and Readers in *Gulliver's Travels*," in *Gulliver's Travels*, by Jonathan Swift, ed. Albert J. Rivero (New York: Norton, 2002), 432.

61. Tuveson, "Swift," 77.

CHAPTER 4. THE ANIMAL

1. Michel Foucault, *The Order of Things: An Archaeology of the Human Sciences* (New York: Random House, 1970), 160. See also 265–79.

2. Francis Coventry, *The History of Pompey the Little: or, The Life and the History of a Lapdog* (London: M. Cooper, 1751), 8.

3. On the trope of the lapdog in this period, and its status "as that seeming oxymoron[,] a feeling thing," see Markman Ellis, "Suffering Things," 92–116, on 96. For related discussions of anxieties around gender, species, and the practice of pet keeping (and, especially, of keeping lapdogs), see Tague, *Animal Companions*, 91–137, and Laura Brown, "Immoderate Love: The Lady and the Lapdog," in *Homeless Dogs and Melancholy Apes*, 65–90. Both Tague and Brown understand Coventry's *Pompey the Little* as a narrative that turns both formally and thematically on the status of the living animal and the pet in particular (an active, feeling subject that is also an object of exchange). See Tague, *Animal Companions*, 131–37; Brown, *Homeless Dogs and Melancholy Apes*, 123–29.

4. One significant exception is Catherine Packham's *Eighteenth-Century Vitalism*, which identifies Locke as an early figure in an emerging tradition of eighteenth-century vitalism. See esp. 13–16.

5. Critics very often laud Sterne's novel for what Gerald Bruns calls its "philosophy of composition": to "let every singularity have its say," in "Introduction: Toward a Random Theory of Prose," in *Theory of Prose*, by Viktor Shklovsky (Elmwood Park, Ill.: Dalkey Archive Press, 1990), xi. For many of its best readers, *Tristram Shandy*'s celebration of singularity is a philosophy of life and personhood as well as of composition. See, for example, Fred Parker, *Scepticism and Literature: An Essay on Pope, Hume, Sterne, and Johnson* (Oxford: Oxford University Press, 2003), 211, 217; Jonathan Lamb, "Sterne and Irregular Oratory," in *Laurence Sterne's "Tristram Shandy": A Casebook*, ed. Thomas Keymer (Oxford: Oxford University Press, 2006), 235; John Traugott's introduction to *Laurence Sterne: A Collection of Critical Essays*, ed. John Traugott (Englewood Cliffs, N.J.: Prentice Hall, 1968), 11; Patricia Meyer Spacks, *Imagining a Self: Autobiography and Novel in Eighteenth-Century England* (Cambridge, Mass.: Harvard University Press, 1976), 134; and Marshall Brown, *Preromanticism* (Stanford, Calif.: Stanford University Press, 1991), 276.

6. For a summary of the critical positions on Sterne's attitude toward Locke, see Peter M. Briggs, "Locke's *Essay* and the Tentativeness of *Tristram Shandy*," in *Critical Essays on Laurence Sterne*, ed. Melvin New (New York: G. K. Hall, 1998), 87–109. For readings that link Sterne to Locke but understand him more in the spirit of Hume, see John Traugott, *Tristram Shandy's World: Sterne's Philosophical Rhetoric* (Berkeley: University of California Press, 1954); Parker, *Scepticism and Literature*, 190–231; and Christina Lupton, "Tristram Shandy, David Hume, and Epistemological Fiction," *Philosophy and Literature* 27.1 (2003): 98–115.

7. Laurence Sterne, *The Life and Opinions of Tristram Shandy, Gentleman*, ed. Ian Campbell Ross (Oxford: Oxford University Press, 1983), 7; hereafter cited parenthetically in the text.

8. Quintilian, *Institutes*, 2:415.

9. Foucault, *Order of Things*, 277, 44. On the enigmatic form of animality, "with its hidden structures, its buried organs, so many invisible functions, and that distant force . . . which keeps it alive" see also 276–78, quote on 277.

10. The identity of the Lockean "person" with the first person, and its nonidentity with "man" or the third person, is most apparent when Locke crosses his terms. Imagining an objection to his account of first-person consciousness, Locke writes: "suppose I wholly lose the memory of some parts of my Life, beyond a possibility of retrieving them, so that perhaps I shall never be conscious of them again; yet am I not the same Person, that did those Actions, had those Thoughts, that I was once conscious of, though I have now forgot them? . . . To which I answer, that we must here take notice what the Word *I* is applied to, which in this case is the Man only" (*Essay*, 342). As Michael Ayers points out, by Locke's logic "I" cannot be applied to "the Man," because that would be "to suppose that the 'man' could be thinking and talking about itself while the 'person' is keeping silent." See Ayers, *Locke*, vol. 2, *Ontology* (London: Routledge, 1991), 283–84.

11. Charles Taylor, *Sources of the Self: The Making of Modern Identity* (Cambridge, Mass.: Harvard University Press, 1989), 176.

12. See C. B. Macpherson, *The Political Theory of Possessive Individualism: Hobbes to Locke* (Oxford: Clarendon, 1962).

13. For a compelling reading of Locke's "owner-person," see Jonathan Lamb, "Locke's Wild Fancies: Empiricism, Personhood, and Fictionality," *Eighteenth Century* 48.3 (2007): 187–204; esp. 194–95; see also Jonathan Lamb, *Things Things Say*, esp. 129–50.

14. On Locke's extension of the *suum*, the domain of one's own, see Karl Olivecrona, "Locke's Theory of Appropriation," *Philosophical Quarterly* 24.96 (1974): 220–34. On the audacity of Locke's achievement in removing all natural restrictions on private property, see

C. B. Macpherson, "Locke on Capitalist Appropriation," *Western Political Quarterly* 4.4 (1951): 550–66.

15. Deidre Lynch puts the point similarly in "Personal Effects and Sentimental Fictions," in *The Secret Life of Things: Animals, Objects, and It-Narratives in Eighteenth-Century England*, ed. Mark Blackwell (Lewisburg, Pa.: Bucknell University Press, 2007), 68.

16. I am grateful to both David Brewer and Jonathan Elmer for pressing me to think about Tristram's concluding dash, and to Jesse Molesworth for underscoring the sadness as well as humor it implies.

17. G. E. M. Anscombe, "The First Person," in *Mind and Language*, ed. Samuel Guttenplan (Oxford: Clarendon, 1975), 45; hereafter cited parenthetically in the text.

18. For a discussion of contemporary reactions to Locke's separation of self from substance, see Christopher Fox, *Locke and the Scriblerians: Identity and Consciousness in Early Eighteenth-Century Britain* (Berkeley: University of California Press, 1988).

19. In his discussion of the form of animal life, Michael Thompson says something similar about the term "self-movement": "an appeal to 'self-movement' is not illuminating. The reflexive is simply one of the means our language gives us for marking the different relation posited between subject and predicate, thing and event. It does not by itself tell us what this relation is." See Thompson, "The Representation of Life," in *Virtues and Reasons: Phillipa Foot and Moral Theory*, ed. Rosalind Hursthouse, Gavin Lawrence, and Warren Quinn (Oxford: Clarendon, 1995), 264.

20. Wolfram Schmidgen also argues that Locke's chapter on identity proceeds from analogy to "blur the lines" between life and consciousness, and ends "on the verge of completing the growing association of life and consciousness" (212, 213). In Schmidgen, "The Politics and Philosophy of Mixture: John Locke Recomposed," *Eighteenth Century* 48.3 (2007): 205–23. See also Schmidgen, "Locke's Mixed Liberty," in his *Exquisite Mixture: The Virtues of Impurity in Early Modern England* (Philadelphia: University of Pennsylvania Press, 2013), 101–45.

21. In "'Possessive Individualism,' Reversed: From Locke to Derrida," Etienne Balibar proposes that we rethink possessive individualism (and Lockean property) in ways that resonate with my own efforts to rethink the person of Locke's *Essay*, suggesting that we might understand "the essential 'subject' of liberty in Locke., i.e., the agency that creates, distributes, and regulates the various forms of power" as "property itself, in the abstract," which he also refers to as "*the movement of life* that penetrates things and assimilates them" (302, 303). For Balibar, the person is the "bearer and agent" of this "constituent property," so called because it constitutes the person as such, forming his essence as the "internal capacity or power to act—what Locke calls *life* and also *labor*" (303, 302). See Balibar, "'Possessive Individualism,' Reversed: From Locke to Derrida," *Constellations* 9.3 (2002): 299–317.

22. In a letter to David Garrick from January 1762, Sterne writes that d'Holbach's "house, is now, as yours was to me, my own"; in March, he sends a letter to Garrick via William Shippen, an American physician who met both Sterne and Buffon during his time in Paris in 1761–62 (and who, incidentally, delivered America's first course of lectures on anatomy the following year). See *Letters of Laurence Sterne*, ed. Lewis Perry Curtis (Oxford: Clarendon, 1935), 151, 158n2. On Buffon's fame, see Peter Hans Reill, *Vitalizing Nature in the Enlightenment* (Berkeley: University of California Press, 2005), 34; and Jacques Roger, *Buffon: A Life in Natural History* (Ithaca, N.Y.: Cornell University Press, 1997), 184. I know of only two essays that draw a link between the writings of Sterne and Buffon: John Bender's "Enlightenment Fiction and the Scientific Hypothesis," *Representations* 61 (1998): 6–28, which associates both writers with a midcentury "turn toward manifest fictionality" (19); and J. Rodgers, "'Life' in the Novel:

Tristram Shandy and Some Aspects of Eighteenth-Century Physiology," *Eighteenth-Century Life* 6.1 (1980): 1–20.

23. See Reill, *Vitalizing Nature in the Enlightenment*. The quotation that describes Buffon as "the turning point" in period notions of life comes from Jacques Roger, "The Living World," in *The Ferment of Knowledge: Studies in the Historiography of Eighteenth-Century Science*, ed. G. S. Rousseau and Roy Porter (Cambridge: Cambridge University Press, 1980), 274. My account of Buffon and of Buffon's vitalism is indebted throughout to Reill and Roger, as it is to the work of Philip Sloan and Joanna Stalnaker, cited below.

24. Philip Sloan, "From Logical Universals to Historical Individuals: Buffon's Idea of Biological Species," in Scott Atran et al., *Histoire du concept d'espèce dans les sciences de la vie* (Paris: Fondation Singer-Polignac, 1987), 122. See also Sloan, "The Buffon-Linnaeus Controversy," *Isis* 67.3 (1976): 356–75.

25. The significance of Buffon's newly biological notion of species—constituted by reproduction and thus restricted to living beings—was recognized in its own moment. In its entry on the natural-historical sense of "species," for example, Diderot and D'Alembert's *Encyclopédie* simply reprinted a long passage from Buffon's "The Ass." Buffon's species concept continues to receive attention today because it seems to anticipate questions more central to post-Darwinian biology: in particular, whether "species" are logical individuals (rather than classes). The literature on this question is extensive. The claim that species are logical individuals is sometimes called the "Ghiselin-Hull hypothesis," for its two original defenders. See Michael Ghiselin's influential opening salvo, "A Radical Solution to the Species Problem," *Systematic Zoology* 23.4 (1974): 536–44; and David Hull, "A Matter of Individuality," *Philosophy of Science* 45. 3 (1978): 335–60, and "Are Species Really Individuals?" *Systematic Zoology* 25.2 (1976): 174–91. See also Jean Gayon, "The Individuality of the Species: A Darwinian Theory?—from Buffon to Ghiselin, and Back to Darwin," *Biology and Philosophy* 11 (1996): 215–44. Those who argue against this hypothesis include David Stamos, "Buffon, Darwin, and the Non-Individuality of Species—A Reply to Jean Gayon," *Biology and Philosophy* 13 (1998): 443–70. See also Arthur Lovejoy, "Buffon and the Problem of Species," in *Forerunners of Darwin: 1745–1859*, ed. Bentley Glass, Owsei Temkin, and William L. Straus Jr. (Baltimore: Johns Hopkins University Press, 1959), 84–113.

26. Louis Landa, "The Shandean Homunculus: The Background of Sterne's 'Little Gentleman,'" in *Restoration and Eighteenth-Century Essays in Honour of Alan Dugald McKillop*, ed. Carrol Camden (Chicago: University of Chicago Press, 1963), 49–68. Roy Porter also writes about Sterne's knowledge of contemporary medicine, natural philosophy and natural history in "'The Whole Secret of Health': Mind, Body and Medicine in *Tristram Shandy*," in *Nature Transfigured: Science and Literature, 1700–1900*, ed. John Christie and Sally Shuttleworth (Manchester: Manchester University Press, 1989), 61–84. See also J. Rodgers, "'Life' in the Novel."

27. On the debate between preformationist and epigenesist theories in the mid- and late eighteenth-century—and on the epigenesist poetics of writers from Smart to Keats—see Gigante, *Life*, esp. 1–48.

28. Aristotle, "Politics," in *The Basic Works of Aristotle*, ed. Richard McKeon (New York: Modern Library, 2001), 1128.

29. See Peter Godman, *From Poliziano to Machiavelli: Florentine Humanism in the High Renaissance* (Princeton, N.J.: Princeton University Press, 1998), 122.

30. Hesiod, *Works and Days*, trans. Hugh G. Evelyn-White, 1914, accessed online at http://www.sacred-texts.com/cla/hesiod/works.htm, lines 405–6, my emphasis.

31. Godman, *From Poliziano*, 122.

32. On Aristotle's categories of "woman" and "slave," see Elizabeth V. Spelman, *Inessential Woman: Problems of Exclusion in Feminist Thought* (Boston: Beacon, 1988), 37–56.

33. Virgil, *Georgics*, in *The Works of Virgil: Containing his pastorals, Georgics and Æneis. Translated into English verse by Mr. Dryden. In three volumes.* London: J. and R. Tonson, 1763, book 2, lines 498, 493, 500, 497. Quote on pages 258–59.

34. Critics from Deidre Lynch to Jonathan Lamb have argued that Sterne insists on an essential distinction between persons and things. I am arguing that the episode with the ox suggests that this distinction depends on another, which Walter and Walter's Locke both elide: the distinction between the living and the nonliving. See Lynch, "Personal Effects and Sentimental Fictions"; and Jonathan Lamb, "Modern Metamorphoses and Disgraceful Tales," *Critical Inquiry* 28.1 (2001): 133–66.

35. In his translation of the *Natural History*, William Smellie inserts a footnote after Buffon's first use of "reproduction," which explains (I think too simply and somewhat inaccurately) that Buffon uses "reproduction" to "signif[y] the power of producing and propagating in general," and "generation" to signify "a species of reproduction peculiar to animated beings," to animals rather than plants (2.2–3).

36. Roger, *Living World*, 187.

37. The *OED* dates the first and most general meaning of reproduction—"the action or process of forming, creating, or bringing into existence again"—to the mid-seventeenth century. It dates the two other primary senses of the term—"A copy, an exact equivalent; *esp.* a copy of a picture or other work of art by means of engraving, photography, or similar processes"; and, "*Biol.* The production by living organisms of new individuals or offspring; the perpetuation of a species by this process; the power of reproducing in this way"—to 1701 and 1713, respectively. "reproduction, n.," *OED Online*. Oxford University Press, September 2015. http://www.oed .com.proxy.uchicago.edu/view/Entry/163102?redirectedFrom=reproduction.

38. Reill, *Vitalizing Nature*, 45.

39. For an interesting reading of the concluding lines of *Tristram Shandy*, and of their animal imagery in particular, see Mark Loveridge, "Stories of Cocks and Bulls: The Ending of *Tristram Shandy*," *Eighteenth-Century Fiction* 5.1 (1992): 35–54.

40. There are good reasons to consider matters of writing when one thinks about Buffon. For one thing, central terms of Buffon's vitalism—like composition and reproduction—are also terms of writing and representation. For another, Buffon is perhaps most widely known for his "Discourse on Style," a lecture delivered to the French Academy in 1753, which remains a classic of French letters and composition textbooks. In the "Discourse," Buffon repeatedly invokes the analogy of living form to characterize the well-formed work of literature. But frequently, the living form on which Buffon models literary form sounds more like life as described by preformation than it does the life of Buffon's own reproductive vitalism. It unfolds from an original germ that is always already whole and everywhere develops in precisely the same and fixed manner, according to "a successive development, a sustained gradation, a uniform movement." In Buffon, "Discourse on Style," in *Theories of Style: With Especial Reference to Prose Composition*, ed. Lane Cooper (New York: Macmillan, 1907), 173. Joanna Stalnaker makes a similar point in *The Unfinished Enlightenment: Description in the Age of the Encyclopedia* (Ithaca, N.Y.: Cornell University Press, 2010), 67, and takes this to mark the evolution of Buffon's natural-philosophical ideas over the course of his life.

41. On the invisibility of women in Sterne, the classic essay is Ruth Perry's "Words for Sex: The Verbal-Sexual Continuum in *Tristram Shandy*," *Studies in the Novel* 20 (1988): 27–42. See

also Carol Kay, *Political Constructions: Defoe, Richardson, and Sterne in Relation to Hobbes, Hume, and Burke* (Ithaca, N.Y.: Cornell University Press, 1988), 230–36.

42. Plato, *Apology*, trans. Benjamin Jowett (Champaign, Ill.: Project Gutenberg), 19.

43. Plato, *Apology*, 23.

44. Quintilian, *Institutes*, 2:415.

45. Derrida, *Animal That Therefore I Am*, 92.

46. As I understand it, Thompson's work ultimately aims to establish a foundation for a normative naturalism, an ethics grounded in "human being" that would not be vulnerable to charges of biologism. To this end, he reworks some basic thinking about what it is to be human, and to be a living being. Thompson's work follows on that of Anscombe, whom he identifies as the first to call for the kind of "analytical Aristotelianism" that he seeks to develop. Thompson also follows Anscombe in making the Wittgensteinian move to questions of representation: in Thompson's case, the shift from the question of "What is a life form, a species, a *psuche*?" to "How is such a thing described?" ("Representation of Life," 279). Much of Thompson's work on the representation of life has recently been published, in slightly revised form, as the first section of his *Life and Action: Elementary Structures of Practice and Practical Thought* (Cambridge, Mass.: Harvard University Press, 2008).

47. Thompson argues that "the concept *life form* is more akin to such logical or quasi-logical notions as *object, property, relation, fact*, or *process*." See Thompson, "Apprehending Human Form," 63. To explain the logical notion of the life form that is represented by natural-historical description, Thompson considers the statement "The mayfly breeds shortly before dying." He insists that "the mayfly" is a general form that cannot be reduced to a statistical average or a typical specimen. Statements can be true of "the mayfly" that are not true for most mayflies: "although 'the mayfly' breeds shortly before dying, *most* mayflies die long before breeding. . . . A natural historical judgment may be true though individuals falling under both the subject- and predicate- concepts are as rare as one likes, statistically speaking" ("Representation of Life," 284–85). Elsewhere, he puts the point this way, "The look beyond the individual in the framing of a vital description is not to the 'community' of bearers of the life form but to the life form itself" ("Apprehending Human Form," 65n10).

48. Thompson, "Representation of Life," 272.

49. Thompson, "Apprehending Human Form," 67.

50. On this "wider context," see Thompson, "Representation of Life," 271–79.

51. Thompson, "Apprehending Human Form," 66.

52. Thompson, "Apprehending Human Form," 68.

53. Thompson, "Representation of Life," 277. On the difference between thinking species biologically and philosophically, see also "Apprehending Human Form," 66n10.

54. Thompson, "Apprehending Human Form," 68.

55. Tristram and the ass are a variation on the pair of Tristram (the self-styled "Jack Asse") and Jenny (329). The ass in this scene is also the ass of Buridan's parable, a figure for man in his rational faculty. In Buridan's parable, the ass is presented with two equal choices: a bucket of hay and a pail of water, each equidistant from where he stands. Both hungry and thirsty, the ass has no way to decide between two exactly equal and opposite reasons to move. He stands still, neither eating nor drinking, until he dies. Like Buridan's ass, Sterne's animal also stands still, and he brings Tristram to a stand with him. But from there, Sterne's scene unfolds quite differently—into a sentimental conversation between two animate creatures, who move and are moved in turn.

56. Joseph Addison, "An Essay on Virgil's *Georgics*," in *Miscellaneous Works in Verse and Prose, of the Late Right Honourable Joseph Addison, Esq.*, vol. 1 (Edinburgh: J. Robertson, [1769]),

237. The line from Virgil comes from Dryden's translation of the *Georgics*, book 3, line 456. My understanding of the georgic, here, owes much to Kevis Goodman's *Georgic Modernity and British Romanticism*.

57. Angelo Poliziano, "The Countryman," in *Silvae*, ed. and trans. Charles Fantazzi (Cambridge, Mass.: Harvard University Press, 2004), 42, line 180.

58. Laurence Sterne, *A Sentimental Journey Through France and Italy by Mr. Yorick* (Oxford: Oxford University Press, 1968), 28.

59. For an extended look at the way that the sentimental tradition "refocused the very question of what it means to 'move' and be moved," see James Chandler, "Moving Accidents: The Emergence of Sentimental Probability," in *The Age of Cultural Revolutions: Britain and France 1750–1820*, ed. Colin Jones and Dror Wahrman (Berkeley: University of California Press, 2002), quote on 139.

60. Sterne, *Sentimental Journey*, 114.

61. See Georg Lukács, "Richness, Chaos and Form: A Dialogue Concerning Laurence Sterne," in his *Soul and Form*, trans. Anna Bostock (London: Merlin 1974), and Kay, *Political Constructions*, 196–246, esp. 204–26.

62. See Jesse Molesworth, *Chance and the Eighteenth-Century Novel: Realism, Probability, Magic* (Cambridge: Cambridge University Press, 2010), 189–205.

63. This line comes from the original and much longer French passage: "On me demandera sans doute pourquoi je ne veux pas que ces corps mouvans qu'on trouve dans les liqueurs séminales, soient des animaux, puisque tous ceux qui les ont observez les ont regardez comme tels, et que Leeuwenhoek et les autres observateurs s'accordent à les appeller animaux, qu'il ne paroît même pas qu'ils aient eu le moindre doute, le moindre scrupule sur cela. On pourra me dire aussi qu'on ne conçoit pas trop ce que c'est que des parties organique vivantes, à moins que de les regarder comme des animalcules, et que de supposer qu'un animal est composé de petite animaux, est à peu près la même chose que de dire qu'un être organize est composé de parties organique vivantes." In Georges-Louis Leclerc de Buffon, *Histoire Naturelle, Générale et Particulière, Avec la Description du Cabinet du Roy*, vol. 2, 259, accessed online at http://www.buffon.cnrs.fr/?lang=en.

64. Buffon, "Initial Discourse," 161.

65. Buffon, "Initial Discourse," 161.

CHAPTER 5. THE CHILD

1. Mary Wollstonecraft, *Thoughts on the Education of Daughters* (Bristol: Thoemmes, 1995), 16.

2. Before the mid-eighteenth century, English literature written specifically for children often (though not exclusively) meant religious or conduct manuals, rather than what F. J. Harvey Darton refers to as "works produced ostensibly to give children spontaneous pleasure." See Darton, *Children's Books in England: Five Centuries of Social Life* (Cambridge: Cambridge University Press, 1982), 1. The rise of children's literature as a recognizable body of writing and a significant part of the book market is frequently traced to Locke's writings on education and human understanding, and to educational publishers who were influenced by them, especially John Newbery. See also Robert Bator, "Out of the Ordinary Road: John Locke and English Juvenile Fiction in the Eighteenth Century," *Children's Literature* 1 (1972): 46–53; and Samuel F. Pickering Jr., *John Locke and Children's Books in Eighteenth-Century England* (Knoxville: University of Tennessee Press, 1981).

3. Critics tend to divide late eighteenth-century children's writers into two camps: those influenced by Locke, and those influenced by Rousseau. Rousseau's camp, which includes pedagogues like Thomas Day and Richard Edgeworth, is generally taken to be familiar with the ideas it deploys; Locke's is not. In *Children's Books in England*, for example, Darton writes, "During that period, writers for children were, educationally, disciples of either Locke or Rousseau. If they followed Locke, it was, as likely as not, without knowing it. That was inevitable, because with his acceptance of facts as the basis of theory, Locke was typically English, down to the smallest practical detail. . . . Locke knew exactly what strict but not unkind English mothers did. . . . If tiny points like those appear in later books by the Kilners, Lady Fenn, Mrs Trimmer, and others, it is not because the writers thought Locke out, but because Locke knew their long-established habits beforehand" (112).

4. Charles Lamb, *The Letters of Charles and Mary Anne Lamb*, ed. Edwin W. Marrs Jr., 3 vols. (Ithaca, N.Y.: Cornell University Press, 1976), 2.81–82; qtd. in Christine Kenyon-Jones, *Kindred Brutes*, 51–52.

5. Many critics still follow Lamb's characterization of the "Barbauld Crew," dismissing this generation of children's writers as politically conservative and aesthetically impoverished. Notable exceptions include Anne Chandler, "Wollstonecraft's *Original Stories*: Animal Objects and the Subject of Fiction," in *The Eighteenth Century Novel*, ed. Albert J. Rivero (New York: AMS Press, 2002), 325–51; Mitzi Myers, "Impeccable Governesses, Rational Dames, and Moral Mothers: Mary Wollstonecraft and the Female Tradition in Georgian Children's Books," *Children's Literature* 14 (1986): 31–59; and Mitzi Myers, "Romancing the Moral Tale: Maria Edgeworth and the Problematics of Pedagogy," in *Romanticism and Children's Literature in Nineteenth-Century England*, ed. James Holt McGavran Jr. (Athens: University of Georgia Press, 1991), 96–128. Works that do chart the rise of children's literature according to what Myers terms the "Whiggish view of children's literary history as a progress toward pure amusement and imaginative fantasy" ("Impeccable Governesses," 31) include Isaac Kramnick, "Children's Literature and Bourgeois Ideology: Observations on Culture and Industrial Capitalism in the Later Eighteenth Century," in *Culture and Politics from Puritanism to the Enlightenment*, ed. Perez Zagorin (Berkeley: University of California Press, 1980), 203–40; Geoffrey Summerfield, *Fantasy and Reason: Children's Literature in the Eighteenth Century* (Athens: University of Georgia Press, 1984); and, to a degree, Darton's *Children's Books in England*. In his illuminating essay "Wordsworth, Fairy Tales, and the Politics of Children's Reading" (in *Romanticism and Children's Literature in Nineteenth-Century England*, ed. James Holt McGavran Jr. [Athens: University of Georgia Press, 1991], 34–53), Alan Richardson tells a similar story about the development from reason to fantasy but reverses the Romantic and post-Romantic valuation of its terms, reminding us that, "at a time when debates on children's literature were highly politicized, the Barbauld 'crew' was dominated by liberal and radical figures like the Aikins, the Edgeworths, Joseph Priestley, Thomas Beddoes, Mary Wollstonecraft, and William Godwin. . . . The Romantic advocates of fairyland, on the other hand, had already turned from Godwin and their youthful radicalism toward the conservative social and political stances that would mark their later careers" (40). See also Richardson's *Literature, Education, and Romanticism: Reading as Social Practice, 1780–1832* (Cambridge: Cambridge University Press, 1995).

6. James Boswell, *Life of Johnson*, ed. R. W. Chapman (Oxford: Oxford University Press, 1980), 662; qtd. in Norma Clarke, "'The Cursed Barbauld Crew': Women Writers and Writing for Children in the Late Eighteenth Century," in *Opening the Nursery Door: Reading, Writing and Childhood 1600–1900*, ed. Mary Hilton, Morag Styles, and Victor Watson (London: Routledge, 1997), 94.

7. On the innovation and influence of Barbauld's age-graded readers, see Pickering, *John Locke and Children's Books*, 192; and Frances Ferguson, "Educational Rationalization / Sublime Reason," in *The Sublime and Education*, ed. J. Jennifer Jones, August 2010, Romantic Circles, http://www.rc.umd.edu/praxis/sublime_education/ferguson/ferguson.html.

8. Anna Letitia Barbauld, *Lessons for Children*, 4 vols. (London: J. Johnson, 1787–88) 1.7; hereafter cited parenthetically in the text by volume and page number.

9. Tess Cosslett also raises this question in the first chapter of her *Talking Animals in British Children's Fiction: 1786–1914*, and her answers overlap with my own. Cosslett links animal stories to the educational ideas of Locke and Rousseau, to the traditions of the Aesopian fable, natural theology, and sensibility, as well as to widespread changes in cultural attitudes toward both animals and children. See 9–36. While she focuses mainly on nineteenth-century children's fiction, Cosslett begins with a sharp reading of Trimmer's *Fabulous Histories*—whose title, Cosslett writes, "signals the basic contradiction" with which her book is concerned: "how and why does anyone write stories about talking animals for children in an age of Enlightenment and Reason, of Progress and Modernity?" (37).

10. John Locke, *Some Thoughts Concerning Education*, ed. John W. and Jean S. Yolton (Oxford: Clarendon, 1989), 242.

11. A number of excellent studies of the political fable voice some version of this lament. See, for example Annabel Patterson, *Fables of Power: Aesopian Writing and Political History* (Durham, N.C.: Duke University Press, 1991), 1, 137; Lewis, *The English Fable*, 186; Marc Shell, "The Lie of the Fox: Rousseau's Theory of Verbal, Monetary, and Political Representation" *SubStance* 10 (1974): 111.

12. Ritvo, *The Animal Estate*, 4. Jacques Derrida, *Animal That I Therefore Am*, 37. Derrida returns to the fable at great length in *The Beast and the Sovereign*, trans. Geoffrey Bennington, vol. 1 (Chicago: University of Chicago Press, 2009), especially in the first two lectures (1–62), which focus on La Fontaine's fable of "The Wolf and the Lamb," and the "becoming-fabulous of political action and discourse" (35).

13. Locke, *Some Thoughts*, 212.

14. [Eleanor Fenn], *Fables in Monosyllables by Mrs. Teachwell; to which are added Morals, in dialogues, between a mother and children* (London: John Marshall, 1783), 25–27.

15. Fenn, *Fables*, 32–33.

16. William Godwin, *Fables, Ancient and Modern: Adapted for the Use of Children* (London: T. Hodgkins, 1805), 10–11.

17. Pickering, *John Locke and Children's Books*, 29. Pickering's characterization of Trimmer's representativeness is repeated in many accounts of the rise of children's literature, which set Trimmer at the helm of a literary establishment that aimed to induct children into a set social order by teaching them lessons of "kindness" in the sense both of recognizing their own (superior) species and treating other species well. Darton writes in a similar if more scathing vein: "The importance of Sarah Trimmer is that she *was* important. . . . She stood for all that solidity and stolidity which defeated Napoleon by not understanding him or realizing how huge was the menace of change. Stupid and intelligent at once . . . she lived an honourable career without doubts of herself or hesitation about public conduct" (*Children's Books in England*, 158).

18. Sarah Trimmer, *Fabulous Histories: Designed for the Instruction of Children, Respecting their Treatment of Animals* (London: T. Longman, 1786), ix–x; hereafter cited parenthetically in the text.

19. On this sort of translation of the animal body into expressive and moving speech, see Menely, *Animal Claim*, esp. 1–18, 124–63.

20. In the *Essay*, Locke occasionally envisions the individual life to proceed through different orders of being, from vegetable to animal to human (and finally, in the case of the old man who loses his ability to perceive or to move, to mollusk). See 117, 148. In *Some Thoughts Concerning Education*, Locke variously compares children to wax, paper, water, dogs, and horses; his metaphors for education include imprinting, directing, and training (see, for example, 83, 104, 265).

21. Citing evidence mainly from French visual and literary culture, but extending his conclusions to the West more generally, Ariès traces the "discovery of childhood" to the impact of seventeenth-century social and economic changes to the family unit. See Philippe Ariès, *Centuries of Childhood*, trans. Robert Baldick (London: Jonathan Cape, 1962). In *Forgotten Children: Parent-Child Relations from 1500–1900* (Cambridge: Cambridge University Press, 1983), Linda Pollock gives a comprehensive account of the literature both in favor of and against the Ariès thesis. For accounts that largely agree with Ariès, see Lawrence Stone, *The Family, Sex and Marriage in England, 1500–1800* (New York: Harper, 1979), and J. H. Plumb, "The New World of Children," in *The Birth of a Consumer Society: The Commercialization of Eighteenth-Century England*, ed. Neil McKendrick, John Brewer, and J. H. Plumb (London: Europa, 1982), 286–315.

22. Ala A. Alryyes, *Original Subjects: The Child, the Novel, and the Nation* (Cambridge, Mass.: Harvard University Press, 2001), 124. Alryyes's picture of childhood echoes Ariès's account of an earlier, premodern understanding of childhood as a primarily social status; see Ariès' *Centuries of Childhood*, 26.

23. Lewis, *English Fable*, 8.

24. On the children's genre of the it-narrative (though this is not his term), see Pickering, *John Locke and Children's Books*, 84–103; and Lynn Festa, "The Moral Ends of Eighteenth- and Nineteenth-Century Object Narratives," in *The Secret Life of Things: Animals, Objects, and It-Narratives in Eighteenth-Century England*, ed. Mark Blackwell (Lewisburg, Pa.: Bucknell University Press, 2007), 309–28.

25. Dorothy Kilner, *The Life and Perambulation of a Mouse*, 2 vols. (London: John Marshall, c. 1785), 1.viii; hereafter cited parenthetically in the text by volume and page number.

26. Mary Wollstonecraft, *Original Stories, from Real Life; with Conversations, Calculated to Regulate the Affections, and Form the Mind to Truth and Goodness* (London: J. Johnson, 1788), 48; hereafter cited parenthetically in the text.

27. In a related reading of Wollstonecraft's *Original Stories*, Anne Chandler argues that Wollstonecraft's self-consciousness about the form of her text complicates its assertions of species difference and hierarchy. See Chandler, "Wollstonecraft's *Original Stories*."

28. For a discussion of the quasi-figurative logic of pethood—which argues that the logic of pethood is necessarily opposed to an ethics of "life" more broadly—see Marc Shell, "The Family Pet," *Representations* 15 (1986): 121–53. Shell also insists that pets are never exactly or entirely animals. On his view, they are better understood as allegorical figures for relations between human beings, and for the operations by which human beings are organized into relations of kin and kind. At the same time, Shell acknowledges that the logic of (animal) vehicle and (human) tenor may not always be clear—especially, Shell imagines, to children: "Family pets are generally mythological beings on the line between human kin and animal kind, or beings thought of as being on the line between. Yet sometimes we *really* cannot tell whether a being is essentially human or animal—say, when we were children, or when we shall become extraterrestrial explorers. Sometimes we *really* cannot tell whether a being is our kind or not our kind, our kin or not our kin; we cannot tell what we are and to whom" (142).

29. Frances Ferguson, "Reading Morals: Locke and Rousseau on Education and Inequality," *Representations* 6 (1984): 77.

30. Ferguson, "Reading Morals," 76.

31. Ferguson, "Reading Morals," 76.

32. In *Food for Thought*, Louis Marin characterizes the fable similarly, as the literary equivalent of the philosophical genre of the state of nature narrative, used by contract theorists like Hobbes, Locke, and Rousseau to figure the origin of political society. By converting eating into speaking, fables would enact the basic move of social contract, in which civil society replaces an original state of nature and distributes power differently. Marin argues that fables tend to reveal this transformation to be an illusion, ultimately resolving speaking into eating, right into might. (See Marin, *Food for Thought*, esp. 74.) Jayne Lewis makes a related point in *The English Fable*: the fabulous animal who speaks, eats, and is eaten reveals language to be grounded "in the realm of frequently brutal power relations. And thereby fables weld together the material, the political, and the symbolic" (8).

33. Jean-Jacques Rousseau, "Discourse on the Origin and Foundations of Inequality Among Men," in *Rousseau's Political Writings*, ed. Alan Ritter and Julia Conaway Bondanella (New York: Norton, 1988), 39.

34. Rousseau, "Discourse on Inequality," 10.

35. On Rousseau's effort to realize a properly human being (and properly human politics), see Tracy B. Strong, *Jean-Jacques Rousseau: The Politics of the Ordinary* (Lanham, Md.: Rowman and Littlefield, 2002). Throughout this section, I am indebted to Strong's understanding of Rousseau. In at least two key respects, however, his account differs from my own. First, his account of pity is uninterested in the figure of the animal on which Rousseau often focuses; indeed, Strong glosses Rousseau's notion of pity as "the capacity humans have of recognizing another human being as like oneself, rather than as a dog or a tree" (42). Second, he takes the view that Emile and the reader of *Emile* are in quite different positions (conceding that Emile or at least Emile's environment is everywhere manipulated by the preceptor, but setting the reader at a more critical and comfortable distance) (108). My own sense that Emile and the reader are far more closely identified bears some resemblance to Strong's description of Rousseau's more general effort "to make available a text that is experienced as if directly by the reader" (Strong, *Jean-Jacques Rousseau*, 9).

36. For a sensitive reading of Rousseau's effort to imagine a way out of relations of dependence and domination, and the role that the animal plays in this effort, see Nancy Yousef's chapter "Rousseau's Autonomous Beast: Natural Man as Imaginary Animal," in her *Isolated Cases*, 63–95.

37. On the apparent discrepancy between Rousseau's different discussions of pity, see John T. Scott's introduction to *Essay on the Origin of Languages and Writings Related to Music*, in *The Collected Writings of Rousseau*, vol. 7 (Hanover, N.H.: University Press of New England, 1998), xxix–xxx.

38. See, for example, Janie Vanpée's work on reading in *Emile*: "Reading Lessons in Rousseau's *Emile ou de l'éducation*," *Modern Language Studies* 20.3 (1990): 40–49; and "Rousseau's *Emile ou de l'éducation*: Resistance to Reading," *Yale French Studies* 77 (1990): 156–76.

39. Rousseau, "Discourse on Inequality," 29.

40. In *Of Grammatology*, Derrida characterizes Rousseau's notion of pity along similar lines, as a relation of both identity and difference: "What concerns us here about the status of pity, the root of the love of others, is that it is neither the source itself, nor a secondary stream of passion, one acquired passion among others. It is *the first diversion* of the love of self. It is *almost* primitive, and it is in the difference between absolute proximity and absolute identity that all the problematics of pity are lodged." In Jacques Derrida, *Of Grammatology*, trans. Gayatri Chakravorty Spivak (Baltimore: Johns Hopkins University Press, 1998), 174. See also 205–6.

41. For a related reading of the centrality and complexity of *Robinson Crusoe* to the course of Emile's education, see Brian McGrath, "Rousseau's Crusoe; or, On Learning to Read as Not Myself," *Eighteenth-Century Fiction* 23.1 (2010): 119–39. McGrath is also interested in "the extent to which [Emile] learns to think of himself no longer as Émile but as Robinson Crusoe" (122), but he sees this as more of a problem for Rousseau's purposes than I do.

42. Ferguson, "Educational Rationalization," par. 17. In particular, Ferguson argues that Barbauld's age-graded *Lessons* responds directly to Rousseau's critique of fable, carefully calibrating each volume to the conceptual and linguistic skills of a different developmental stage in order to prevent the sort of interpretive overreaching (and resulting dependence) that so worried Rousseau.

43. Ferguson, "Educational Rationalization," par. 18.

44. Ferguson, "Educational Rationalization," par. 27.

45. Lévi-Strauss, *Totemism*, 99.

46. Lévi-Strauss, *Totemism*, 101.

CODA

1. Anna Letitia Barbauld, "The Caterpillar," in Anna Letitia Barbauld, *Selected Poetry and Prose*, ed. William McCarthy and Elizabeth Kraft (Peterborough, Ontario: Broadview, 2002), 179–80; hereafter cited parenthetically in the text by line number. McCarthy and Kraft identify 1816 as a likely date of composition. In "Pests, Parasites, and Positionality," *Studies in Romanticism* 43.2 (2004), Alice Den Otter argues that it was likely 1815.

2. Swift, *Gulliver's Travels*, 80.

3. Cowper, *Task*, 3.334.

4. Quoted from William McCarthy and Elizabeth Kraft's introduction to *The Poems of Anna Letitia Barbauld*, ed. McCarthy and Kraft (Athens: University of Georgia Press, 1994), xxiv.

5. William McCarthy, *Anna Letitia Barbauld: Voice of the Enlightenment* (Baltimore: Johns Hopkins University Press, 2008), 407. In this biography of Barbauld, McCarthy uses the poem as evidence of her life—"Anna Letitia became a zealous gardener, keen on exterminating pests. Such, at least, is implied by a poem she wrote during an infestation of caterpillars"—and then uses that life to read the poem: "She went after the caterpillars furiously, . . . but in the midst of her rampage a single caterpillar caught her notice, and she paused to study it. She records that moment of strange intimacy between her and an alien fellow creature" (406). Den Otter also imagines the poem to be prompted by a real-life incident, arguing for 1815 rather than 1816 as a likely date of composition by reasoning, in part, that the summer of 1816 was unusually cool, so there would have been few caterpillars in Barbauld's garden for her to encounter. See "Pests, Parasites, and Positionality," 212n9.

6. For an incisive reading of Barbauld that makes a related argument about "Eighteen Hundred and Eleven" in particular, see Alexis Chema, "'A Tongue in Every Star': Barbauld and the Persuasive Figure," unpublished ms., cited by permission of the author.

7. I take Barbauld to be making a point similar to Roberto Esposito's, when he takes up Simone Weil's warning about the dangers of the first-person plural, "we," and its connection to (a certain form of) the first-person singular: "The part of the person that should be rejected is precisely the one that says 'I' or 'we'; better still, the logical thread that ties individual self-consciousness to collective consciousness in the grammatical mode of the first person" (*Third Person: Politics of Life and Philosophy of the Impersonal*, trans. Zakiya Hanafi [Cambridge: Polity,

2012], 102). The problem for Esposito (and I think also for Barbauld) is that "we" is never truly plural; in Esposito's terms, it is a personal rather than impersonal form.

8. Rousseau, *Emile*, 223.

9. Den Otter makes a related point, arguing that Barbauld's poem "wins the emotional acquiescence of her audience, only to challenge their morality from the inside out" ("Pests, Parasites, and Positionality," 213).

10. See Esposito on the third person as a way of redirecting "the 'I'" away from "the simultaneously inclusive and exclusive circle of the 'we'" (*Third Person*, 102).

11. Johnson, *Dictionary*, s.v. "Caterpillar"; qtd. in Den Otter, "Pests, Parasites, and Positionality," 214. On the notion of "vermin" (as well as that of "fellow-creature"), see Diamond, "Eating Meat and Eating People," 476.

12. "Caprice, n.," *OED Online*. Oxford University Press, September 2015. http://www.oed .com.proxy.uchicago.edu/view/Entry/27549?redirectedFrom=caprice.

13. "Caprice," in Ephraim Chambers, *Cyclopædia: Or, an universal dictionary of arts and sciences; . . . By E. Chambers, F.R.S. With the supplement, and modern improvements, incorporated into one alphabet. By Abraham Rees, D. D. In four volumes*, vol. 1 (London: W. Strahan, J. F. and C. Rivington, et al., 1778–88), unpaginated; "capriccio, n.," *OED Online*. Oxford University Press, September 2015. http://www.oed.com.proxy.uchicago.edu/view/Entry/27547. It is worth noting that *caprice* is also a term of art, and specifically of musical composition. Again, from Rees' supplement to Chambers: "an irregular composition, which succeeds rather by the force of genius, than by observations of the rules of art."

Works Cited

Abrams, M. H. *The Mirror and the Lamp: Romantic Theory and the Critical Tradition*. New York: Oxford University Press, 1953.

Addison, Joseph. "An Essay on Virgil's *Georgics*." In *Miscellaneous Works in Verse and Prose, of the Late Right Honourable Joseph Addison, Esq.* 4 vols. Edinburgh: J. Robertson, 1769. 1.228–39.

Agamben, Giorgio. *The Open: Man and Animal*. Trans. Kevin Attell. Stanford, Calif.: Stanford University Press, 2004.

Alryyes, Ala A. *Original Subjects: The Child, the Novel, and the Nation*. Cambridge, Mass.: Harvard University Press, 2001.

Anscombe, G. E. M. "The First Person." In *Mind and Language*. Ed. Samuel Guttenplan. Oxford: Clarendon, 1975. 45-65.

Aravamudan, Srinivas. *Tropicopolitans: Colonialism and Agency, 1688–1804*. Durham, N.C.: Duke University Press, 1999.

Ariès, Philippe. *Centuries of Childhood*. Trans. Robert Baldick. London: Jonathan Cape, 1962.

Aristotle. "Politics." In *The Basic Works of Aristotle*. Ed. Richard McKeon. New York: Modern Library, 2001. 1113–1316.

Armstrong, Nancy. *Desire and Domestic Fiction: A Political History of the Novel*. New York: Oxford University Press, 1987.

Ayers, Michael. *Locke*. Vol. 2, *Ontology*. London: Routledge, 1991.

Balibar, Etienne. "'Possessive Individualism,' Reversed: From Locke to Derrida." *Constellations* 9.3 (2002): 299–317.

Barbauld, Anna Letitia. *Lessons for Children*. 4 vols. London: J. Johnson, 1787–88.

———. *The Poems of Anna Letitia Barbauld*. Ed. William McCarthy and Elizabeth Kraft. Athens: University of Georgia Press, 1994.

———. *Selected Poetry and Prose*. Ed. William McCarthy and Elizabeth Kraft. Peterborough, Ontario: Broadview, 2002.

Barrell, John. *English Literature in History 1730–80: An Equal, Wide Survey*. New York: St. Martin's, 1983.

———. *The Idea of Landscape and the Sense of Place 1730–1840: An Approach to the Poetry of John Clare*. Cambridge: Cambridge University Press, 1972.

Bator, Robert. "Out of the Ordinary Road: John Locke and English Juvenile Fiction in the Eighteenth Century." *Children's Literature* 1 (1972): 46–53.

Beattie, James. *Essays: On poetry and music, as they affect the mind; on laughter, and ludicrous composition; on the usefulness of classical learning*. 3rd ed. London: printed for E. and C. Dilly, 1779.

Beesemeyer, Irene Basey. "Crusoe the *ISOLATO*: Daniel Defoe Wrestles with Solitude." *1650–1850: Ideas, Aesthetics, and Inquiries in the Early Modern Era* 10 (2004): 79–102.

Bender, John. "Enlightenment Fiction and the Scientific Hypothesis." *Representations* 61 (1998): 6–28.

Bennett, Jane. *Vibrant Matter: A Political Ecology of Things.* Durham, N.C.: Duke University Press, 2010.

Bergson, Henri. *Les Deux Sources de la morale et de la religion.* 88e édition. Paris: PUF, 1958.

Blackwell, Mark, ed. *The Secret Life of Things: Animals, Objects, and It-Narratives in Eighteenth-Century England.* Lewisburg, Pa.: Bucknell University Press, 2007.

Blair, Hugh. *Lectures on Rhetoric and Belles Lettres.* 3 vols. Dublin: printed for Messrs. White-stone, Colles, Burnet, et al., 1783.

Bogel, Fredric V. *The Difference Satire Makes: Rhetoric and Reading from Jonson to Byron.* Ithaca, N.Y.: Cornell University Press, 2001.

Boswell, James. *Life of Johnson.* Ed. R. W. Chapman. Oxford: Oxford University Press, 1980.

Briggs, Peter M. "Locke's *Essay* and the Tentativeness of *Tristram Shandy.*" In *Critical Essays on Laurence Sterne.* Ed. Melvin New. New York: G. K. Hall, 1998. 87–109.

Brown, Homer O. "The Displaced Self in the Novels of Daniel Defoe." *ELH* 38.4 (1971): 562–90.

Brown, Laura. *Homeless Dogs and Melancholy Apes: Humans and Other Animals in the Modern Literary Imagination.* Ithaca, N.Y.: Cornell University Press, 2010.

Brown, Marshall. *Preromanticism.* Stanford, Calif.: Stanford University Press, 1991.

Bruns, Gerald. "Allegory and Satire: A Rhetorical Mediation." *New Literary History* 11.1 (1979): 121–32.

―――. "Introduction: Toward a Random Theory of Prose." In *Theory of Prose.* By Viktor Shklovsky. Elmwood Park, Ill.: Dalkey Archive Press, 1990. ix-xv.

Brunström, Conrad, and Katherine Turner. "'I Shall Not Ask Jean-Jacques Rousseau': Anthro-pomorphism in the Cowperian Bestiary." *Journal for Eighteenth-Century Studies* 33.4 (2010): 453–68.

Buell, Lawrence. *The Environmental Imagination: Thoreau, Nature Writing, and the Formation of American Culture.* Cambridge, Mass.: Harvard University Press, 1995.

Buffon, Georges-Louis Leclerc de. "Discourse on Style." In *Theories of Style: With Especial Reference to Prose Composition.* Ed. Lane Cooper. New York: Macmillan, 1907. 169-79.

―――. *Histoire Naturelle, Générale et Particulière, Avec La Description du Cabinet du Roy.* http://www.buffon.cnrs.fr/?lang=en.

―――. "Initial Discourse." [From *Histoire Naturelle.*] Trans. John Lyon. *Journal of the History of Biology* 9.1 (1976): 133–81.

―――. *Natural History, General and Particular, by the Count de Buffon, translated into English. Illustrated with above 260 copper-plates, and occasional notes and observations by the translator.* 9 vols. Trans. William Smellie. Edinburgh: William Creech, [1780–85].

Cameron, Sharon. *Impersonality: Seven Essays.* Chicago: University of Chicago Press, 2007.

Carnochan, W. B. *Lemuel Gulliver's Mirror for Man.* Berkeley: University of California Press, 1968.

Cast Away. Dir. Robert Zemeckis. 20th Century Fox, 2000.

Castle, Terry. "Why the Houyhnhnms Don't Write: Swift, Satire, and the Fear of the Text." *Essays in Literature* 7 (1980): 31–44.

Cavell, Stanley. *Cities of Words: Pedagogical Letters on a Register of the Moral Life.* Cambridge, Mass.: Belknap Press of Harvard University Press, 2004.

―――. *The Claim of Reason: Wittgenstein, Skepticism, Morality, and Tragedy.* Oxford: Oxford University Press, 1999.

Chambers, Ephraim. *Cyclopædia: Or, an universal dictionary of arts and sciences; . . . In two volumes.* London: James and John Knapton et al., 1728.

―――. *Cyclopædia: Or, an universal dictionary of arts and sciences; . . . By E. Chambers, F.R.S. With the supplement, and modern improvements, incorporated into one alphabet. By Abraham Rees, D. D. In four volumes.* London: W. Strahan, J. F. and C. Rivington et al., 1778–88.

Chandler, Anne. "Wollstonecraft's *Original Stories:* Animal Objects and the Subject of Fiction." In *The Eighteenth Century Novel.* Ed. Albert J. Rivero. New York: AMS, 2002. 325–51.

Chandler, James. "Moving Accidents: The Emergence of Sentimental Probability." In *The Age of Cultural Revolutions: Britain and France 1750–1820.* Ed. Colin Jones and Dror Wahrman. Berkeley: University of California Press, 2002. 137–70.

Chapin, Chester. *Personification in Eighteenth-Century English Poetry.* New York: King's Crown, 1955.

Chema, Alexis. "A Tongue in Every Star: Barbauld and the Persuasive Figure." Unpublished ms.

Chudgar, Neil. "Swift's Gentleness." *ELH* 78.1 (Spring 2011): 137–61.

Clark, Kenneth. *Landscape into Art.* London: John Murray, 1949.

Clarke, Norma. "'The Cursed Barbauld Crew': Women Writers and Writing for Children in the Late Eighteenth Century." In *Opening the Nursery Door: Reading, Writing and Childhood 1600–1900.* Ed. Mary Hilton, Morag Styles, and Victor Watson. London: Routledge, 1997. 91–103.

Coetzee, J. M. *Elizabeth Costello.* New York: Penguin, 2003.

―――. "He and His Man." http://www.nobelprize.org/nobel_prizes/literature/laureates/2003/coetzee-lecture-e.html.

Cohen, Ralph. *The Art of Discrimination: Thomson's "The Seasons" and the Language of Criticism.* Berkeley: University of California Press, 1964.

―――. *The Unfolding of "The Seasons."* Baltimore: Johns Hopkins University Press, 1970.

Cole, Lucinda, ed. "Animal, All Too Animal." Special issue, *Eighteenth Century* 52.1 (2011).

―――. "Introduction: Human-Animal Studies and the Eighteenth Century." In "Animal, All Too Animal." Ed. Lucinda Cole. Special issue, *Eighteenth Century* 52.1 (2011): 1–10.

Coleridge, Samuel Taylor. *Biographia Literaria; or, Biographical Sketches of My Literary Life and Opinions.* Ed. James Engell and W. Jackson Bate. Vol. 7 of *The Collected Works of Samuel Taylor Coleridge.* Princeton, N.J.: Princeton University Press, 1985.

―――. *Coleridge's Miscellaneous Criticism.* Ed. Thomas Middleton Raysor. London: Constable, 1936.

Comte, Auguste. *Oeuvres D'Auguste Comte.* 12 vols. Paris: Éditions Anthropos, 1968–71.

Cosslett, Tess. *Talking Animals in British Children's Fiction: 1786–1914.* Aldershot: Ashgate, 2006.

Cottingham, John. "'A Brute to the Brutes?': Descartes' Treatment of Animals." *Philosophy* 53.206 (1978): 551–59.

Coventry, Francis. *The History of Pompey the Little: or, The Life and the History of a Lapdog.* London: M. Cooper, 1751.

Cowper, William. *The Letters and Prose Writings of William Cowper.* Ed. James King and Charles Ryskamp. 5 vols. Oxford: Clarendon, 1979–86.

―――. *The Poems of William Cowper.* 3 vols. Ed. John D. Baird and Charles Ryskamp. Oxford: Clarendon, 1980–95.

Darton, F. J. Harvey. *Children's Books in England: Five Centuries of Social Life.* Cambridge: Cambridge University Press, 1982.

Darwin, Erasmus. *The Botanic Garden, containing The Loves of the Plants.* Lichfield: J. Jackson, 1789.

Defoe, Daniel. *Robinson Crusoe.* Ed. Michael Shinagel. New York: Norton, 1975.

―――. *Serious Reflections During the Life and Surprising Adventures of Robinson Crusoe with His Vision of the Angelick World. Written by Himself.* London: W. Taylor, 1720.

Den Otter, Alice. "Pests, Parasites, and Positionality." *Studies in Romanticism* 43.2 (2004): 209–30.

Derrida, Jacques. *The Animal That Therefore I Am*. Ed. Marie-Louise Mallet. Trans. David Wills. New York: Fordham University Press, 2008.

———. *The Beast and the Sovereign*. Trans. Geoffrey Bennington. 2 vols. Chicago: University of Chicago Press, 2009.

———. *Of Grammatology*. Trans. Gayatri Chakravorty Spivak. Baltimore: Johns Hopkins University Press, 1998.

Descartes, René. *Discourse on the Method*. In *The Philosophical Writings of Descartes*. 2 vols. Trans. John Cottingham, Robert Stoothoff, and Dugald Murdoch. Cambridge: Cambridge University Press, 1984–85.

Diamond, Cora. "Eating Meat and Eating People." *Philosophy* 53.206 (1978): 465–79.

Diderot, Denis, and Louis Jean-Marie Daubenton. "Animal." In *Encyclopédie ou Dictionnaire raisonné des sciences, des arts et des métiers, par une Société de Gens de lettres*. Ed. Denis Diderot and Jean Le Rond d'Alembert. 1751–72. ARTFL Encyclopédie Project. http://artflx .uchicago.edu/cgi-bin/philologic/getobject.pl?c.1:1101.encyclopedie0311.

Doody, Margaret Anne. "Insects, Vermin, and Horses: *Gulliver's Travels* and Virgil's *Georgics*." In *Augustan Studies: Essays in Honor of Irvin Ehrenpreis*. Ed. Douglas Lane Patey and Timothy Keegan. Cranbury, N.J.: Associated University Presses, 1985. 145–74.

Elliot, Robert C. *The Literary Persona*. Chicago: University of Chicago Press, 1982.

Ellis, Markman. "Suffering Things: Lapdogs, Slaves, and Counter-Sensibility." In *The Secret Life of Things: Animals, Objects, and It-Narratives in Eighteenth-Century England*. Ed. Mark Blackwell. Lewisburg, Pa.: Bucknell University Press, 2007. 92–116.

Esposito, Roberto. *Third Person: Politics of Life and Philosophy of the Impersonal*. Trans. Zakiya Hanafi. Cambridge, UK: Polity, 2012.

Fabricant, Carole. "Speaking for the Irish Nation: The Drapier, the Bishop, and the Problems of Colonial Representation." *ELH* 66.2 (1999): 337–72.

[Fenn, Eleanor]. *Fables in Monosyllables by Mrs. Teachwell; to which are added Morals, in dialogues, between a mother and children*. London: John Marshall, 1783.

Ferguson, Frances. "Canons, Poetics, and Social Value: Jeremy Bentham and How to Do Things with People." *MLN* 100.5 (1995): 1148–64.

———. "Educational Rationalization / Sublime Reason." In *The Sublime and Education*. Ed. J. Jennifer Jones. August 2010. Romantic Circles. http://www.rc.umd.edu/praxis/sublime _education/ferguson/ferguson.html.

———. "Reading Morals: Locke and Rousseau on Education and Inequality." *Representations* 6 (1984): 66–84.

———. *Wordsworth: Language as Counter-Spirit*. New Haven, Conn.: Yale University Press, 1977.

Festa, Lynn. "The Moral Ends of Eighteenth- and Nineteenth-Century Object Narratives." In *The Secret Life of Things: Animals, Objects, and It-Narratives in Eighteenth-Century England*. Ed. Mark Blackwell. Lewisburg, Pa.: Bucknell University Press, 2007. 309–28.

———. "Person, Animal, Thing: The 1796 Dog Tax and the Right to Superfluous Things." *Eighteenth-Century Life* 33.2 (2009): 1–44.

———. *Sentimental Figures of Empire in Eighteenth-Century Britain and France*. Baltimore: Johns Hopkins University Press, 2006.

Flynn, Carol Houlihan. *The Body in Swift and Defoe*. Cambridge: Cambridge University Press, 1990.

Foucault, Michel. *The Order of Things: An Archaeology of the Human Sciences*. New York: Random House, 1970.

——. *Security, Territory, Population: Lectures at the Collège de France, 1977–78*. Ed. Michel Senellart. Trans. Graham Burchell. Houndmills, Basingstoke: Palgrave Macmillan, 2007.

Fox, Christopher. *Locke and the Scriblerians: Identity and Consciousness in Early Eighteenth-Century Britain*. Berkeley: University of California Press, 1988.

Fraiman, Susan. "Shelter Writing: Desperate Housekeeping from Crusoe to Queer Eye." *New Literary History* 37.2 (2006): 341–59.

Freud, Sigmund. "Animism, Magic and the Omnipotence of Thought." In *Totem and Taboo: Some Points of Agreement Between the Mental Lives of Savages and Neurotics*. Vol. 13 of *The Standard Edition of the Complete Psychological Works of Sigmund Freud*. Ed. James Strachey. 24 vols. London: Hogarth, 1953–74. 75-99.

Frost, Samantha. "Faking It: Hobbes's Thinking-Bodies and the Ethics of Dissimulation," *Political Theory* 29.1 (2001): 30–57.

——. *Lessons from a Materialist Thinker: Hobbesian Reflections on Ethics and Politics*. Stanford, Calif.: Stanford University Press, 2008.

Gallagher, Catherine. *Nobody's Story: The Vanishing Acts of Women Writers in the Marketplace, 1670–1820*. Berkeley: University of California Press, 1995.

——. "The Rise of Fictionality." In *The Novel*. Vol. 1, *History Geography, and Culture*. Ed. Franco Moretti. Princeton, N.J.: Princeton University Press, 2006. 336–63.

Gayon, Jean. "The Individuality of the Species: A Darwinian Theory?—from Buffon to Ghiselin, and Back to Darwin." *Biology and Philosophy* 11 (1996): 215–44.

Ghiselin, Michael. "A Radical Solution to the Species Problem." *Systematic Zoology* 23.4 (1974): 536–44.

Gigante, Denise. *Life: Organic Form and Romanticism*. New Haven, Conn.: Yale University Press, 2009.

Gildon, Charles. *The Life and Strange Surprizing Adventures of Mr. D—— De F——*. London, 1719.

Godman, Peter. *From Poliziano to Machiavelli: Florentine Humanism in the High Renaissance*. Princeton, N.J.: Princeton University Press, 1998.

Godwin, William. *Enquiry Concerning Political Justice*. Ed. Isaac Kramnick. Harmondsworth: Penguin, 1976.

——. *Fables, Ancient and Modern: Adapted for the Use of Children*. London: T. Hodgkins, 1805.

Goodman, Kevis. *Georgic Modernity and British Romanticism: Poetry and the Mediation of History*. Cambridge: Cambridge University Press, 2004.

Hallam, Henry. *Introduction to the Literature of Europe, in the Fifteenth, Sixteenth and Seventeenth Centuries*. 4 vols. London: John Murray, 1837–39.

Hammond, Brean. "Swift's Reading." In *Cambridge Companion to Jonathan Swift*. Ed. Christopher Fox. Cambridge: Cambridge University Press, 2003. 73–86.

Haraway, Donna. *The Companion Species Manifesto: Dogs, People, and Significant Otherness*. Chicago: Prickly Paradigm, 2003.

Harrison, Peter. "Descartes on Animals." *Philosophical Quarterly* 42.167 (1992): 219–27.

Hawes, Clement. "Three Times Round the Globe: Gulliver and Colonial Discourse." *Cultural Critique* 18 (1991): 187–214.

Hazlitt, William. *Lectures on English Poets and The Spirit of the Age*. London: J. M. Dent, 1910.

Heath, John. *The Talking Greeks: Speech, Animals, and the Other in Homer, Aeschylus, and Plato.*
    Cambridge: Cambridge University Press, 2005.
Hesiod, *Works and Days*. Trans. Hugh G. Evelyn-White. 1914. http://www.sacred-texts.com/cla
    /hesiod/works.htm.
Hobbes, Thomas. *Leviathan*. London: Penguin, 1985.
———. *Leviathan, with Selected Variants from the Latin Edition of 1668*. Ed. Edwin Curley.
    Indianapolis: Hackett, 1994.
Holmes, Oliver Wendell. *The Common Law*. New York: Dover, 1991.
Hull, David. "A Matter of Individuality." *Philosophy of Science* 45.3 (1978): 335–60.
———. "Are Species Really Individuals?" *Systematic Zoology* 25.2 (1976): 174–91.
Hulme, Peter. *Colonial Encounters: Europe and the Native Caribbean 1492–1797*. London:
    Methuen, 1986.
Hume, David. *A Treatise of Human Nature*. Ed. P. H. Nidditch. Oxford: Oxford University
    Press, 1978.
Hunter, J. Paul. *Before Novels: The Cultural Contexts of Eighteenth-Century English Fiction*. New
    York: Norton, 1990.
———. "*Gulliver's Travels* and the Later Writings." In *Cambridge Companion to Jonathan Swift*.
    Ed. Christopher Fox. Cambridge: Cambridge University Press, 2003. 216–40.
———. "*Gulliver's Travels* and the Novel." In *The Genres of* Gulliver's Travels. Ed. Frederik N.
    Smith. Newark: University of Delaware Press, 1990. 56–74.
———. *The Reluctant Pilgrim: Defoe's Emblematic Method and the Quest for Form in "Robinson
    Crusoe."* Baltimore: Johns Hopkins University Press, 1966.
Hutchings, W. B. "'Can Pure Description Hold the Place of Sense?': Thomson's Landscape
    Poetry." In *James Thomson: Essays for the Tercentenary*. Ed. Richard Terry. Liverpool: Liver-
    pool University Press, 2000. 35–66.
Inglesfield, Robert. "Thomson and Shaftesbury." In *James Thomson: Essays for the Tercentenary*.
    Ed. Richard Terry. Liverpool: Liverpool University Press, 2000. 67–92.
Jager, Eric. "The Parrot's Voice: Language and the Self in Robinson Crusoe." *Eighteenth-Century
    Studies* 21.3 (1988): 316–33.
Jaynes, Julian. "The Problem of Animate Motion in the Seventeenth Century." *Journal of the
    History of Ideas* 31.2 (1970): 219–34.
Johnson, Barbara. "Anthropomorphism in Lyric and Law." In *Persons and Things*. By Johnson.
    Cambridge, Mass.: Harvard University Press, 2010. 188–207.
Johnson, Samuel. *A Dictionary of the English language: In which the words are deduced
    from their originals, and illustrated in their different significations by examples from the best
    writers. To which are prefixed, a history of the language, and an English grammar*. 2 vols.
    2nd ed. London: printed by W. Strahan, for J. and P. Knapton, T. and L. Longman et al.,
    1755–56.
———. *Lives of the English Poets*. 3 vols. Oxford: Clarendon, 1950.
Joyce, James. "Daniel Defoe." In *Robinson Crusoe*. By Defoe. Ed. Michael Shinagel. New York:
    Norton, 1975. 354–57.
Kahn, Victoria. *Wayward Contracts: The Crisis of Political Obligation in England, 1640–1674*.
    Princeton, N.J.: Princeton University Press, 2004.
Kames, Henry Home, Lord. *Elements of Criticism*. 3 vols. Edinburgh: printed for A. Millar,
    A. Kincaid and J. Bell, 1762.
Kaul, Suvir. *Poems of Nation, Anthems of Empire: English Verse in the Long Eighteenth Century*.
    Charlottesville: University of Virginia Press, 2000.

Kay, Carol. *Political Constructions: Defoe, Richardson, and Sterne in Relation to Hobbes, Hume, and Burke.* Ithaca, N.Y.: Cornell University Press, 1988.

Kelly, Ann Cline. "Gulliver as Pet and Pet Owner: Conversations with Animals in Book 4." *ELH* 74.2 (2007): 323–49.

Kenyon-Jones, Christine. *Kindred Brutes: Animals in Romantic Period Writing.* Aldershot: Ashgate, 2001.

Kilner, Dorothy. *The Life and Perambulation of a Mouse.* 2 vols. London: John Marshall, c. 1785.

Knapp, Stephen. *Personification and the Sublime: Milton to Coleridge.* Cambridge, Mass.: Harvard University Press, 1985.

Kramnick, Isaac. "Children's Literature and Bourgeois Ideology: Observations on Culture and Industrial Capitalism in the Later Eighteenth Century." In *Culture and Politics from Puritanism to the Enlightenment.* Ed. Perez Zagorin. Berkeley: University of California Press, 1980. 203–40.

Kunin, Aaron. "Characters Lounge." *Modern Language Quarterly* 70.3 (2009): 291–317.

Lamb, Charles. *The Letters of Charles and Mary Anne Lamb.* Ed. Edwin W. Marrs Jr. 3 vols. Ithaca, N.Y.: Cornell University Press, 1976.

Lamb, Jonathan. "Locke's Wild Fancies: Empiricism, Personhood, and Fictionality." *Eighteenth Century* 48.3 (2007): 187–204.

———. "Modern Metamorphoses and Disgraceful Tales." *Critical Inquiry* 28.1 (2001): 133–66.

———. "Sterne and Irregular Oratory." In *Laurence Sterne's "Tristram Shandy": A Casebook.* Ed. Thomas Keymer. Oxford: Oxford University Press, 2006. 213–39.

———. "Swift, *Leviathan*, and the Persons of Authors." In *Swift's Travels: Eighteenth-Century Satire and Its Legacies.* Ed. Nicholas Hudson and Aaron Santesso. Cambridge: Cambridge University Press, 2008. 25–38.

———. *The Things Things Say.* Princeton, N.J.: Princeton University Press, 2011.

Landa, Louis. "The Shandean Homunculus: The Background of Sterne's 'Little Gentleman.'" In *Restoration and Eighteenth-Century Essays in Honour of Alan Dugald McKillop.* Ed. Carrol Camden. Chicago: University of Chicago Press, 1963. 49–68.

Landry, Donna. *Noble Brutes: How Eastern Horses Transformed English Culture.* Baltimore: Johns Hopkins University Press, 2009.

Latour, Bruno. *Reassembling the Social: An Introduction to Actor-Network-Theory.* Oxford: Oxford University Press, 2005.

———. *We Have Never Been Modern.* Trans. Catherine Porter. Cambridge, Mass.: Harvard University Press, 1993.

Levin, Samuel. "Allegorical Language." In *Allegory, Myth, and Symbol.* Ed. Morton W. Bloomfield. Cambridge, Mass.: Harvard University Press, 1981. 23–38.

Lévi-Strauss, Claude. *The Savage Mind.* Chicago: University of Chicago Press, 1966.

———. *Totemism.* Trans. Rodney Needham. Boston: Beacon, 1963.

Lewis, Jayne. *The English Fable: Aesop and Literary Culture, 1651–1740.* Cambridge: Cambridge University Press, 1996.

Locke, John. *An Essay Concerning Human Understanding.* Ed. Peter H. Nidditch. Oxford: Oxford University Press, 1975.

———. *Some Thoughts Concerning Education.* Ed. John W. Yolton and Jean S. Yolton. Oxford: Oxford University Press, 1989.

———. *Two Treatises of Government.* Ed. Peter Laslett. Cambridge: Cambridge University Press, 1988.

Lovejoy, Arthur. "Buffon and the Problem of Species." In *Forerunners of Darwin: 1745–1859.* Ed. Bentley Glass, Owsei Temkin, and William L. Straus Jr. Baltimore: Johns Hopkins University Press, 1959. 84–113.

Loveridge, Mark. *A History of Augustan Fable.* Cambridge: Cambridge University Press, 1998.

———. "Stories of Cocks and Bulls: The Ending of *Tristram Shandy.*" *Eighteenth-Century Fiction* 5.1 (1992): 35–54.

Lukács, Georg. "Richness, Chaos and Form: A Dialogue Concerning Laurence Sterne." In *Soul and Form.* By Lukács. Trans. Anna Bostock. London: Merlin, 1974. 124–51.

Lupton, Christina. "Tristram Shandy, David Hume, and Epistemological Fiction." *Philosophy and Literature* 27.1 (2003): 98–115.

Lupton, Julia Reinhard. *Citizen Saints: Shakespeare and Political Theology.* Chicago: University of Chicago Press, 2005.

Lynch, Deidre Shauna. *The Economy of Character: Novels, Market Culture and the Business of Inner Meaning.* Chicago: University of Chicago Press, 1998.

———. "Personal Effects and Sentimental Fictions." In *The Secret Life of Things: Animals, Objects, and It-Narratives in Eighteenth-Century England.* Ed. Mark Blackwell. Lewisburg, Pa.: Bucknell University Press, 2007. 63–91.

———. "'Young Ladies Are Delicate Plants': Jane Austen and Greenhouse Romanticism." *ELH* 77 (2010): 689-729.

Macpherson, C. B. "Locke on Capitalist Appropriation." *Western Political Quarterly* 4.4 (1951): 550–66.

———. *The Political Theory of Possessive Individualism: Hobbes to Locke.* Oxford: Clarendon, 1962.

Macpherson, Sandra. *Harm's Way: Tragic Responsibility and the Novel Form.* Baltimore: Johns Hopkins University Press, 2010.

Mandeville, Bernard. *The Fable of the Bees; or, Private Vices, Public Benefits.* Indianapolis: Liberty Fund, 1988.

Marin, Louis. *Food for Thought.* Trans. Mette Hjort. Baltimore: Johns Hopkins University Press, 1989.

Marshall, David. "Autobiographical Acts in *Robinson Crusoe.*" *ELH* 71 (2004): 899–920.

Marx, Karl. *Capital: A Critique of Political Economy.* 3 vols. Oxford: Oxford University Press, 1976–81.

McCarthy, William. *Anna Letitia Barbauld: Voice of the Enlightenment.* Baltimore: Johns Hopkins University Press, 2008.

McGrath, Brian. "Rousseau's Crusoe; or, On Learning to Read as Not Myself." *Eighteenth-Century Fiction* 23.1 (2010): 119–39.

McKeon, Michael. *Origins of the English Novel 1600–1740.* Baltimore: Johns Hopkins University Press, 2002.

———. *The Secret History of Domesticity: Public, Private, and the Division of Knowledge.* Baltimore: Johns Hopkins University Press, 2005.

McKillop, Alan Dugald. *The Background of Thomson's "Seasons."* Minneapolis: University of Minnesota Press, 1942.

Menely, Tobias. *The Animal Claim: Sensibility and the Creaturely Voice.* Chicago: University of Chicago Press, 2015.

———. "Animal Signs and Ethical Significance: Expressive Creatures in the British Georgic." *Mosaic* 39.4 (2006): 111–27.

———. "Zoophilpsychosis: Why Animals Are What's Wrong with Sentimentality." *Symploke* 15.1–2 (2007): 244–67.

Michie, Allen. "Gulliver the Houyahoo: Swift, Locke, and the Ethics of Excessive Individualism." In *Humans and Other Animals in Eighteenth-Century British Culture*. Ed. Frank Palmeri. Aldershot: Ashgate, 2006. 67–82.

Milne, Anne. *"Lactilla Tends Her Fav'rite Cow": Ecocritical Readings of Animals and Women in Eighteenth-Century British Labouring-Class Women's Poetry*. Lewisburg, Pa.: Bucknell University Press, 2008.

Molesworth, Jesse. *Chance and the Eighteenth-Century Novel: Realism, Probability, Magic*. Cambridge: Cambridge University Press, 2010.

Montag, Warren. *The Unthinkable Swift: The Spontaneous Philosophy of a Church of England Man*. London: Verso, 1994.

Montaigne, Michel de. "The Apologie for Raymond Sebond." In *The Essayes of Montaigne: John Florio's Translation*. Ed. J. I. M. Stewart. New York: Modern Library, 1933. 385-547.

Myers, Mitzi. "Impeccable Governesses, Rational Dames, and Moral Mothers: Mary Wollstonecraft and the Female Tradition in Georgian Children's Books." *Children's Literature* 14 (1986): 31–59.

———. "Romancing the Moral Tale: Maria Edgeworth and the Problematics of Pedagogy." In *Romanticism and Children's Literature in Nineteenth-Century England*. Ed. James Holt McGavran Jr. Athens: University of Georgia Press, 1991. 96–128.

Nash, Richard. "Joy and Pity: Reading Animal Bodies in Late Eighteenth-Century Culture." *Eighteenth-Century* 52.1 (2011): 47–67.

———. *Wild Enlightenment: The Borders of Human Identity in the Eighteenth Century*. Charlottesville: University of Virginia Press, 2003.

The New Princeton Encyclopedia of Poetry and Poetics. Ed. Alex Preminger and T. V. F. Brogan. Princeton, N.J.: Princeton University Press, 1993.

Olivecrona, Karl. "Locke's Theory of Appropriation." *Philosophical Quarterly* 24.96 (1974): 220–34.

Packham, Catherine. *Eighteenth-Century Vitalism: Bodies, Culture, Politics*. Houndmills, Basingstoke: Palgrave Macmillan, 2012.

Palmeri, Frank. "The Autocritique of Fables." In *Humans and Other Animals in Eighteenth-Century British Culture*. Ed. Frank Palmeri. Aldershot: Ashgate, 2006. 83–100.

———, ed. *Humans and Other Animals in Eighteenth-Century British Culture: Representation, Hybridity, Ethics*. Aldershot: Ashgate, 2006.

———. *Satire in Narrative: Petronius, Swift, Gibbon, Melville, and Pynchon*. Austin: University of Texas Press, 1990.

Parker, Fred. *Scepticism and Literature: An Essay on Pope, Hume, Sterne, and Johnson*. Oxford: Oxford University Press, 2003.

Patterson, Annabel. *Fables of Power: Aesopian Writing and Political History*. Durham, N.C.: Duke University Press, 1991.

Paulson, Ronald. *The Fictions of Satire*. Baltimore: Johns Hopkins University Press, 1967.

Paxson, James J. *The Poetics of Personification*. Cambridge: Cambridge University Press, 1994.

Perkins, David. *Romanticism and Animal Rights*. Cambridge: Cambridge University Press, 2007.

Perry, Ruth. "Words for Sex: The Verbal-Sexual Continuum in *Tristram Shandy*." *Studies in the Novel* 20 (1988): 27–42.

Picciotto, Joanna. "Reading People." Unpublished ms.

Pick, Anat. *Creaturely Poetics: Animality and Vulnerability in Literature and Film*. New York: Columbia University Press, 2011.

Pickering, Samuel F., Jr., *John Locke and Children's Books in Eighteenth-Century England.* Knoxville: University of Tennessee Press, 1981.

Pinch, Adela. *Strange Fits of Passion: Epistemologies of Emotion, Hume to Austen.* Stanford, Calif.: Stanford University Press, 1996.

Pitkin, Hannah. "Hobbes's Concept of Representation." Parts 1 and 2. *American Political Science Review* 58 (1964): 328–40, 902–18.

Plato. *Apology.* Trans. Benjamin Jowett. Champaign, Ill.: Project Gutenberg.

———. *Statesman.* Ed. Julia Annas and Robin Waterfield. Trans. Robin Waterfield. Cambridge: Cambridge University Press, 1995.

Plumb, J. H. "The New World of Children." In *The Birth of a Consumer Society: The Commercialization of Eighteenth-Century England.* Ed. Neil McKendrick, John Brewer, and J. H. Plumb. London: Europa, 1982. 286–315.

Poliziano, Angelo. *Silvae.* Ed. and trans. Charles Fantazzi. Cambridge, Mass.: Harvard University Press, 2004.

Pollock, Linda. *Forgotten Children: Parent-Child Relations from 1500–1900.* Cambridge: Cambridge University Press, 1983.

Pope, Alexander. *Poetry and Prose of Alexander Pope.* Ed. Aubrey Williams. Boston: Houghton Mifflin, 1969.

Porter, Roy. "'The Whole Secret of Health': Mind, Body and Medicine in *Tristram Shandy.*" In *Nature Transfigured: Science and Literature, 1700–1900.* Ed. John Christie and Sally Shuttleworth. Manchester: Manchester University Press, 1989. 61–84.

Priestley, Joseph. *A Course of Lectures on Oratory and Criticism.* London: printed for J. Johnson, 1777.

Quintilian. *Institutes: M. Fabius Quinctilianus his Institutes of eloquence: or, the art of speaking in public, . . . Translated into English, . . . with notes, critical and explanatory, by William Guthrie, Esq; in two volumes.* London: printed for T. Waller, 1756.

Rawson, Claude. *God, Gulliver, and Genocide: Barbarism and the European Imagination, 1492–1945.* Oxford: Oxford University Press, 2001.

———. "Gulliver and Others: Reflections on Swift's 'I' Narrators." In *Gulliver's Travels.* By Jonathan Swift. Ed. Albert J. Rivero. New York: Norton, 2002. 480–99.

———. *Gulliver and the Gentle Reader.* London: Routledge, 1973.

Reill, Peter Hans. *Vitalizing Nature in the Enlightenment.* Berkeley: University of California Press, 2005.

Richardson, Alan. *Literature, Education, and Romanticism: Reading as Social Practice, 1780–1832.* Cambridge: Cambridge University Press, 1995.

———. "Wordsworth, Fairy Tales, and the Politics of Children's Reading." In *Romanticism and Children's Literature in Nineteenth-Century England.* Ed. James Holt McGavran Jr. Athens: University of Georgia Press, 1991. 34–53.

Richetti, John. *Defoe's Narratives: Situations and Structures.* Oxford: Clarendon, 1975.

———. "Secular Crusoe: The Reluctant Pilgrim Re-Visited." In *Eighteenth-Century Genre and Culture: Serious Reflections on Occasional Forms.* Ed. Dennis Todd and Cynthia Wall. Newark: University of Delaware Press, 2001. 58–78.

Ridley, Glynis, ed. "Animals in the Eighteenth Century." Special issue, *Journal for Eighteenth-Century Studies* 33.4 (2010).

Riskin, Jessica. "The Defecating Duck; or, The Ambiguous Origins of Artificial Life." *Critical Inquiry* 29.4 (2003): 599–633.

Ritvo, Harriet. *The Animal Estate: The English and Other Creatures in the Victorian Age*. Cambridge, Mass.: Harvard University Press, 1987.

———. "Possessing Mother Nature: Genetic Capital in Eighteenth-Century Britain." In *Early Modern Conceptions of Property*. Ed. John Brewer and Susan Staves. London: Routledge, 1995. 413–26.

Robbins, Louise. *Elephant Slaves and Pampered Parrots: Exotic Animals in Eighteenth-Century Paris*. Baltimore: Johns Hopkins University Press, 2002.

Rochlin, Margy. "Marooned on an Island, Out on a Limb." *New York Times* 5 November 2000, late ed.: 2A.1.

Rodgers, J. "'Life' in the Novel: *Tristram Shandy* and Some Aspects of Eighteenth-Century Physiology." *Eighteenth-Century Life* 6.1 (1980): 1–20.

Rodino, Richard H. "Authors, Characters, and Readers in *Gulliver's Travels*." In *Gulliver's Travels*. By Jonathan Swift. Ed. Albert J. Rivero. New York: Norton, 2002. 427–50.

Roger, Jacques. *Buffon: A Life in Natural History*. Ithaca, N.Y.: Cornell University Press, 1997.

———. "The Living World." In *The Ferment of Knowledge: Studies in the Historiography of Eighteenth-Century Science*. Ed. G. S. Rousseau and Roy Porter. Cambridge: Cambridge University Press, 1980. 255–84.

Rousseau, Jean-Jacques. "Discourse on the Origin and Foundations of Inequality Among Men." In *Rousseau's Political Writings*. Ed. Alan Ritter and Julia Conaway Bondanella. New York: Norton, 1988. 3-57.

———. *Emile; or, On Education*. Trans. Allan Bloom. New York: Basic, 1979.

Said, Edward. "Swift as Intellectual." In *The World, the Text and the Critic*. Cambridge, Mass.: Harvard University Press, 1984. 72–89.

Santner, Eric. *On Creaturely Life: Rilke, Benjamin, Sebald*. Chicago: University of Chicago Press, 2006.

Schmidgen, Wolfram. *Eighteenth-Century Fiction and the Law of Property*. Cambridge: Cambridge University Press, 2002.

———. *Exquisite Mixture: The Virtues of Impurity in Early Modern England*. Philadelphia: University of Pennsylvania Press, 2013.

———. "The Politics and Philosophy of Mixture: John Locke Recomposed." *Eighteenth Century* 48.3 (2007): 205–23.

Schonhorn, Manuel. *Defoe's Politics: Parliament, Power, Kingship, and "Robinson Crusoe."* Cambridge: Cambridge University Press, 1991.

Scott, John T. Introduction. In *Essay on the Origin of Languages and Writings Related to Music*. By Jean-Jacques Rousseau. Ed. and trans. John T. Scott. *The Collected Writings of Rousseau*. Vol. 7. Hanover, N.H.: University Press of New England, 1998. xiii–xlii.

Shaftesbury, Anthony Ashley Cooper, third Earl of. "An Inquiry Concerning Virtue or Merit." In *Characteristics of Men, Manners, Opinions, Times*. Ed. Lawrence E. Klein. Cambridge: Cambridge University Press, 1999. 163–230.

———. "The Moralists, a Philosophical Rhapsody, Being a Recital of Certain Conversations on Natural and Moral Subjects." In *Characteristics of Men, Manners, Opinions, Times*. Ed. Lawrence E. Klein. Cambridge: Cambridge University Press, 1999. 231–338.

Shannon, Laurie. *The Accommodated Animal: Cosmopolity in Shakespearean Locales*. Chicago: University of Chicago Press, 2013.

———. "Poor, Bare, Forked: Animal Sovereignty, Human Negative Exceptionalism, and the Natural History of King Lear." *Shakespeare Quarterly* 60.2 (2009): 168–96.

Shell, Marc. "The Family Pet." *Representations* 15 (1986): 121–53.

———. "The Lie of the Fox: Rousseau's Theory of Verbal, Monetary, and Political Representation." *Sub-Stance* 10 (1974): 111–23.

Shevelow, Kathryn. *For the Love of Animals: The Rise of the Animal Protection Movement.* New York: Henry Holt, 2008.

Singer, Peter. *Animal Liberation.* New York: Harper Collins, 1975.

———. Foreword. "Animals in the Eighteenth Century." Ed. Glynis Ridley. Special issue, *Journal for Eighteenth-Century Studies* 33.4 (2010): 427–30.

Sitter, John. *The Cambridge Introduction to Eighteenth-Century Poetry.* Cambridge: Cambridge University Press, 2011.

Skinner, Quentin. *Visions of Politics.* Vol. 3, *Hobbes and Civil Science.* Cambridge: Cambridge University Press, 2002.

Slaughter, Joseph R. *Human Rights, Inc.: The World Novel, Narrative Form, and International Law.* New York: Fordham University Press, 2007.

Sloan, Philip. "The Buffon-Linnaeus Controversy." *Isis* 67.3 (1976): 356–75.

———. "From Logical Universals to Historical Individuals: Buffon's Idea of Biological Species." In Scott Atran et al., *Histoire du concept d'espèce dans les sciences de la vie.* Paris: Fondation Singer-Polignac, 1987. 101–40.

Spacks, Patricia Meyer. *Imagining a Self: Autobiography and Novel in Eighteenth-Century England.* Cambridge, Mass.: Harvard University Press, 1976.

———. *The Insistence of Horror: Aspects of the Supernatural in Eighteenth-Century Poetry.* Cambridge, Mass.: Harvard University Press, 1962.

Spelman, Elizabeth V. *Inessential Woman: Problems of Exclusion in Feminist Thought.* Boston: Beacon, 1988.

Spencer, Jane. "Creating Animal Experience in Late Eighteenth-Century Narrative." *Journal for Eighteenth-Century Studies* 33.4 (2010): 469–86.

Stalnaker, Joanna. *The Unfinished Enlightenment: Description in the Age of the Encyclopedia.* Ithaca, N.Y.: Cornell University Press, 2010.

Stamos, David. "Buffon, Darwin, and the Non-Individuality of Species—A Reply to Jean Gayon." *Biology and Philosophy* 13 (1998): 443–70.

Starr, G. A. *Defoe and Spiritual Autobiography.* Princeton, N.J.: Princeton University Press, 1965.

Starr, G. Gabrielle. *Lyric Generations: Poetry and the Novel in the Long Eighteenth Century.* Baltimore: Johns Hopkins University Press, 2004.

———. "Objects, Imaginings, and Facts: Going Beyond Genre in Behn and Defoe." *Eighteenth-Century Fiction* 16.4 (2004): 499–518.

Steffe, John. *Five Letters: Containing . . . for religious knowledge, piety, and devotion.* London: printed for J. Buckland, at the Buck in Pater-noster Row; T. Toft in Chelmsford, 1757.

Sterne, Laurence. *The Letters of Laurence Sterne.* Ed. Lewis Perry Curtis. Oxford: Clarendon, 1935.

———. *The Life and Opinions of Tristram Shandy, Gentleman.* Ed. Ian Campbell Ross. Oxford: Oxford University Press, 1983.

———. *A Sentimental Journey Through France and Italy by Mr. Yorick.* Oxford: Oxford University Press, 1968.

Stone, Lawrence. *The Family, Sex and Marriage in England, 1500–1800.* New York: Harper, 1979.

Strong, Tracy B. "How to Write Scripture: Words, Authority, and Politics in Thomas Hobbes." *Critical Inquiry* 20.1 (1993): 128–59.

———. *Jean-Jacques Rousseau: The Politics of the Ordinary.* Lanham, Md.: Rowman and Littlefield, 2002.

Summerfield, Geoffrey. *Fantasy and Reason: Children's Literature in the Eighteenth Century*. Athens: University of Georgia Press, 1984.

Swift, Jonathan. *Correspondence of Jonathan Swift*. 5 vols. Ed. Harold Williams. Oxford: Clarendon. 1963–65.

———. *Gulliver's Travels*. Ed. Albert J. Rivero. New York: Norton, 2002.

———. *Jonathan Swift: The Complete Poems*. Ed. Pat Rogers. New Haven: Yale University Press, 1983.

———. *A Tale of a Tub and Other Works*. Ed. Angus Ross and David Woolley. Oxford: Oxford University Press, 1986.

Tague, Ingrid H. *Animal Companions: Pets and Social Change in Eighteenth-Century Britain*. University Park: Pennsylvania State University Press, 2015.

———. "Dead Pets: Satire and Sentiment in British Elegies and Epitaphs for Animals." *Eighteenth-Century Studies* 41.3 (2008): 289–306.

Tamen, Miguel. *Friends of Interpretable Objects*. Cambridge, Mass.: Harvard University Press, 2001.

Taylor, Charles. *Sources of the Self: The Making of Modern Identity*. Cambridge, Mass.: Harvard University Press, 1989.

Terry, Richard "'Meaner Themes': Mock-Heroic and Providentialism in Cowper's Poetry." *Studies in English Literature, 1500–1900* 34.3 (1994): 617–34.

Thomas, Keith. *Man and the Natural World: Changing Attitudes in England 1500–1800*. New York: Penguin, 1983.

Thompson, Helen. *Ingenuous Subjection: Compliance and Power in the Eighteenth-Century Domestic Novel*. Philadelphia: University of Pennsylvania Press, 2005.

Thompson, Michael. "Apprehending Human Form." In *Modern Moral Philosophy*. Ed. Anthony O'Hear. Cambridge: Cambridge University Press, 2004. 47–74.

———. *Life and Action: Elementary Structures of Practice and Practical Thought*. Cambridge, Mass.: Harvard University Press, 2008.

———. "The Representation of Life." In *Virtues and Reasons: Philippa Foot and Moral Theory*. Ed. Rosalind Hursthouse, Gavin Lawrence, and Warren Quinn. Oxford: Clarendon, 1995. 247–96.

Thomson, James. *Liberty, The Castle of Indolence, and Other Poems*. Ed. James Sambrook. Oxford: Clarendon, 1986.

———. *The Seasons*. Ed. James Sambrook. Oxford: Oxford University Press, 1981.

Todd, Dennis. *Imagining Monsters: Miscreations of the Self in Eighteenth-Century England*. Chicago: University of Chicago Press, 1995.

Trask, Michael. "The Ethical Animal: From Peter Singer to Patricia Highsmith." *Post45*. 2012. http://post45.research.yale.edu/2012/11/the-ethical-animal-from-peter-singer-to-patricia -highsmith/.

Traugott, John, ed. *Laurence Sterne: A Collection of Critical Essays*. Englewood Cliffs, N.J.: Prentice Hall, 1968.

———. *Tristram Shandy's World: Sterne's Philosophical Rhetoric*. Berkeley: University of California Press, 1954.

Trickett, Rachel. "Cowper, Wordsworth, and the Animal Fable." *Review of English Studies* 34.136 (1983): 471–80.

Trimmer, Sarah. *Fabulous Histories: Designed for the Instruction of Children, Respecting their Treatment of Animals*. London: T. Longman, 1786.

Tuveson, Ernest. "Swift: The View from Within the Satire." In *The Satirist's Art*. Ed. H. James Jensen and Malvin R. Zirker. Bloomington: Indiana University Press, 1972. 55-85.

Tylor, Edward. *Primitive Culture: Researches into the Development of Mythology, Philosophy, Religion, Language, Art, and Custom.* 7th ed. 2 vols. New York: Brentano, [1924].

Vanpée, Janie. "Reading Lessons in Rousseau's *Emile ou de l'éducation.*" *Modern Language Studies* 20.3 (1990): 40–49.

———. "Rousseau's *Emile ou de l'éducation*: Resistance to Reading." *Yale French Studies* 77 (1990): 156–76.

Vermeule, Blakey. *Why Do We Care About Literary Characters?* Baltimore: Johns Hopkins University Press, 2011.

Vickers, Ilse. *Defoe and the New Sciences.* Cambridge: Cambridge University Press, 1996.

Virgil. *The Works of Virgil: Containing his Pastorals, Georgics and Æneis. Translated into English verse by Mr. Dryden. In three volumes.* London: J. and R. Tonson, 1763.

Wall, Cynthia. *The Prose of Things: Transformations of Description in the Eighteenth Century.* Chicago: University of Chicago Press, 2006.

Watt, Ian. "The Ironic Tradition in Augustan Prose from Swift to Johnson." In *The Character of Swift's Satire: A Revised Focus.* Ed. Claude Rawson. Newark: University of Delaware Press, 1983. 305–23.

———. *The Rise of the Novel: Studies in Defoe, Richardson, and Fielding.* Berkeley: University of California Press, 2001.

Weil, Kari. *Thinking Animals: Why Animal Studies Now?* New York: Columbia University Press, 2013.

Wheeler, Roxann. "'My Savage,' 'My Man': Racial Multiplicity in *Robinson Crusoe.*" *ELH* 62.4 (1995): 821–61.

Williams, Kathleen M. "Gulliver's Voyage to the Houyhnhnms." *ELH* 18.4 (1951): 275–86.

Williams, R. John. "Naked Creatures: *Robinson Crusoe*, the Beast, and the Sovereign." *Comparative Critical Studies* 2.3 (2005): 337–48.

Wollstonecraft, Mary. *Original Stories, from Real Life; with Conversations, Calculated to Regulate the Affections, and Form the Mind to Truth and Goodness.* London: J. Johnson, 1788.

———. *Thoughts on the Education of Daughters.* Bristol: Thoemmes, 1995.

Woloch, Alex. *The One vs. the Many: Minor Characters and the Space of the Protagonist in the Novel.* Princeton, N.J.: Princeton University Press, 2003.

Woolf, Virginia. "Robinson Crusoe." In *Robinson Crusoe.* By Daniel Defoe. Ed. Michael Shinagel. New York: Norton, 1975. 306–11.

Wordsworth, William. *Lyrical Ballads.* Ed. R. L. Brett and A. R. Jones. New York: Routledge, 1991.

———. *The Prose Works of William Wordsworth.* Ed. W. J. B. Owen and Jane Worthington Smyser. 3 vols. Oxford: Clarendon, 1974.

———. *Wordsworth's Literary Criticism.* Ed. W. J. B. Owen. London: Routledge, 1974.

Yolton, John W. and Jean S. Introduction. In *Some Thoughts Concerning Education.* By Locke. Oxford: Clarendon, 1989. 1–75.

Yousef, Nancy. *Isolated Cases: The Anxieties of Autonomy in Enlightenment Philosophy and Romantic Literature.* Ithaca, N.Y.: Cornell University Press, 2004.

Zimmerman, Everett. "Robinson Crusoe and No Man's Land." *Journal of English and Germanic Philology* 102 (2003): 506–29.

———. *Swift's Narrative Satires: Author and Authority.* Ithaca, N.Y.: Cornell University Press, 1983.

Index

Acknowledgments

I had the good fortune to grow up in a place, and at a time, largely friendly to public education. I wrote this book in a time and place considerably less so. I am profoundly grateful to the many teachers who shepherded me through the first two decades of my life with creativity, dedication, and daily acts of kindness and attention. Everyone should be so lucky.

At McGill University, a few teachers were especially important as I learned to think and write: Maggie Kilgour, Robert Lecker, Kathleen Roberts Skerrett, and Gary Wihl. Above all, I owe immense thanks to Darko Suvin. The intellectual seriousness with which he treated my undergraduate self was bracing, and transformative. I have his model in mind whenever I advise undergraduate students. At the wonderfully imaginative institution that was the London Consortium, marvelous teachers opened up new vistas and new subjects and cemented my sense of where I wanted to go. Thank you to the late Paul Hirst, to Laura Mulvey, and especially to Colin MacCabe. Anyone who knows Colin can appreciate my gratitude for his boundless enthusiasm, his loyal friendship, and his remarkable breadth of knowledge. Colin also taught me the deep pleasures of collaboration, and a capacious sense of what intellectual endeavors might include. Paula Jalfon deserves mention, too, for all she taught me about writing, research, and tenacity. Many of the ideas that made their way into this book began to develop during my time in London, especially during the 2001 foot-and-mouth crisis. Thanks to the friends and colleagues who talked with me then, and encouraged my thinking.

Many cherished friends and colleagues at the University of Chicago have helped to shape or sustain my work. Jim Chandler has read this manuscript more often than anyone. I am moved by his generosity in doing so, and humbled, always, by his astounding powers of synthesis. On more than one occasion, he suggested a reference that made all the difference or asked the question that brought a chapter into focus. This book would have been a far lesser thing without his contribution. Frances Ferguson's incisive, generous reading has been crucial at every stage in the writing and revising of this book. Frances's work has been so important to my own, and I am deeply grateful for the many occasions on which she helped me to sharpen my ideas, to frame my arguments, or to recognize the force of a point in ways I had not. From the moment of my arrival at Chicago, Bill Brown took animals to be an important topic of inquiry, and he took me to have something important to say about them. This was immensely valuable in the early stages of this project especially. Ever since, Bill's extraordinary critical acumen and incomparable sense of style has helped me to strengthen my ideas, and my prose. Finally, this book simply would not have come into being without Sandra Macpherson's dazzling intelligence, and her sustained, close engagement with my ideas. She is the sort of teacher and colleague I aspire to be, someone who makes those around her smarter. I am grateful for the ways that she has always pressed—and enabled—me to think the more difficult, the more interesting thought.

For the conversations and collegiality that make the University of Chicago such a remarkable place to live and work, I am also grateful to Fredrik Albritton Jonsson, Thomas Christensen, Hillary Chute, Bradin Cormack, Robert Devendorf, the late Miriam Hansen, Jim Hevia, Oren Izenberg, Patrick Jagoda, David Levin, Rochona Majumdar, Tom Mitchell, Benjamin Morgan, Daniel Morgan, Sarah Nooter, Elizabeth O'Connor Chandler, Mark Payne, Chicu Reddy, Rick Rosengarten, Martha Roth, Lisa Ruddick, Zach Samalin, Eric Santner, David Simon, Eric Slauter, Justin Steinberg, Richard Strier, Robin Valenza, and especially Maud Ellmann, Beth Helsinger, Mark Miller, and Debbie Nelson. I am particularly grateful to Elaine Hadley for her clear-sighted intelligence; to Lauren Berlant for encouragement at key moments and for her amazing capacity to articulate *the* important question; and to Joshua Scodel, for his immensely helpful reading of an early draft of Chapter 1. Thank you above all to Timothy Campbell, my inestimable colleague, interlocutor, and dear friend.

I have honed many of the ideas in this book in conversations, classes, and workshops with the phenomenally smart graduate students who make this work such a pleasure. Thank you to Matthew Boulette, David Diamond, Caroline Heller, Nana Holtsnider, Andrew Inchiosa, Mabel Mietzelfeld, Stephen Pannuto, Cassidy Picken, Aleks Prigozhin, Samuel Rowe, Lauren Schachter, Tristan Schweiger, Brady Smith, Suzanne Taylor, Allison Turner, and David Womble; and to the founding core of the Animal Studies Workshop: Bill Hutchison, Katharine Mershon, Joela Jacobs, Les Beldo, Ashley Drake, and Agnes Malinowska. Thank you too to the astonishing, creative undergraduates I have had the great good fortune to teach at Chicago, for all the ways your thinking has enriched my own.

Work on this book was supported by a Barbara Thom postdoctoral fellowship at the Huntington Library, which gave me much needed time, and a glorious setting, in which to think and work. It also afforded me the company of a marvelous group of fellows and affiliates, each of whom influenced or encouraged my thinking. Thank you in particular to Heidi Brayman Hackel, Frances Dolan, Elizabeth Eger, Heather James, Peter Stallybrass, Skip Stout, Abigail Swingen, Will West, and especially Elizabeth Allen. For fostering such a congenial environment for intellectual work and exchange, heartfelt thanks to Roy Ritchie and Steve Hindle, outgoing and incoming directors of the Huntington during my fellowship year.

Audiences at the Newberry Library Eighteenth-Century Seminar, the Bloomington Eighteenth-Century Studies Workshop at Indiana University, Vanderbilt University, Wesleyan University, Bard College, College of the Holy Cross, Vassar College, University of Virginia, University of Washington, University of Pittsburgh, University of British Columbia, and the Chicago Humanities Festival have engaged with my work and helped me to make it better. Many tremendous people working in (and around) eighteenth-century studies helped me to find my home in the field, sometimes simply by taking an interest at a critical or early moment. For conversations, friendship, or support, thank you to Mark Blackwell, David Brewer, Marshall Brown, Tony Brown, Deirdre D'Albertis, Robert DeMaria, Jonathan Elmer, Lisa Freeman, Amanda Jo Goldstein, Kevis Goodman, Nicholas Hudson, Paul Hunter, Sarah Tindal Kareem, Anna Kornbluh, Ivan Krielkamp, Aaron Kunin, Tom Lockwood, Christina Lupton, Ruth Mack, Robert Markley, Tobias Menely, Jesse Molesworth, Joanne Myers, Richard Nash, Julie Park, Joanna Picciotto, Andrew Piper, Wolfram Schmidgen, John Shanahan, Helen Thompson, Nick Williams, and Abigail Zitin. John Sitter encouraged me early on, and critically so.

For bringing this book into being, a very big thank you to Jerome Singerman at the University of Pennsylvania Press. Thanks, too, to Noreen O'Connor-Abel for shepherding it through the production process, and to John Hubbard for the beautiful cover design. Thank you, especially, to the wonderful anonymous readers for the press, whose rigor, generosity, and depth of engagement with my work simply floored me. I hope I have honored that engagement in my responses to it. Cynthia Wall read an earlier version of the entire manuscript and provided invaluable comments and suggestions. I am grateful to her for taking the time, and for the countless ways the book was strengthened by her reading. Chapter 3 was read by Helen Deutsch at an early moment and Lynn Festa at a late one; their comments helped me immensely in bringing the chapter together. Melissa Adams-Campbell made writing (and rewriting) the Introduction immensely more pleasurable than it would have been otherwise and helped me tremendously in framing the book. Far flung from the field, but nevertheless crucial, was Daniel Morgan's always insightful reading of the work at various stages. I am grateful for the formative friendships and formidable intelligence of Jenny Ludwig, Rachel Watson, and Nathan Wolff, alongside whom so many of the ideas in this book were first thought. Neil Chudgar remains one of the key interlocutors of the project, and his acuity and generosity of mind is present on every single page. Thank you.

I am thankful for the friends that have sustained me through the years of writing this book (and many more), especially Amanda Antholt, Liz Doggett, Rebecca Durcan, Maggie Grant, Hilary Lewis, Ashley Macguire, Sarah Nooter, and Laura Scholl. I am thankful for the family that has done the same. My greatest debt of gratitude goes to my parents, Val Keenleyside and Ed Keenleyside, and to my brother, Steve Keenleyside, sources of seemingly unending and unconditional love and support. Thank you especially to my parents, and to Karen Williams, Frankie Williams, and Carmen Jones, for all the love and care they have given my children—often when I have been elsewhere, writing this book.

To Michael Green, thanks come nowhere close to the mark. Nevertheless, for your unfailing support and love, for living this joyful and exhausting life with me, for the many nights you didn't sleep so that I could: thank you. My gorgeous, beloved children, Wilder George Keenleyside Green and Simone Mae Keenleyside Green, did nothing at all to contribute to the writing of this book. I thank them for everything else.

An early version of Chapter 1 appeared as "Personification for the People," in *ELH* 76 (2009): 447–72. Portions of Chapter 4 were published as "The First-Person Form of Life: Locke, Sterne, and the Autobiographical Animal," in *Critical Inquiry* 39 (2012): 116–41.